# INUYASHA

## ANI-MANGA VOL. 14

D1366543

CREATED BY
RUMIKO TAKAHASHI

# Inuyasha Ani-Manga™
## Vol. #14

### Created by
### Rumiko Takahashi

Translation based on the VIZ anime TV series
Translation Assistance/Katy Bridges
Lettering/John Clark
Cover Design & Graphics/Hidemi Sahara
Editor/Frances E. Wall

Managing Editor/Annette Roman
Director of Production/Noboru Watanabe
Vice President of Publishing/Alvin Lu
Sr. Director of Acquisitions/Rika Inouye
Vice President of Sales & Marketing/Liza Coppola
Publisher/Hyoe Narita

Printed in the U.S.A.

Published by VIZ Media, LLC
P.O. Box 77010
San Francisco, CA 94107

10 9 8 7 6 5 4 3 2 1
First printing, April 2006

www.viz.com
store.viz.com

# Story thus far

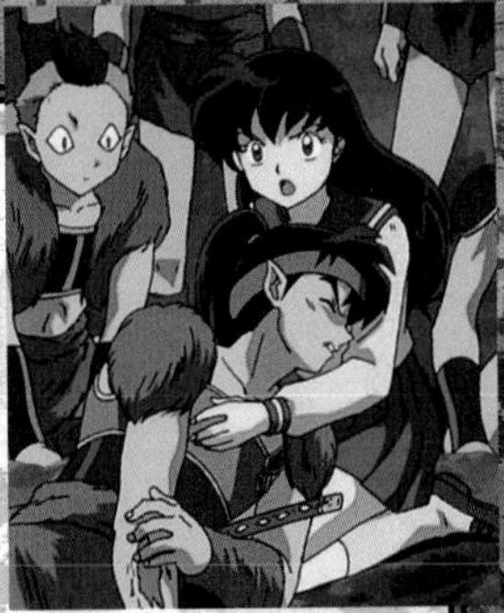

Kagome's mundane teenage existence was turned upside down when she was transported into a mythical version of Japan's medieval past! Kagome is the reincarnation of Lady Kikyo, a great warrior and the defender of the Shikon Jewel, or the Jewel of Four Souls. Kikyo was in love with Inuyasha, a dog-like half-demon who wishes to possess the jewel in order to transform himself into a full-fledged demon. But 50 years earlier, the evil shape-shifting Naraku tricked Kikyo and Inuyasha into betraying one another. The betrayal led to Kikyo's death and Inuyasha's imprisonment under a binding spell...and Inuyasha remained trapped by the spell until Kagome appeared in feudal Japan and unwittingly released him!

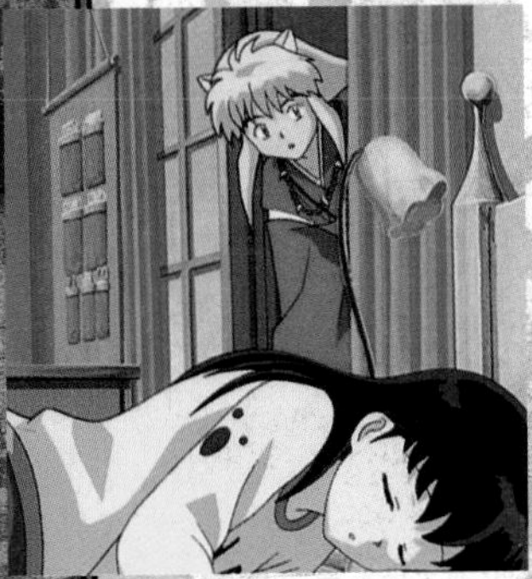

In a skirmish for possession of the Shikon Jewel, it accidentally shatters and is strewn across the land. Only Kagome has the power to find the jewel shards, and only Inuyasha has the strength to defeat the demons who now hold them, so the two unlikely partners are bound together in the quest to reclaim all the pieces of the sacred jewel. To prevent Inuyasha from stealing the jewel, Kikyo's sister, Lady Kaede, puts a magical necklace around Inuyasha's neck that allows Kagome to make him "sit" on command.

Inuyasha and Kagome gradually begin to feel affection for one another, but the situation becomes complicated when Kikyo is raised from the grave through witchcraft. The resurrected Kikyo still burns with hatred and jealousy over Inuyasha's supposed betrayal and his relationship with Kagome, but Inuyasha can't suppress his abiding love for Kikyo. Koga, the leader of a wolf-demon tribe, has kidnapped Kagome, and Inuyasha and the others have come to her rescue. But now Naraku has tricked Koga into pitting himself against Inuyasha in a duel to the death! Is there any hope of escaping Naraku's trap!?

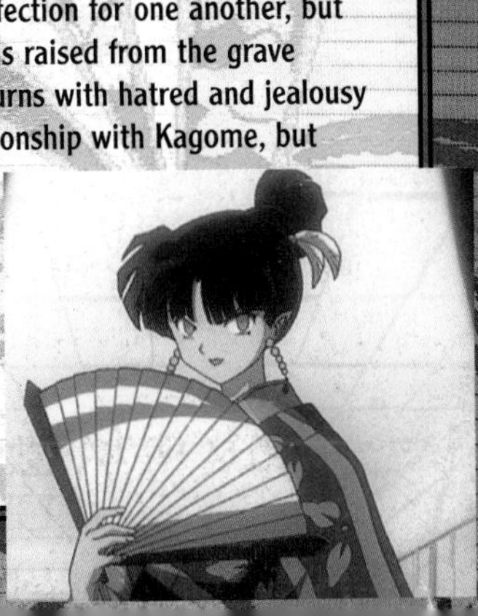

# INUYASHA
## ANI-MANGA ™ Vol. 14

### Contents

# 40
# The Deadly Trap of the Wind Sorceress, Kagura

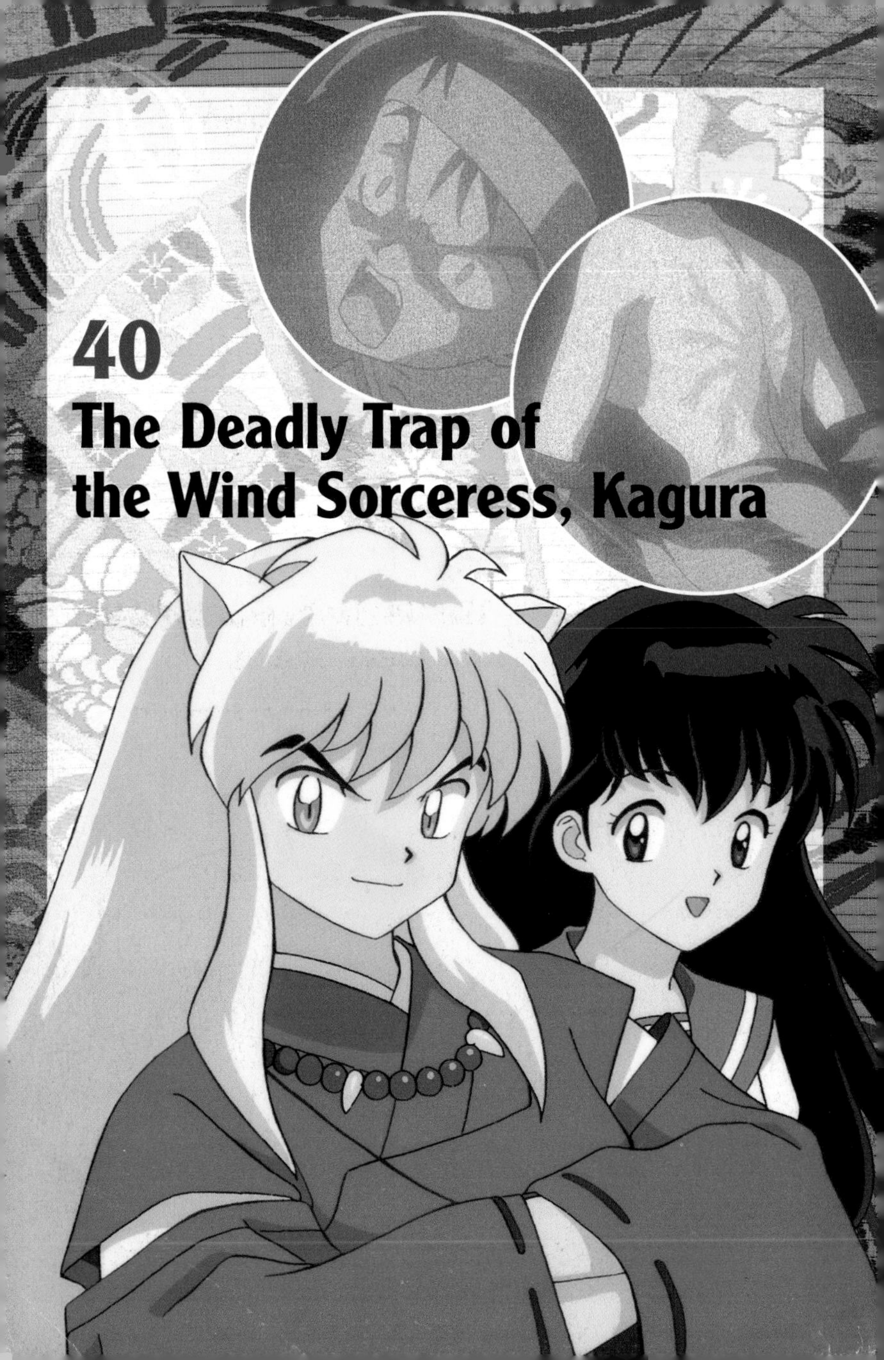

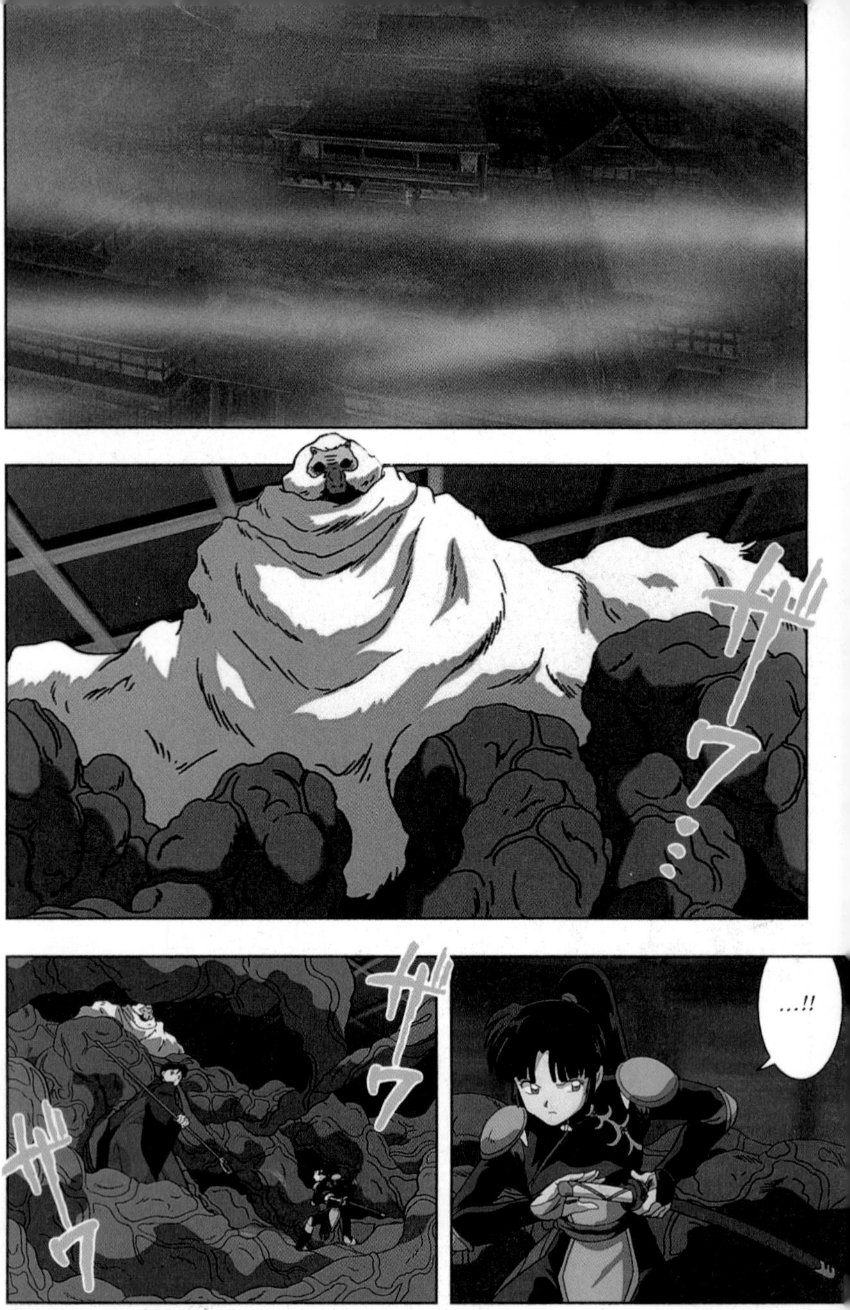
ザワ…
...!!
ザワ
ザワ

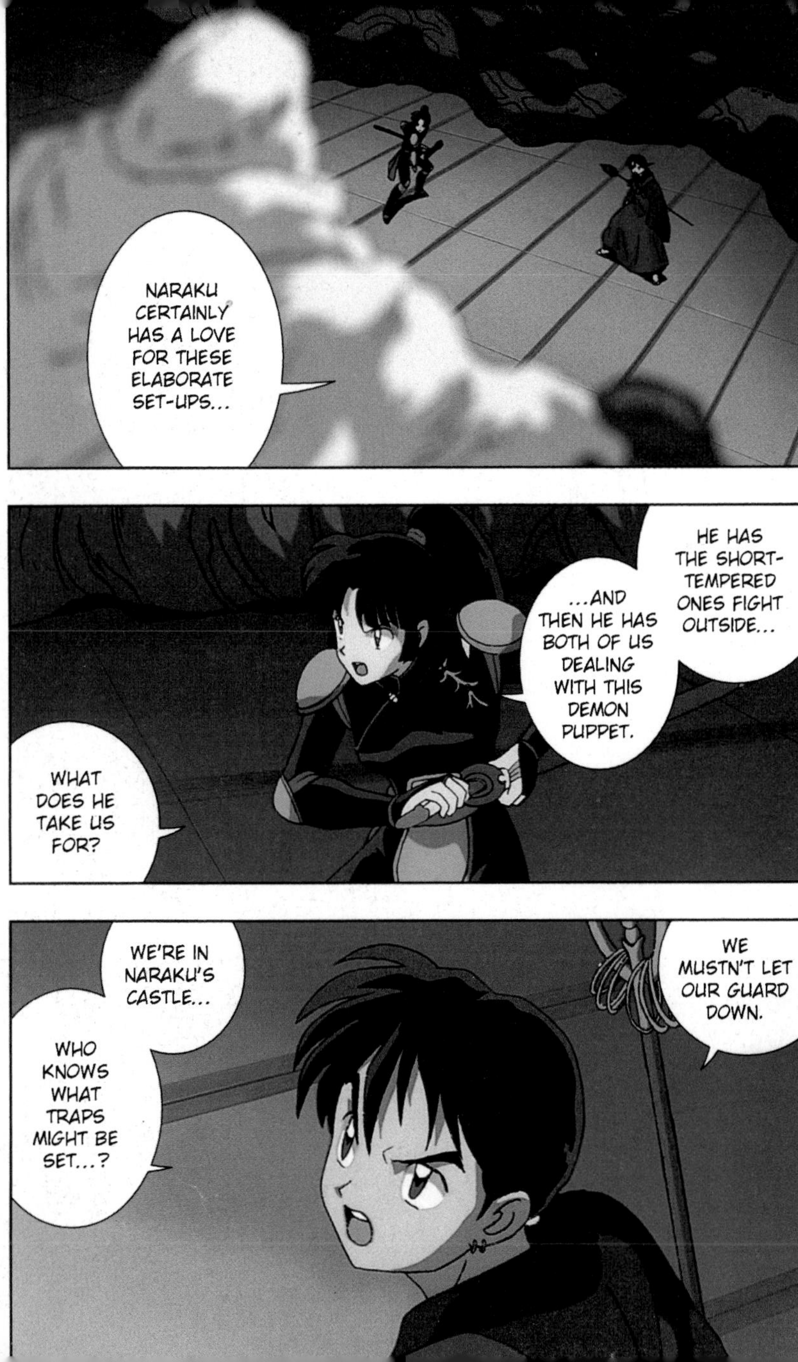
NARAKU CERTAINLY HAS A LOVE FOR THESE ELABORATE SET-UPS...
HE HAS THE SHORT-TEMPERED ONES FIGHT OUTSIDE...
...AND THEN HE HAS BOTH OF US DEALING WITH THIS DEMON PUPPET.
WHAT DOES HE TAKE US FOR?
WE MUSTN'T LET OUR GUARD DOWN.
WE'RE IN NARAKU'S CASTLE...
WHO KNOWS WHAT TRAPS MIGHT BE SET...?

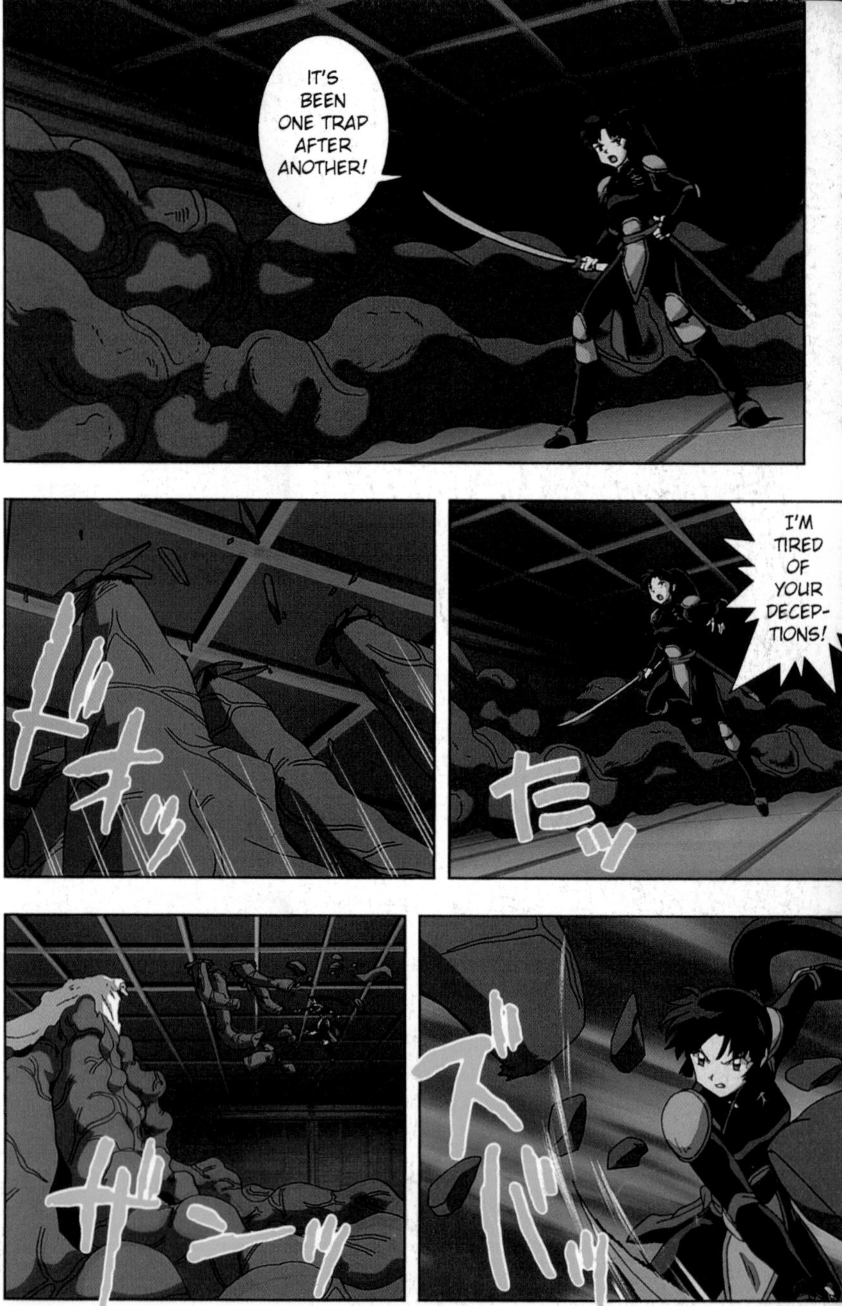
IT'S BEEN ONE TRAP AFTER ANOTHER!
I'M TIRED OF YOUR DECEPTIONS!
たッ
ドオッ
ズバッ
ザンーッ

SHALL WE TEACH THEM A LESSON?

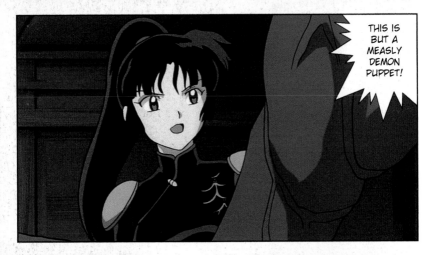

THIS IS BUT A MEASLY DEMON PUPPET!

YAA!!

HYAH!

9

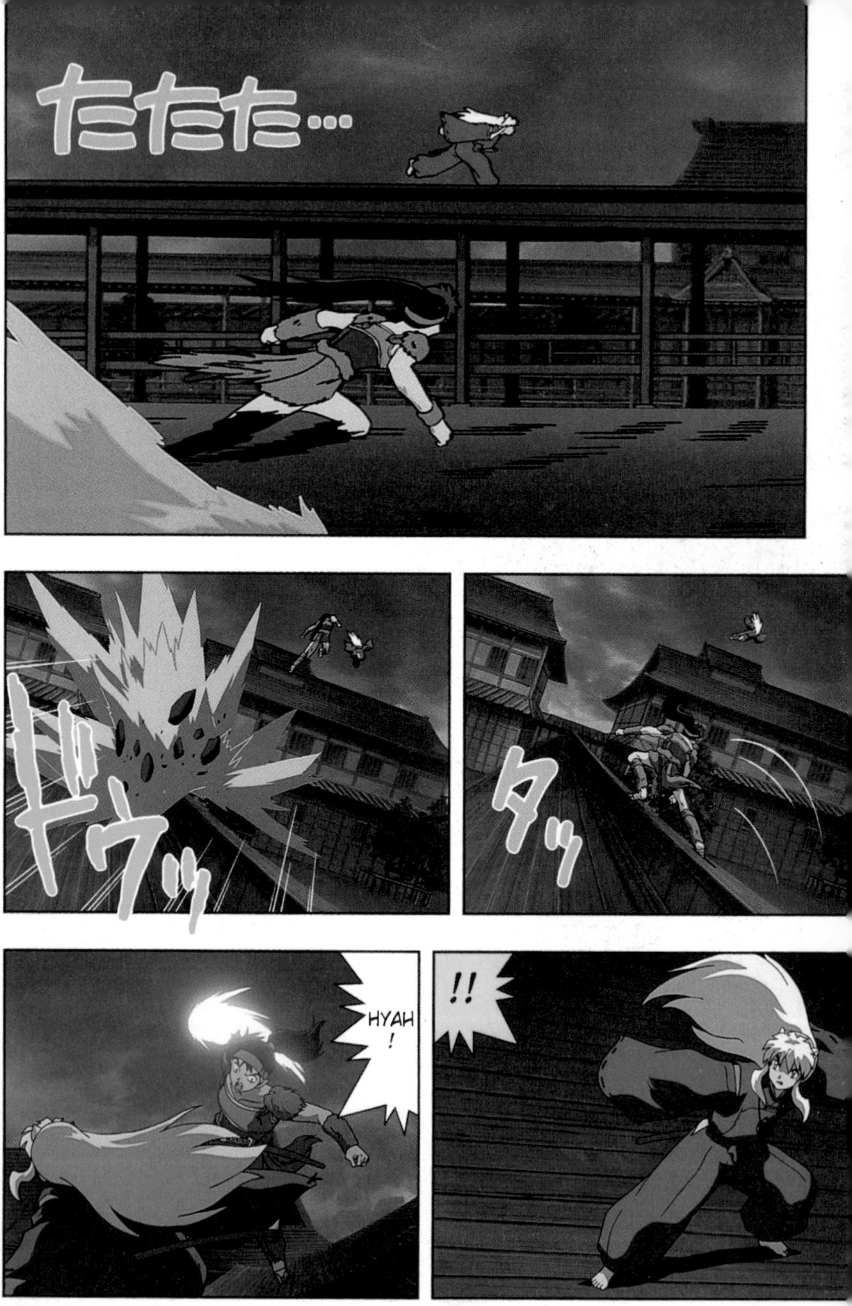
たたたた…
タッ
ドウッ
!!
HYAH!

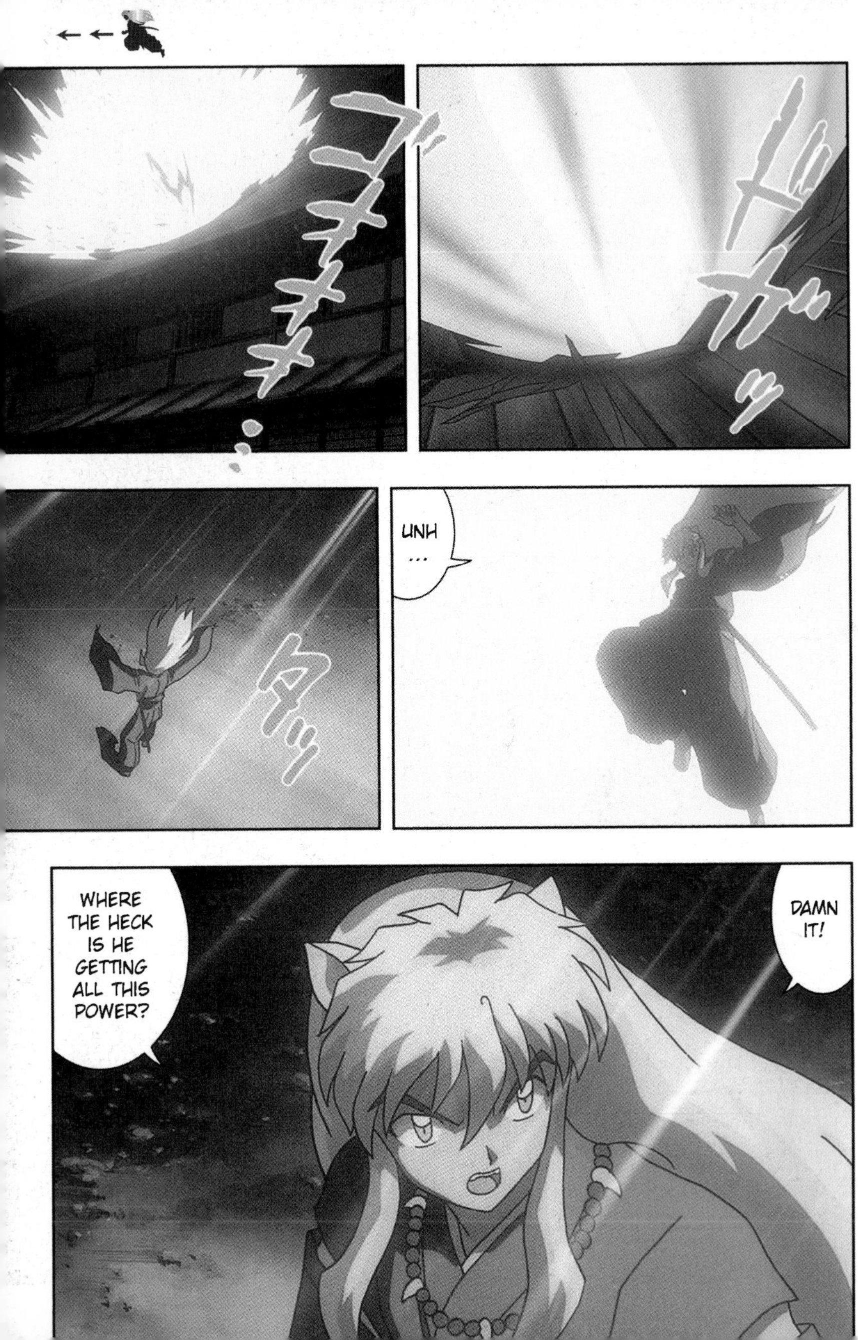

ゴオオオオオ…
ドガガッ
タッ
UNH ...
DAMN IT!
WHERE THE HECK IS HE GETTING ALL THIS POWER?

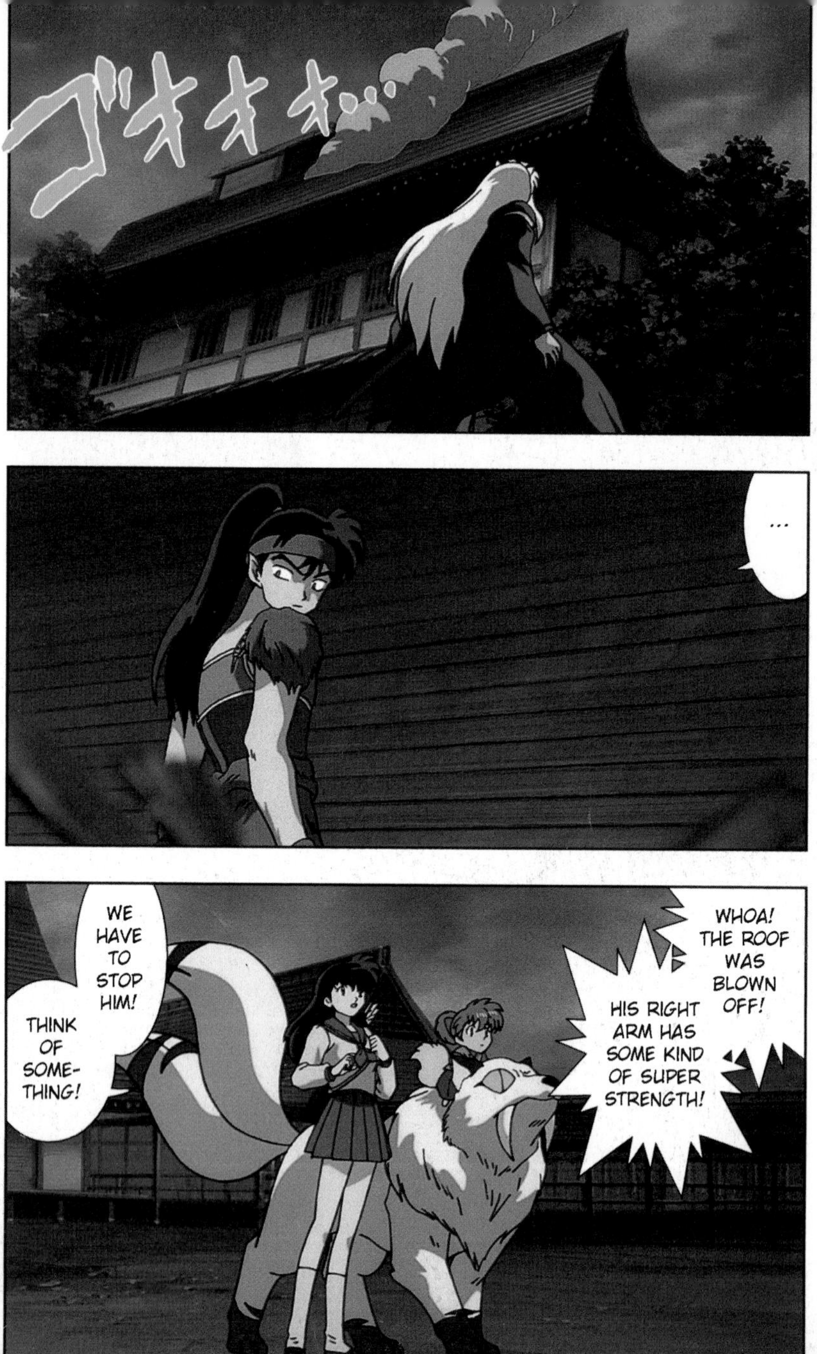
ゴオオオ…
...
WHOA! THE ROOF WAS BLOWN OFF!
HIS RIGHT ARM HAS SOME KIND OF SUPER STRENGTH!
WE HAVE TO STOP HIM!
THINK OF SOMETHING!

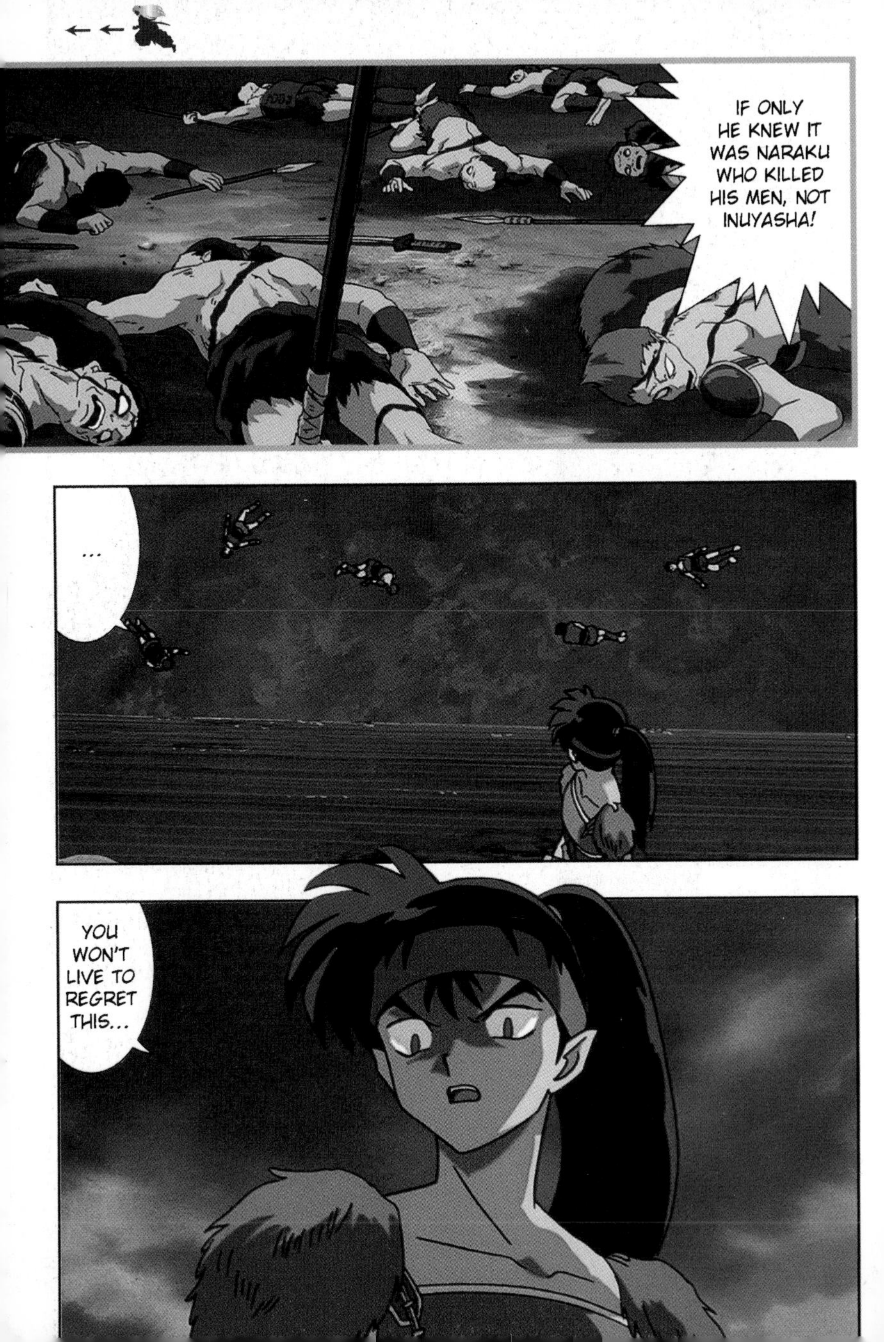
IF ONLY HE KNEW IT WAS NARAKU WHO KILLED HIS MEN, NOT INUYASHA!
...
YOU WON'T LIVE TO REGRET THIS...

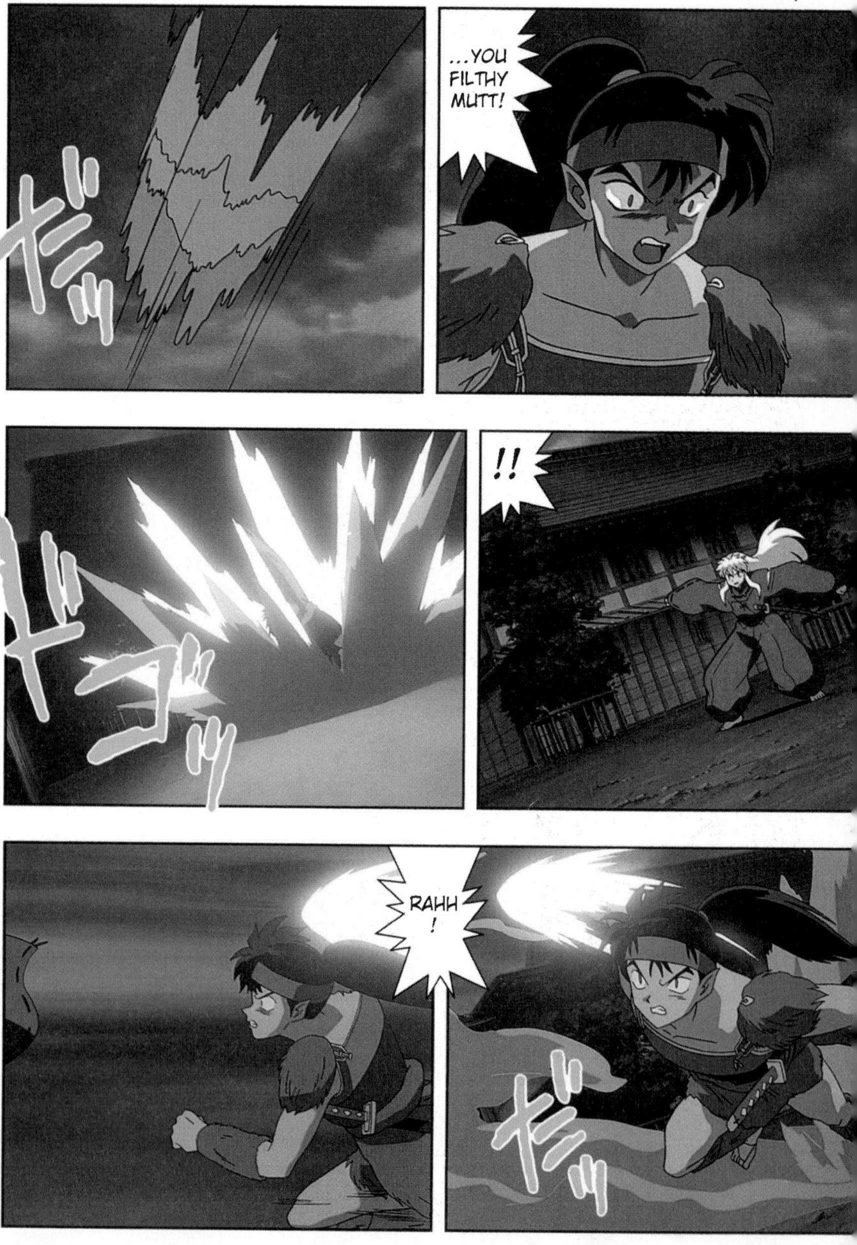
...YOU FILTHY MUTT!
!!
RAHH!

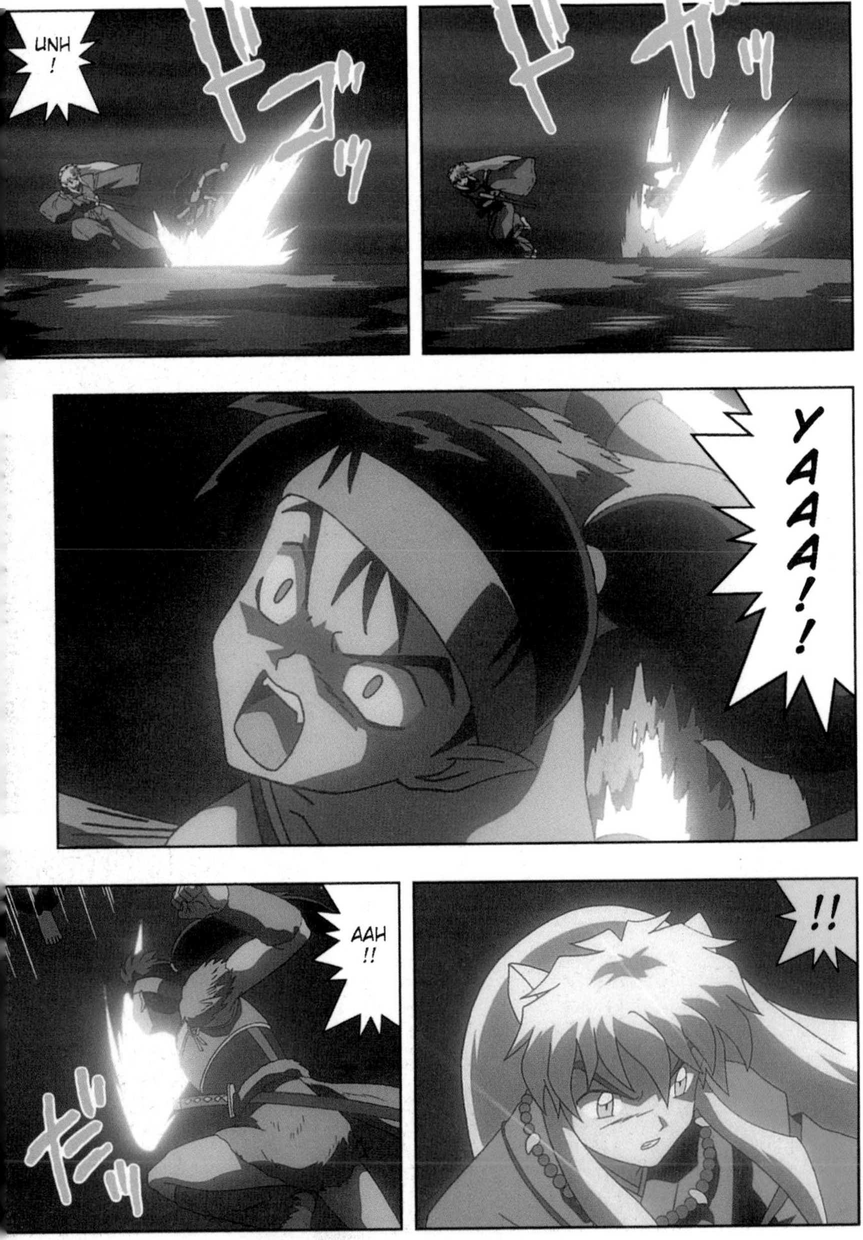
UNH !
YAAAA!!!
!!
AAH !!

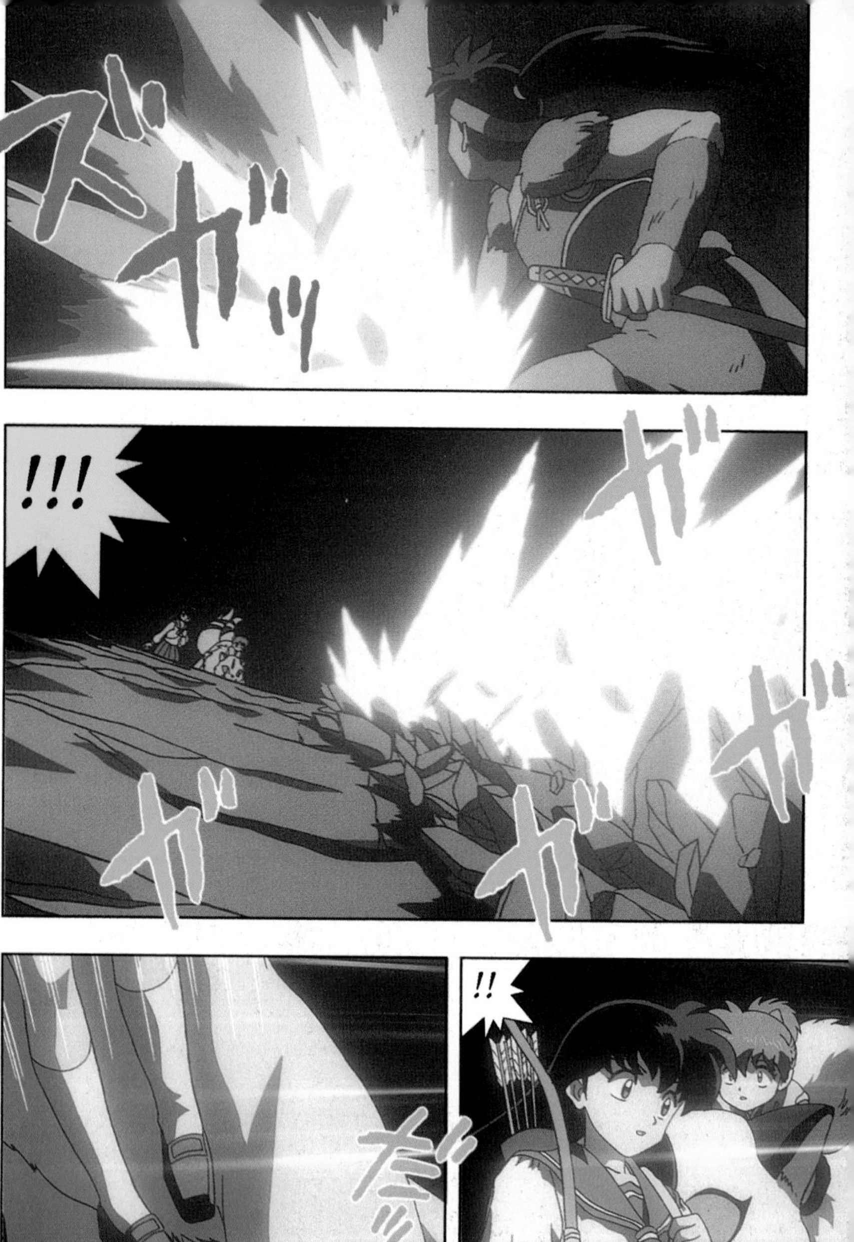
ズガッ
ガガ
ガガ
!!!
!!
だッ

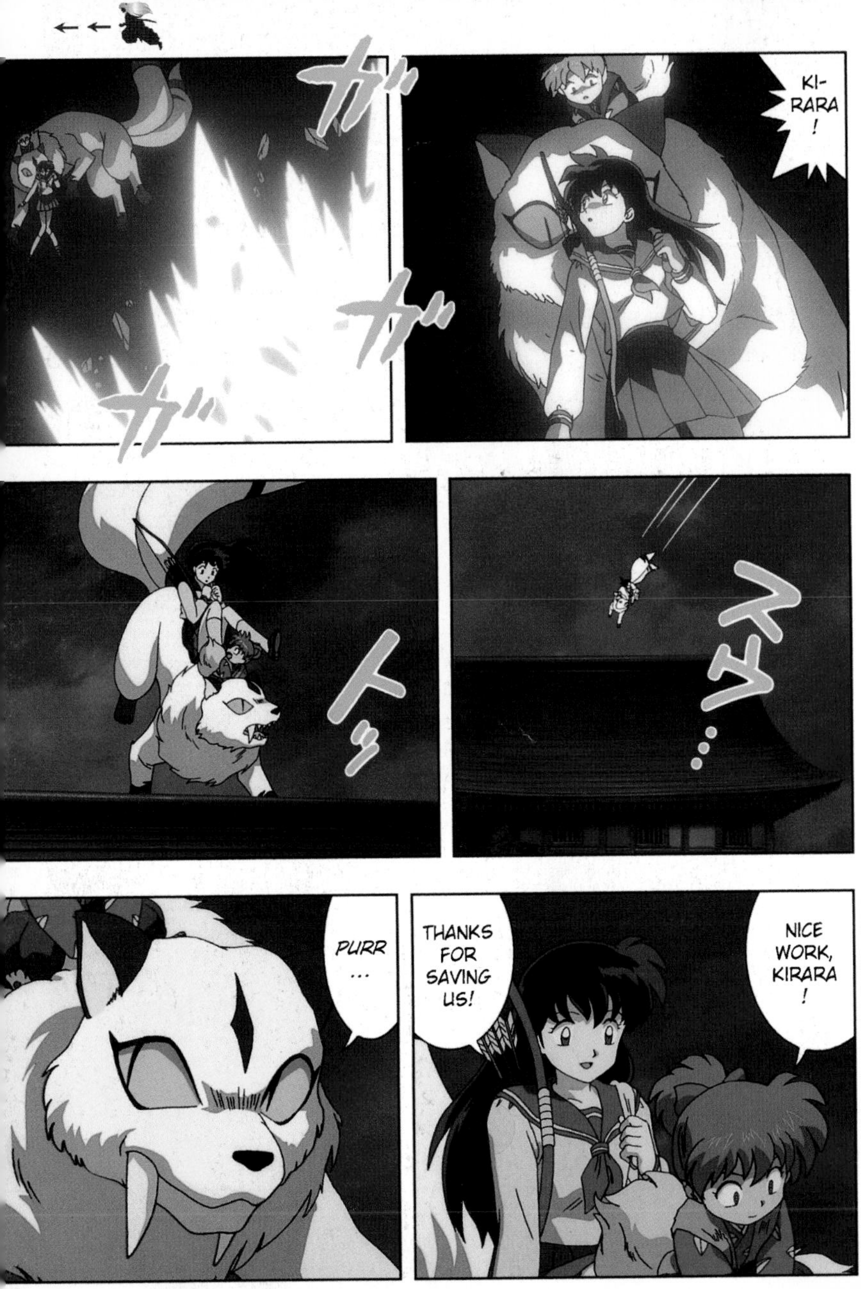
KI-RARA!
ガガガ
スタ…
トッ
NICE WORK, KIRARA!
THANKS FOR SAVING US!
PURR...

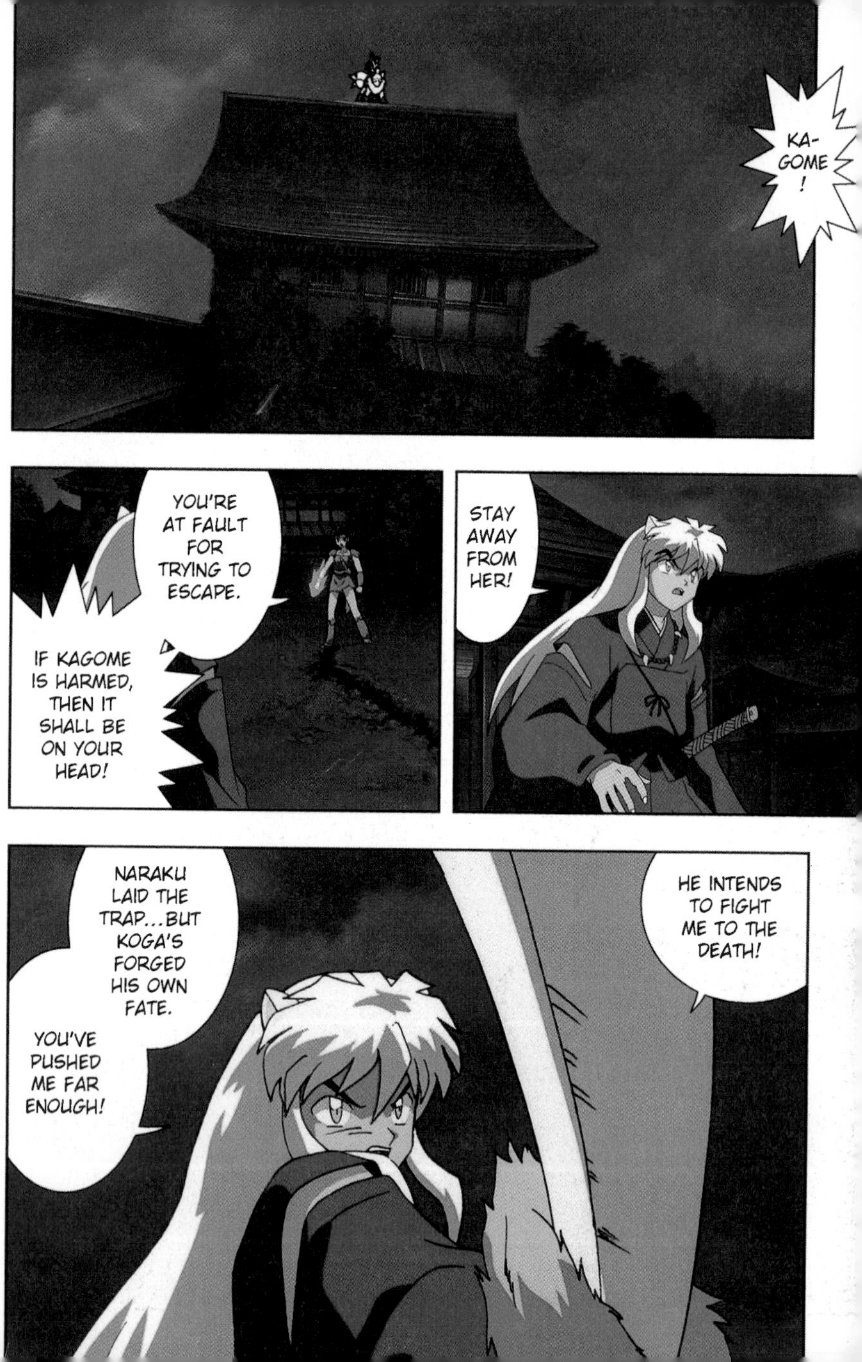
KA-GOME!
STAY AWAY FROM HER!
YOU'RE AT FAULT FOR TRYING TO ESCAPE.
IF KAGOME IS HARMED, THEN IT SHALL BE ON YOUR HEAD!
HE INTENDS TO FIGHT ME TO THE DEATH!
NARAKU LAID THE TRAP...BUT KOGA'S FORGED HIS OWN FATE.
YOU'VE PUSHED ME FAR ENOUGH!

PRE-PARE TO DIE!

HE'S SO FAST !

IN THE NAME OF MY COM-RADES !

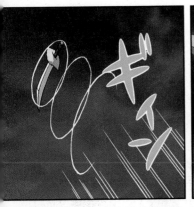

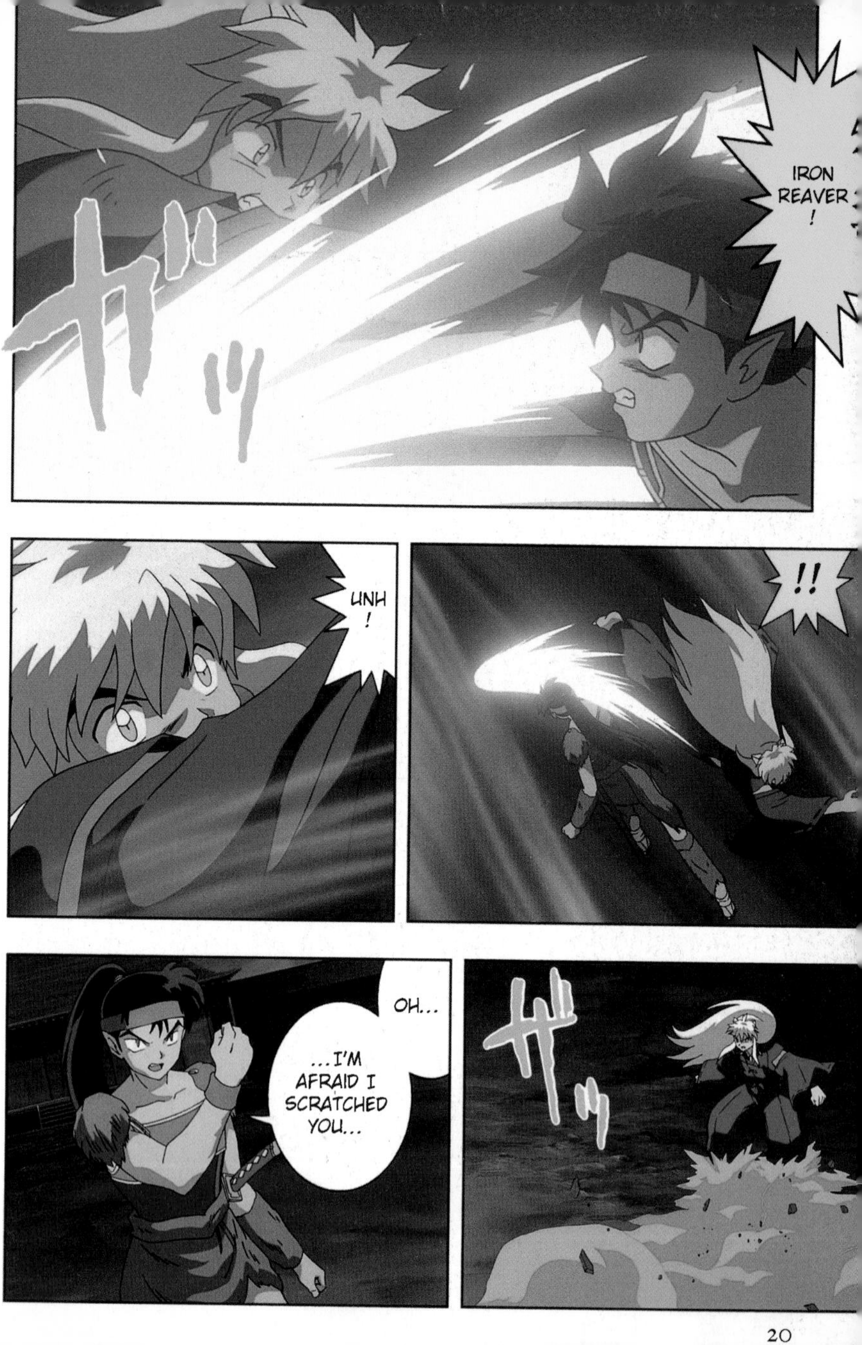
IRON REAVER!
ガッ
!!
UNH!
ザッ
OH...
...I'M AFRAID I SCRATCHED YOU...

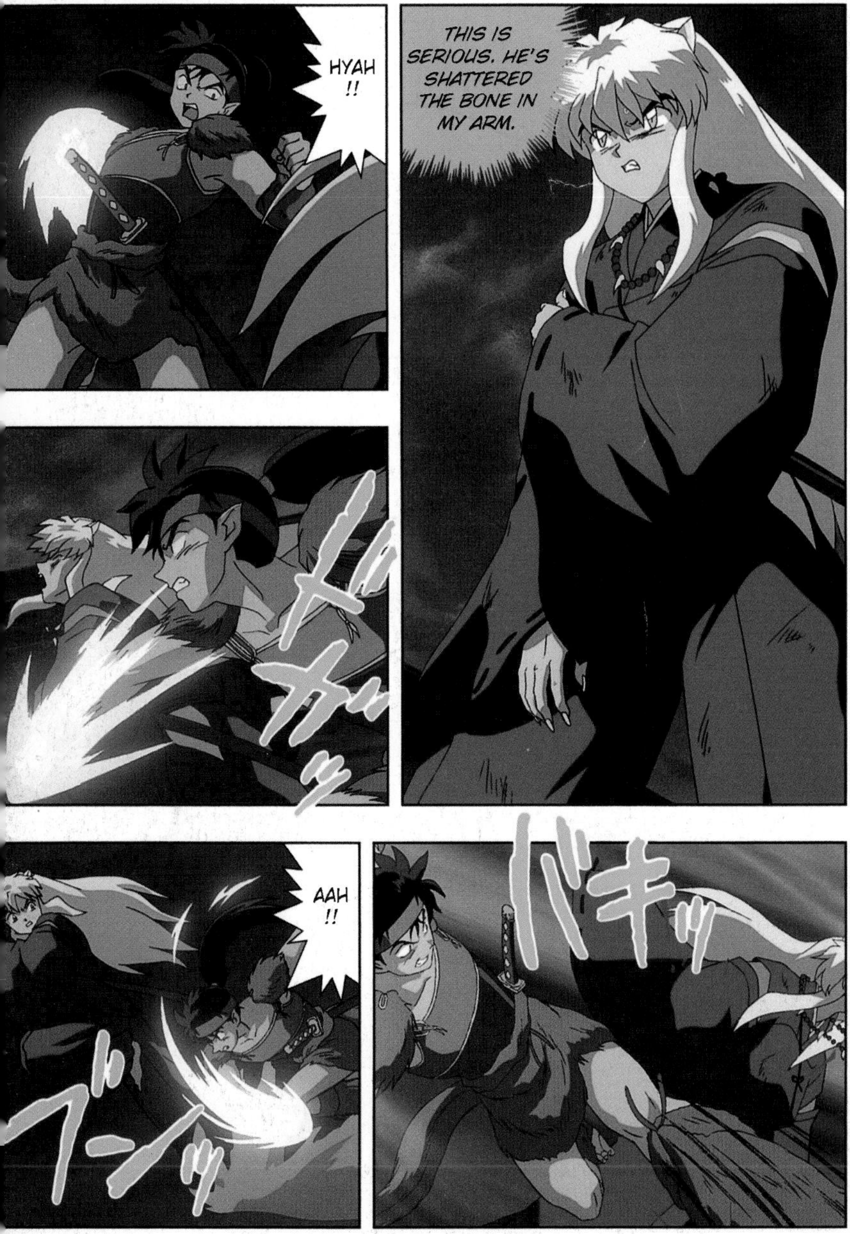
THIS IS SERIOUS. HE'S SHATTERED THE BONE IN MY ARM.
HYAH !!
ドガッ
バキッ
AAH !!
ブンッ

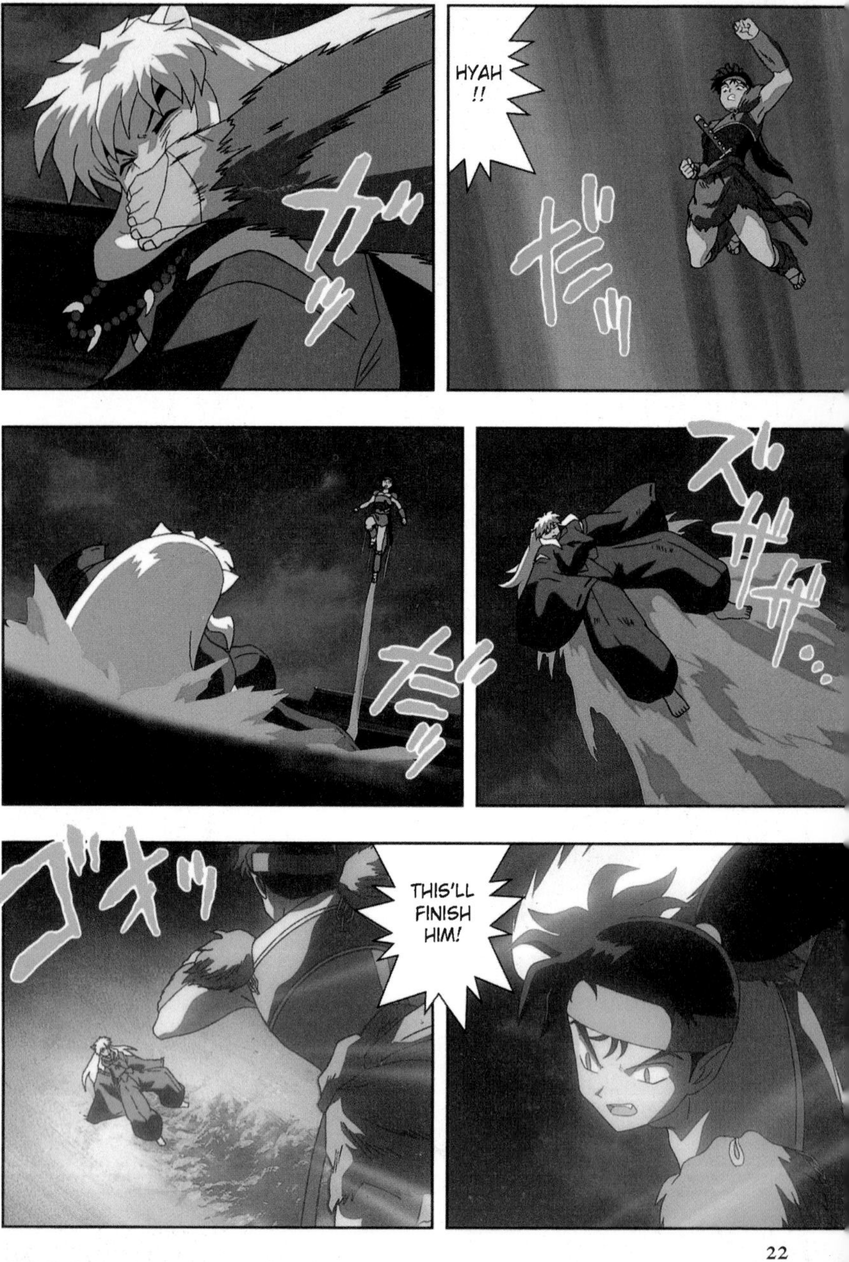
HYAH !!
だッ
ガッ
ズザザザ…
だッ
THIS'LL FINISH HIM!
ゴオッ

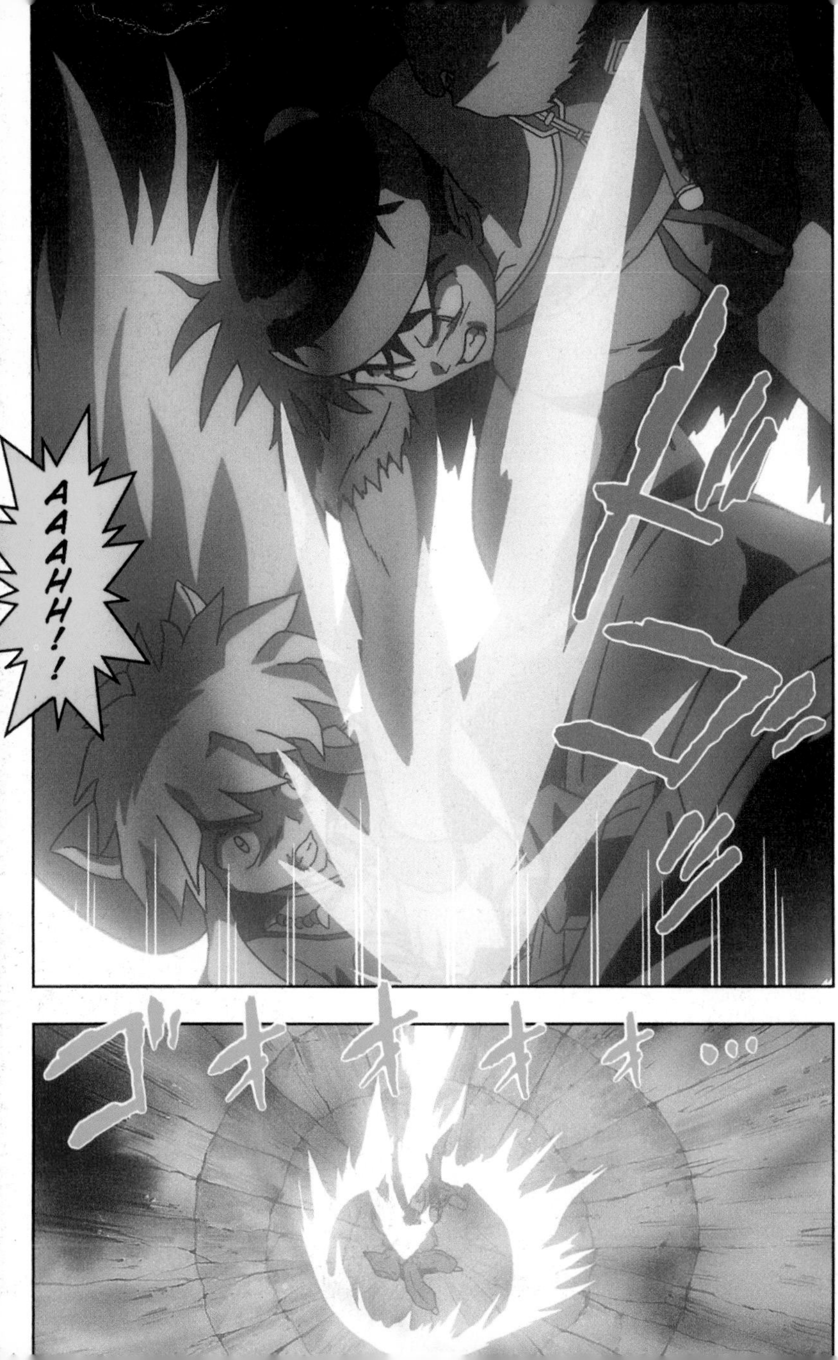
ドゴッ
AAAHH!!
ゴオオオ…

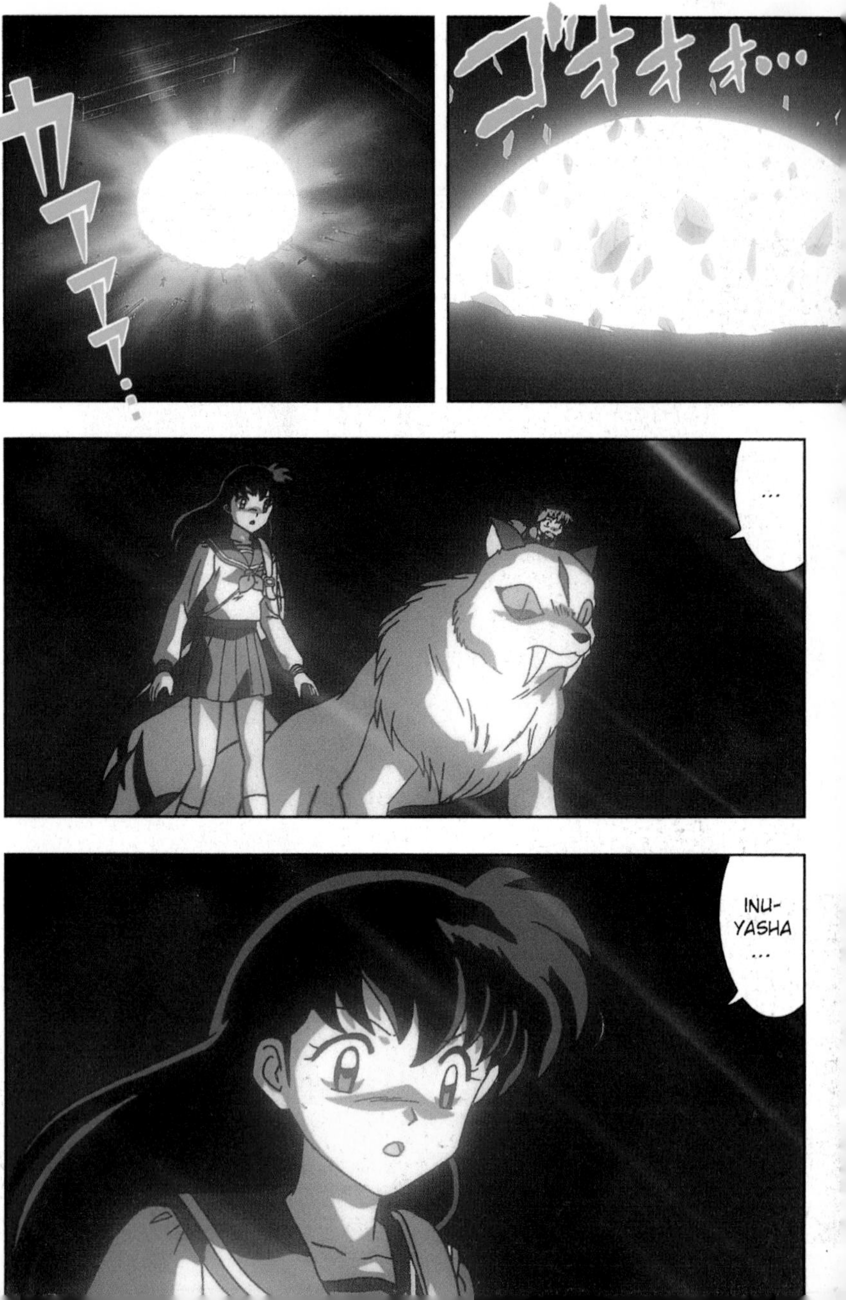
ゴオオォ…
カァァァァ…
...
INU-
YASHA
...

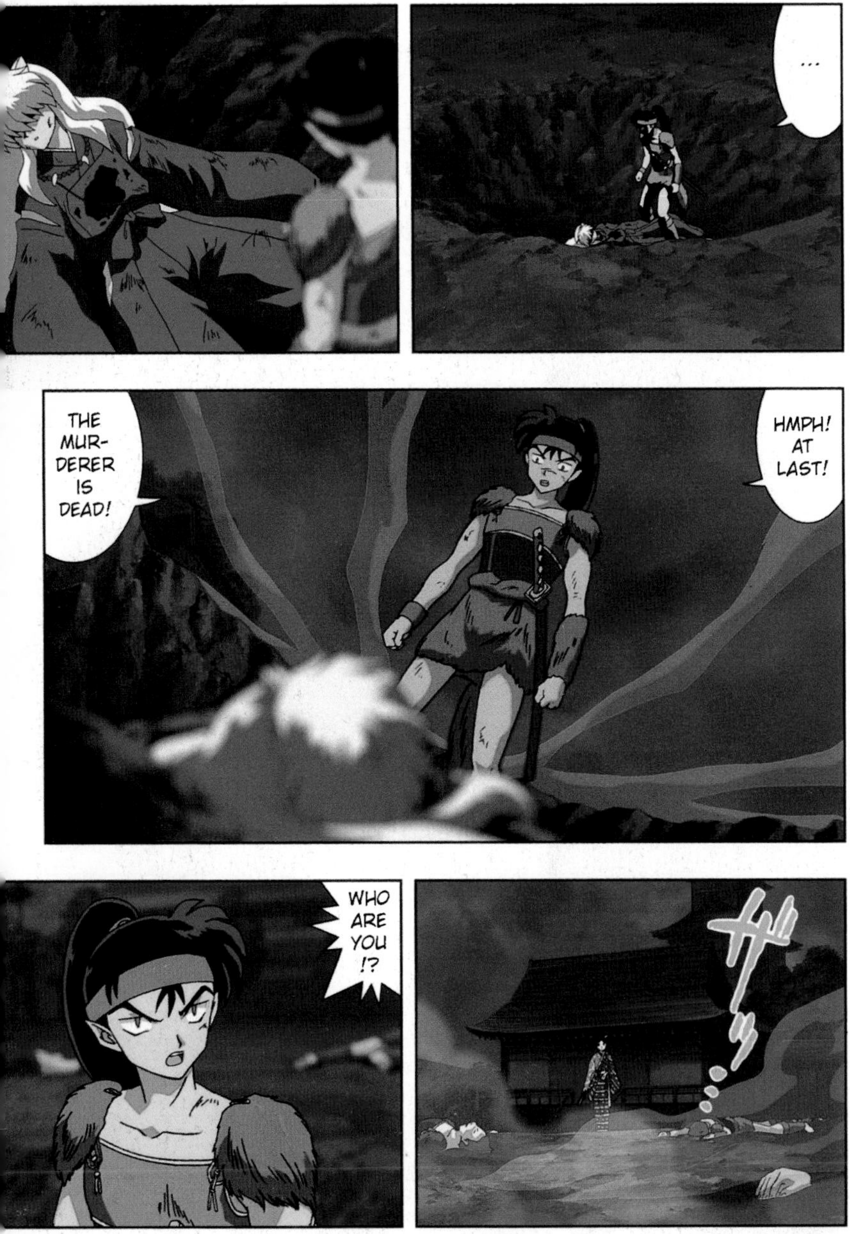
...
HMPH! AT LAST!
THE MUR-DERER IS DEAD!
WHO ARE YOU !?

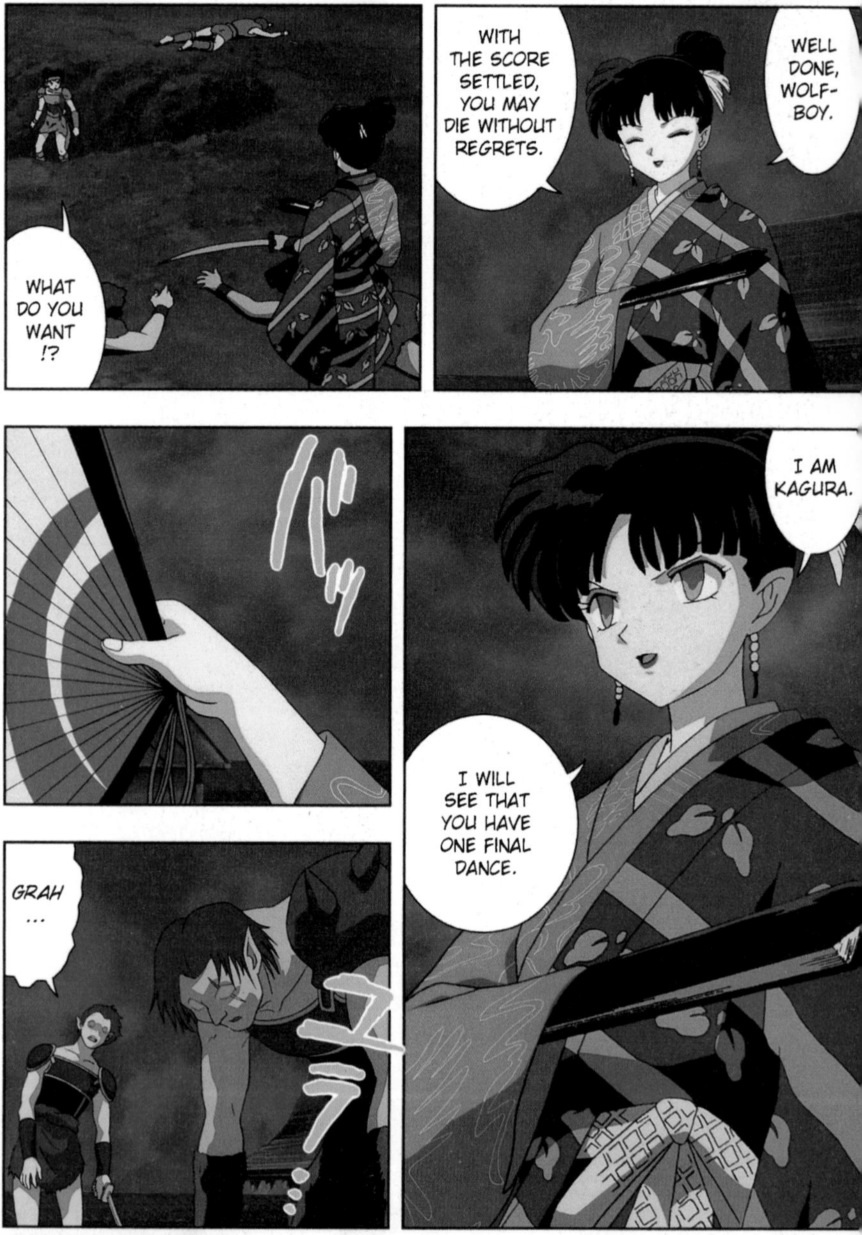
WELL DONE, WOLF-BOY.
WITH THE SCORE SETTLED, YOU MAY DIE WITHOUT REGRETS.
WHAT DO YOU WANT !?
I AM KAGURA.
I WILL SEE THAT YOU HAVE ONE FINAL DANCE.
バッ
GRAH ...
ユラ...

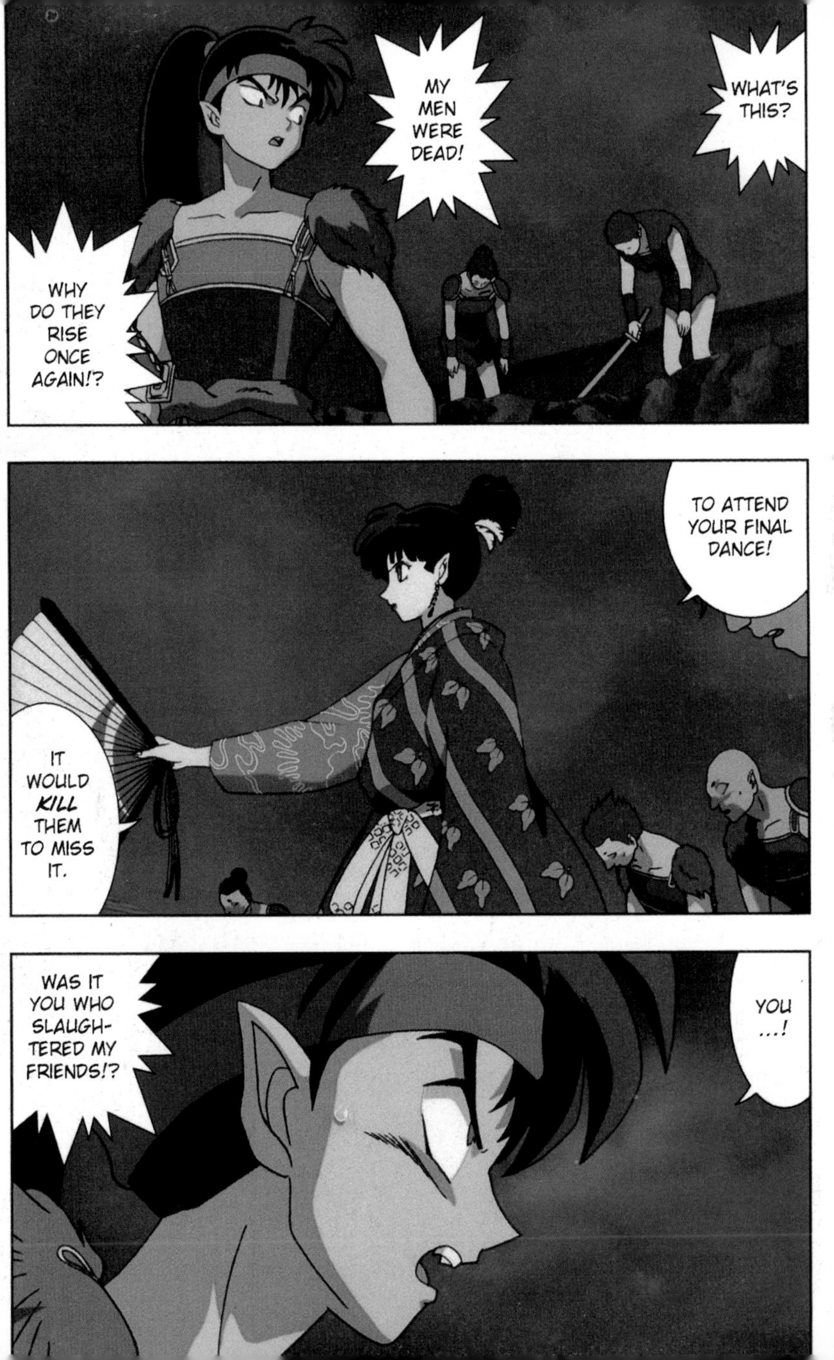
WHAT'S THIS?
MY MEN WERE DEAD!
WHY DO THEY RISE ONCE AGAIN!?
TO ATTEND YOUR FINAL DANCE!
IT WOULD KILL THEM TO MISS IT.
YOU ...!
WAS IT YOU WHO SLAUGH-TERED MY FRIENDS!?

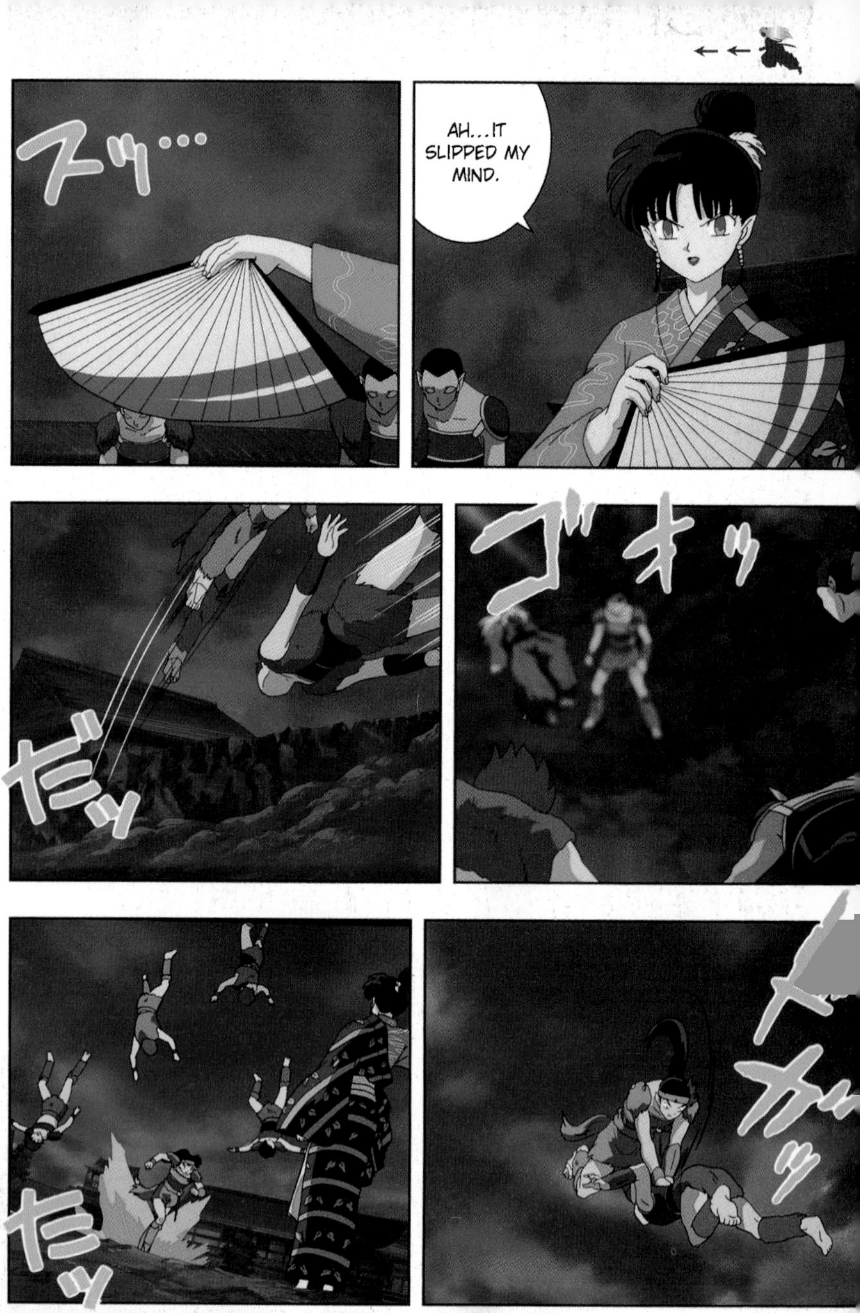
AH...IT SLIPPED MY MIND.
スッ…
ゴオッ
ダッ
タッ
カッ

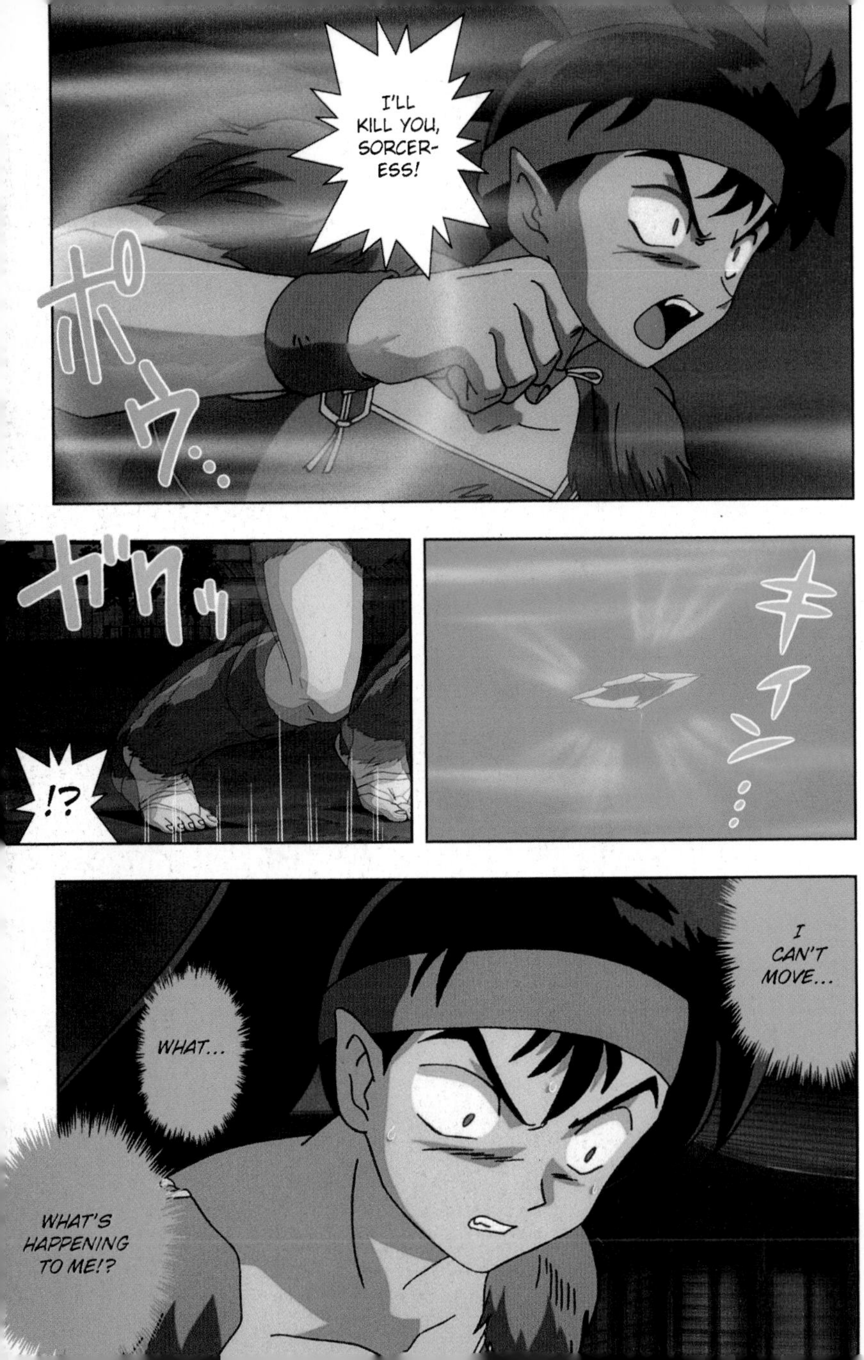
I'LL KILL YOU, SORCERESS!
ポウ...
ガクッ
!?
キイン...
I CAN'T MOVE...
WHAT...
WHAT'S HAPPENING TO ME!?

HEH HEH ...

THE JEWEL SHARD IN YOUR ARM HAS FINALLY RELEASED ITS POISON.

NOW IT'S TIME FOR YOU TO DIE.

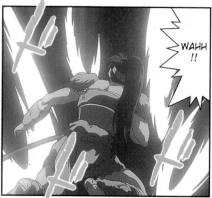

WAHH !!

OHH ...

!!

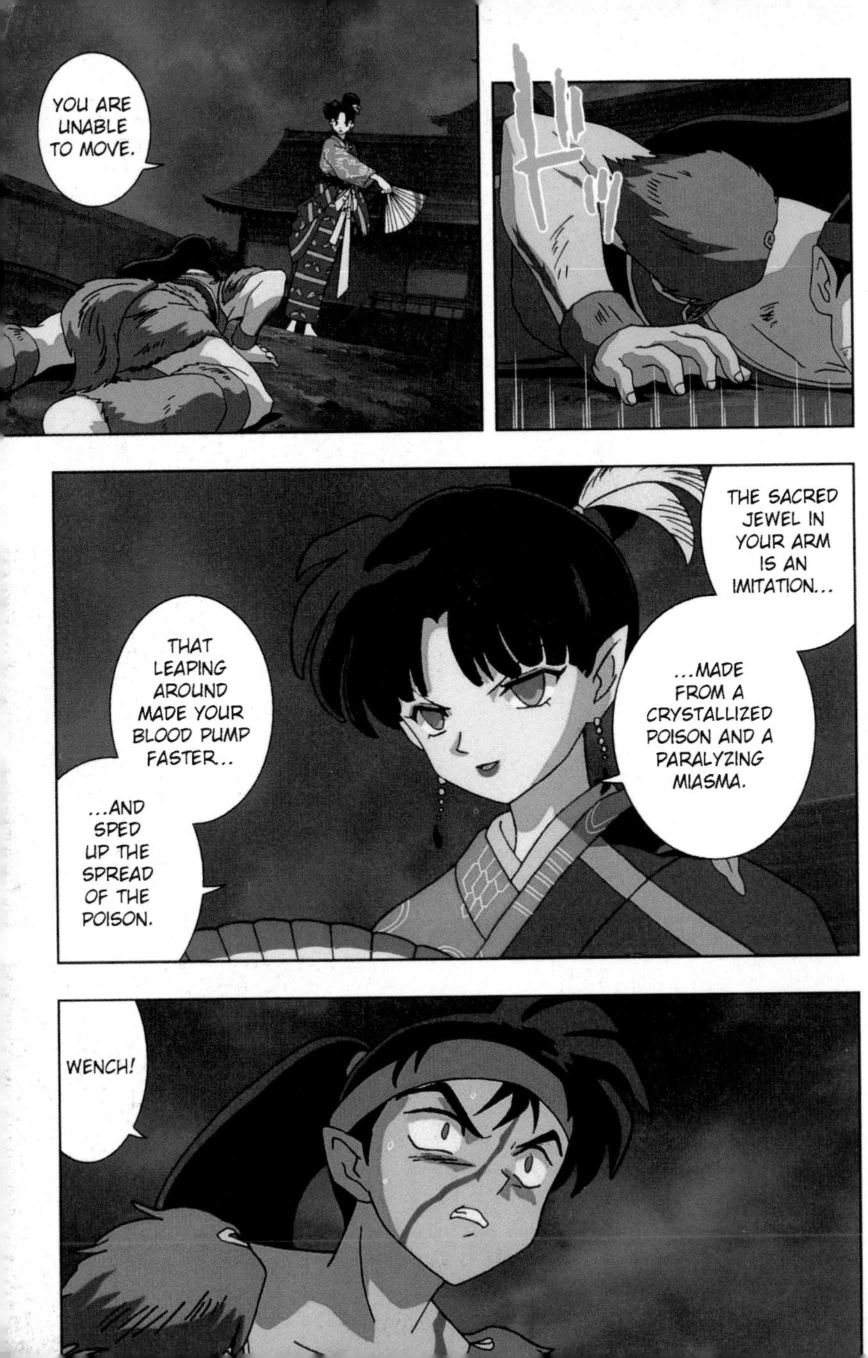
YOU ARE UNABLE TO MOVE.
THE SACRED JEWEL IN YOUR ARM IS AN IMITATION...
...MADE FROM A CRYSTALLIZED POISON AND A PARALYZING MIASMA.
THAT LEAPING AROUND MADE YOUR BLOOD PUMP FASTER..
...AND SPED UP THE SPREAD OF THE POISON.
WENCH!

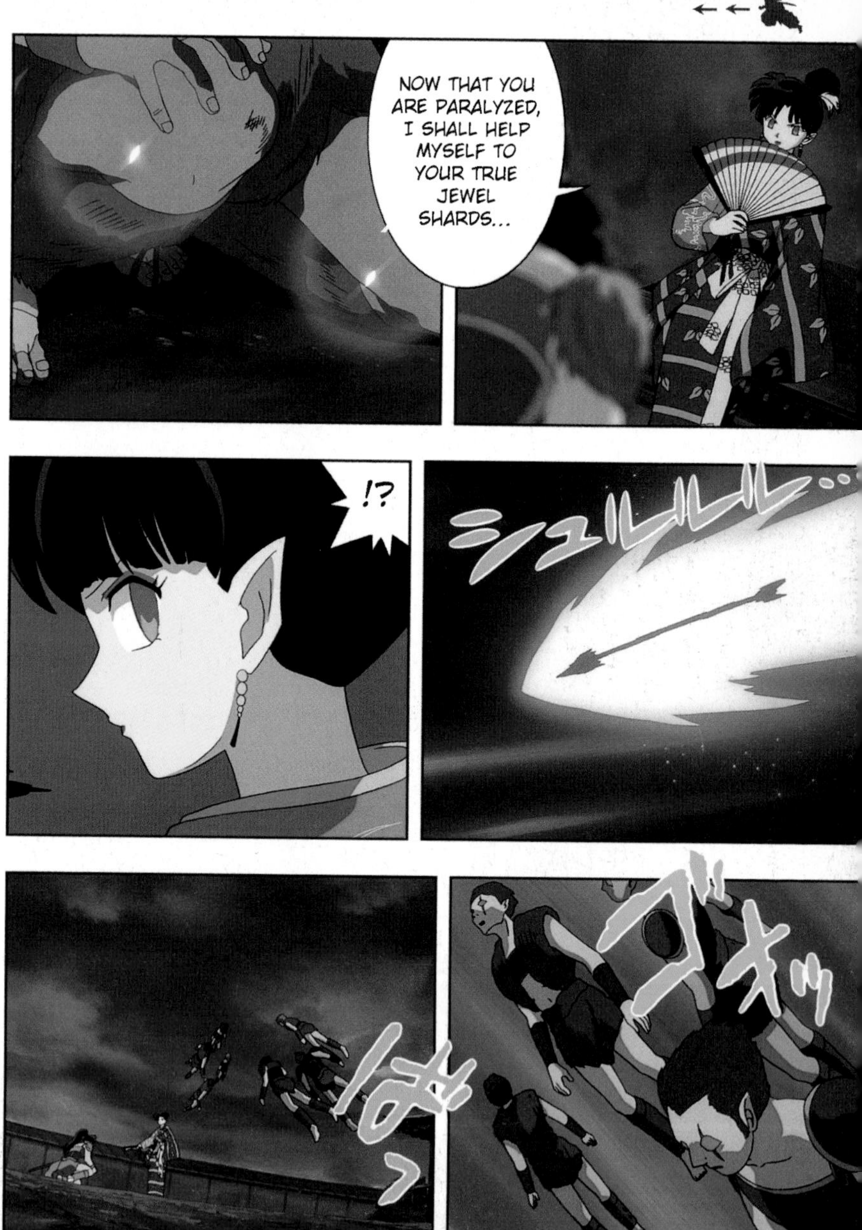
NOW THAT YOU ARE PARALYZED, I SHALL HELP MYSELF TO YOUR TRUE JEWEL SHARDS...
!?
シュルルルル…
ゴオッ
はっ

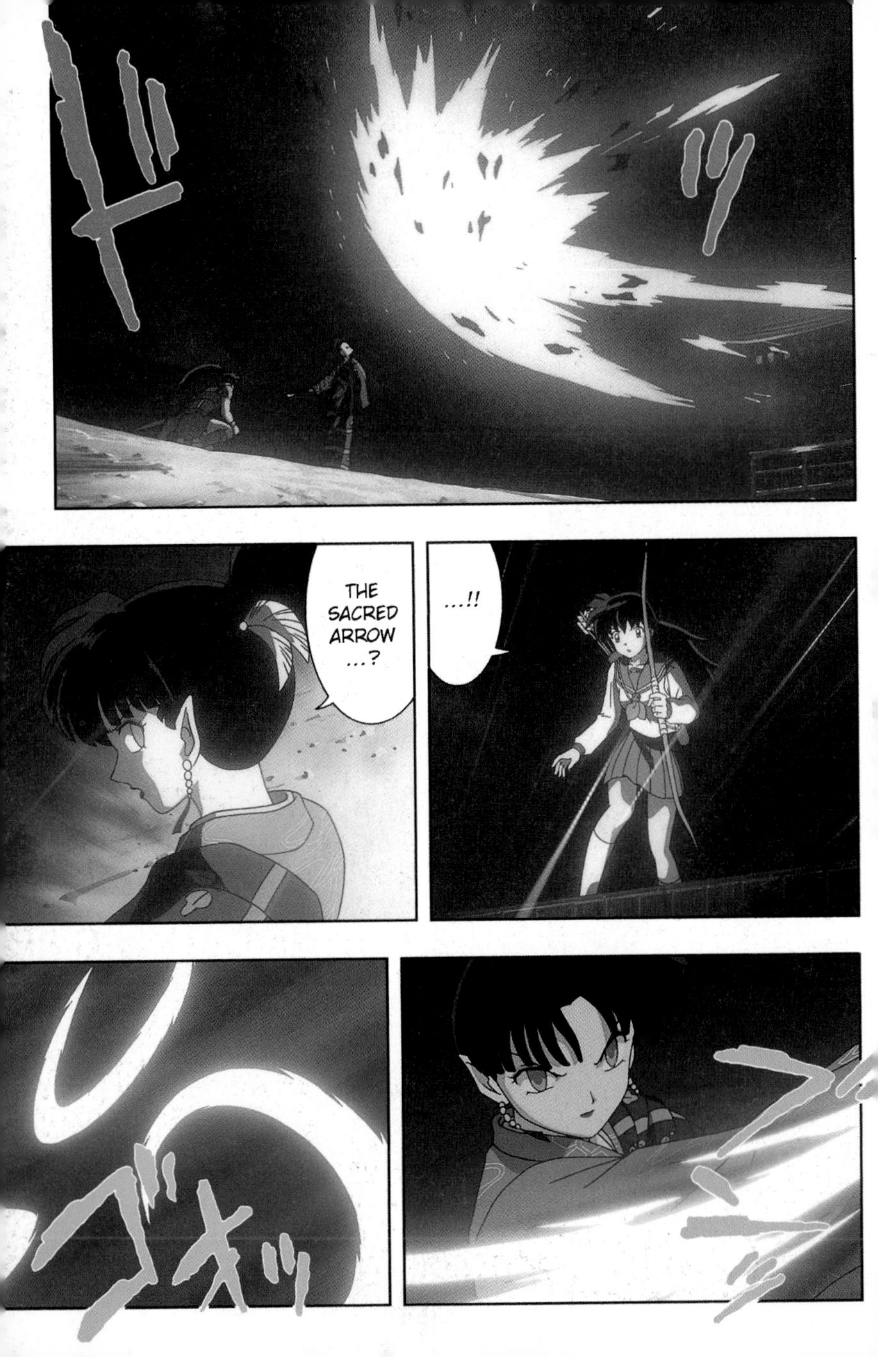
ドッ
...!!
THE SACRED ARROW ...?
ゴオッ

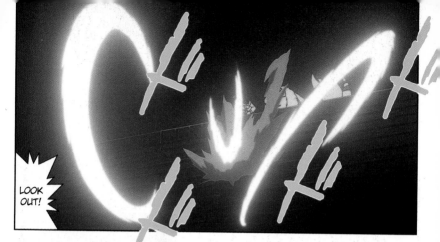

LOOK OUT!

KAGOME, ARE YOU HURT?

NO...I THINK I'M OKAY.

34

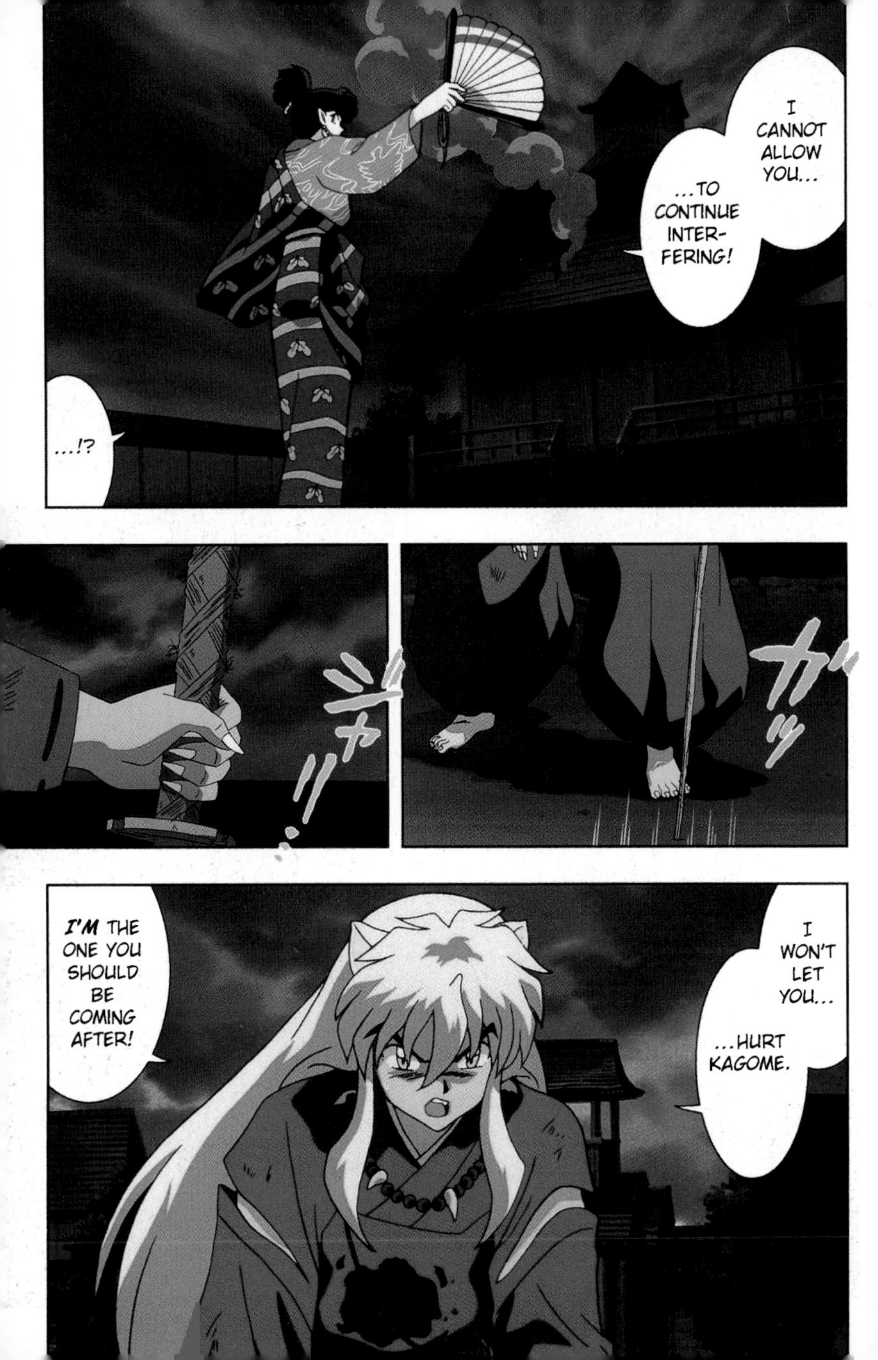

I CANNOT ALLOW YOU...
...TO CONTINUE INTER-FERING!
...!?
ジャリ
ガッ
I WON'T LET YOU...
...HURT KAGOME.
*I'M* THE ONE YOU SHOULD BE COMING AFTER!

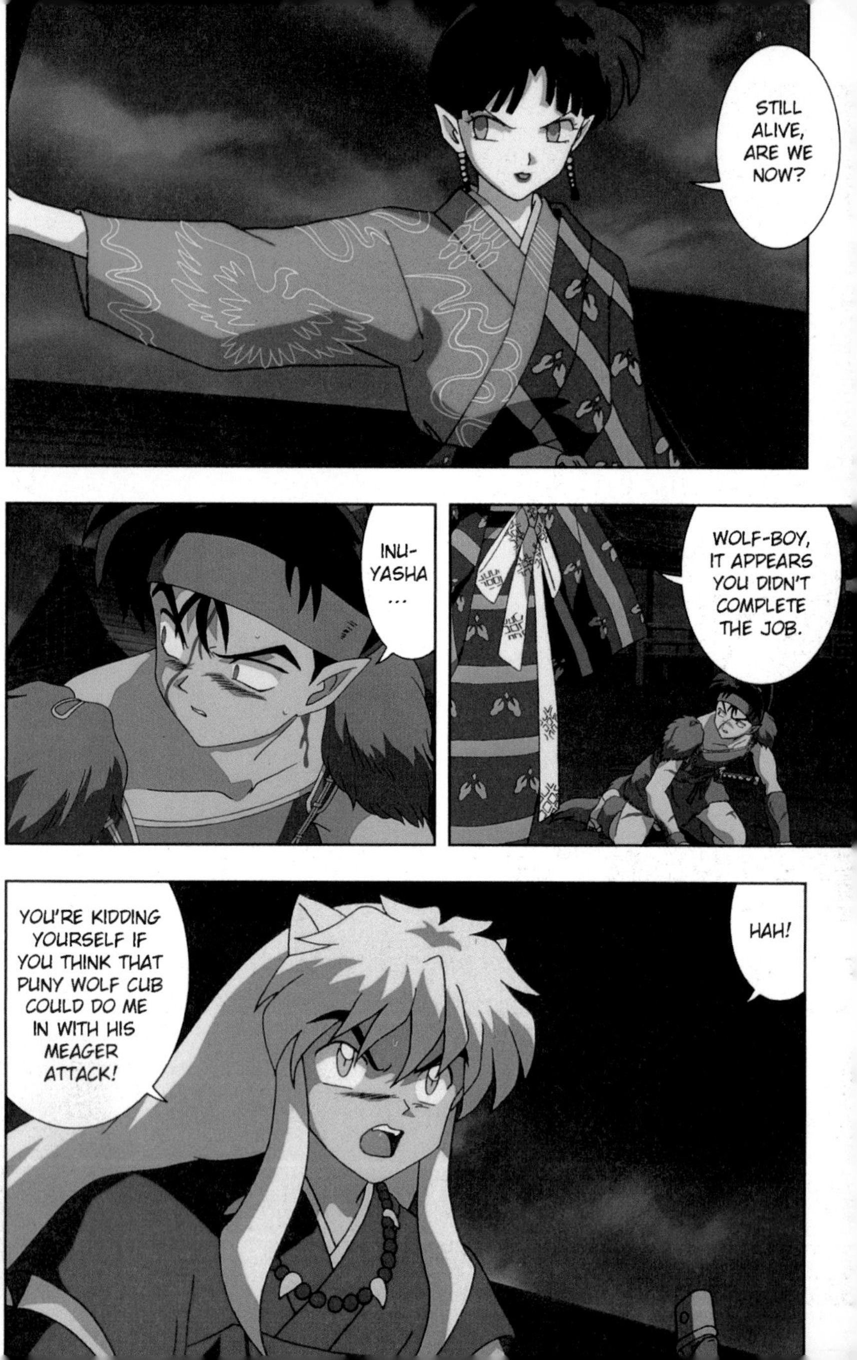
STILL ALIVE, ARE WE NOW?
WOLF-BOY, IT APPEARS YOU DIDN'T COMPLETE THE JOB.
INU-YASHA...
HAH!
YOU'RE KIDDING YOURSELF IF YOU THINK THAT PUNY WOLF CUB COULD DO ME IN WITH HIS MEAGER ATTACK!

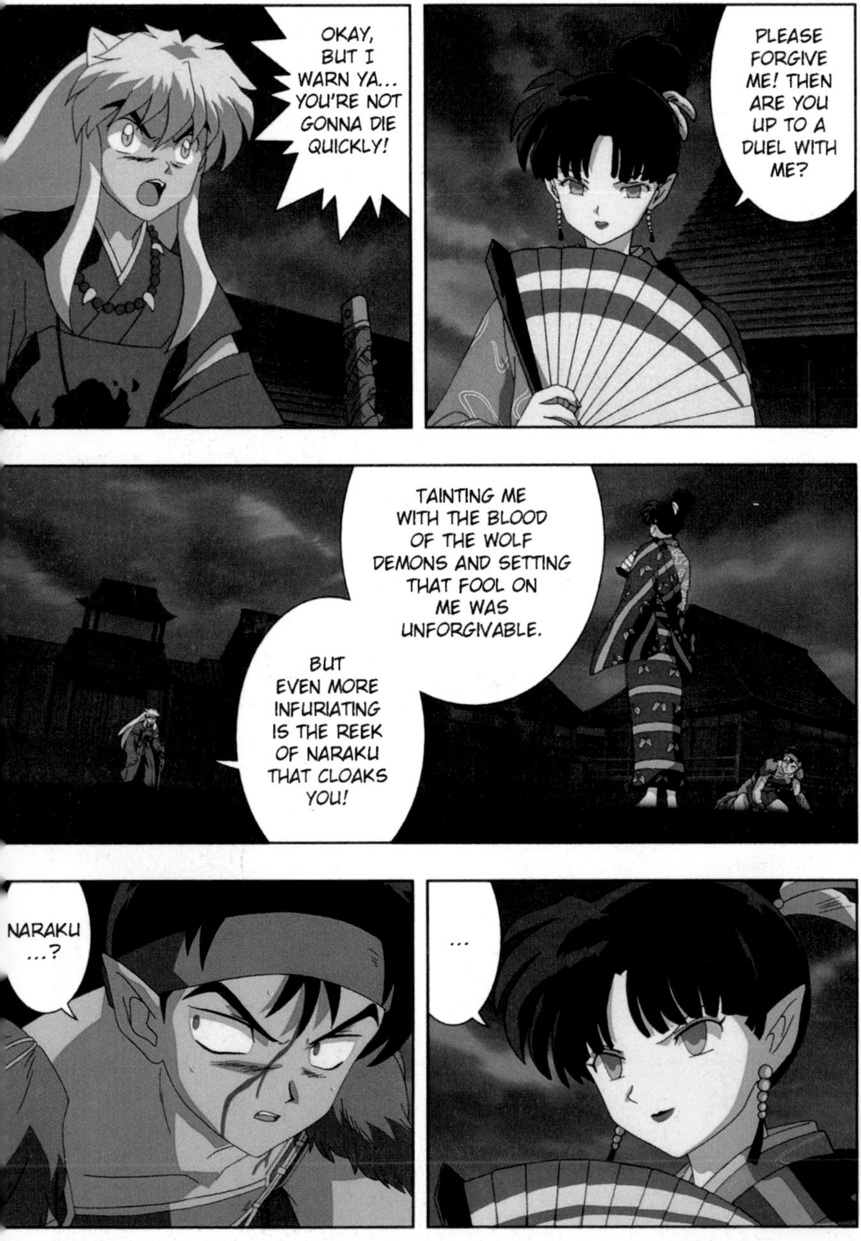
PLEASE FORGIVE ME! THEN ARE YOU UP TO A DUEL WITH ME?
OKAY, BUT I WARN YA... YOU'RE NOT GONNA DIE QUICKLY!
TAINTING ME WITH THE BLOOD OF THE WOLF DEMONS AND SETTING THAT FOOL ON ME WAS UNFORGIVABLE.
BUT EVEN MORE INFURIATING IS THE REEK OF NARAKU THAT CLOAKS YOU!
...
NARAKU ...?

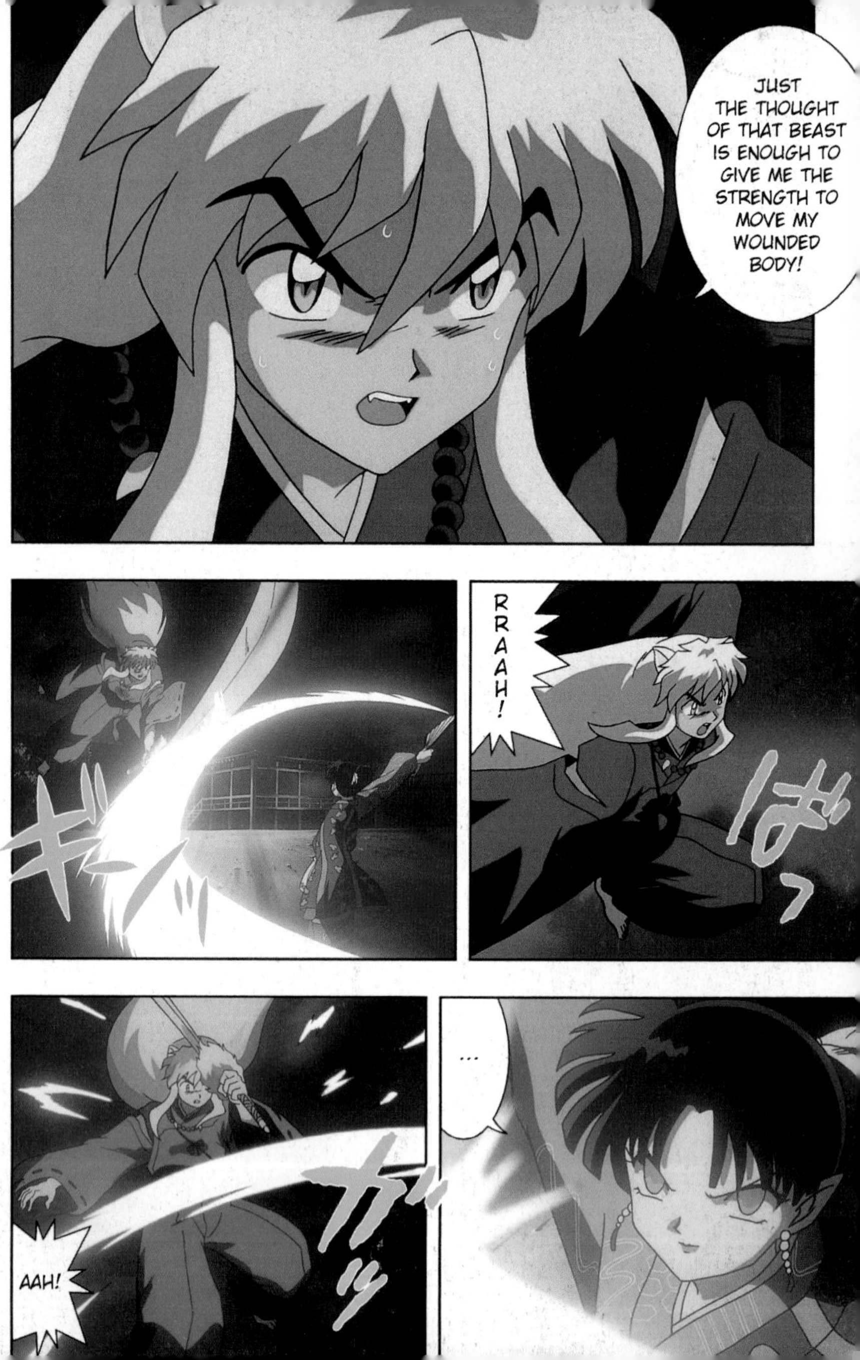
JUST THE THOUGHT OF THAT BEAST IS ENOUGH TO GIVE ME THE STRENGTH TO MOVE MY WOUNDED BODY!
RRAAH!
ばっ
ギン
...
カッ
AAH!

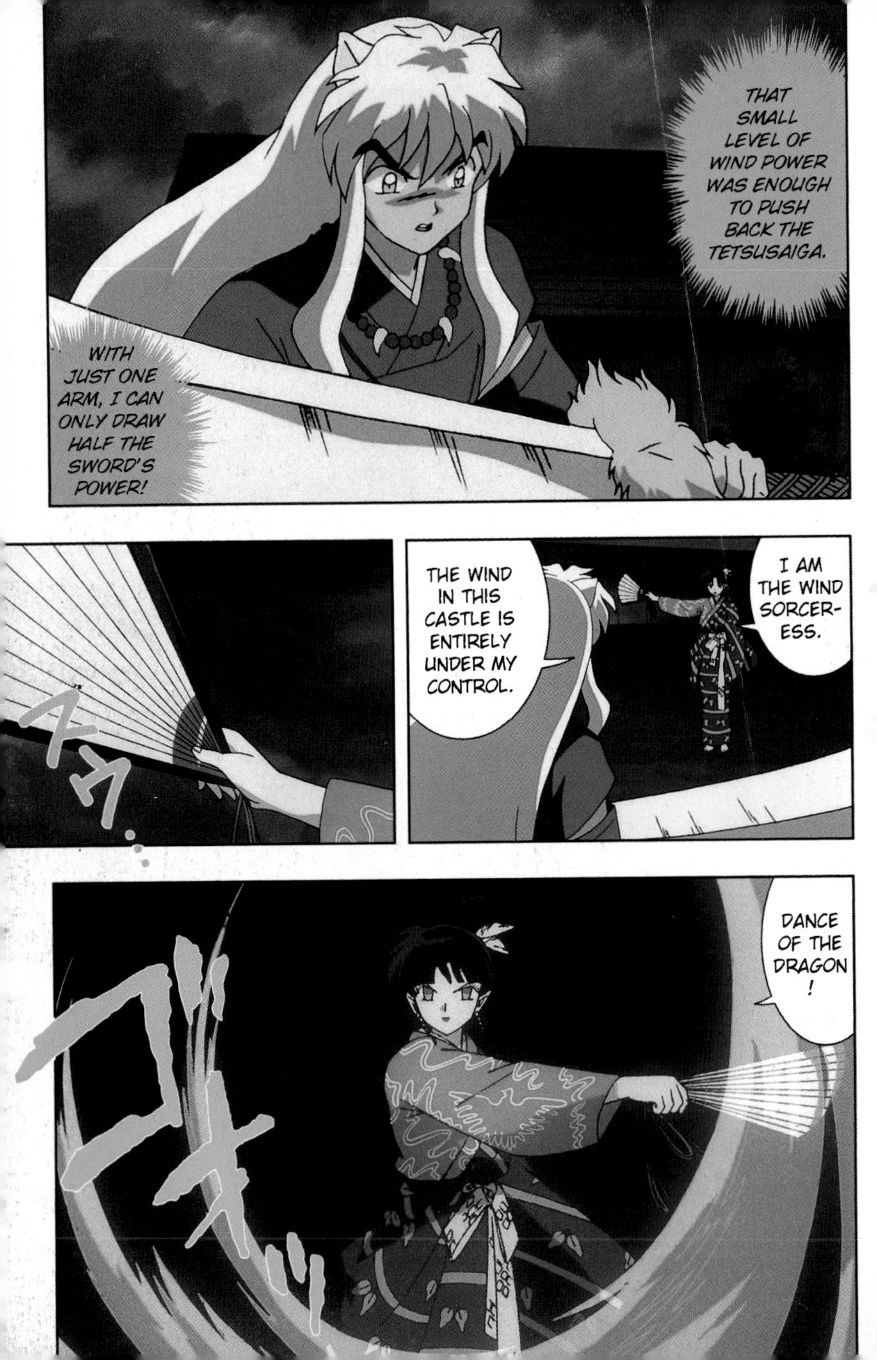
THAT SMALL LEVEL OF WIND POWER WAS ENOUGH TO PUSH BACK THE TETSUSAIGA.
WITH JUST ONE ARM, I CAN ONLY DRAW HALF THE SWORD'S POWER!
I AM THE WIND SORCER-ESS.
THE WIND IN THIS CASTLE IS ENTIRELY UNDER MY CONTROL.
DANCE OF THE DRAGON!

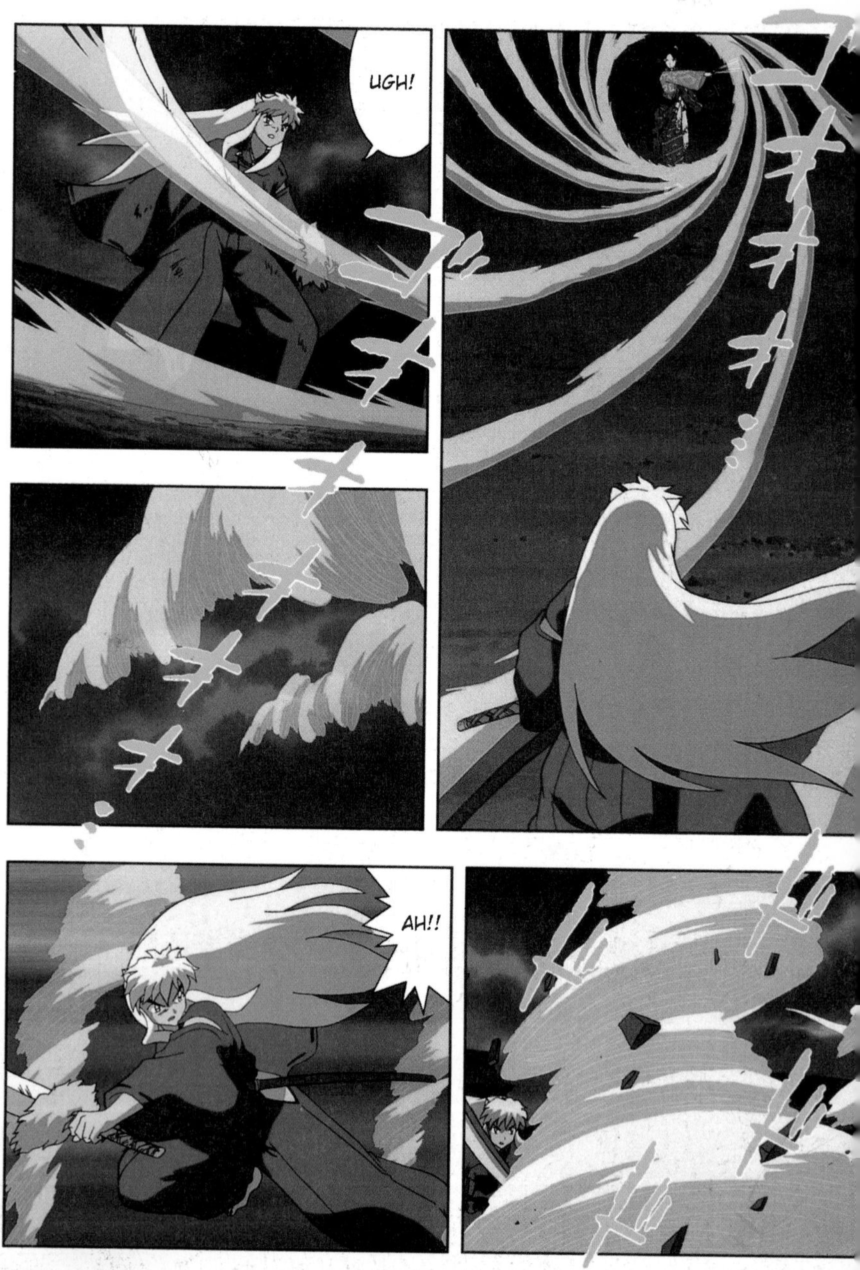
UGH!
AH!!

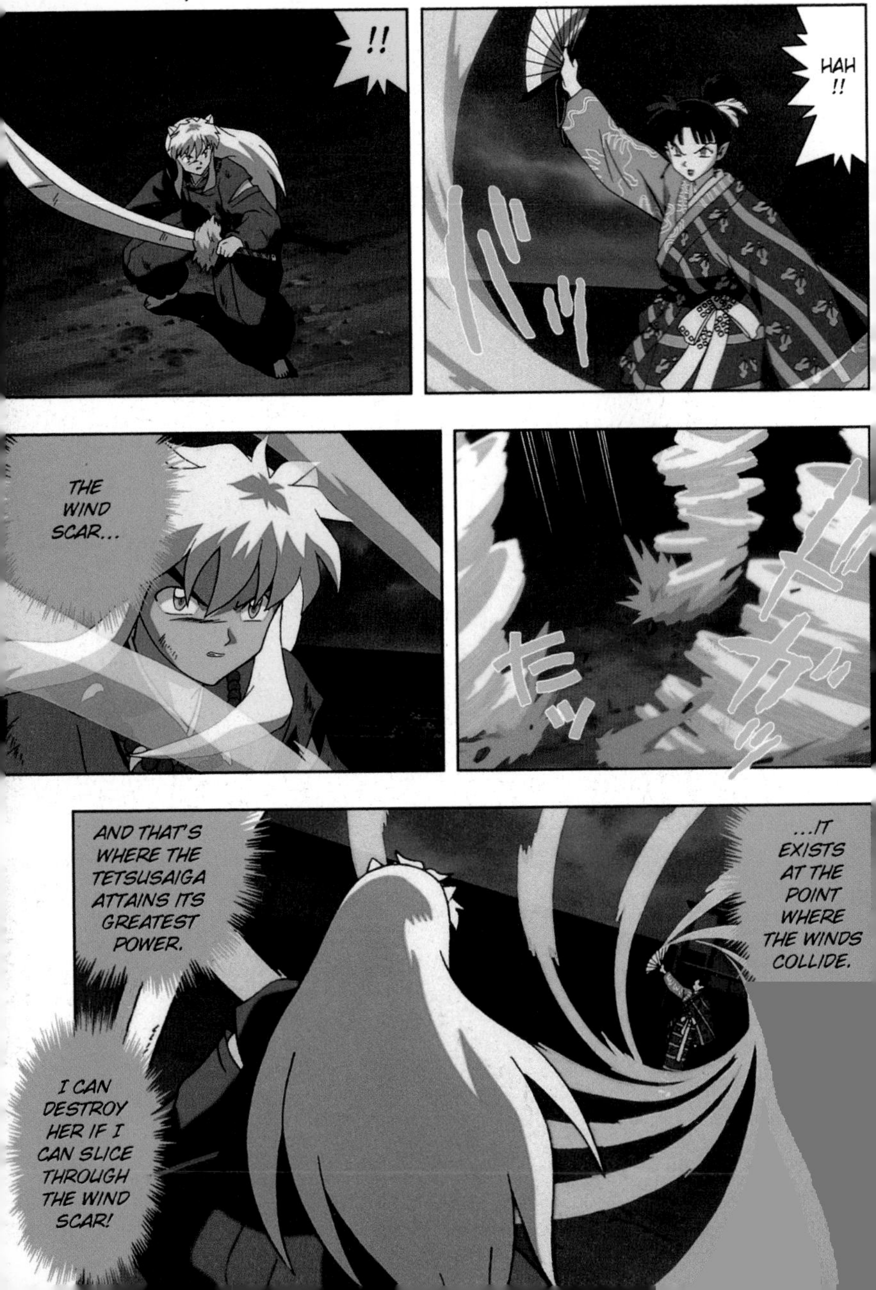
HAH!!
!!
THE WIND SCAR...
...IT EXISTS AT THE POINT WHERE THE WINDS COLLIDE.
AND THAT'S WHERE THE TETSUSAIGA ATTAINS ITS GREATEST POWER.
I CAN DESTROY HER IF I CAN SLICE THROUGH THE WIND SCAR!

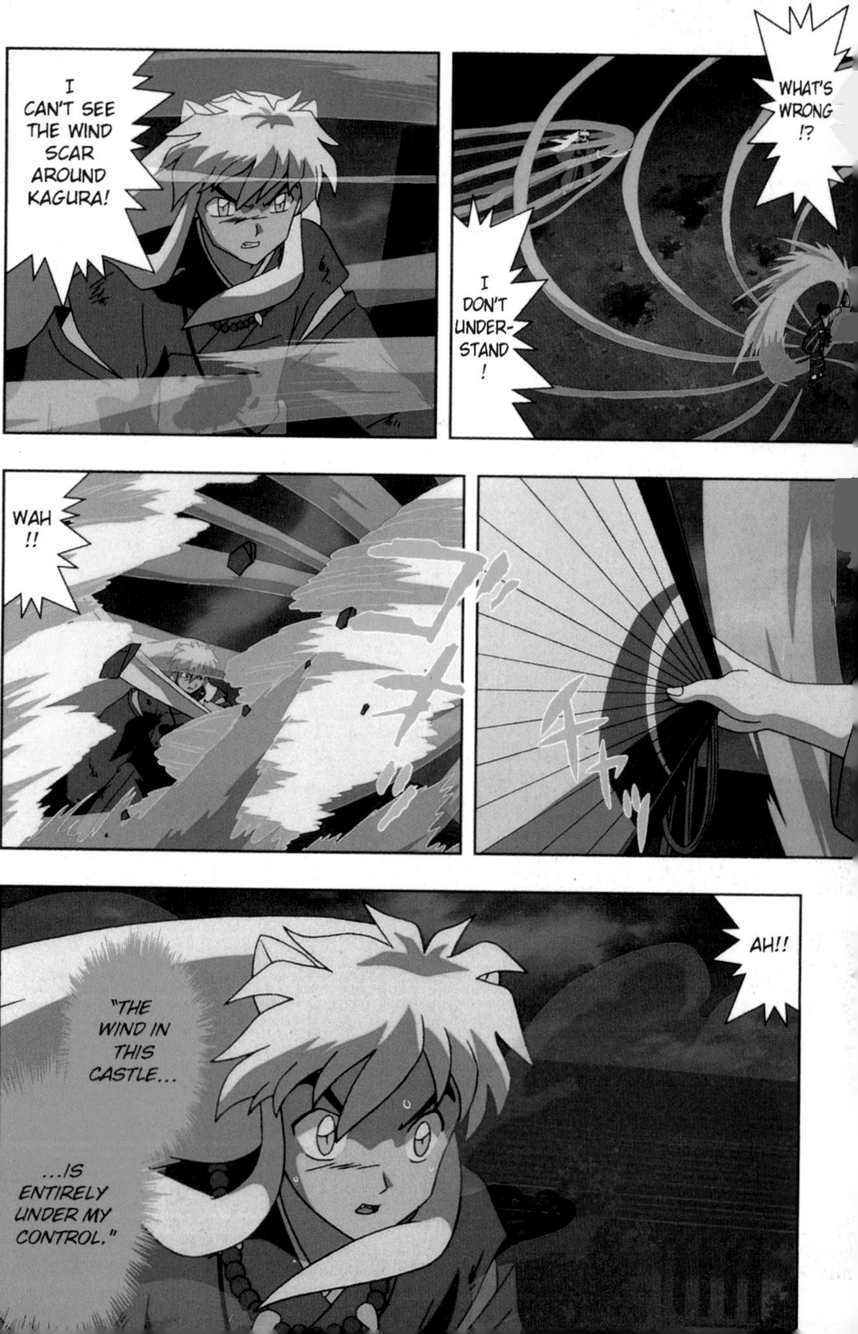
WHAT'S WRONG !?
I DON'T UNDER-STAND !
I CAN'T SEE THE WIND SCAR AROUND KAGURA!
WAH !!
AH!!
"THE WIND IN THIS CASTLE...
...IS ENTIRELY UNDER MY CONTROL."

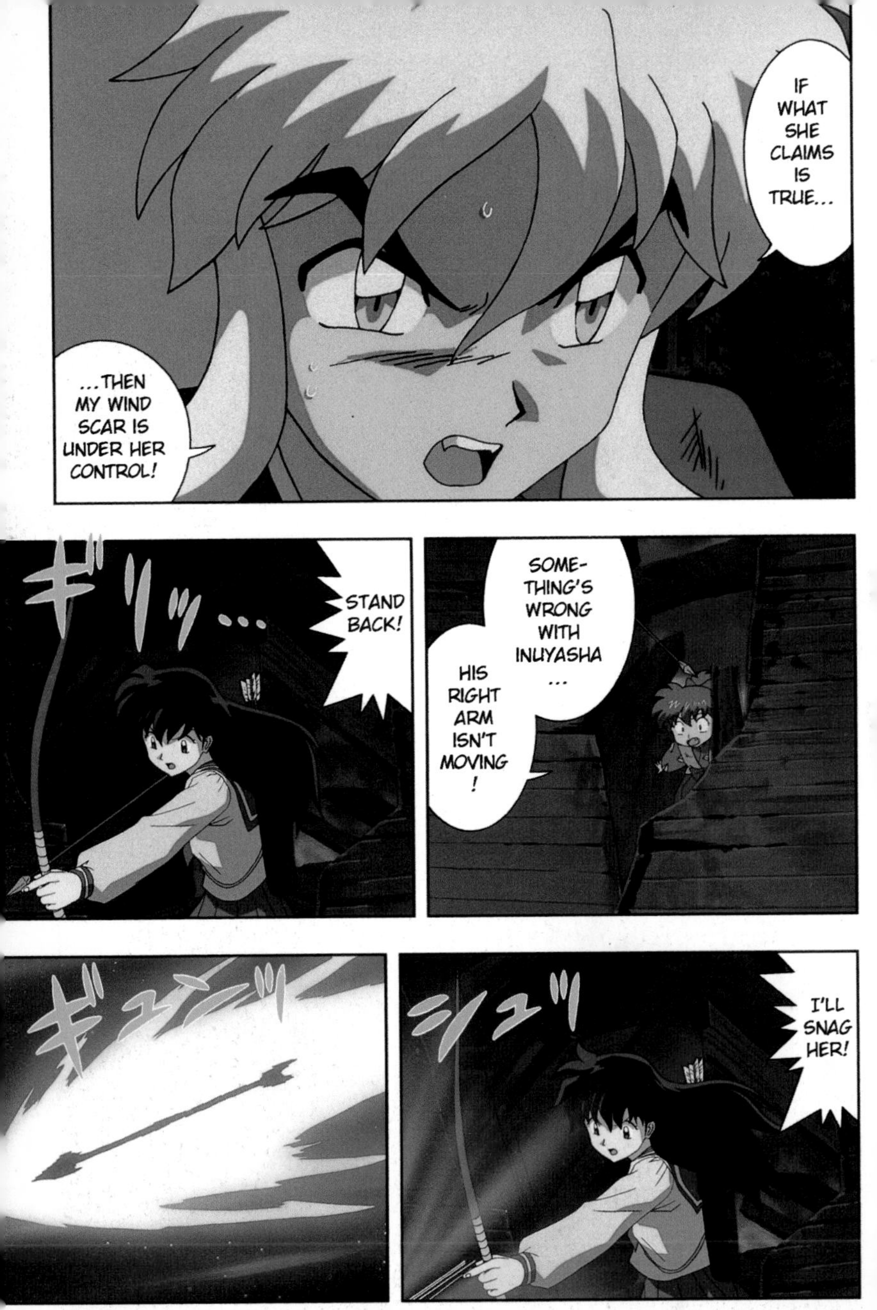
IF WHAT SHE CLAIMS IS TRUE...
...THEN MY WIND SCAR IS UNDER HER CONTROL!
SOME-THING'S WRONG WITH INUYASHA ...
HIS RIGHT ARM ISN'T MOVING !
ギリッ…
STAND BACK!
シュッ
I'LL SNAG HER!
ギューッ

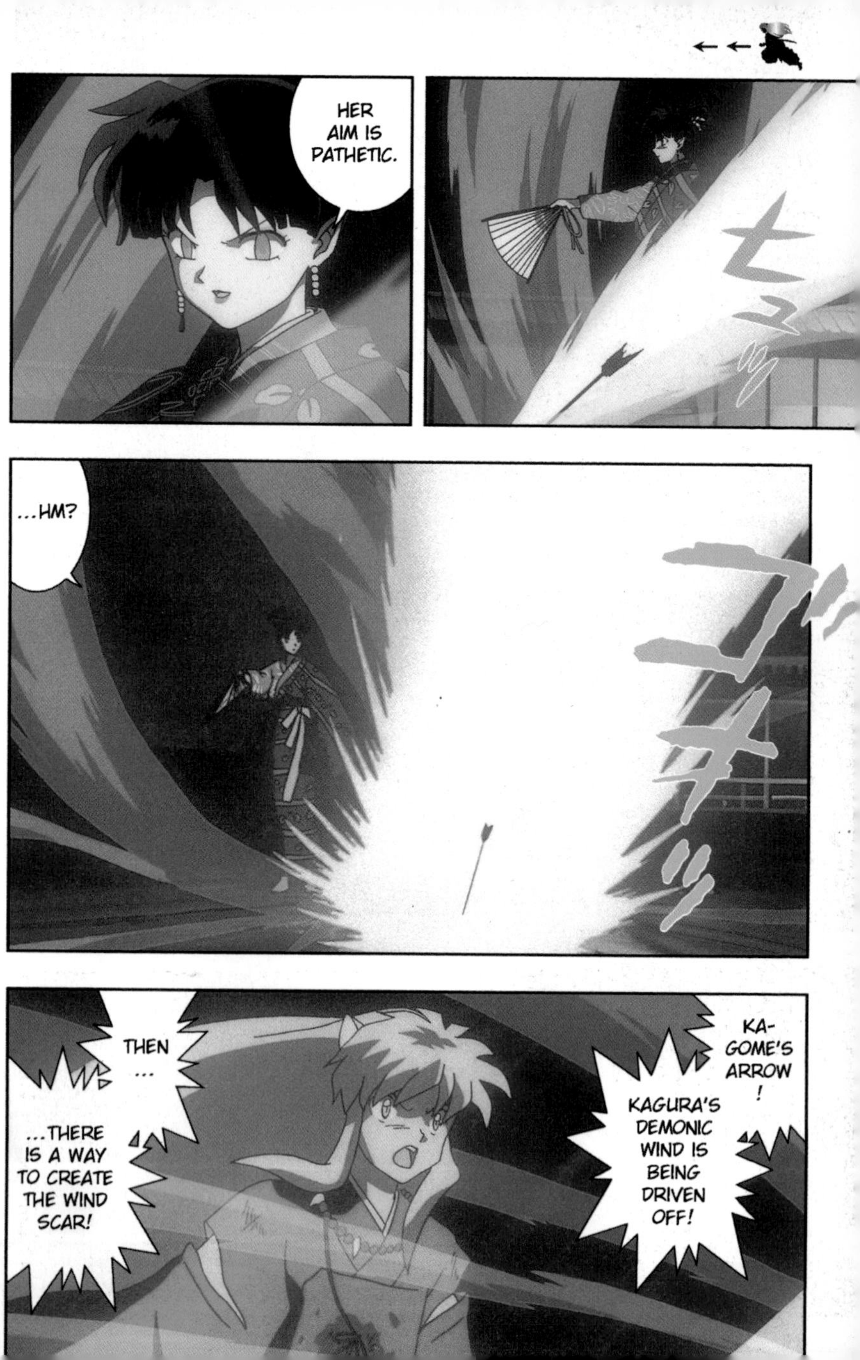
HER AIM IS PATHETIC.
...HM?
KA-GOME'S ARROW!
KAGURA'S DEMONIC WIND IS BEING DRIVEN OFF!
THEN...
...THERE IS A WAY TO CREATE THE WIND SCAR!

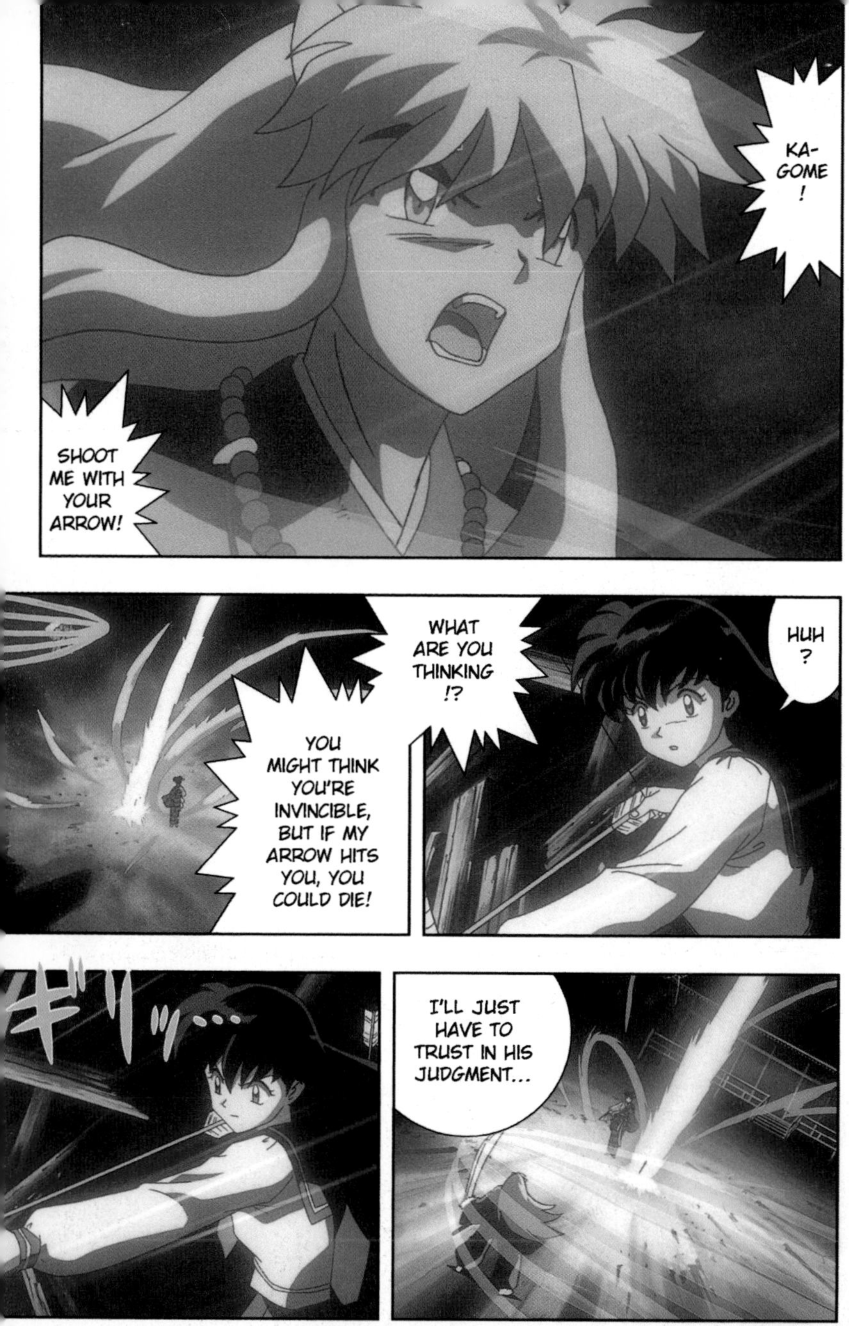
KA-GOME!
SHOOT ME WITH YOUR ARROW!
HUH?
WHAT ARE YOU THINKING!?
YOU MIGHT THINK YOU'RE INVINCIBLE, BUT IF MY ARROW HITS YOU, YOU COULD DIE!
I'LL JUST HAVE TO TRUST IN HIS JUDGMENT...
ギリッ…

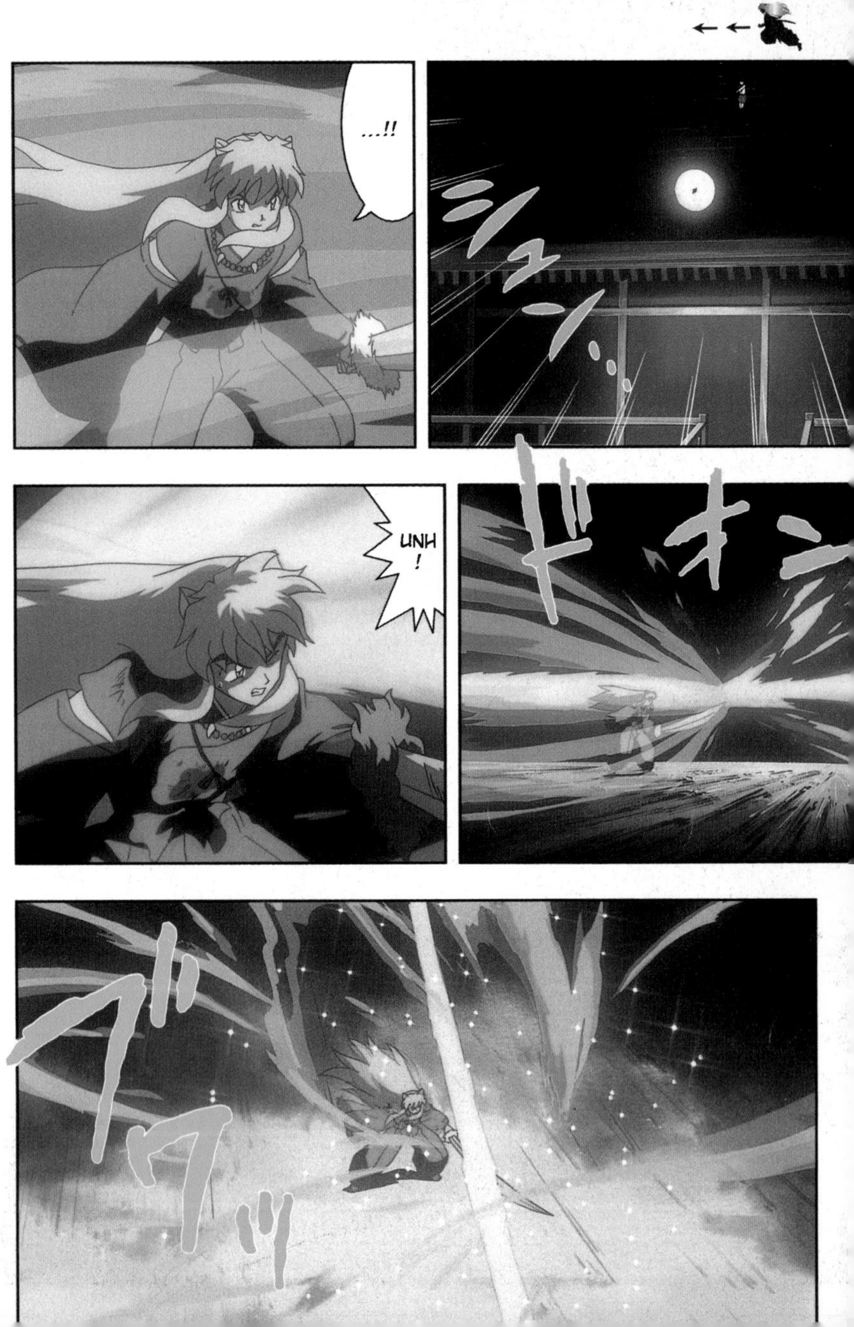
シュン…
...!!
ドオン
UNH!

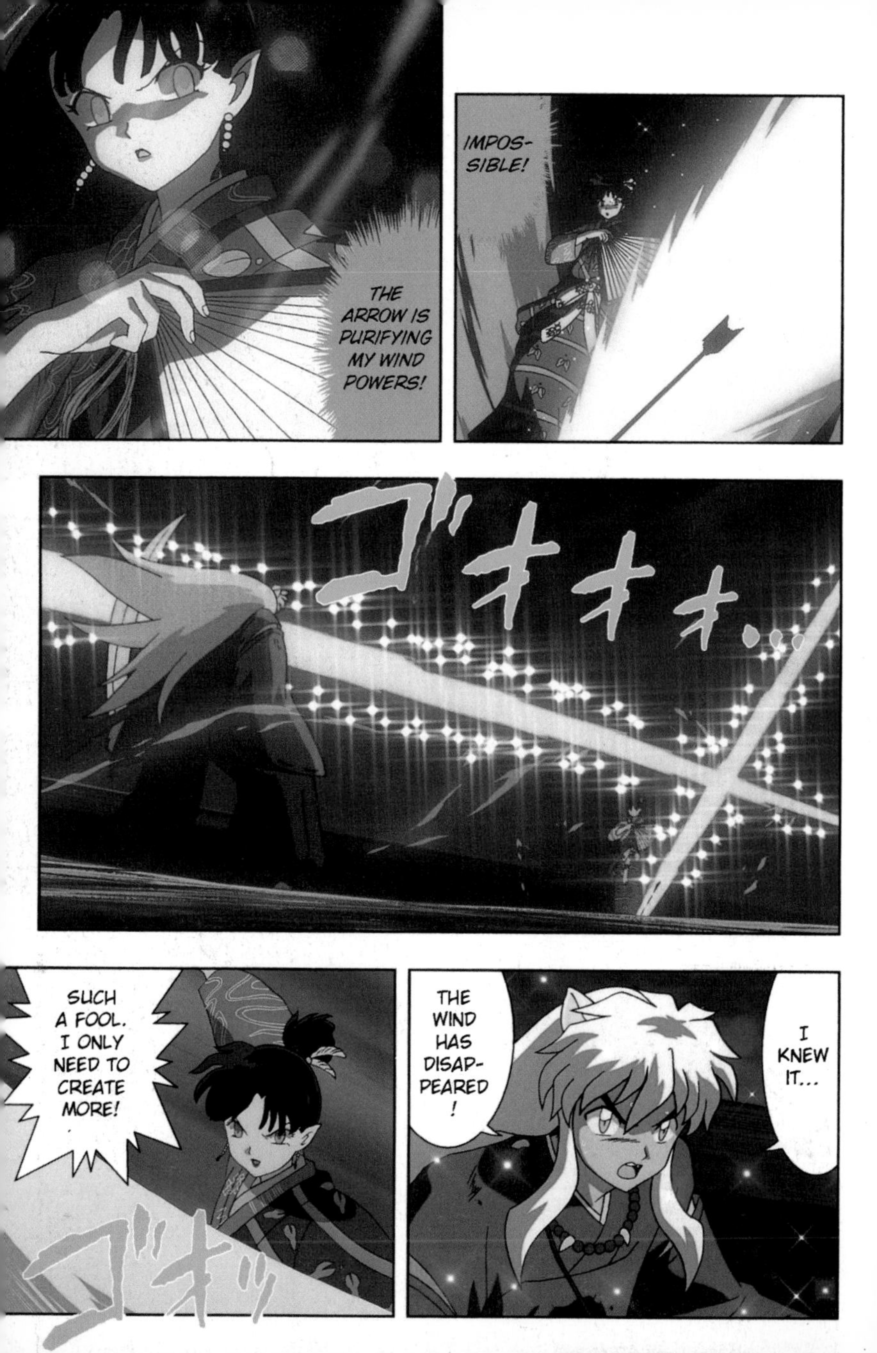
IMPOS-
SIBLE!
THE ARROW IS PURIFYING MY WIND POWERS!
ゴオオォ…
I KNEW IT…
THE WIND HAS DISAP-PEARED!
SUCH A FOOL. I ONLY NEED TO CREATE MORE!
ゴオッ

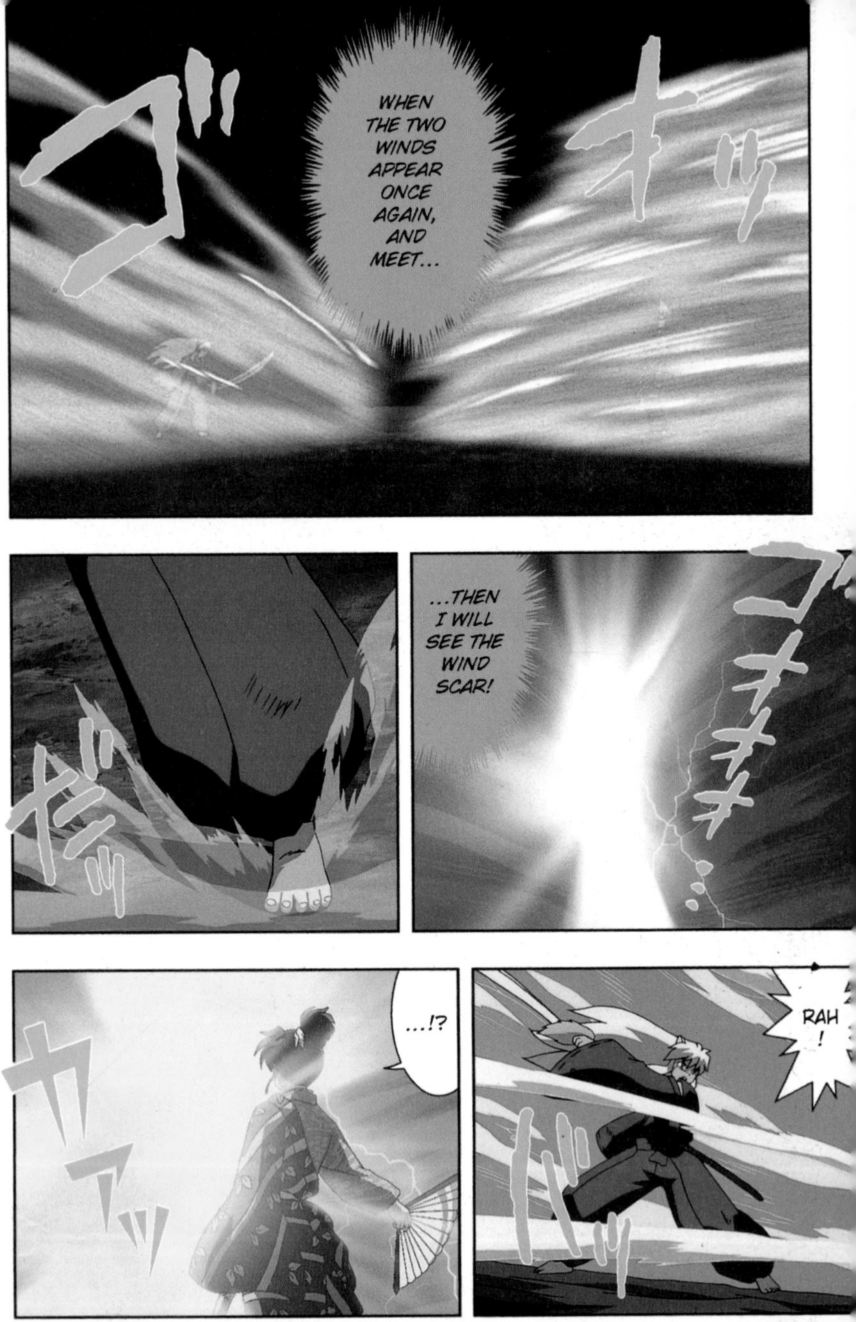

ゴ
オッ
WHEN THE TWO WINDS APPEAR ONCE AGAIN, AND MEET...
ゴ
...THEN I WILL SEE THE WIND SCAR!
ガッ
RAH!
...!?
ヤァッ
バッ

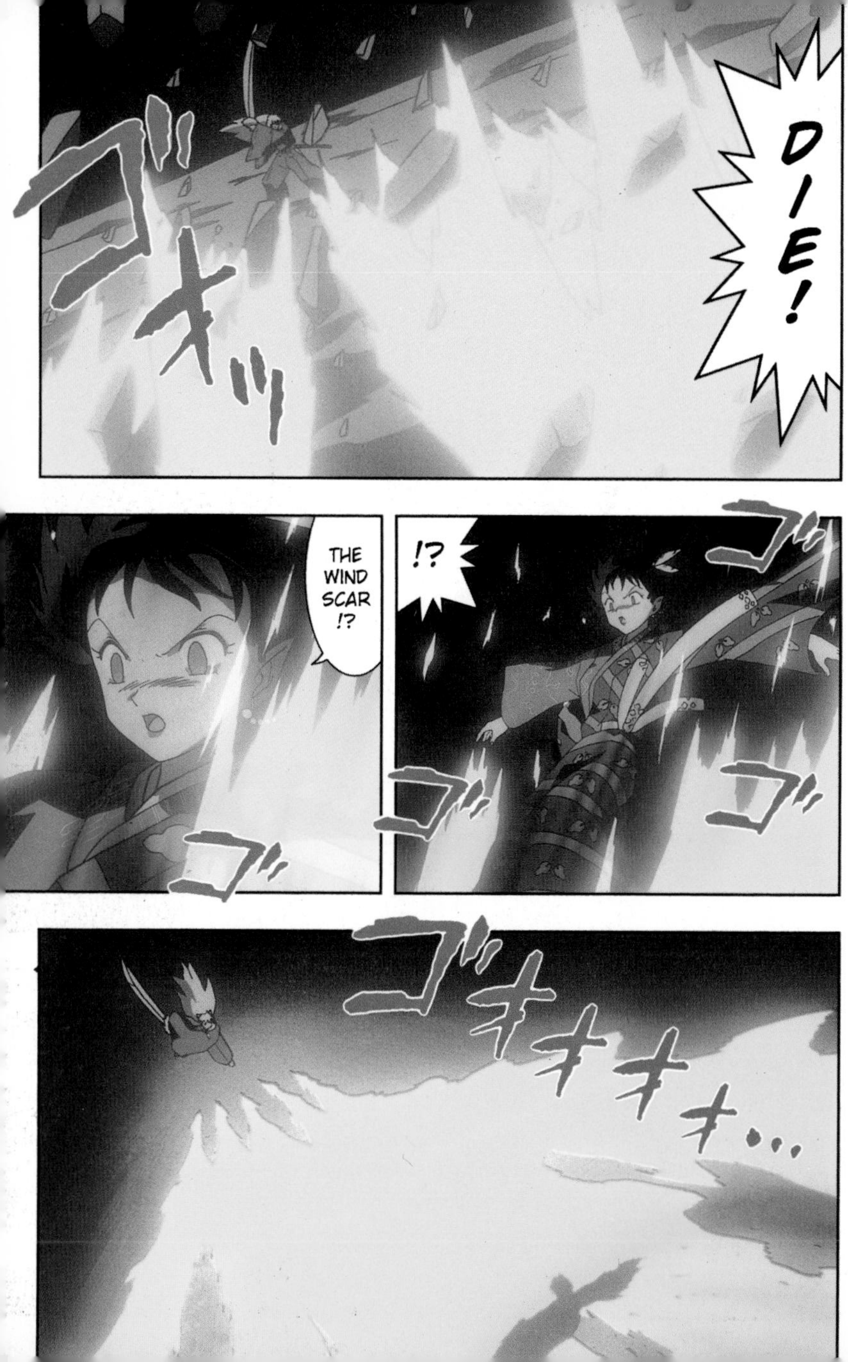

ゴオッ
DIE!
!?
ゴ
ゴ
ゴ
THE WIND SCAR !?
ゴ
ゴオオオオ…

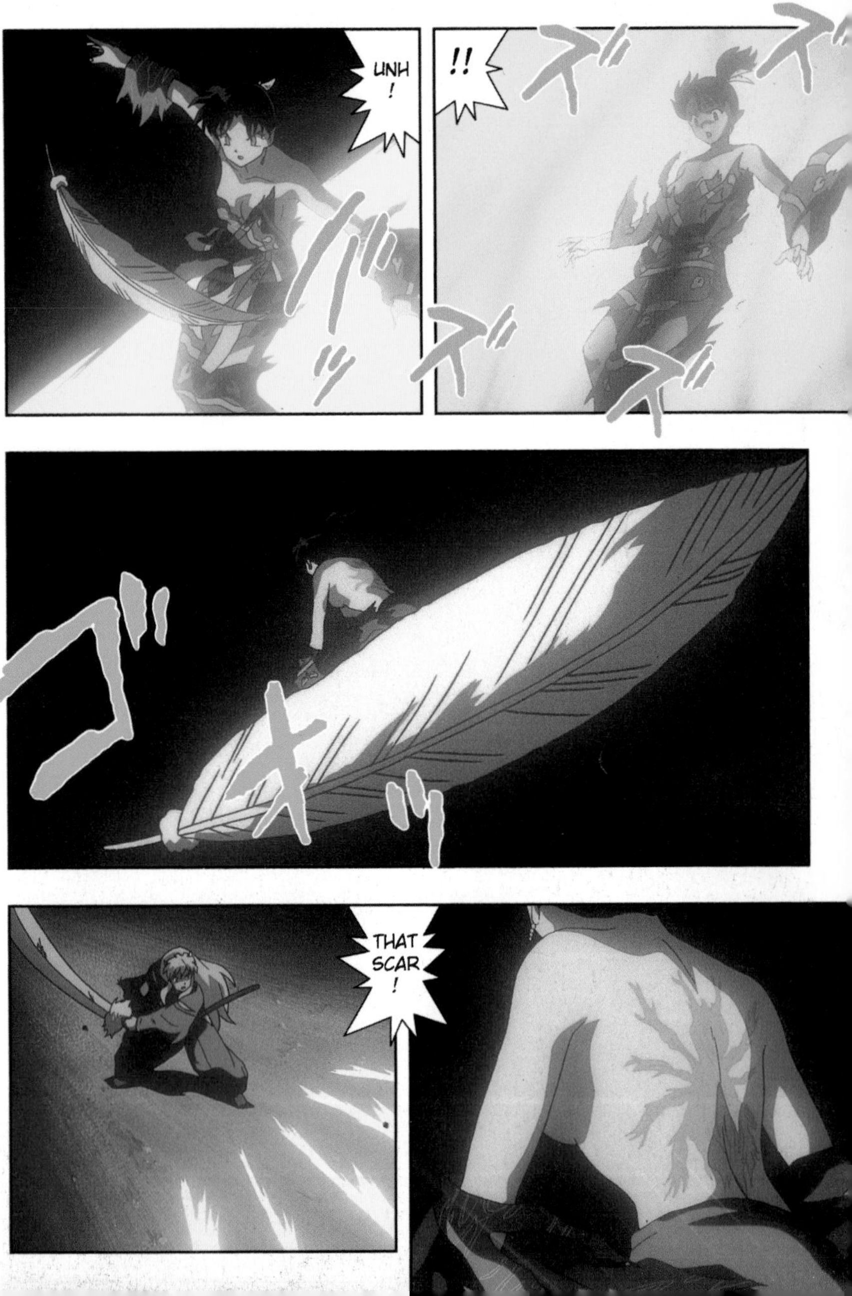
!!
ズ
ズ
ズ
UNH !
バッ
ゴオッ
THAT SCAR !

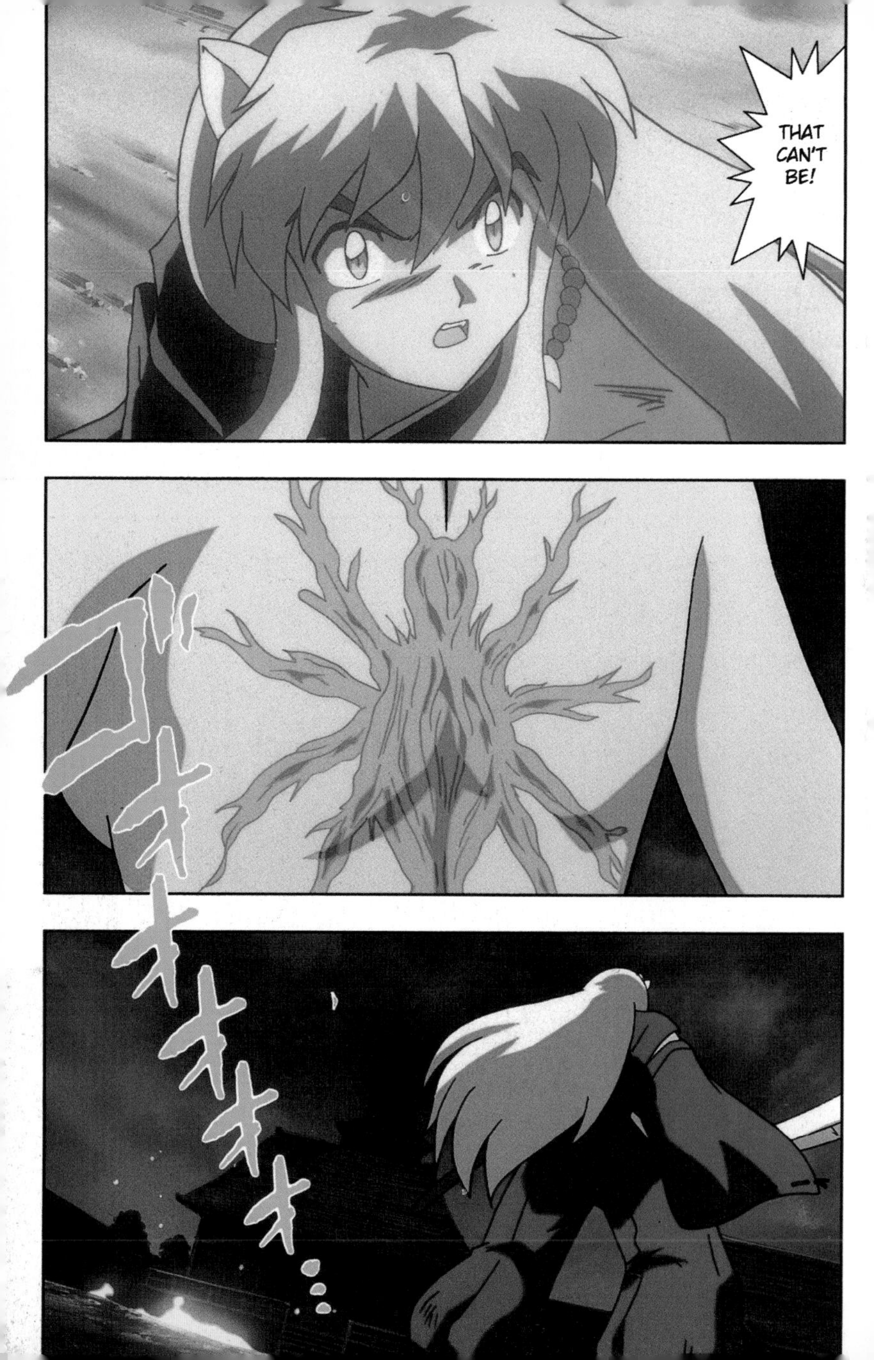
THAT CAN'T BE!
ゴォォォォォ…

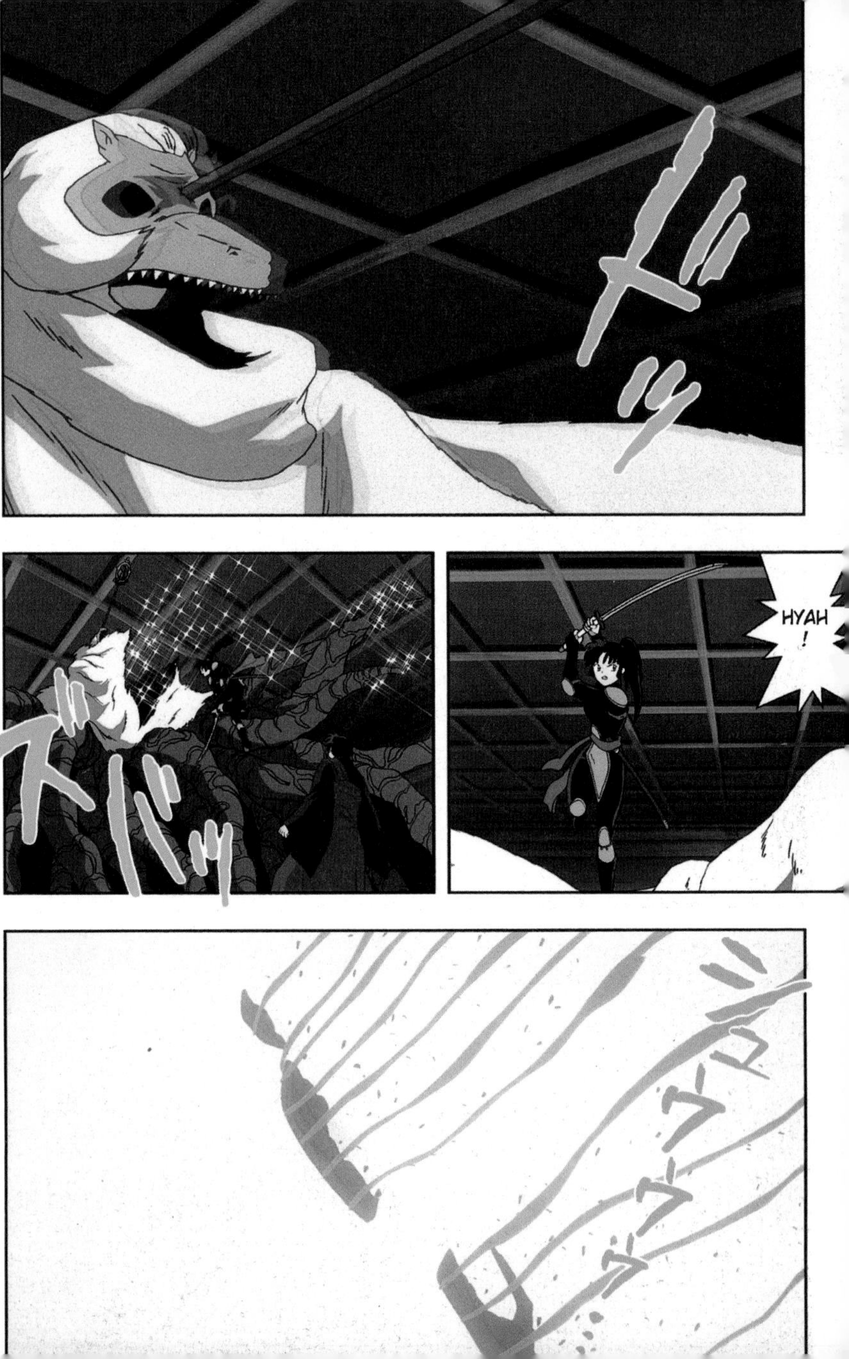
ドッ
ズバッ
HYAH!
シュウウウ

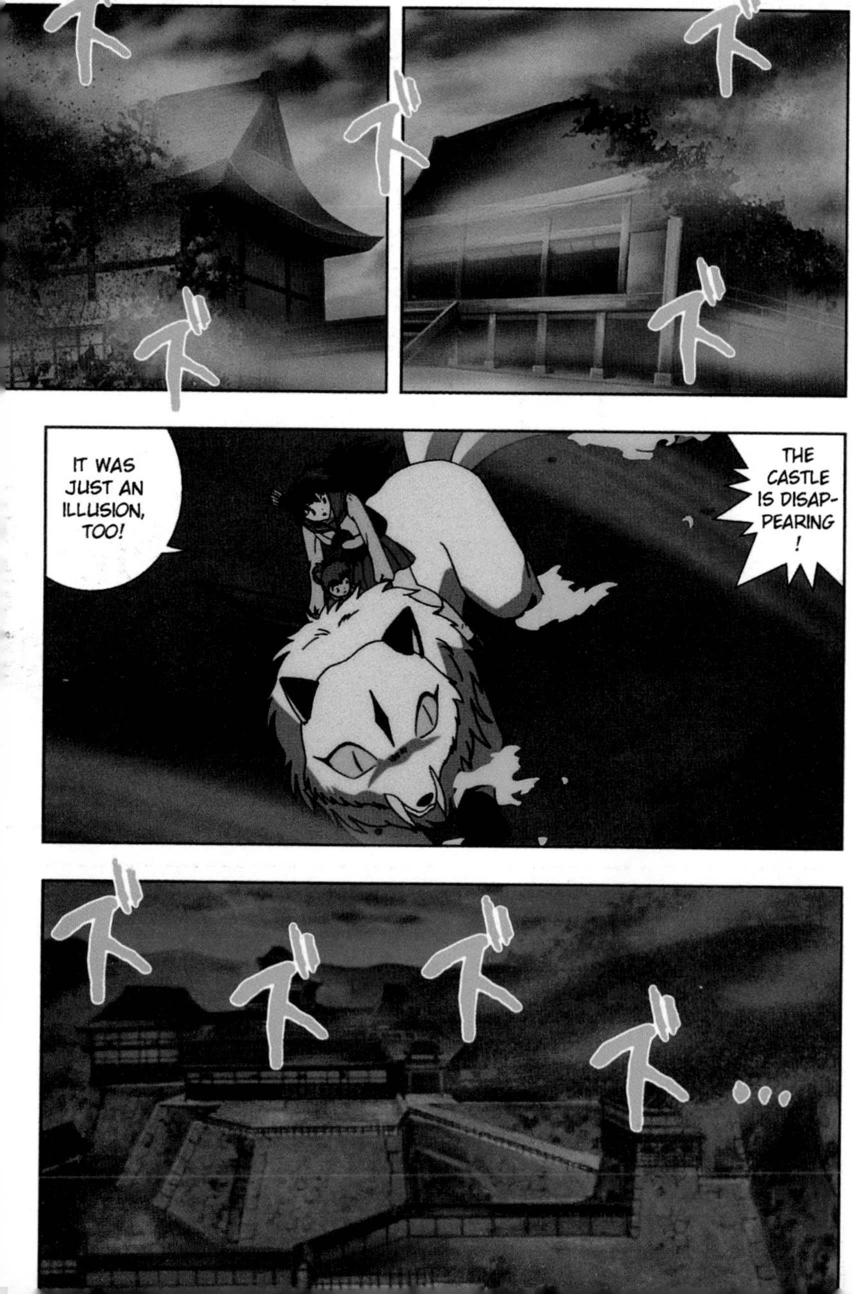
ズ
ズ
ズ
ズ
ズ
THE CASTLE IS DISAPPEARING!
IT WAS JUST AN ILLUSION, TOO!
ズ
ズ
ズ
ズ...

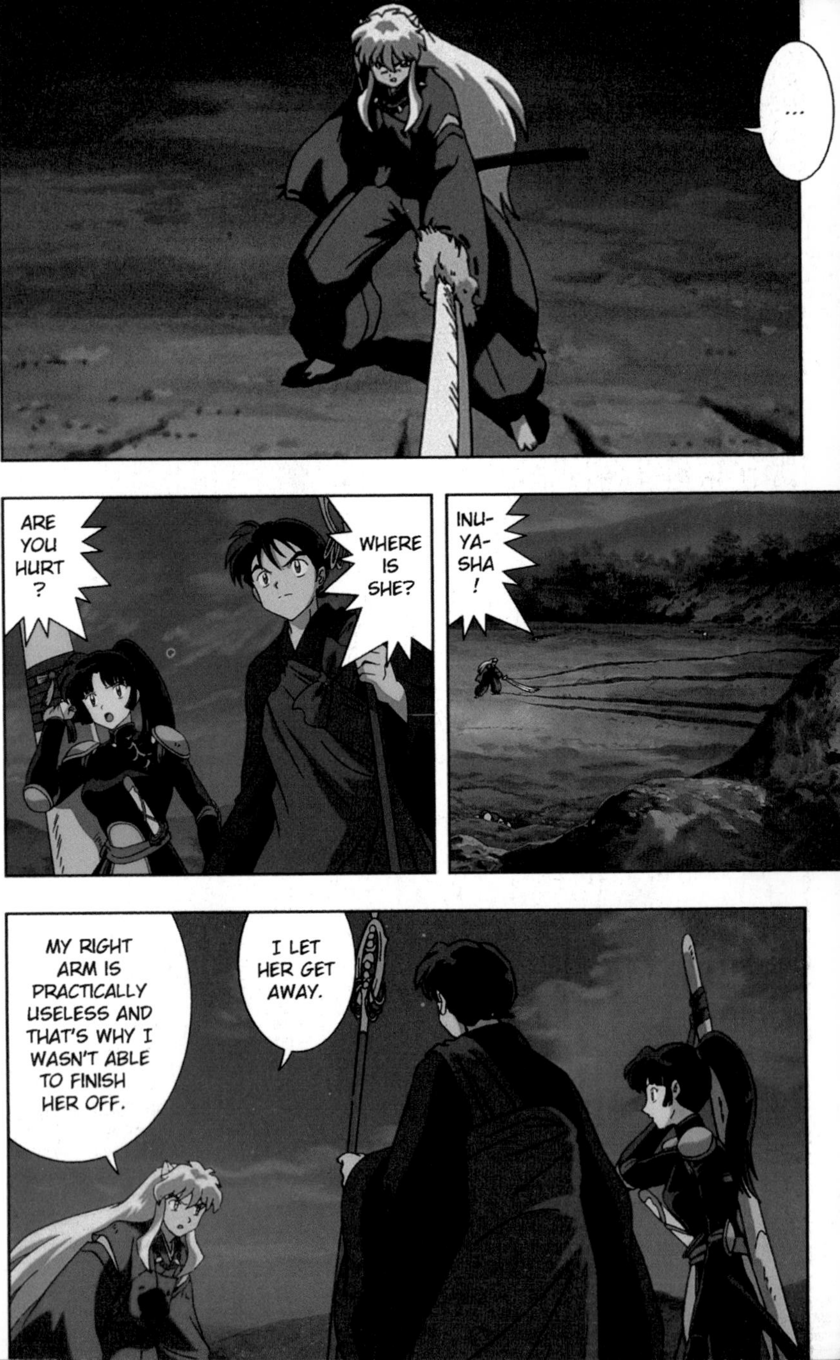
...
INU-YA-SHA!
WHERE IS SHE?
ARE YOU HURT?
I LET HER GET AWAY.
MY RIGHT ARM IS PRACTICALLY USELESS AND THAT'S WHY I WASN'T ABLE TO FINISH HER OFF.

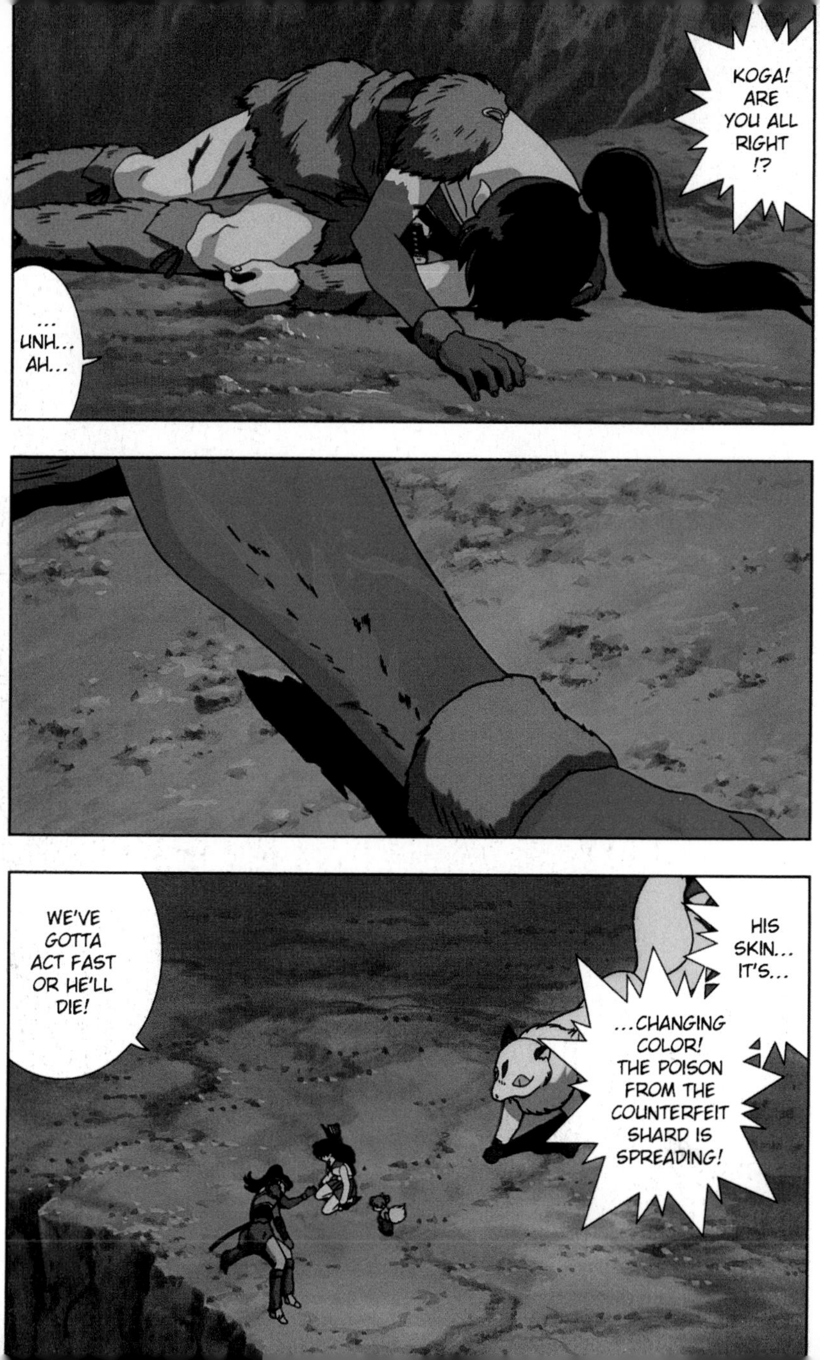
KOGA! ARE YOU ALL RIGHT !?
... UNH... AH...
HIS SKIN... IT'S...
...CHANGING COLOR! THE POISON FROM THE COUNTERFEIT SHARD IS SPREADING!
WE'VE GOTTA ACT FAST OR HE'LL DIE!

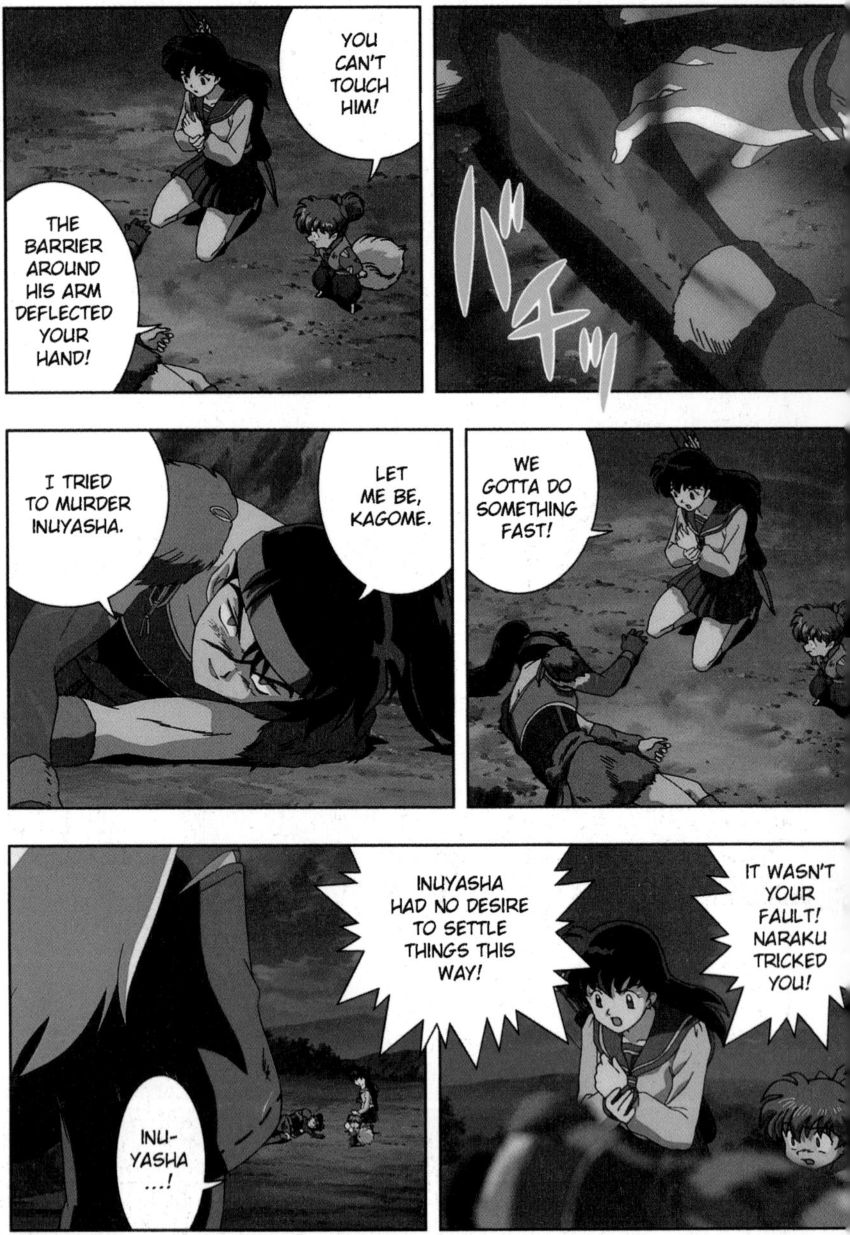
バチッ
YOU CAN'T TOUCH HIM!
THE BARRIER AROUND HIS ARM DEFLECTED YOUR HAND!
WE GOTTA DO SOMETHING FAST!
LET ME BE, KAGOME.
I TRIED TO MURDER INUYASHA.
IT WASN'T YOUR FAULT! NARAKU TRICKED YOU!
INUYASHA HAD NO DESIRE TO SETTLE THINGS THIS WAY!
INU-YASHA ...!

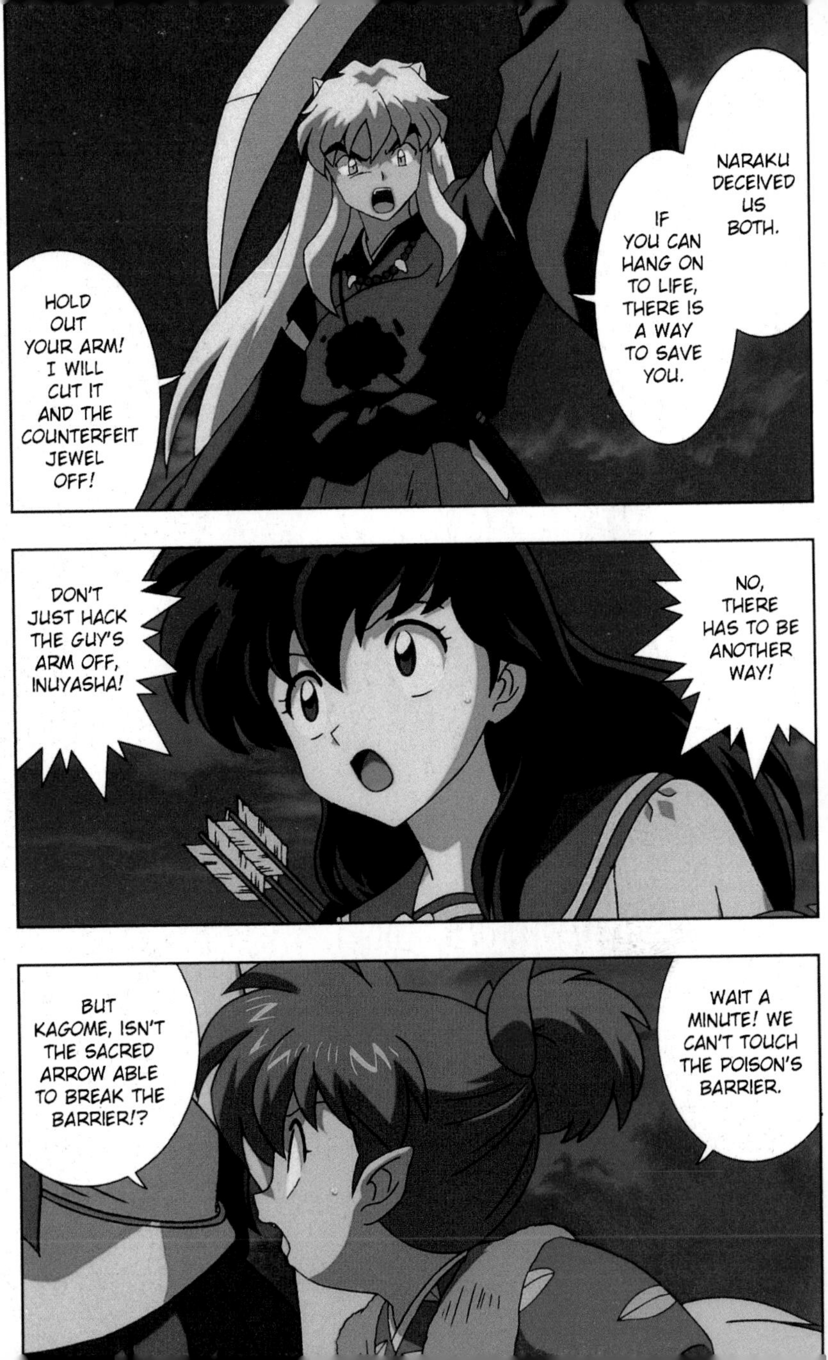
NARAKU DECEIVED US BOTH.
IF YOU CAN HANG ON TO LIFE, THERE IS A WAY TO SAVE YOU.
HOLD OUT YOUR ARM! I WILL CUT IT AND THE COUNTERFEIT JEWEL OFF!
NO, THERE HAS TO BE ANOTHER WAY!
DON'T JUST HACK THE GUY'S ARM OFF, INUYASHA!
WAIT A MINUTE! WE CAN'T TOUCH THE POISON'S BARRIER.
BUT KAGOME, ISN'T THE SACRED ARROW ABLE TO BREAK THE BARRIER!?

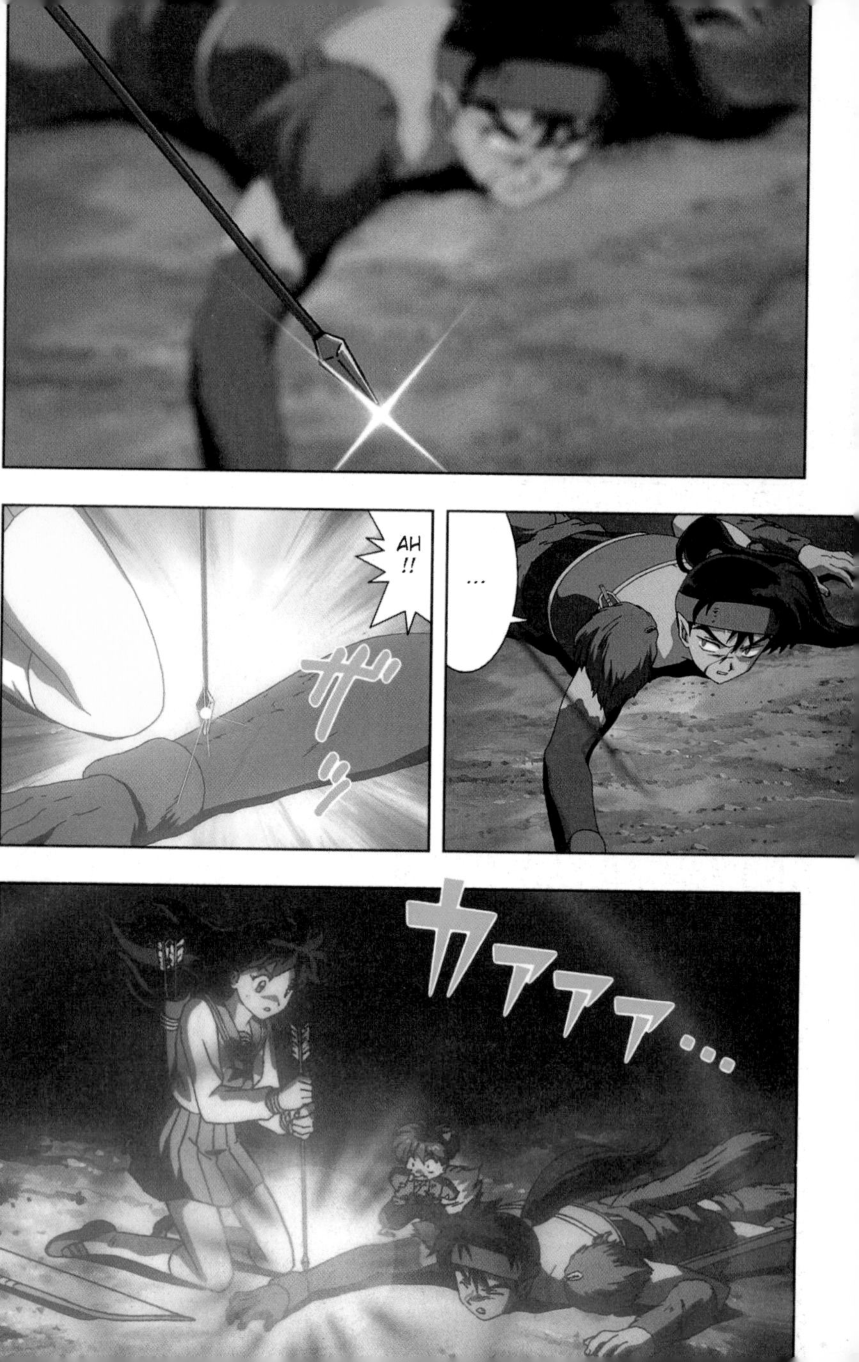
AH !!
...
ザッ
カァァァ...

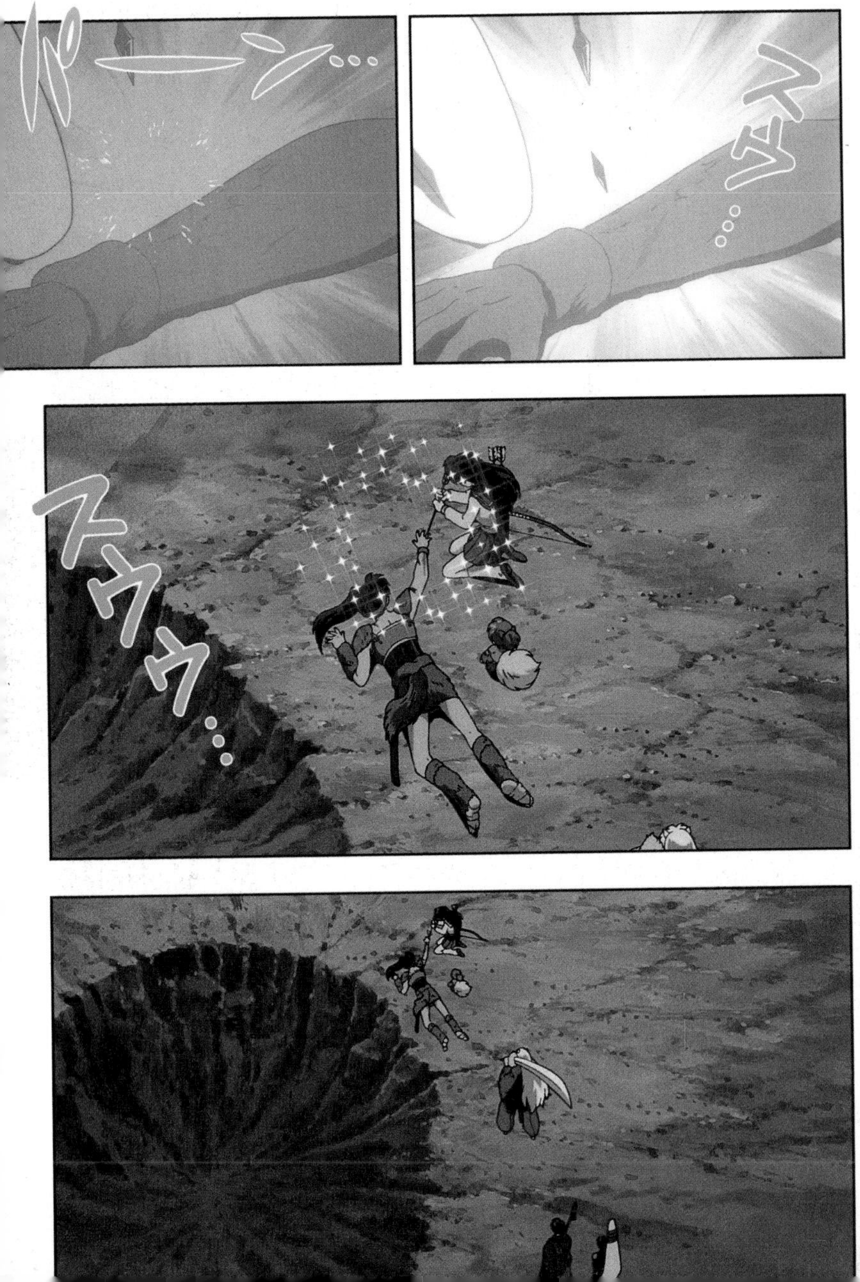
スタ…
パーン…
スウウ…

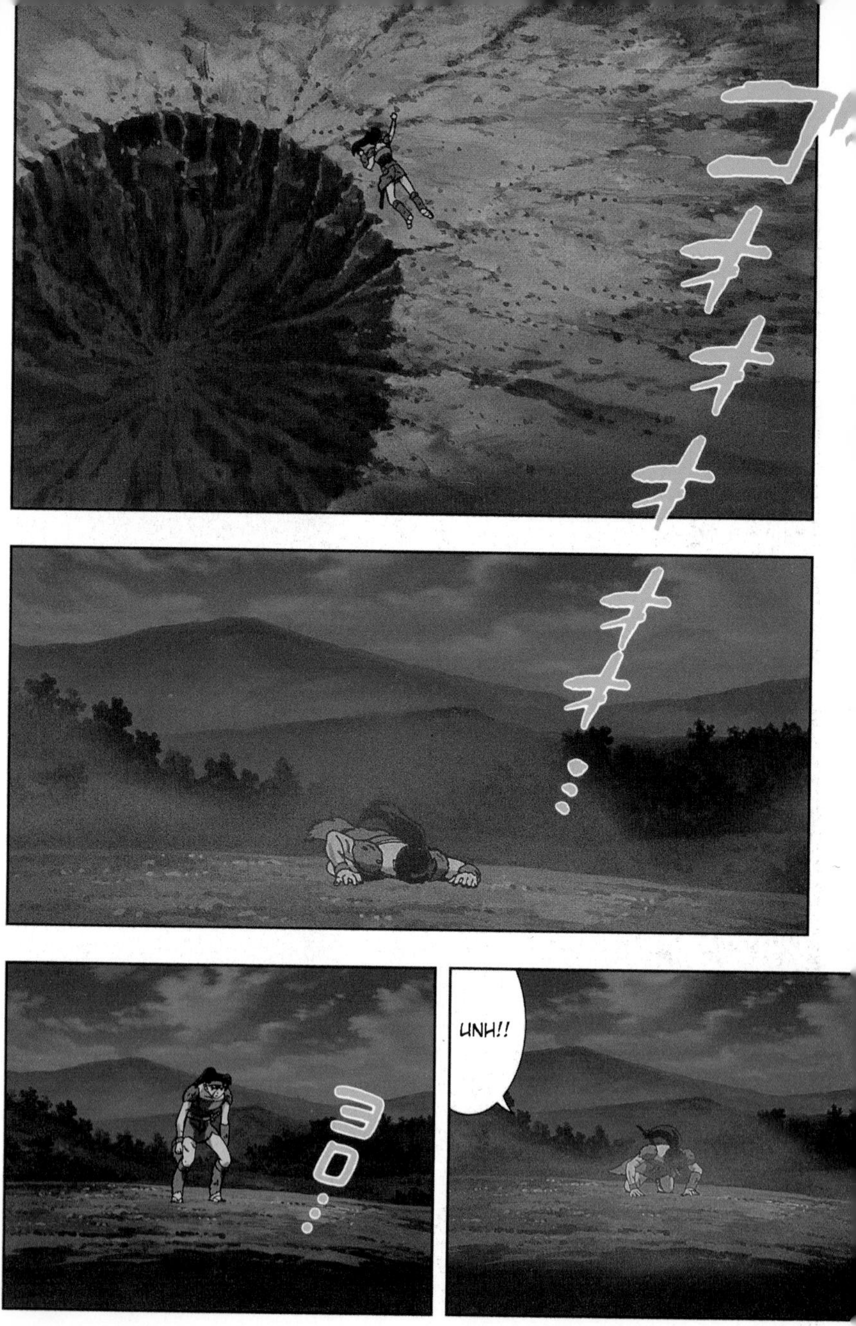
ゴォォォォォ…
ヨロ…
UNH!!

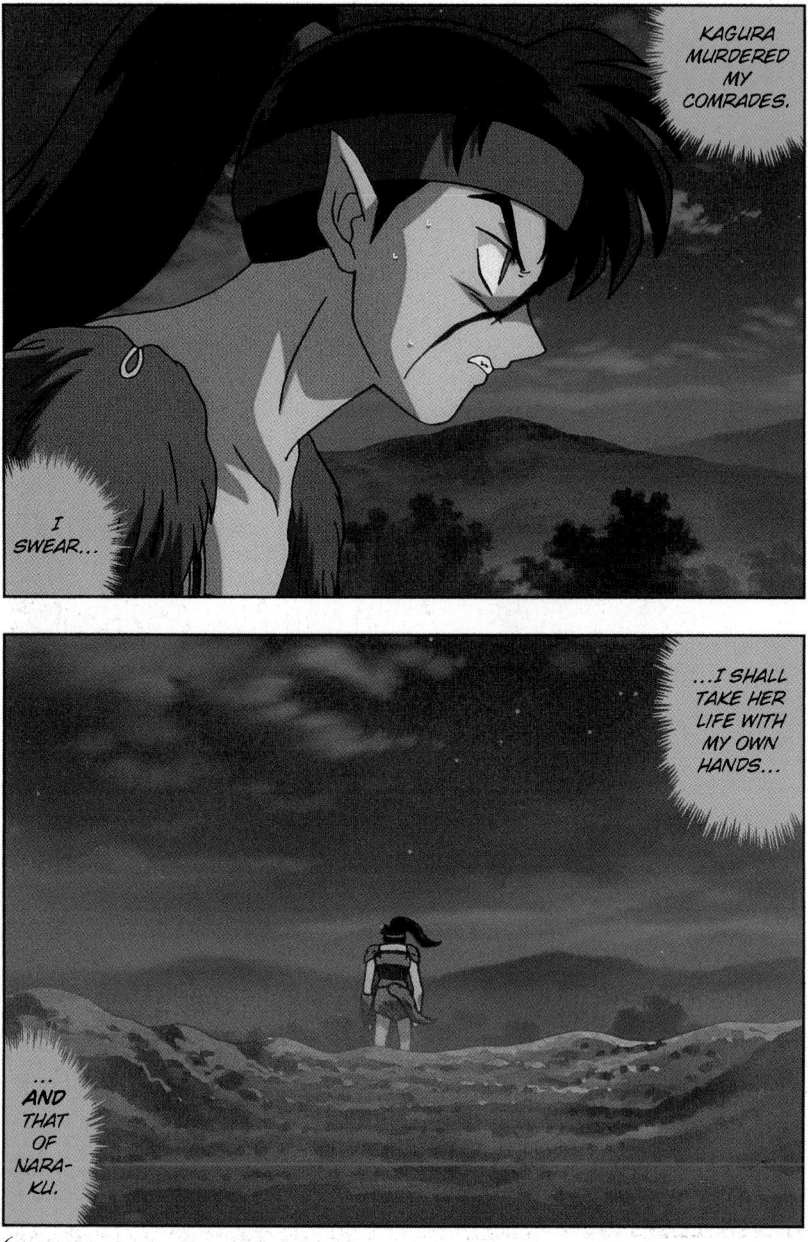
KAGURA MURDERED MY COMRADES.
I SWEAR...
...I SHALL TAKE HER LIFE WITH MY OWN HANDS...
...AND THAT OF NARAKU.

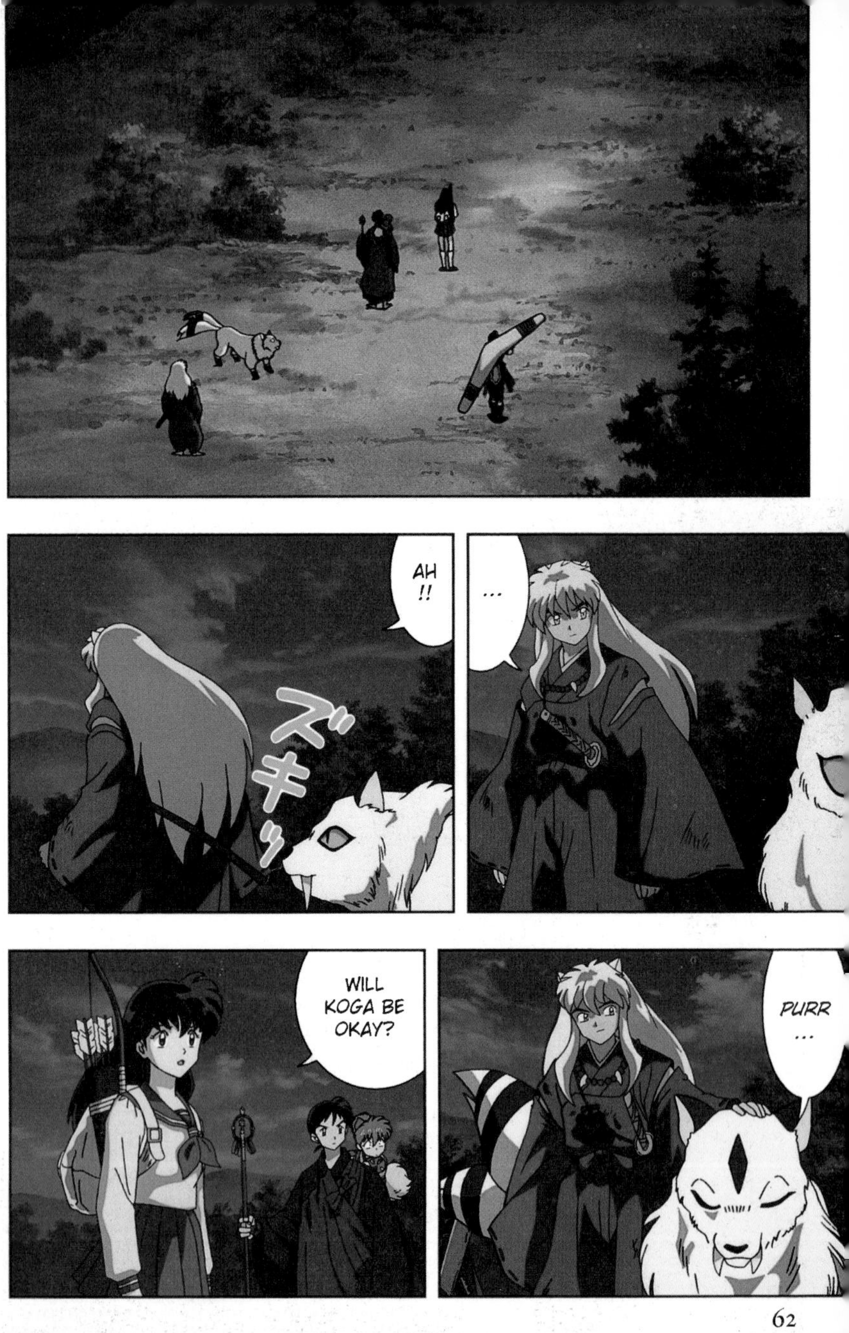
AH !!
ズキッ
...
WILL KOGA BE OKAY?
PURR ...

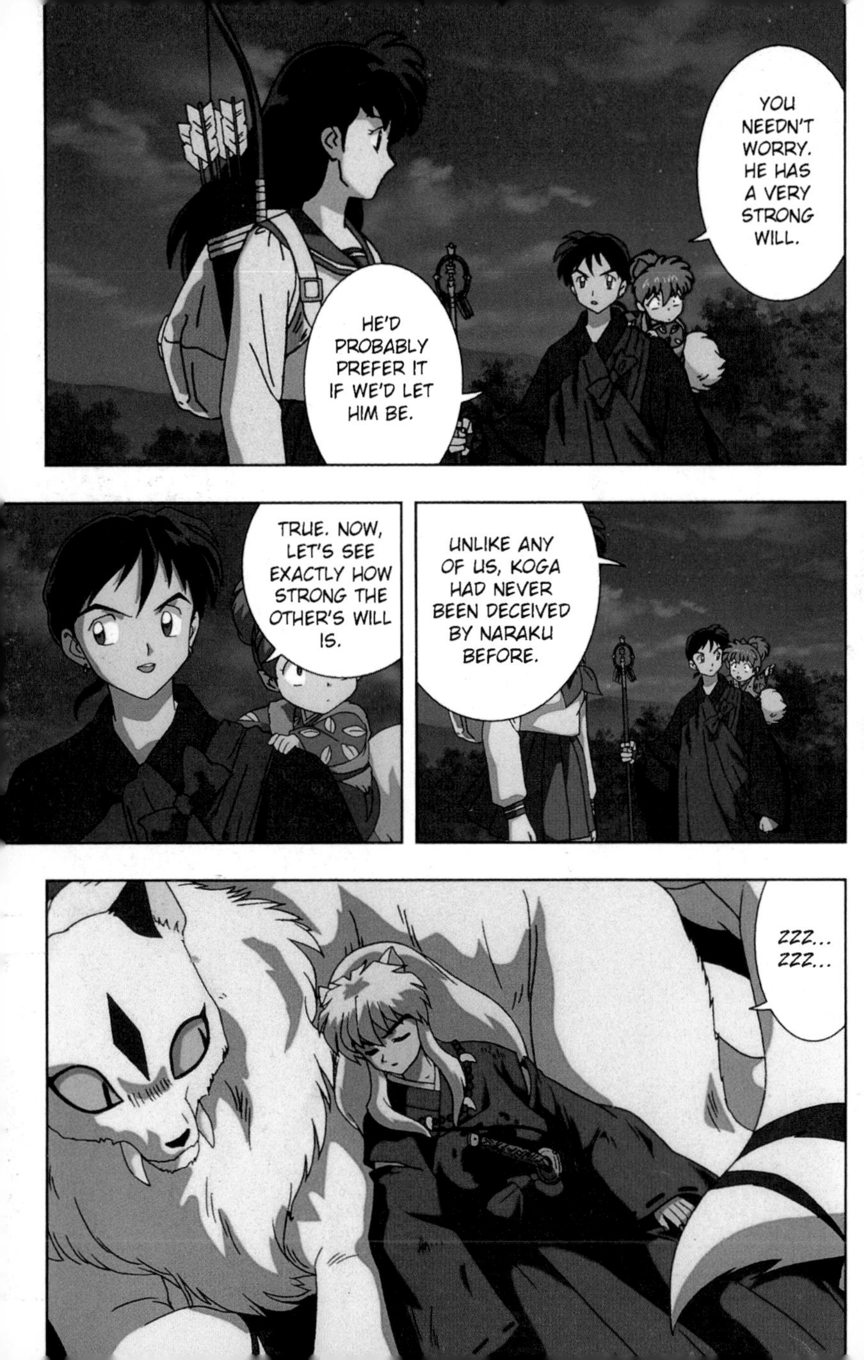
HE'D PROBABLY PREFER IT IF WE'D LET HIM BE.
YOU NEEDN'T WORRY. HE HAS A VERY STRONG WILL.
TRUE. NOW, LET'S SEE EXACTLY HOW STRONG THE OTHER'S WILL IS.
UNLIKE ANY OF US, KOGA HAD NEVER BEEN DECEIVED BY NARAKU BEFORE.
ZZZ... ZZZ...

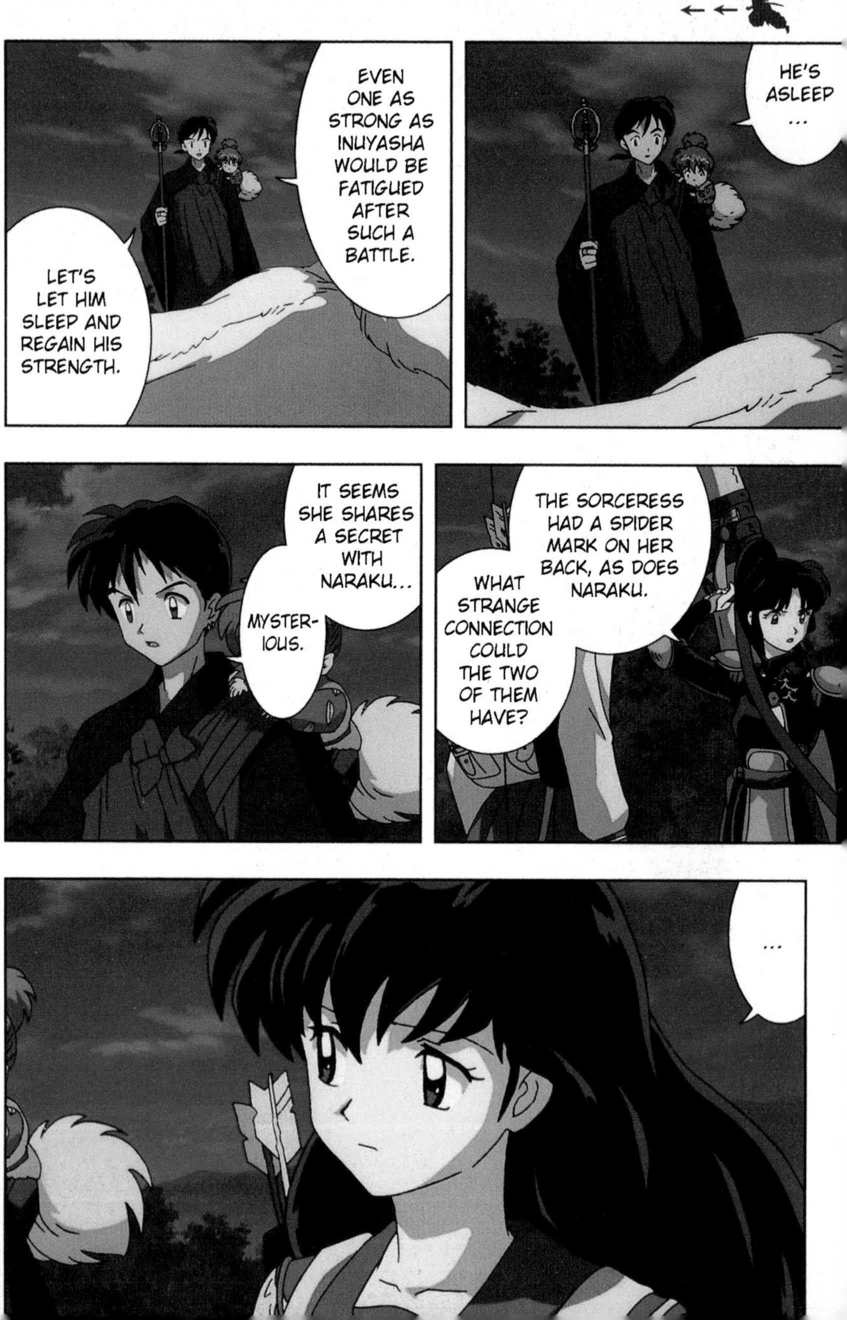
HE'S ASLEEP ...
EVEN ONE AS STRONG AS INUYASHA WOULD BE FATIGUED AFTER SUCH A BATTLE.
LET'S LET HIM SLEEP AND REGAIN HIS STRENGTH.
THE SORCERESS HAD A SPIDER MARK ON HER BACK, AS DOES NARAKU.
WHAT STRANGE CONNECTION COULD THE TWO OF THEM HAVE?
IT SEEMS SHE SHARES A SECRET WITH NARAKU...
MYSTER-IOUS.
...

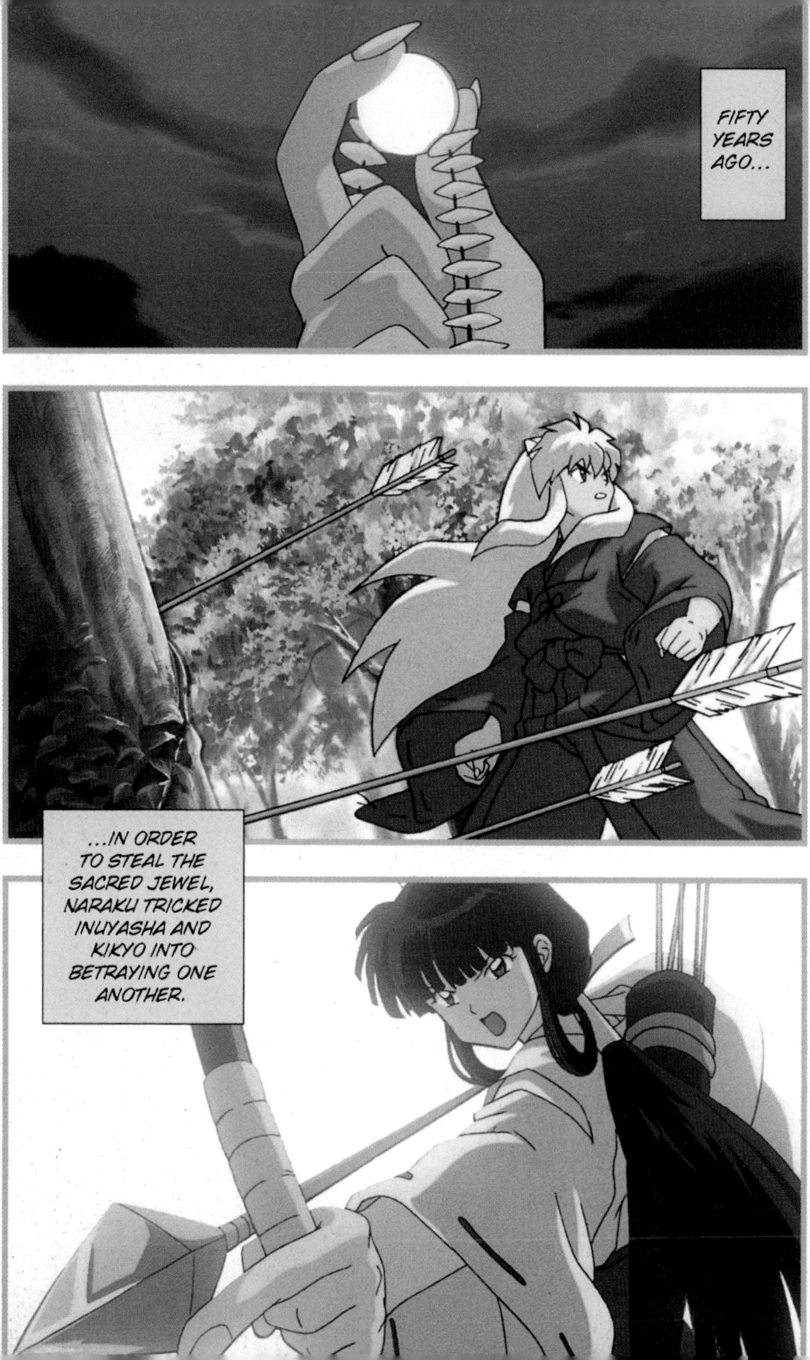
FIFTY YEARS AGO...
...IN ORDER TO STEAL THE SACRED JEWEL, NARAKU TRICKED INUYASHA AND KIKYO INTO BETRAYING ONE ANOTHER.

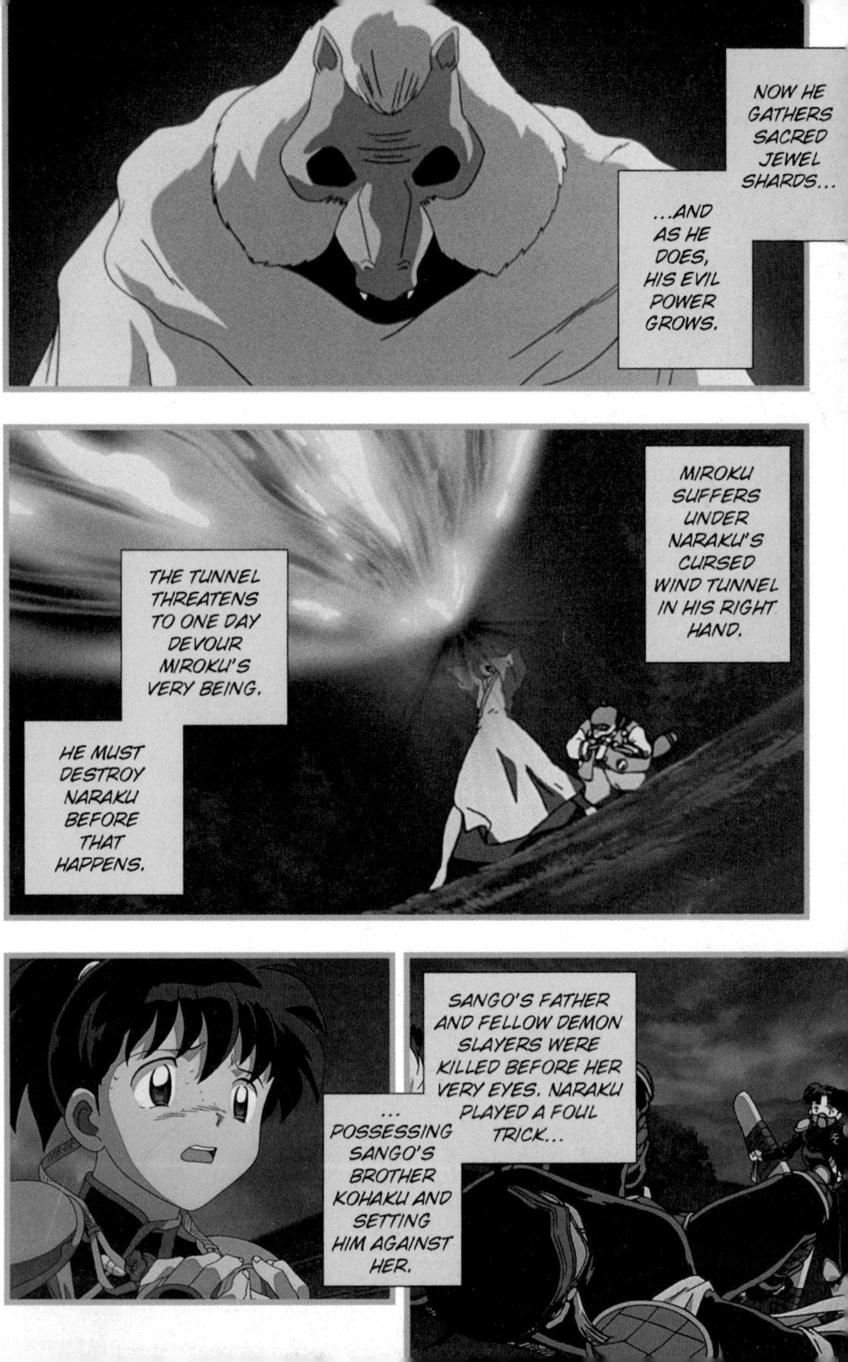
NOW HE GATHERS SACRED JEWEL SHARDS...
...AND AS HE DOES, HIS EVIL POWER GROWS.
MIROKU SUFFERS UNDER NARAKU'S CURSED WIND TUNNEL IN HIS RIGHT HAND.
THE TUNNEL THREATENS TO ONE DAY DEVOUR MIROKU'S VERY BEING.
HE MUST DESTROY NARAKU BEFORE THAT HAPPENS.
SANGO'S FATHER AND FELLOW DEMON SLAYERS WERE KILLED BEFORE HER VERY EYES. NARAKU PLAYED A FOUL TRICK...
...POSSESSING SANGO'S BROTHER KOHAKU AND SETTING HIM AGAINST HER.

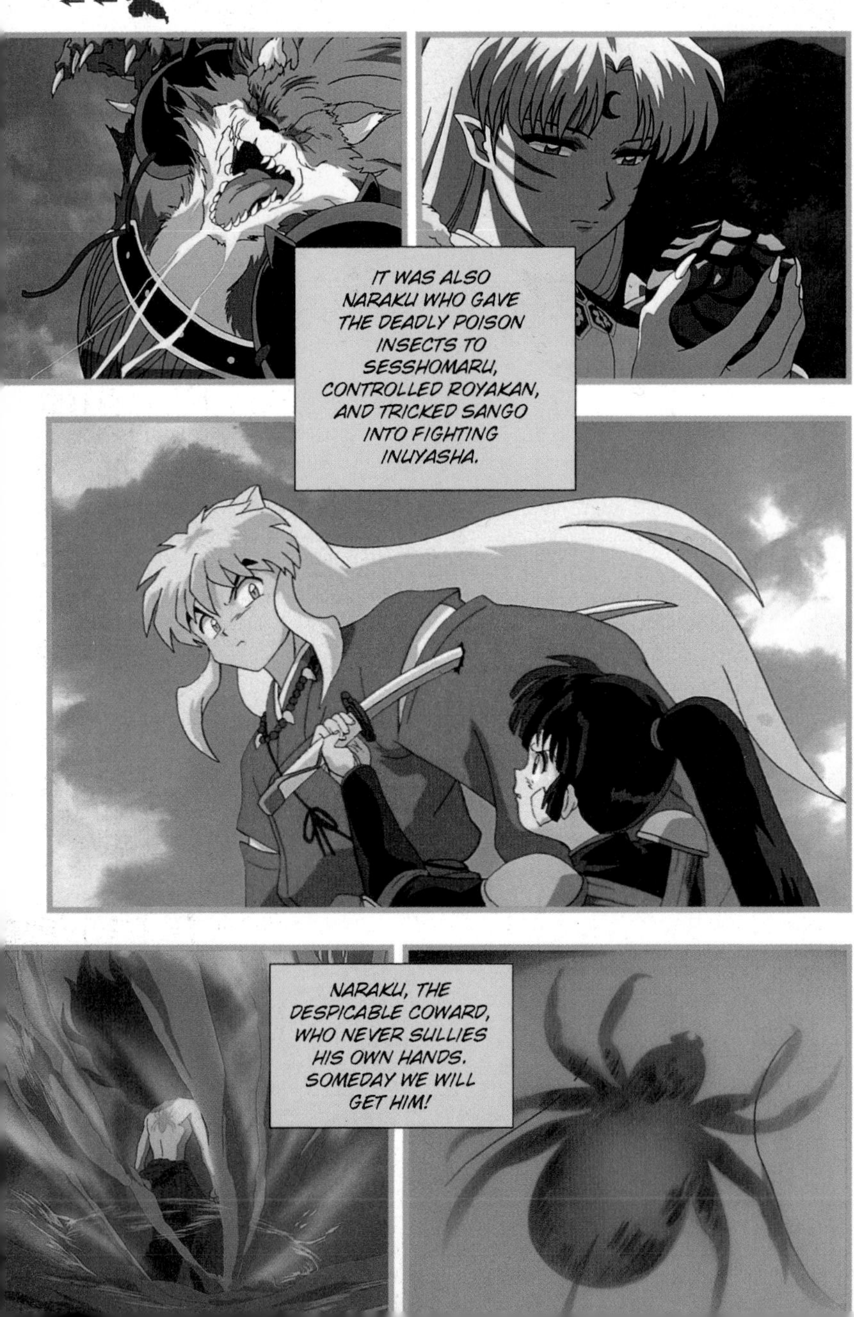
IT WAS ALSO NARAKU WHO GAVE THE DEADLY POISON INSECTS TO SESSHOMARU, CONTROLLED ROYAKAN, AND TRICKED SANGO INTO FIGHTING INUYASHA.
NARAKU, THE DESPICABLE COWARD, WHO NEVER SULLIES HIS OWN HANDS. SOMEDAY WE WILL GET HIM!

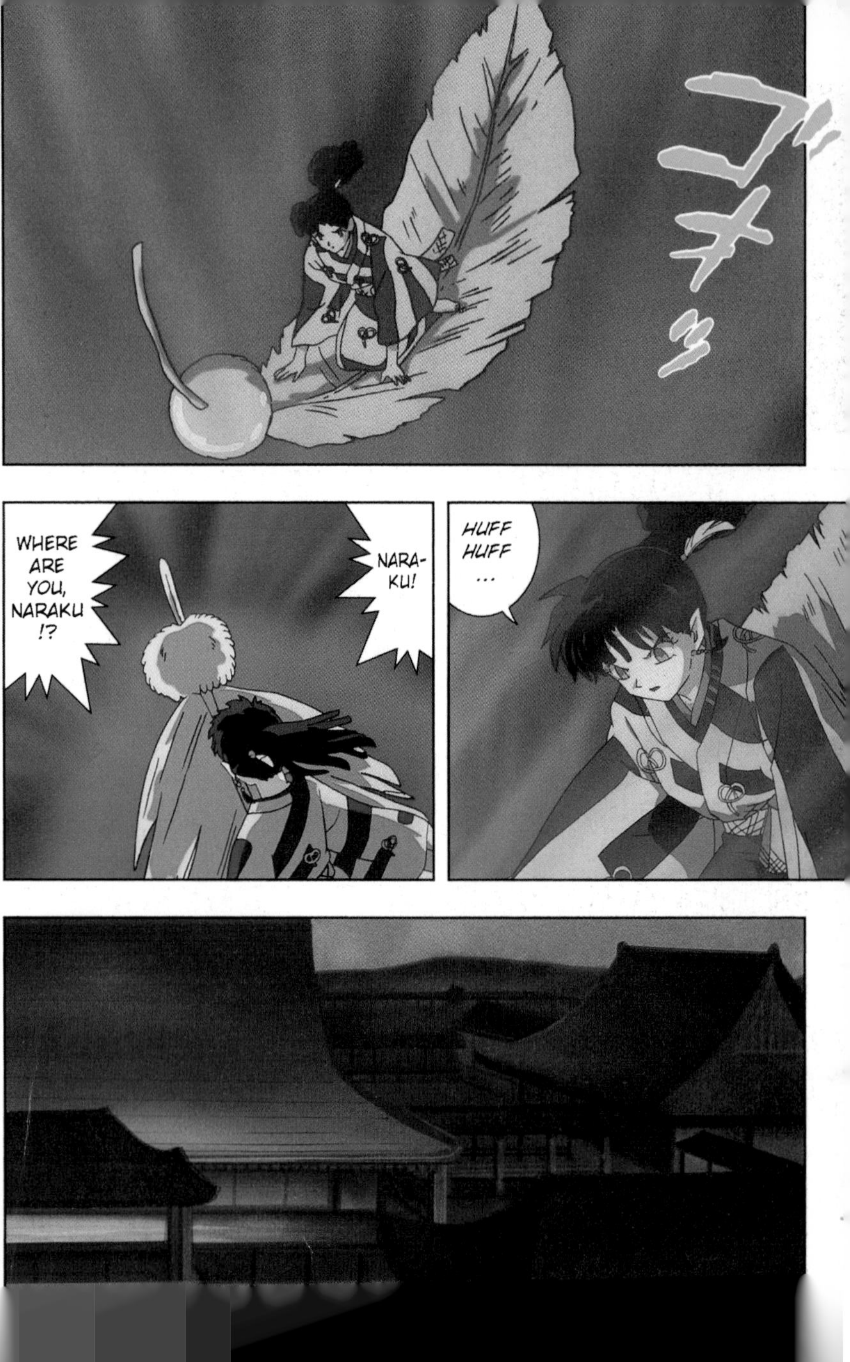
HUFF HUFF ...
NARA-KU!
WHERE ARE YOU, NARAKU!?

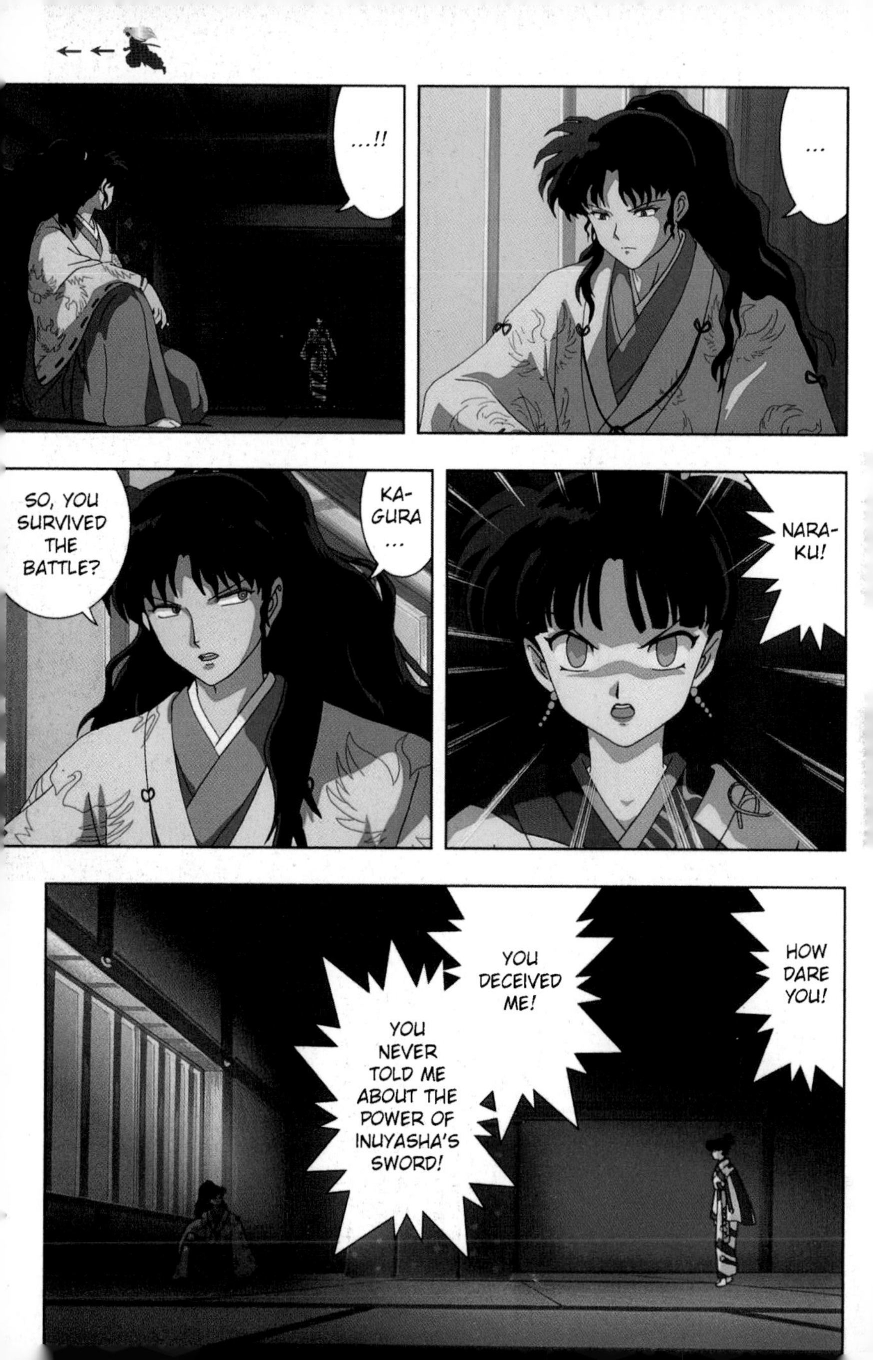
...
...!!
NARA-
KU!
KA-
GURA
...
SO, YOU
SURVIVED
THE
BATTLE?
HOW
DARE
YOU!
YOU
DECEIVED
ME!
YOU
NEVER
TOLD ME
ABOUT THE
POWER OF
INUYASHA'S
SWORD!

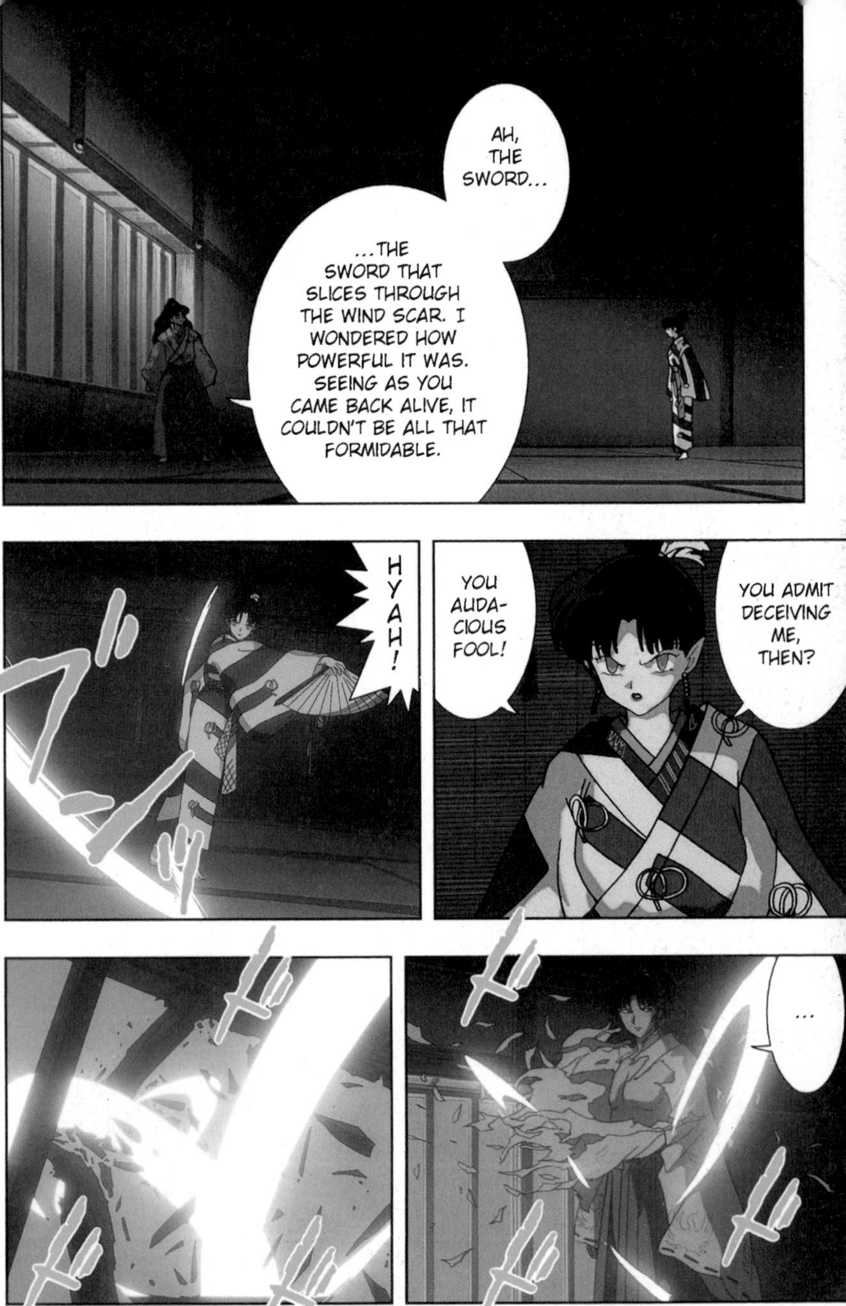
AH, THE SWORD...
...THE SWORD THAT SLICES THROUGH THE WIND SCAR. I WONDERED HOW POWERFUL IT WAS. SEEING AS YOU CAME BACK ALIVE, IT COULDN'T BE ALL THAT FORMIDABLE.
YOU ADMIT DECEIVING ME, THEN?
YOU AUDACIOUS FOOL!
HYAH!
...

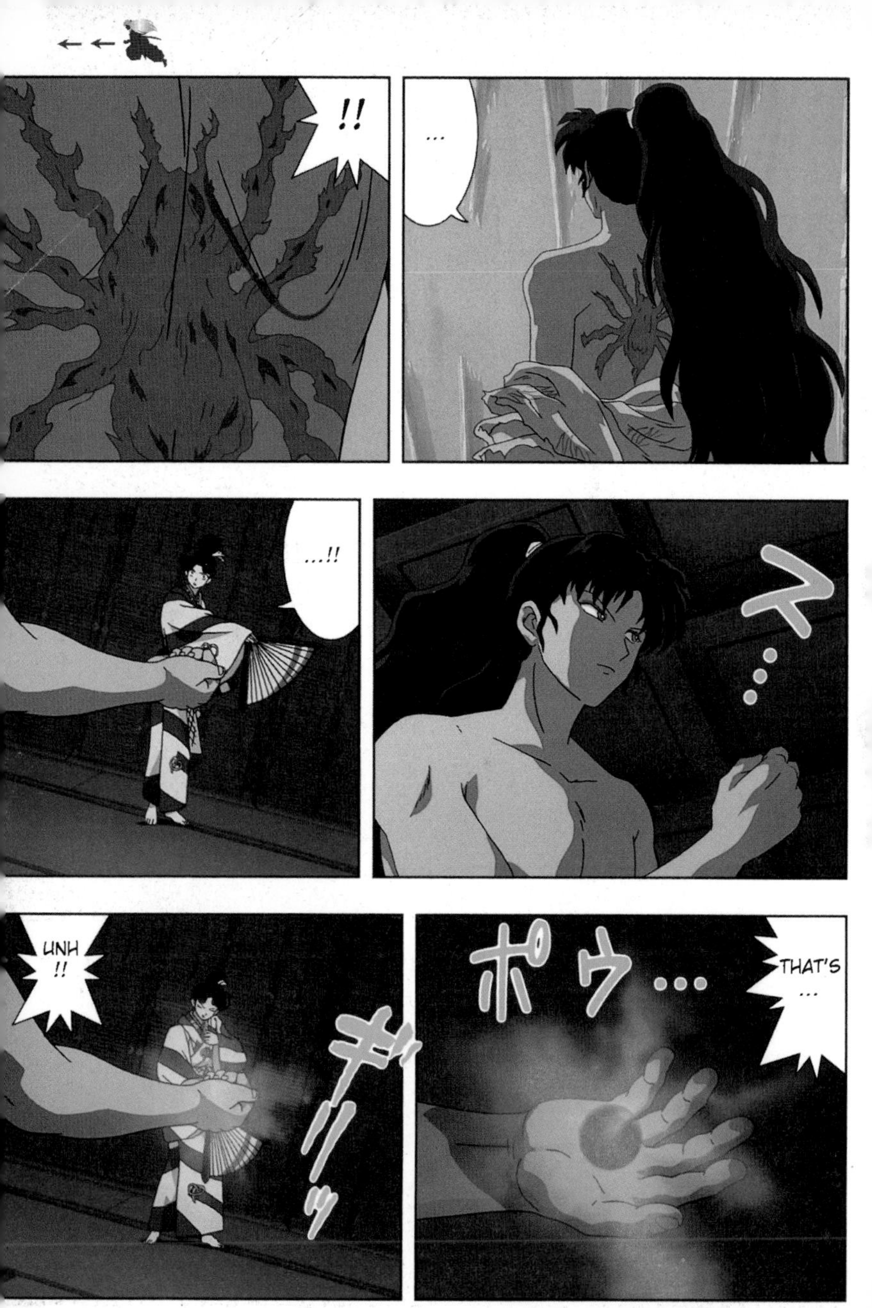
...
!!
...!!
ス...
UNH !!
THAT'S ...
ポウ...
ギリッ

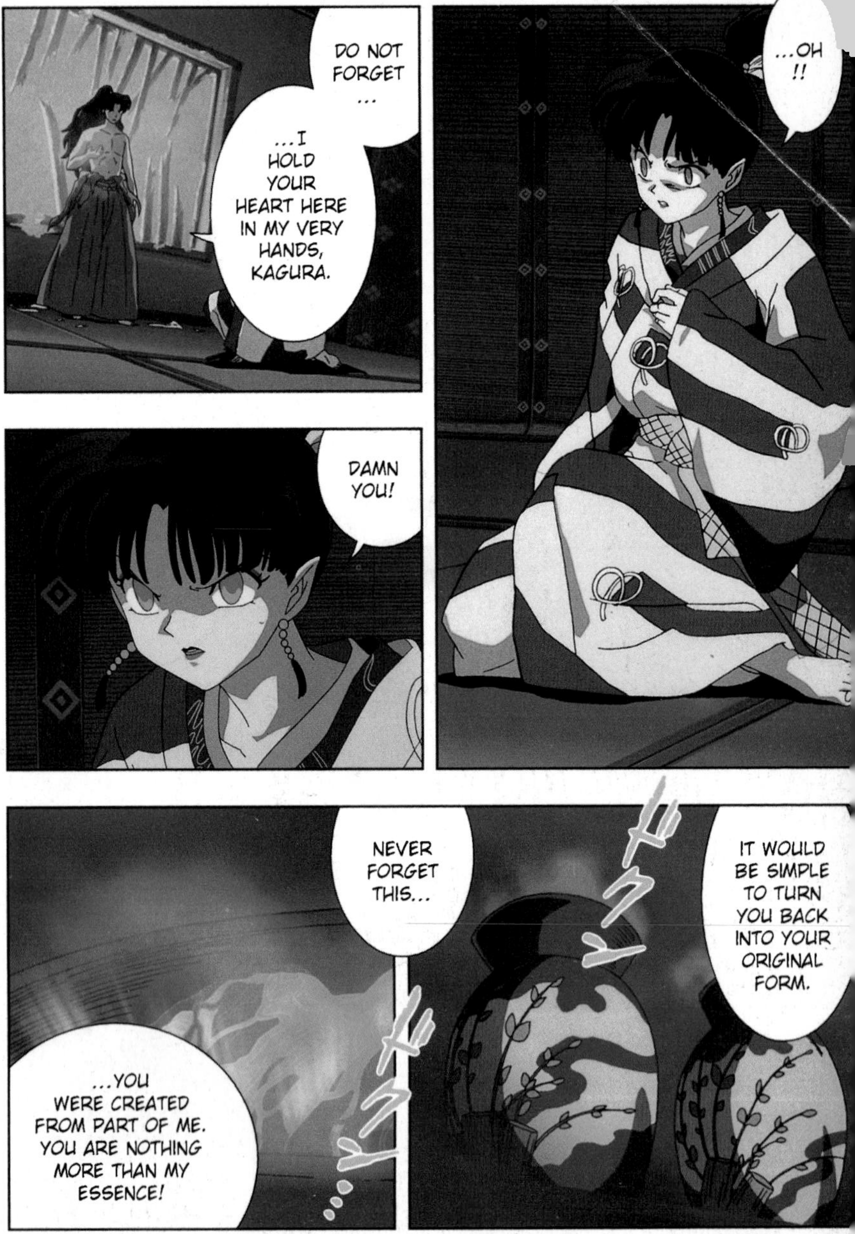

...OH !!
DO NOT FORGET ...
...I HOLD YOUR HEART HERE IN MY VERY HANDS, KAGURA.
DAMN YOU!
IT WOULD BE SIMPLE TO TURN YOU BACK INTO YOUR ORIGINAL FORM.
NEVER FORGET THIS...
...YOU WERE CREATED FROM PART OF ME. YOU ARE NOTHING MORE THAN MY ESSENCE!

# 41 Kagura's Dance and Kanna's Mirror

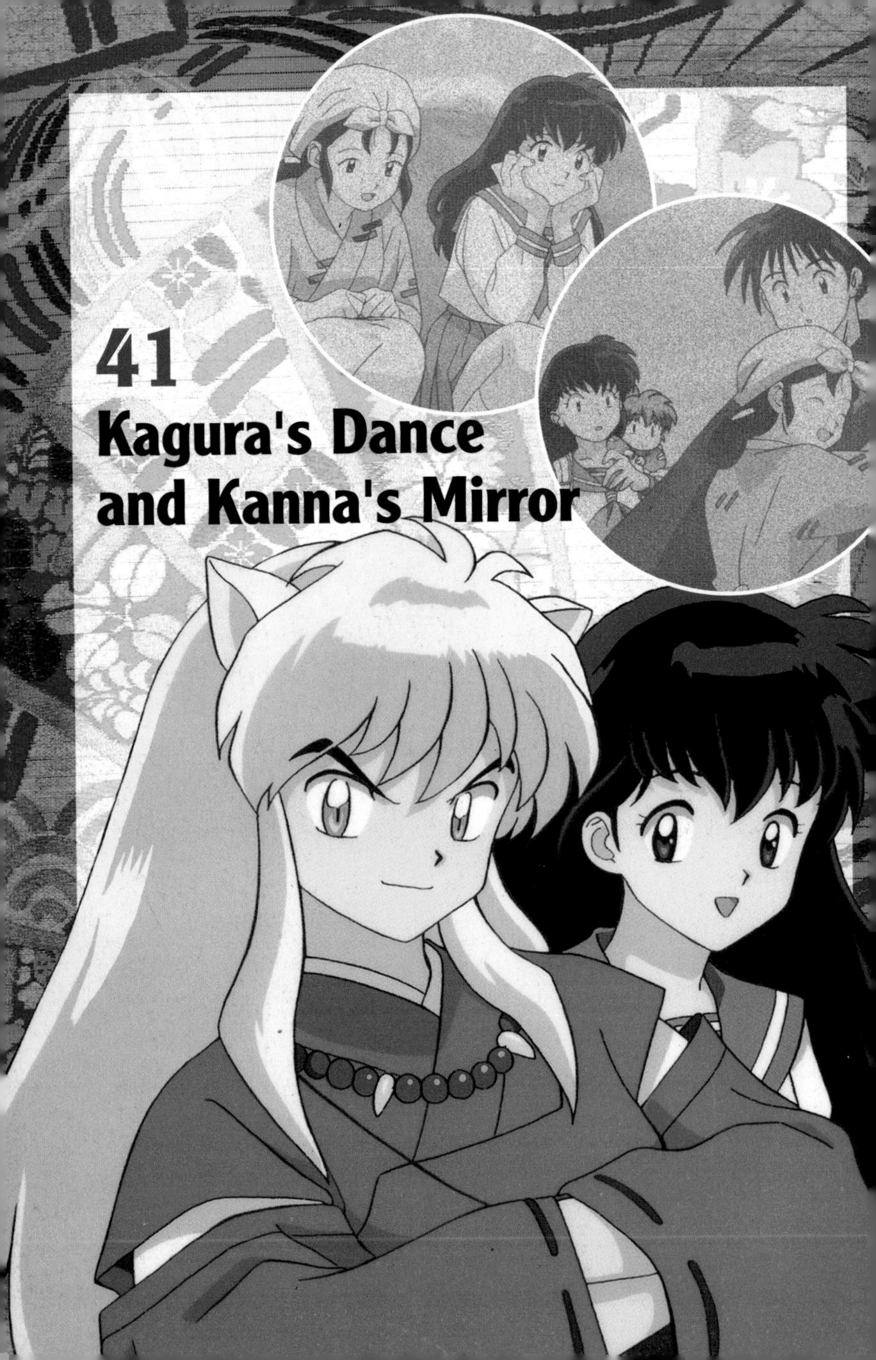

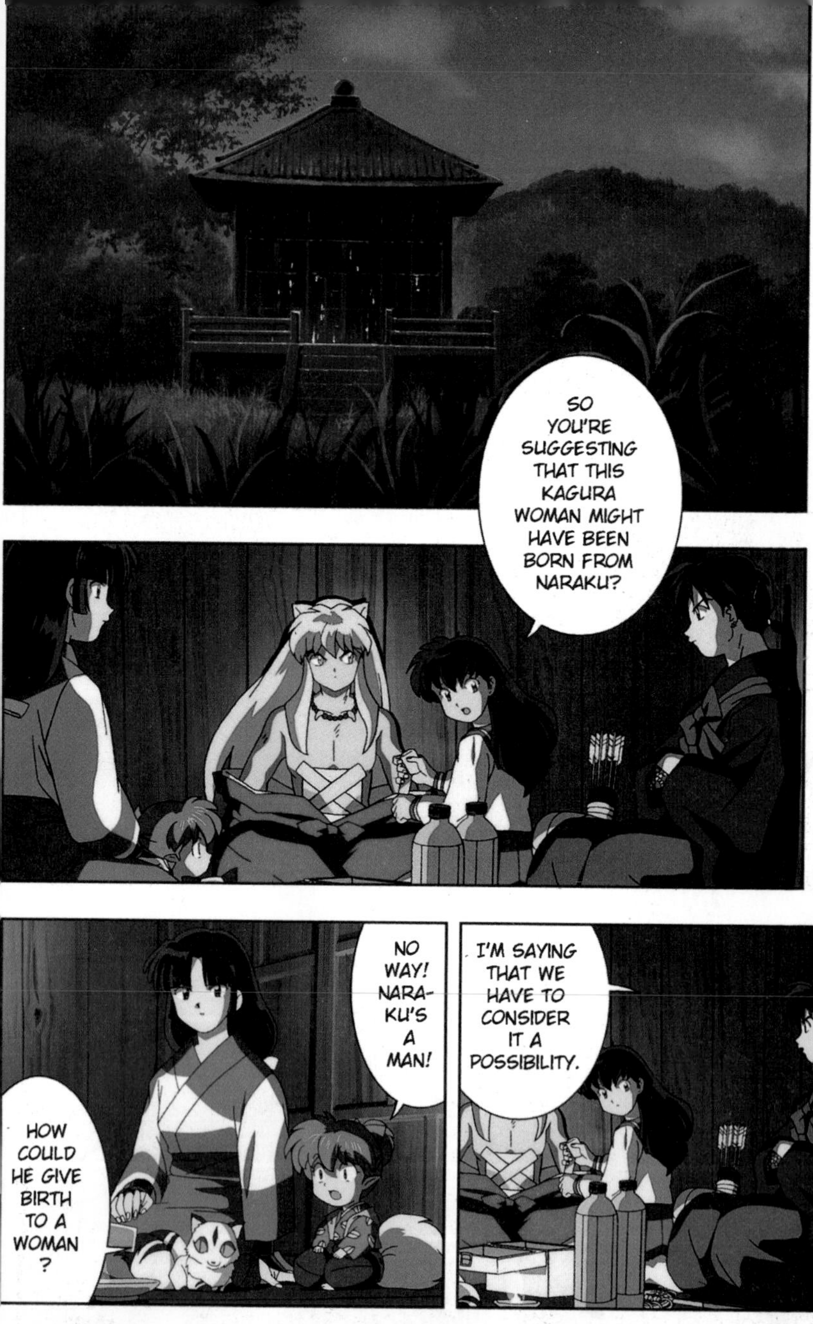
SO YOU'RE SUGGESTING THAT THIS KAGURA WOMAN MIGHT HAVE BEEN BORN FROM NARAKU?
NO WAY! NARA-KU'S A MAN!
HOW COULD HE GIVE BIRTH TO A WOMAN?
I'M SAYING THAT WE HAVE TO CONSIDER IT A POSSIBILITY.

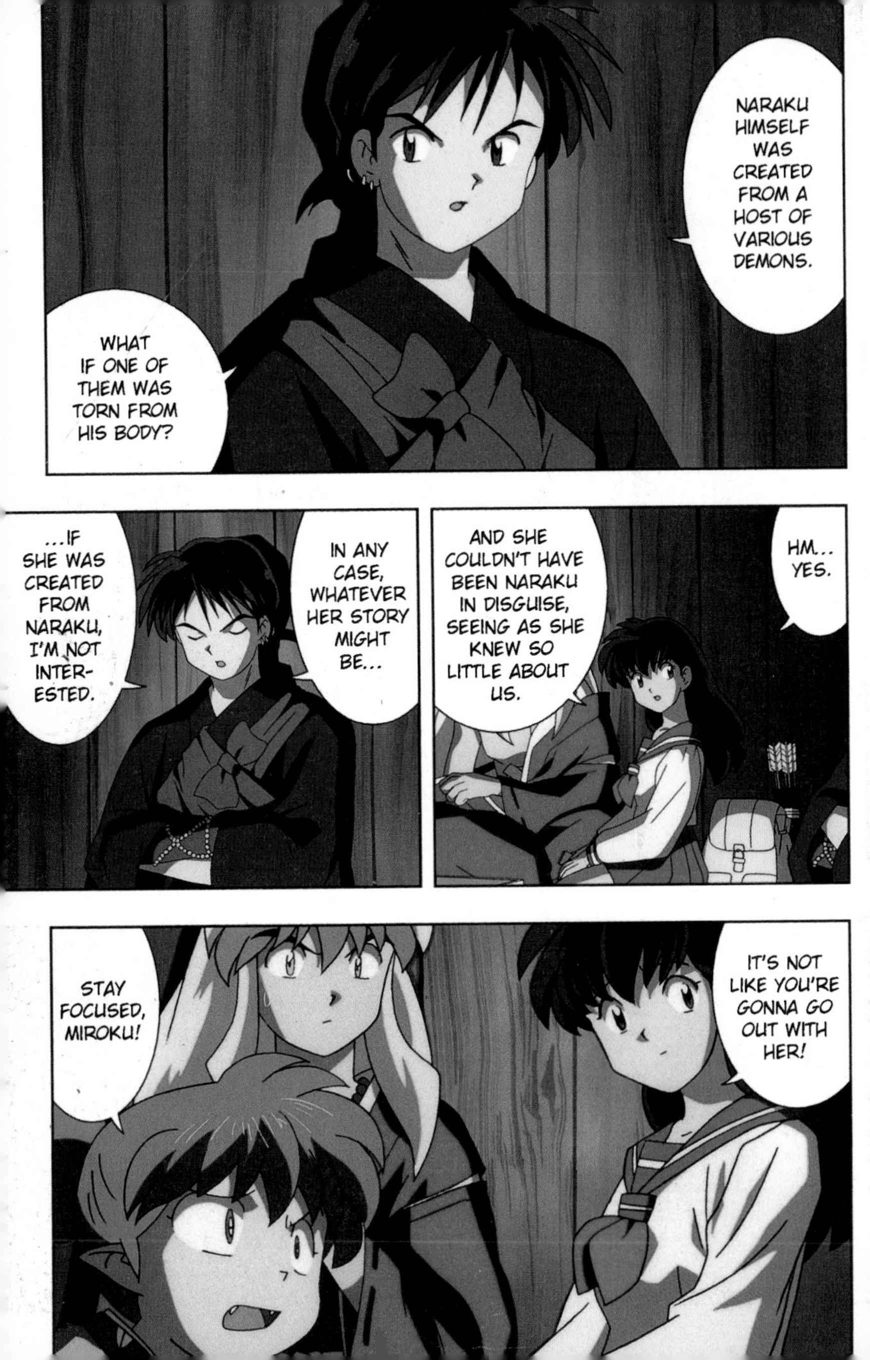
NARAKU HIMSELF WAS CREATED FROM A HOST OF VARIOUS DEMONS.
WHAT IF ONE OF THEM WAS TORN FROM HIS BODY?
HM... YES.
AND SHE COULDN'T HAVE BEEN NARAKU IN DISGUISE, SEEING AS SHE KNEW SO LITTLE ABOUT US.
IN ANY CASE, WHATEVER HER STORY MIGHT BE...
...IF SHE WAS CREATED FROM NARAKU, I'M NOT INTER-ESTED.
IT'S NOT LIKE YOU'RE GONNA GO OUT WITH HER!
STAY FOCUSED, MIROKU!

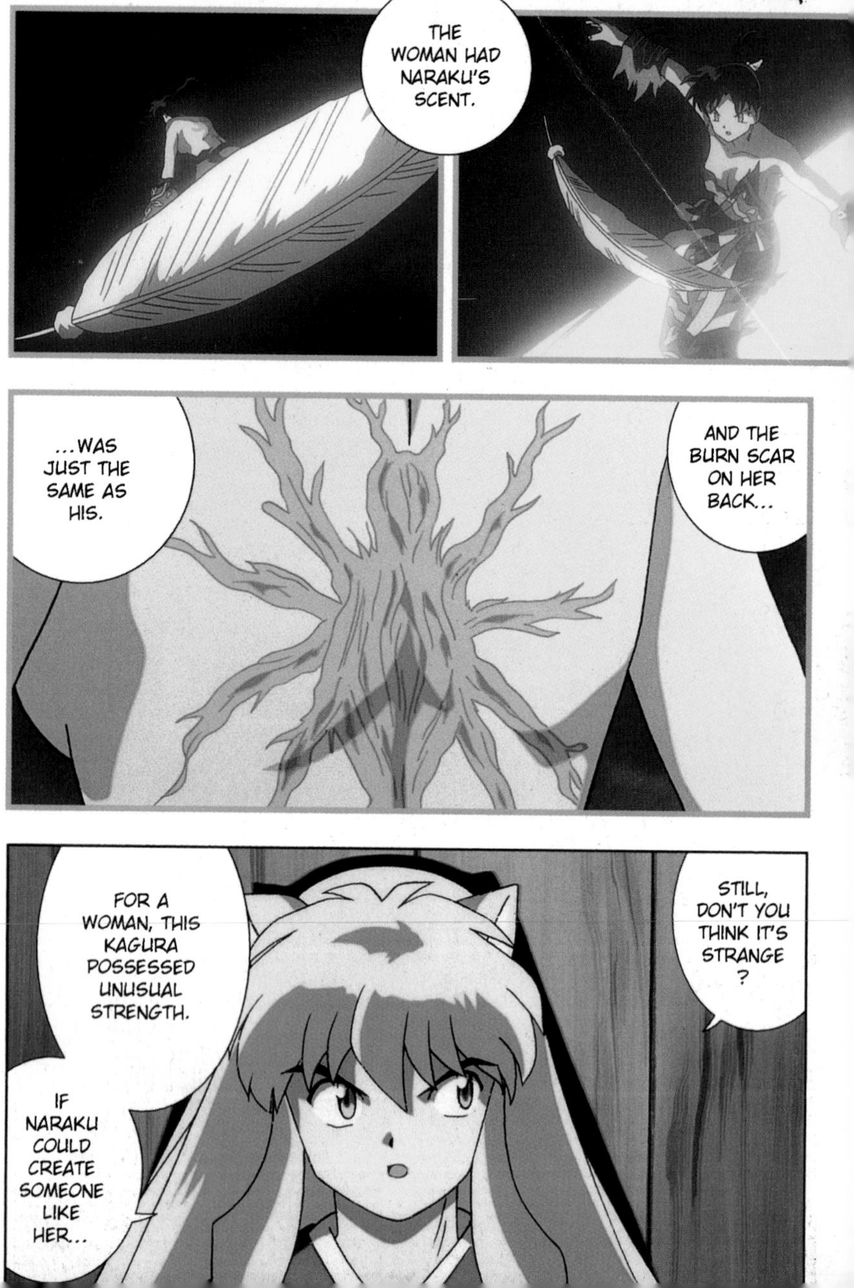
THE WOMAN HAD NARAKU'S SCENT.
AND THE BURN SCAR ON HER BACK...
...WAS JUST THE SAME AS HIS.
STILL, DON'T YOU THINK IT'S STRANGE?
FOR A WOMAN, THIS KAGURA POSSESSED UNUSUAL STRENGTH.
IF NARAKU COULD CREATE SOMEONE LIKE HER...

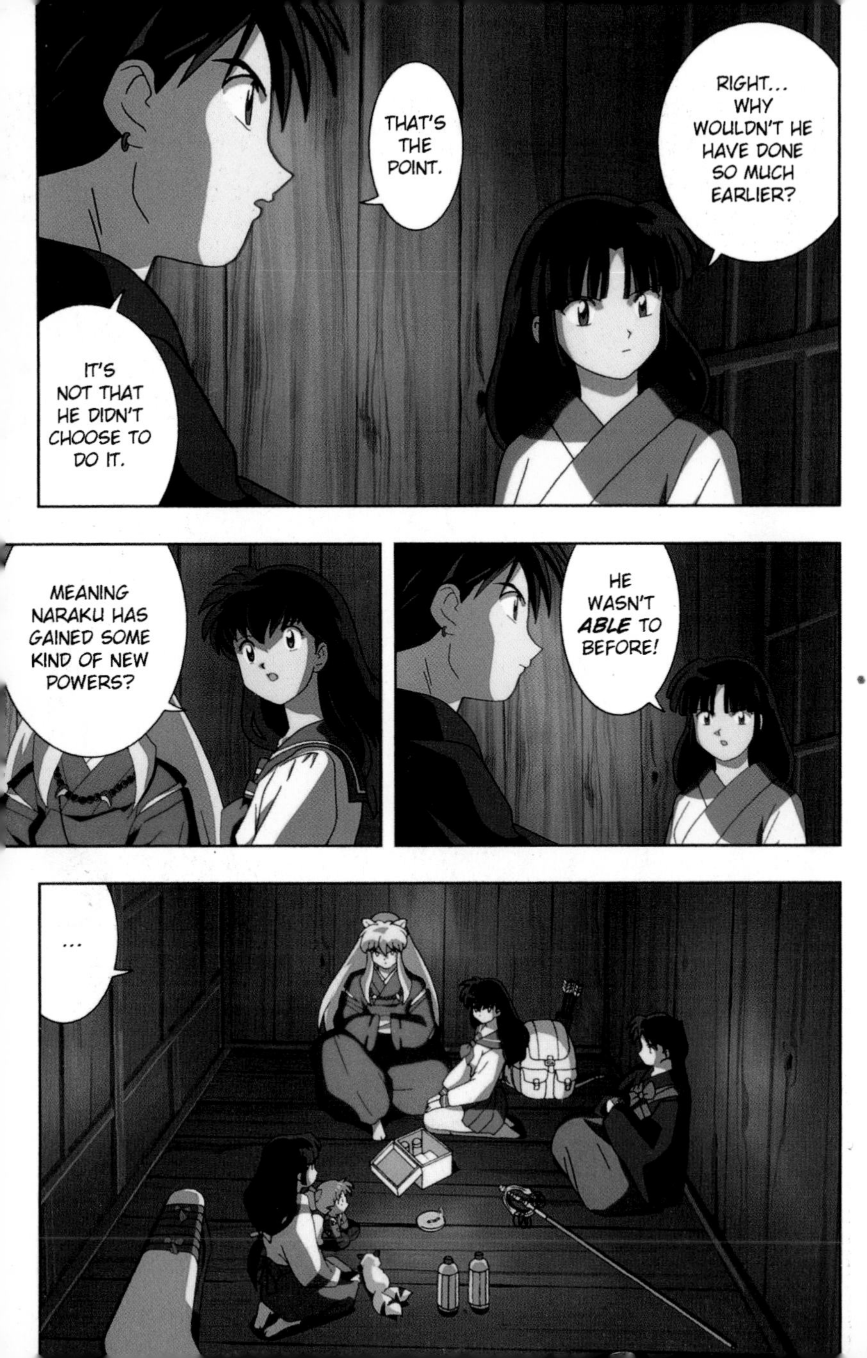
RIGHT... WHY WOULDN'T HE HAVE DONE SO MUCH EARLIER?
THAT'S THE POINT.
IT'S NOT THAT HE DIDN'T CHOOSE TO DO IT.
HE WASN'T ABLE TO BEFORE!
MEANING NARAKU HAS GAINED SOME KIND OF NEW POWERS?
...

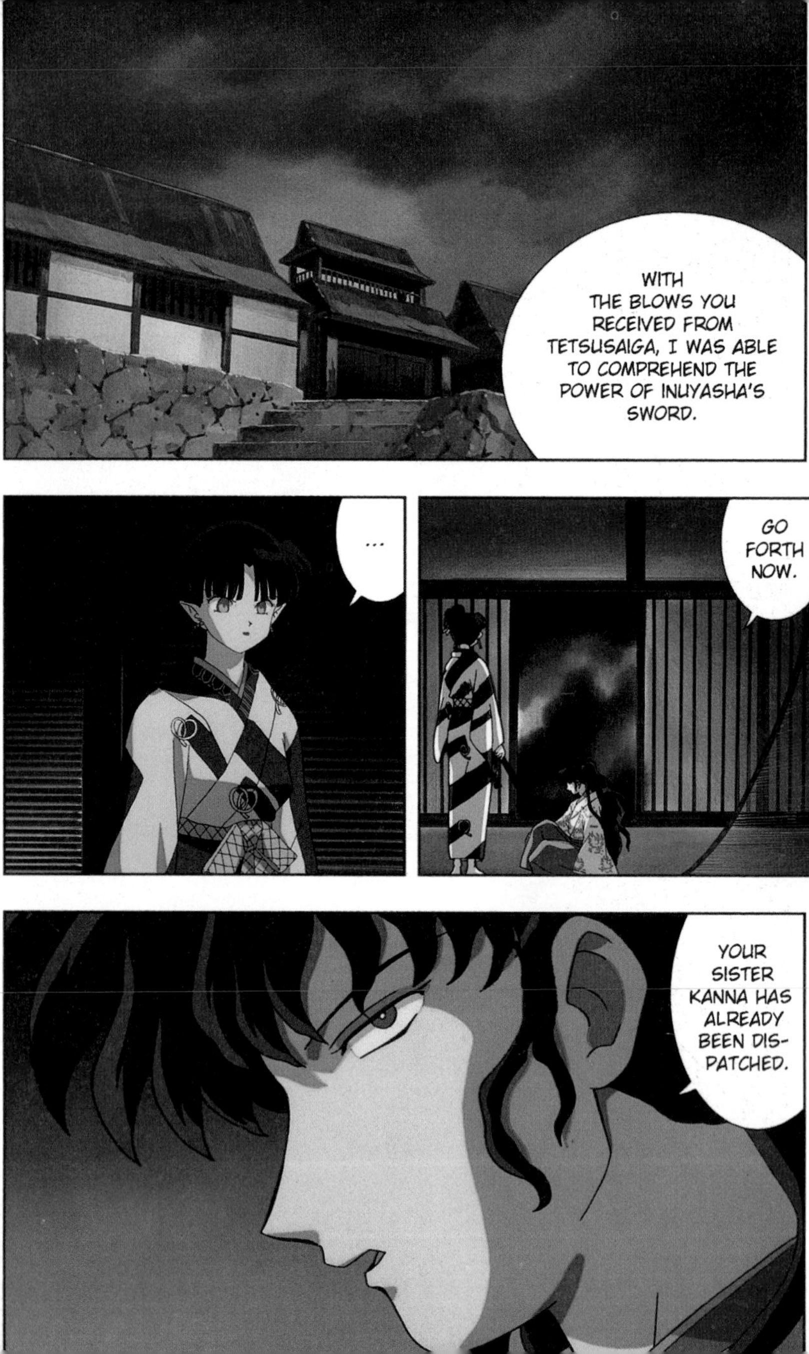
WITH THE BLOWS YOU RECEIVED FROM TETSUSAIGA, I WAS ABLE TO COMPREHEND THE POWER OF INUYASHA'S SWORD.
GO FORTH NOW.
...
YOUR SISTER KANNA HAS ALREADY BEEN DIS-PATCHED.

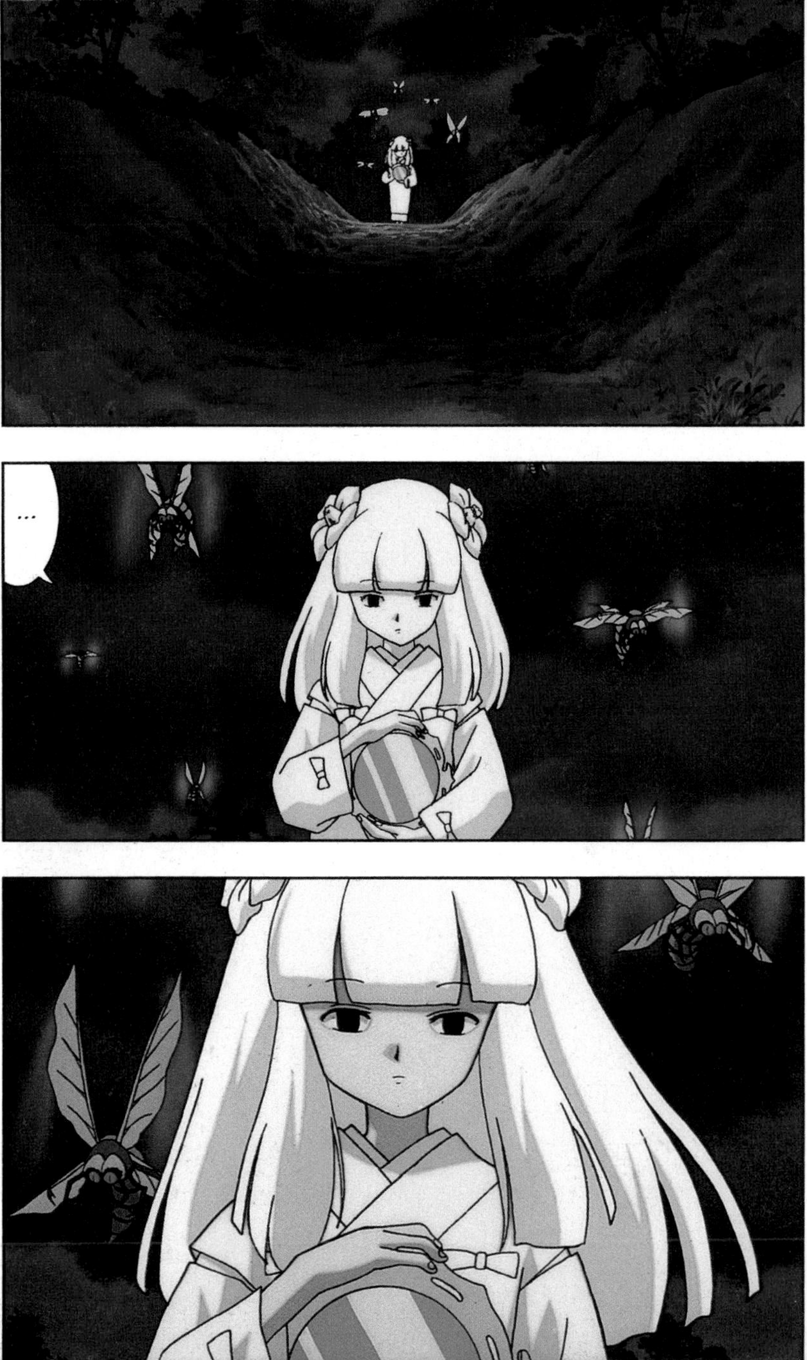
...

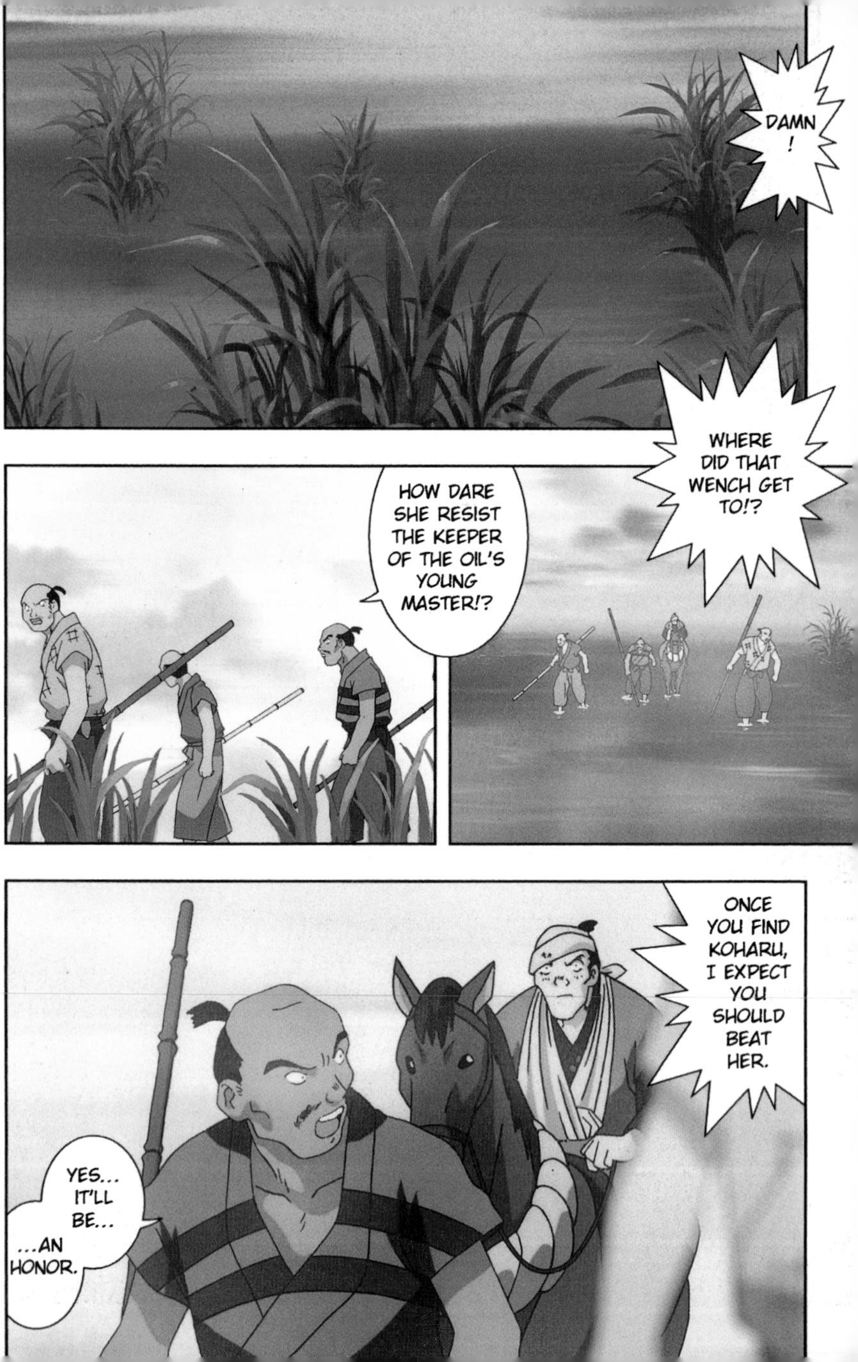
DAMN!
WHERE DID THAT WENCH GET TO!?
HOW DARE SHE RESIST THE KEEPER OF THE OIL'S YOUNG MASTER!?
ONCE YOU FIND KOHARU, I EXPECT YOU SHOULD BEAT HER.
YES... IT'LL BE...
...AN HONOR.

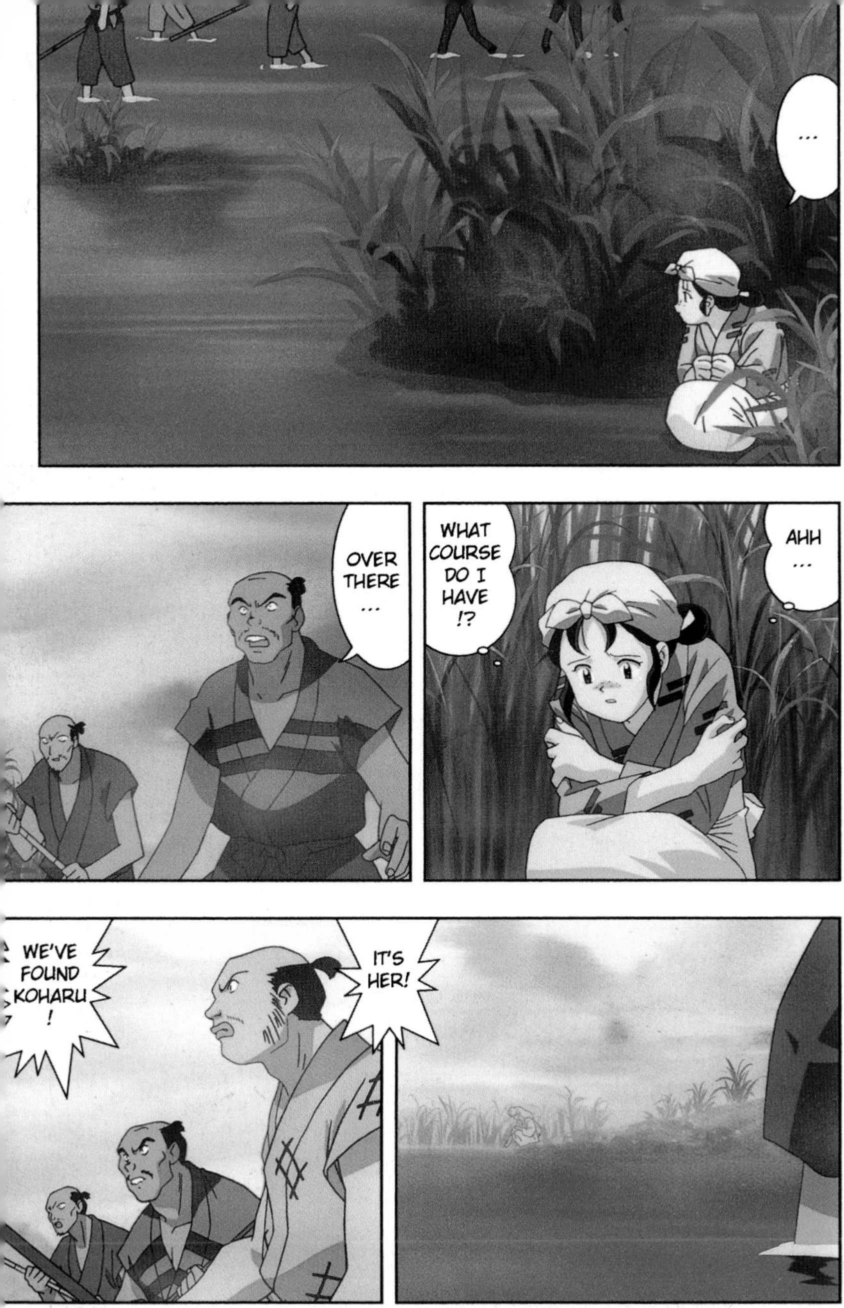
...
AHH ...
WHAT COURSE DO I HAVE !?
OVER THERE ...
IT'S HER!
WE'VE FOUND KOHARU !

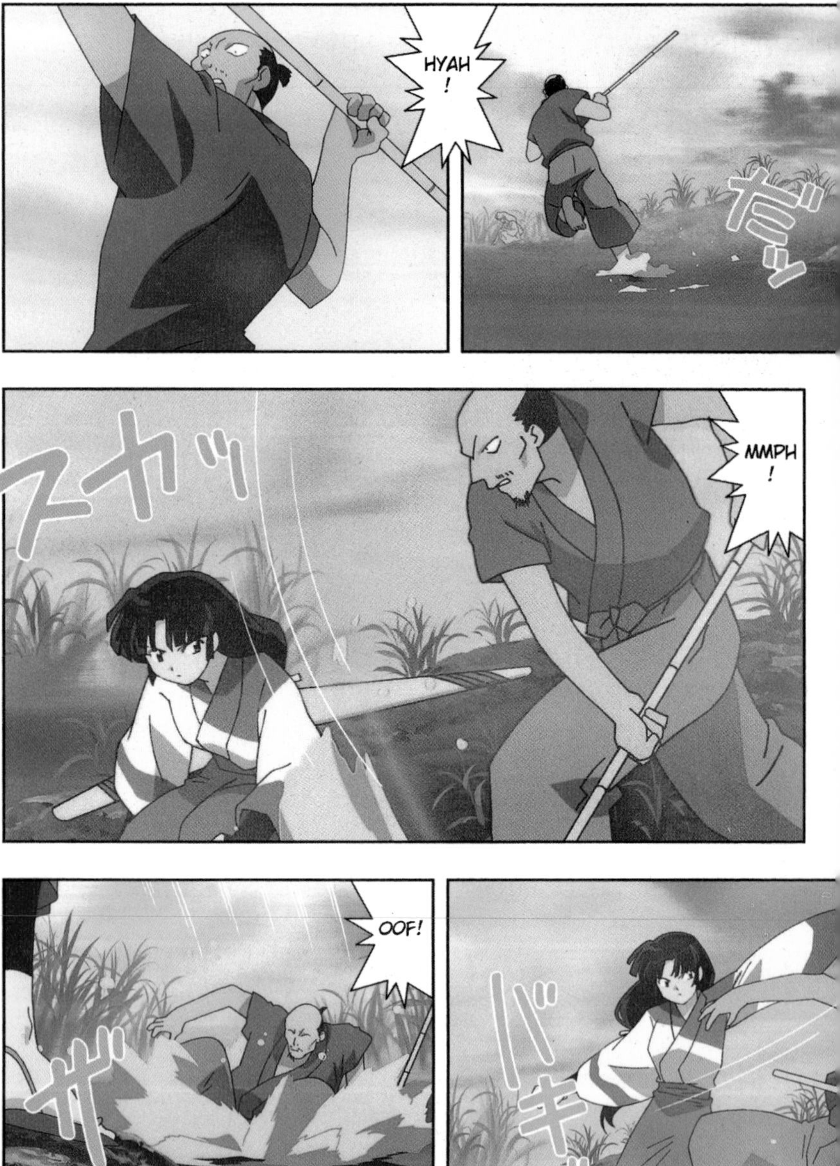

ダッ
HYAH!
MMPH!
スヤッ
バキッ
OOF!
ザッ

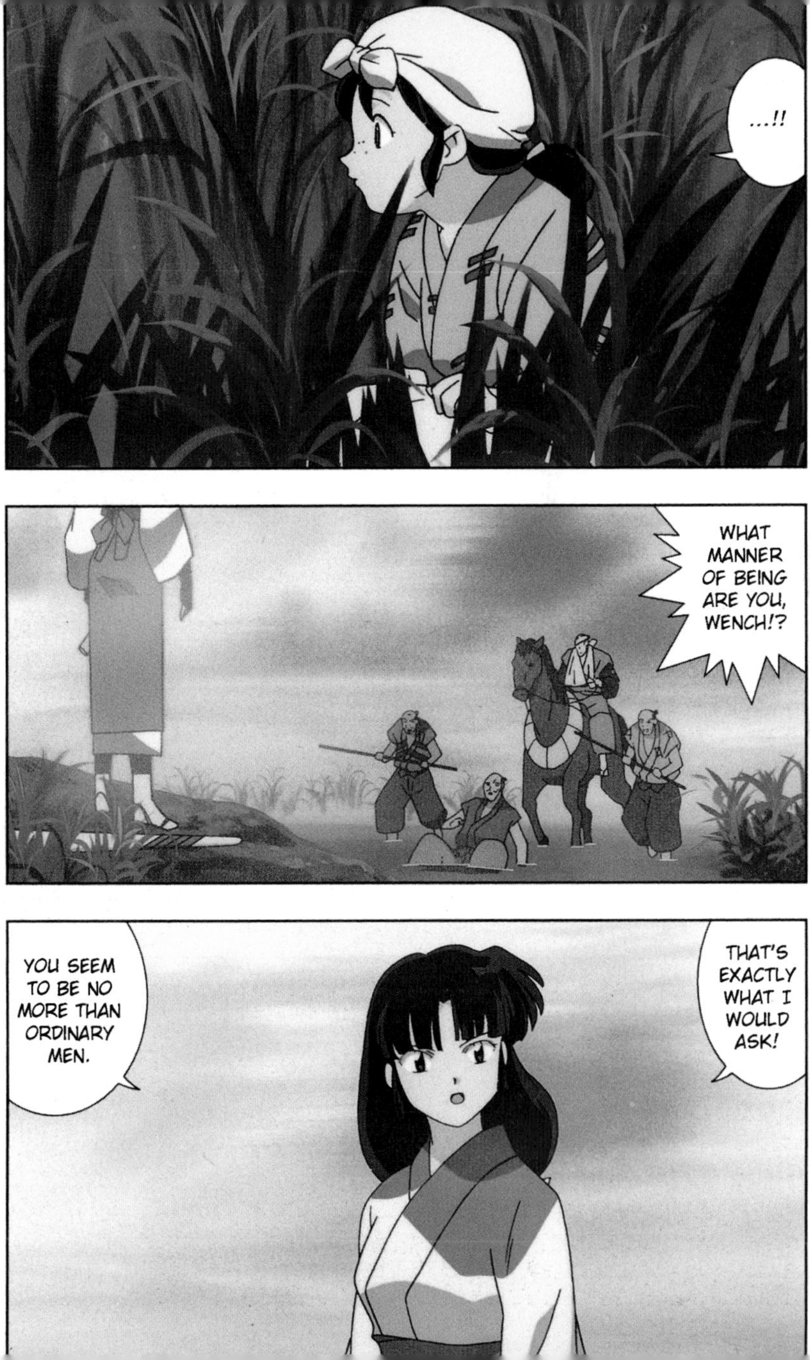
...!!
WHAT MANNER OF BEING ARE YOU, WENCH!?
THAT'S EXACTLY WHAT I WOULD ASK!
YOU SEEM TO BE NO MORE THAN ORDINARY MEN.

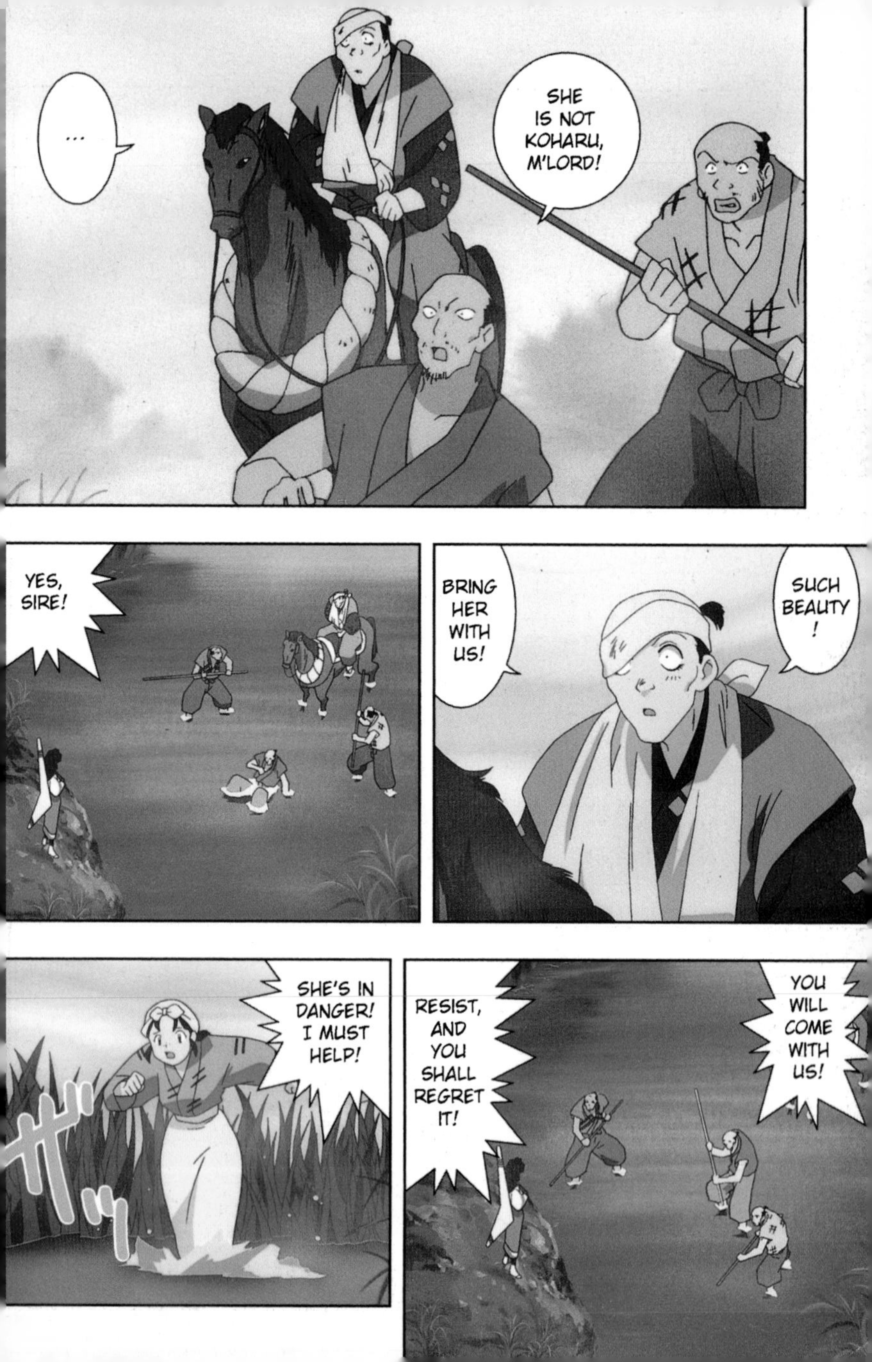
...
SHE IS NOT KOHARU, M'LORD!
SUCH BEAUTY!
BRING HER WITH US!
YES, SIRE!
YOU WILL COME WITH US!
RESIST, AND YOU SHALL REGRET IT!
SHE'S IN DANGER! I MUST HELP!

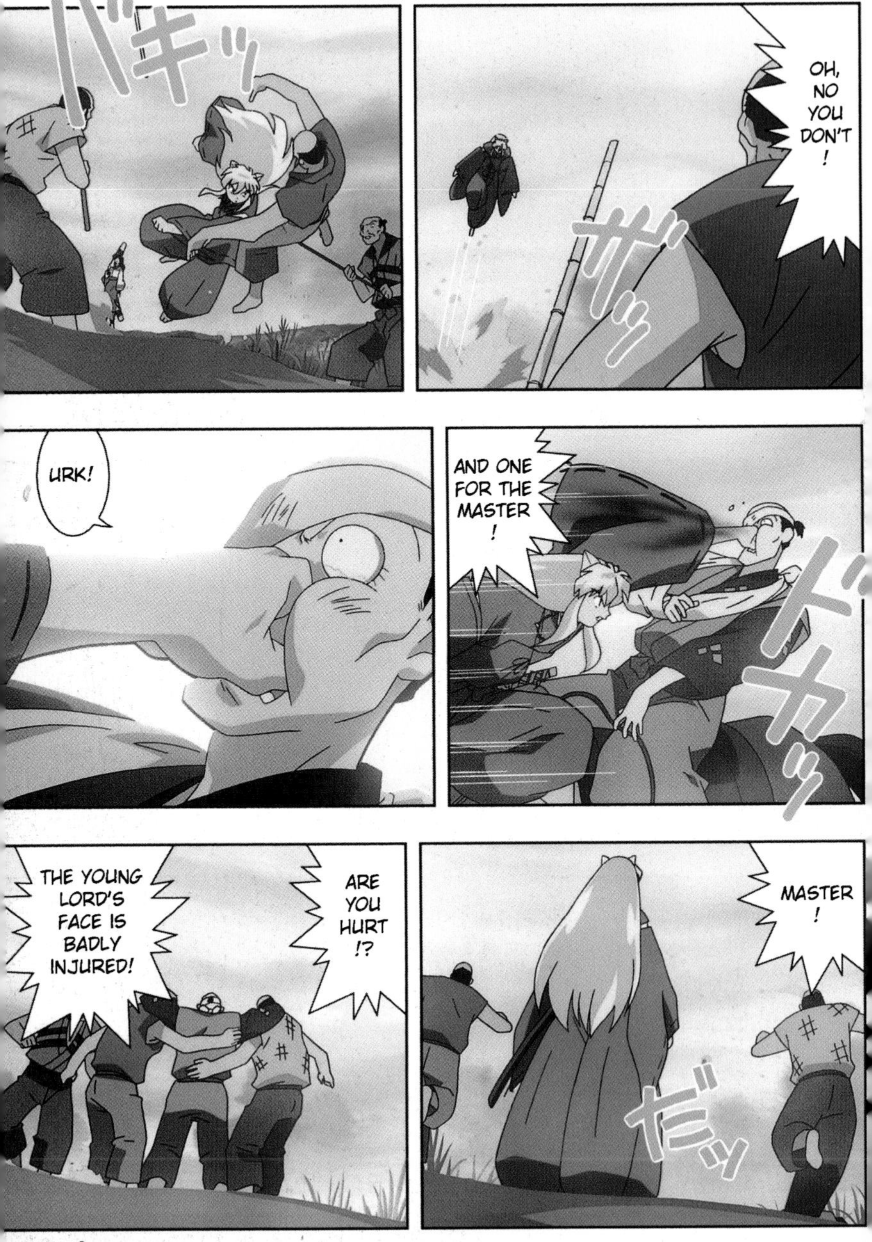

バキッ
OH, NO YOU DON'T!
ザッ
URK!
AND ONE FOR THE MASTER!
ドカッ
THE YOUNG LORD'S FACE IS BADLY INJURED!
ARE YOU HURT!?
MASTER!
だっ

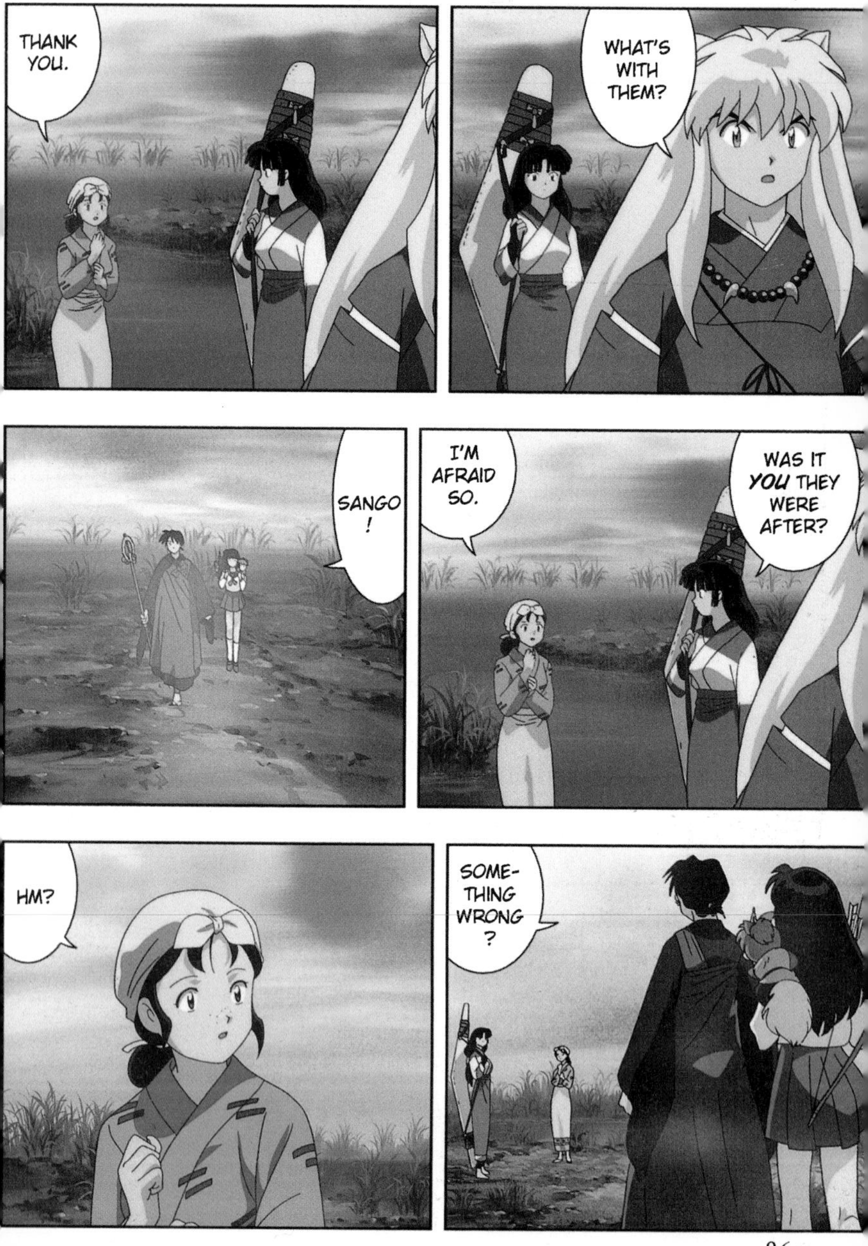
THANK YOU.
WHAT'S WITH THEM?
SANGO!
WAS IT *YOU* THEY WERE AFTER?
I'M AFRAID SO.
HM?
SOME-THING WRONG?

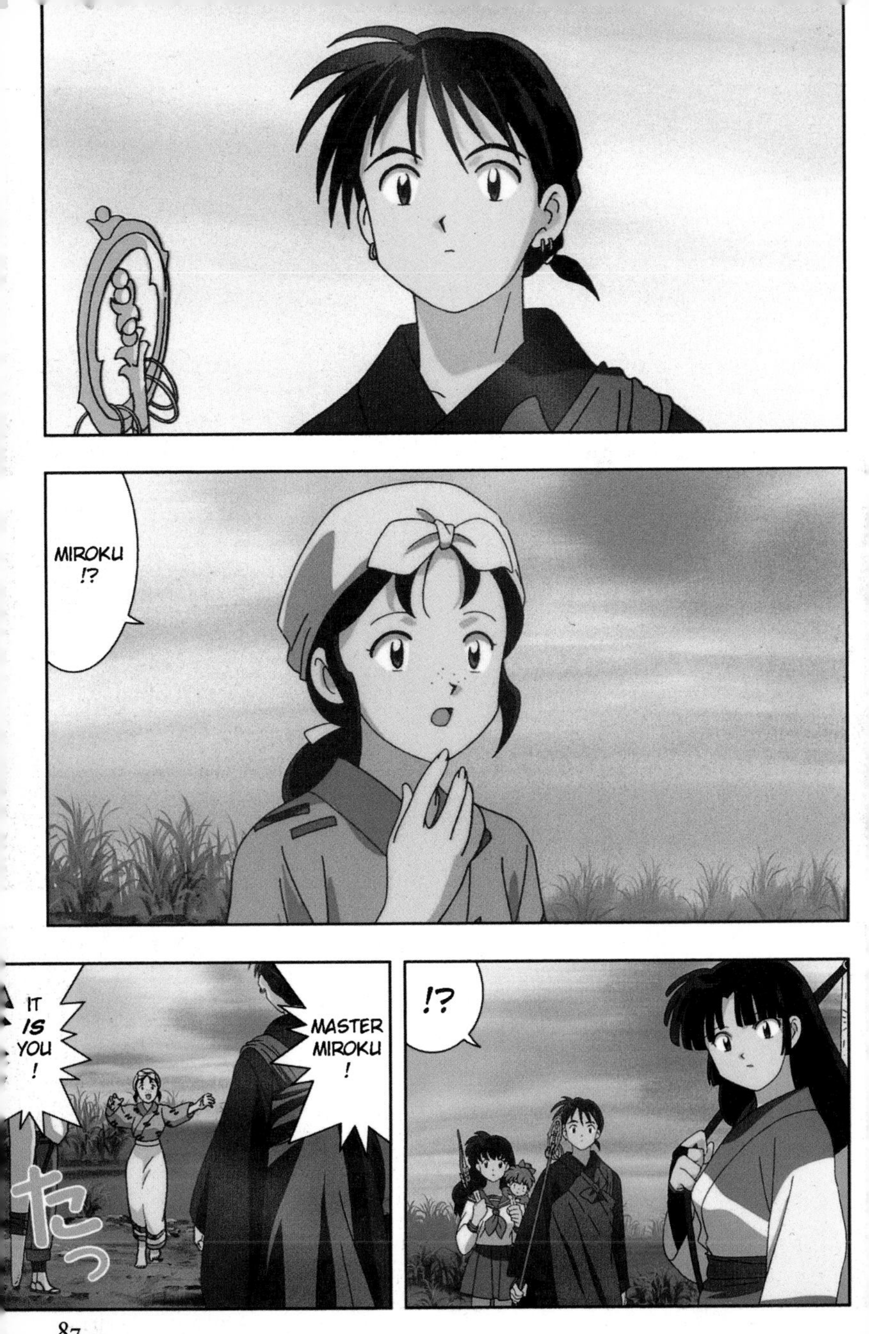
MIROKU !?
MASTER MIROKU !
IT IS YOU !
たっ
!?

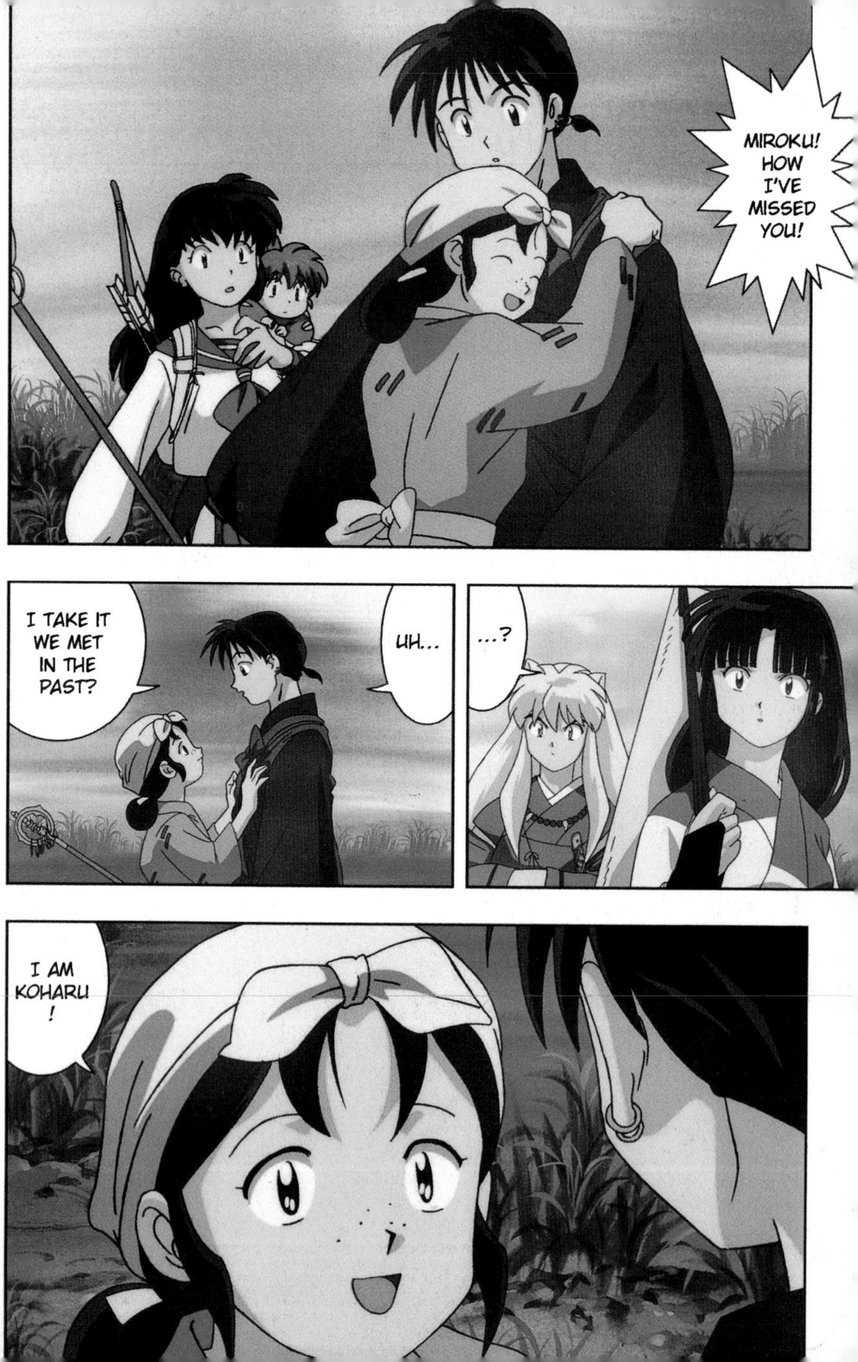
MIROKU! HOW I'VE MISSED YOU!
UH...
I TAKE IT WE MET IN THE PAST?
...?
I AM KOHARU!

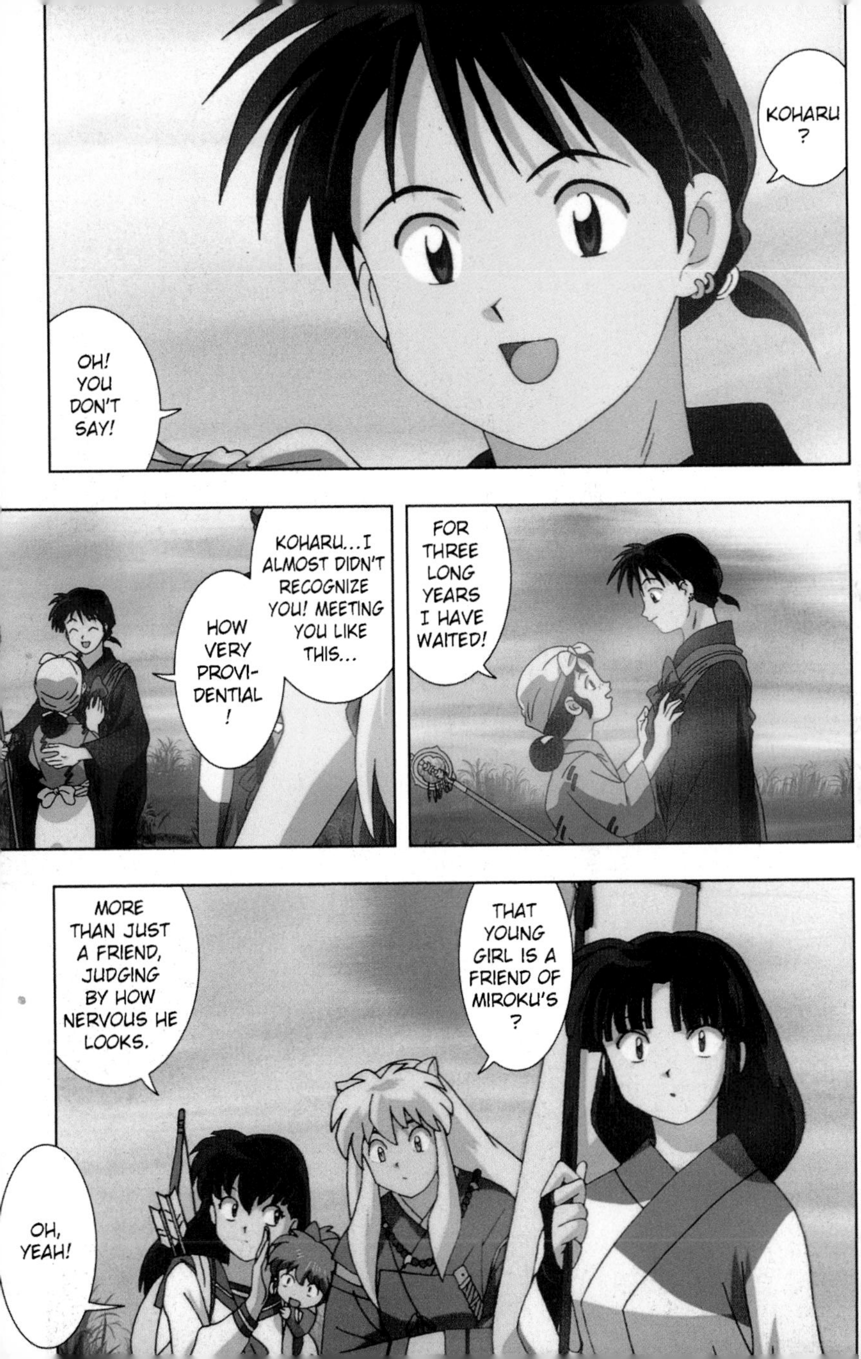
KOHARU?
OH! YOU DON'T SAY!
FOR THREE LONG YEARS I HAVE WAITED!
KOHARU...I ALMOST DIDN'T RECOGNIZE YOU! MEETING YOU LIKE THIS...
HOW VERY PROVI-DENTIAL!
THAT YOUNG GIRL IS A FRIEND OF MIROKU'S?
MORE THAN JUST A FRIEND, JUDGING BY HOW NERVOUS HE LOOKS.
OH, YEAH!

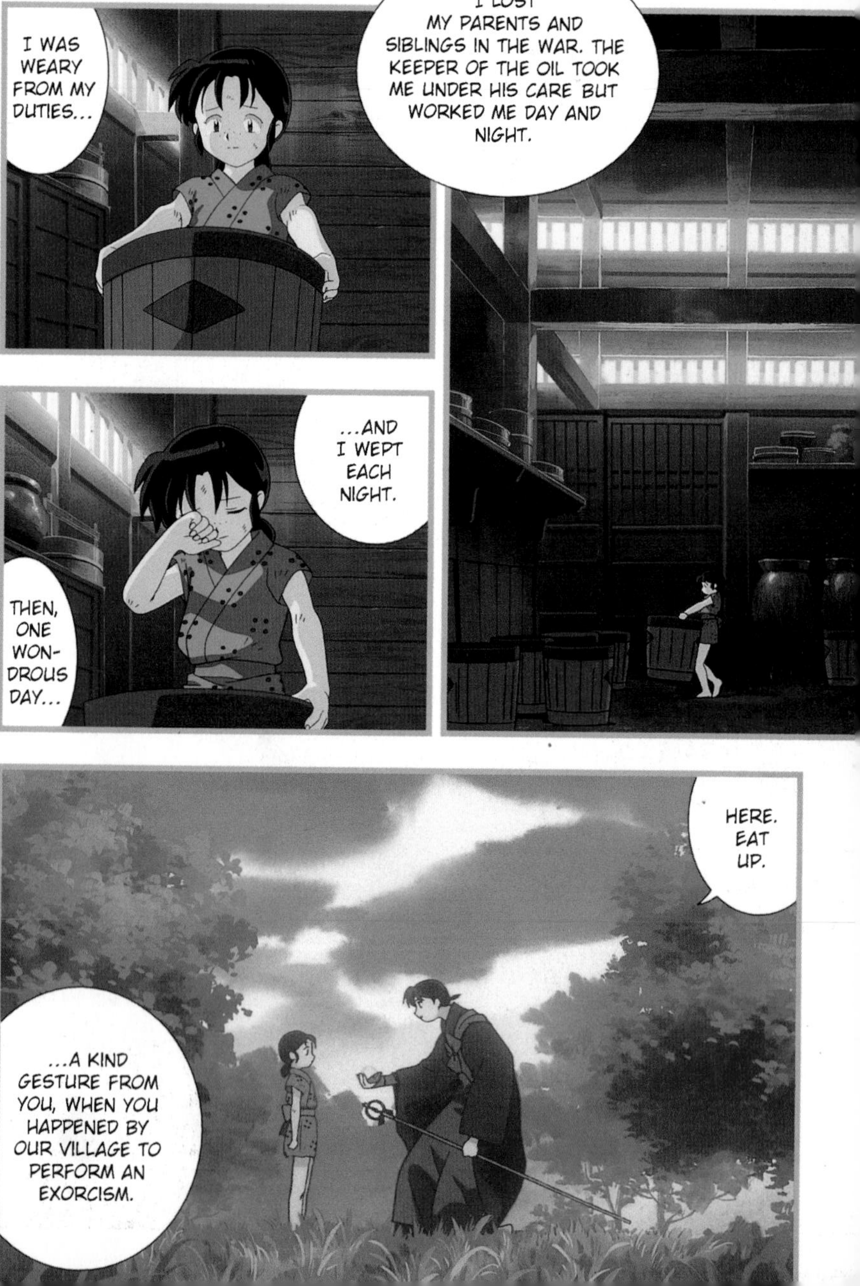
I LOST MY PARENTS AND SIBLINGS IN THE WAR. THE KEEPER OF THE OIL TOOK ME UNDER HIS CARE BUT WORKED ME DAY AND NIGHT.
I WAS WEARY FROM MY DUTIES...
...AND I WEPT EACH NIGHT.
THEN, ONE WON-DROUS DAY...
HERE. EAT UP.
...A KIND GESTURE FROM YOU, WHEN YOU HAPPENED BY OUR VILLAGE TO PERFORM AN EXORCISM.

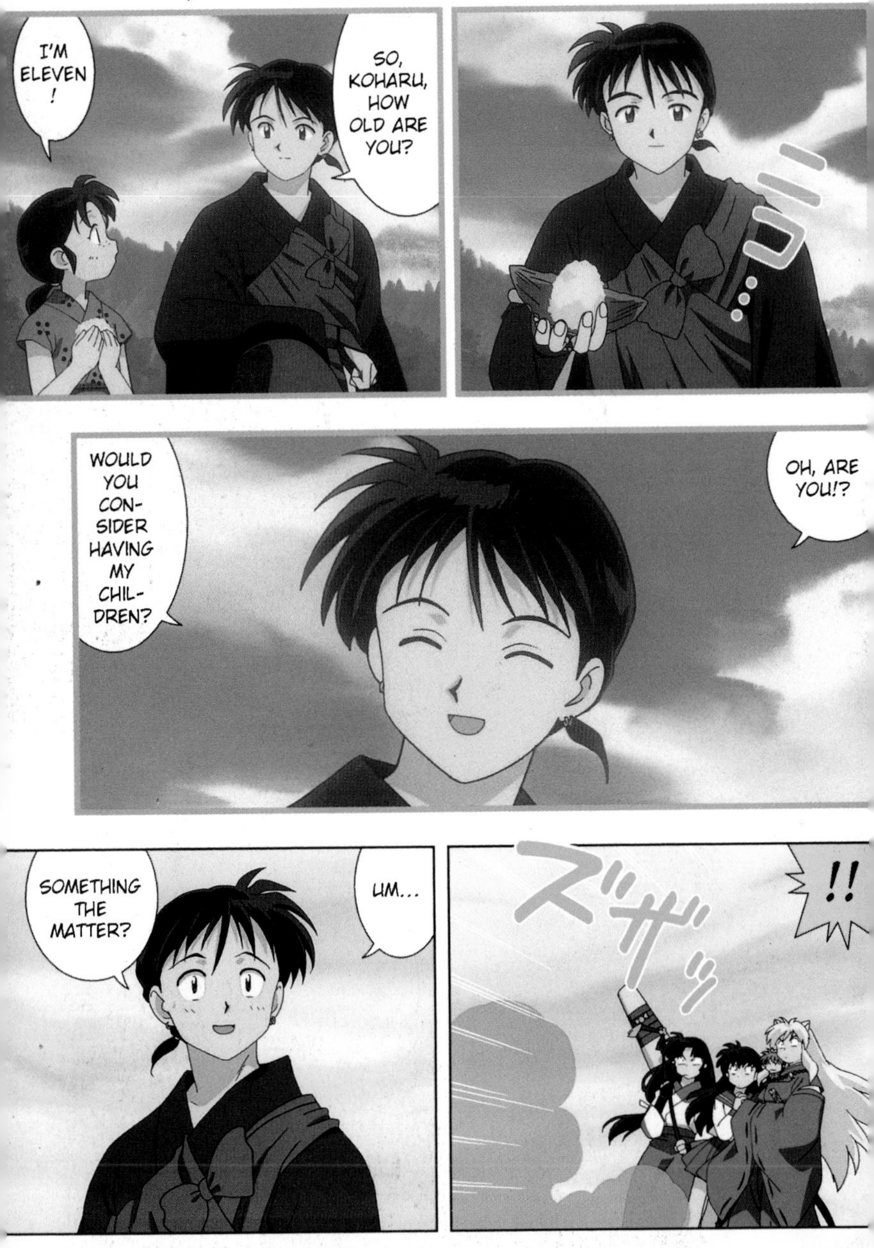
ジ…
SO, KOHARU, HOW OLD ARE YOU?
I'M ELEVEN!
OH, ARE YOU!?
WOULD YOU CONSIDER HAVING MY CHILDREN?
ズザッ
!!
UM...
SOMETHING THE MATTER?

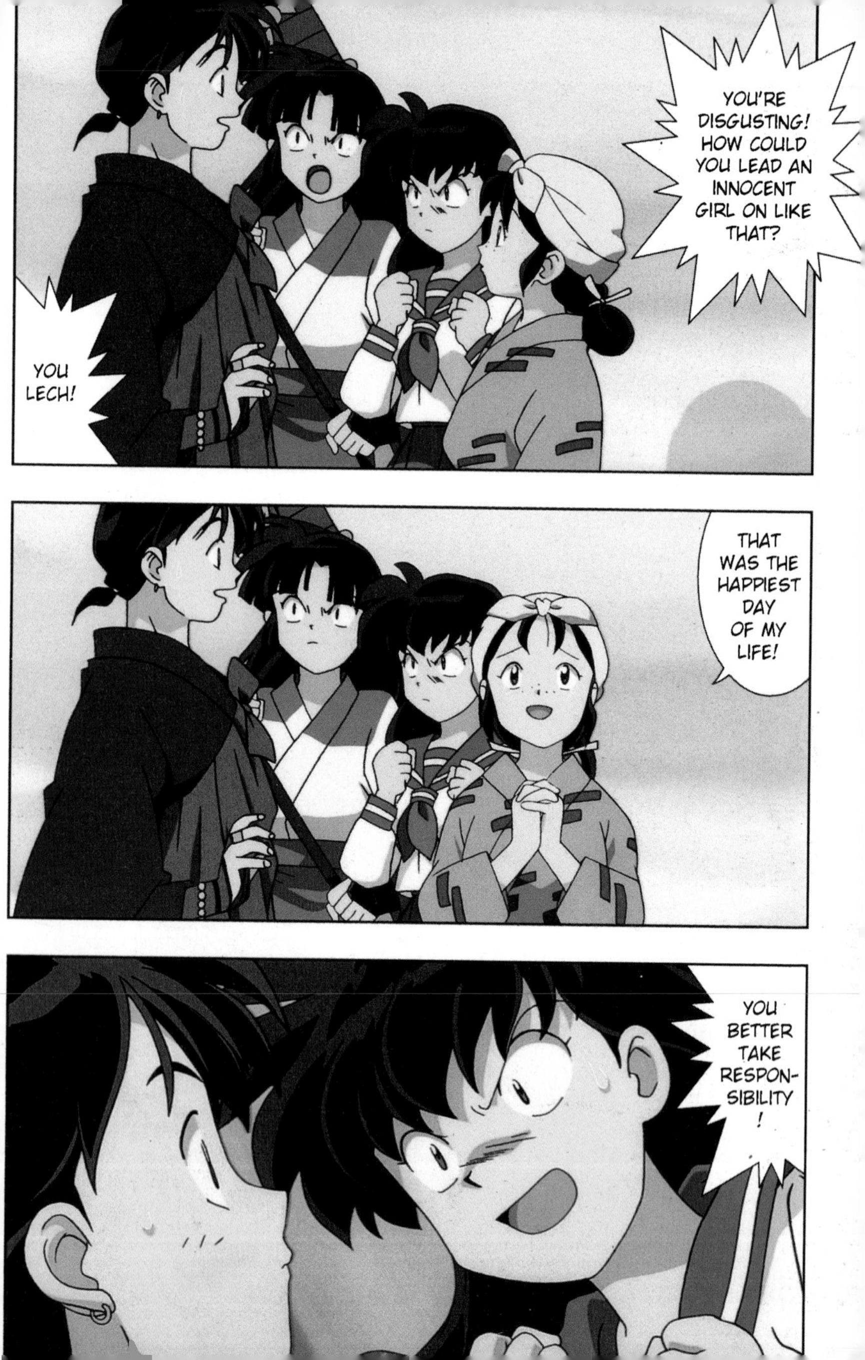
YOU'RE DISGUSTING! HOW COULD YOU LEAD AN INNOCENT GIRL ON LIKE THAT?
YOU LECH!
THAT WAS THE HAPPIEST DAY OF MY LIFE!
YOU BETTER TAKE RESPON-SIBILITY!

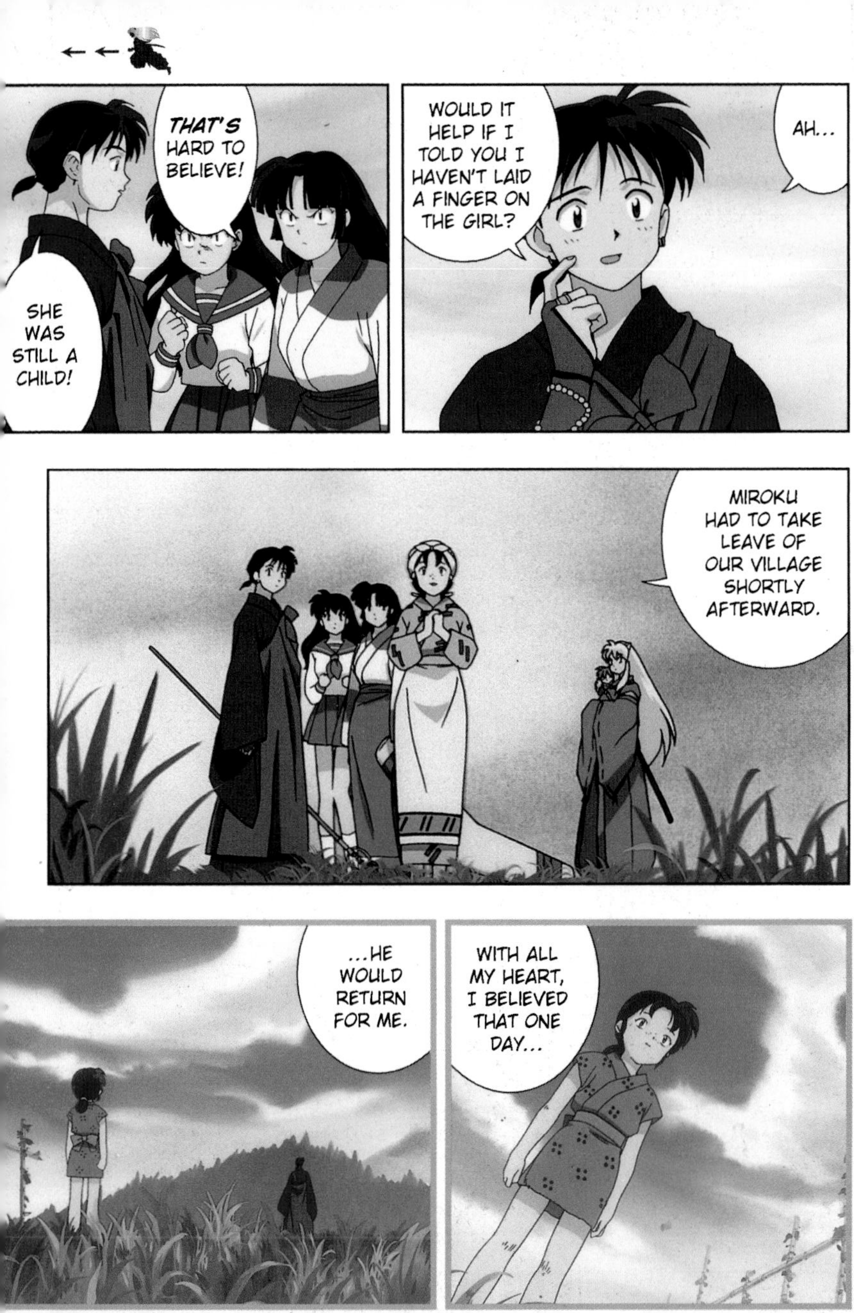
AH...
WOULD IT HELP IF I TOLD YOU I HAVEN'T LAID A FINGER ON THE GIRL?
*THAT'S* HARD TO BELIEVE!
SHE WAS STILL A CHILD!
MIROKU HAD TO TAKE LEAVE OF OUR VILLAGE SHORTLY AFTERWARD.
WITH ALL MY HEART, I BELIEVED THAT ONE DAY...
...HE WOULD RETURN FOR ME.

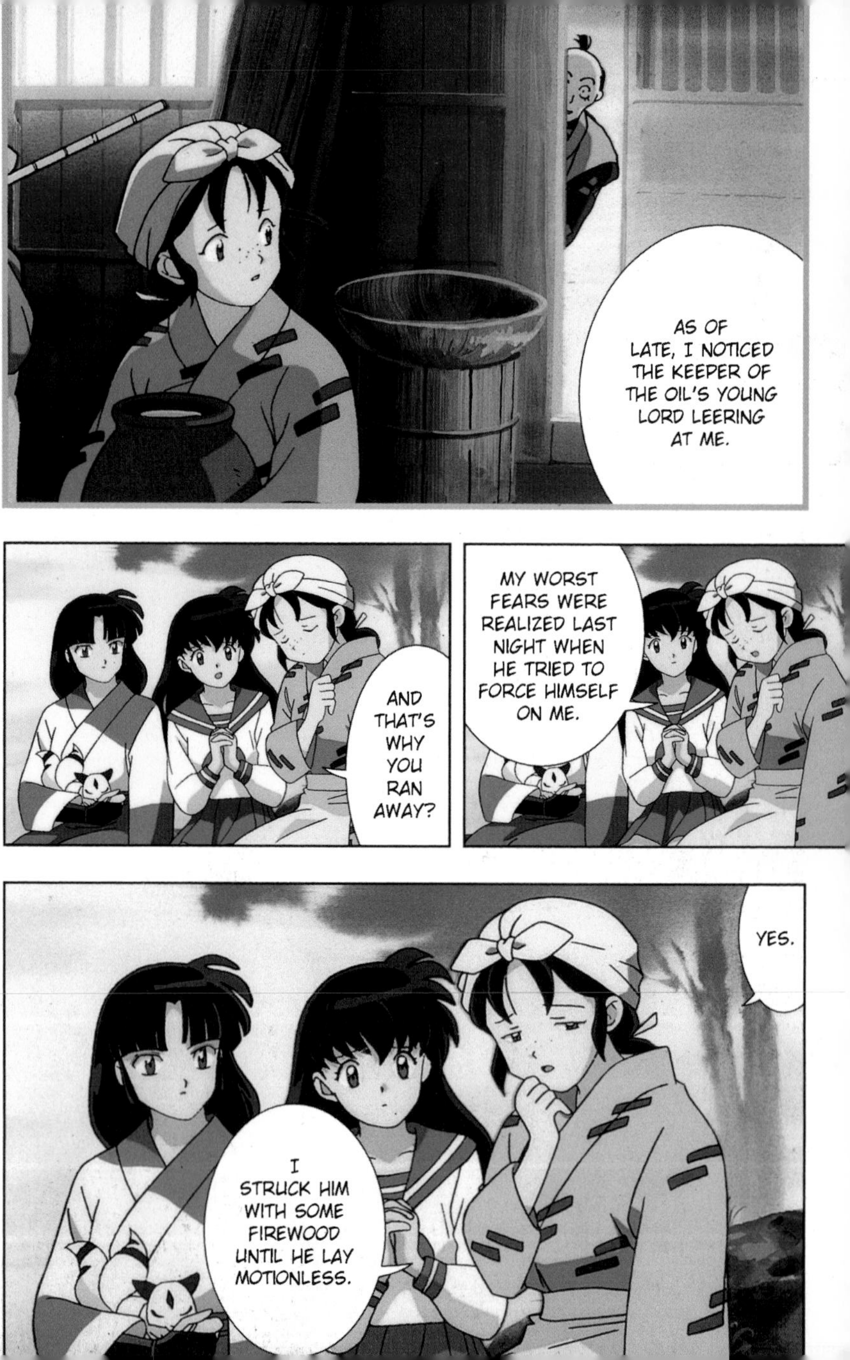
AS OF LATE, I NOTICED THE KEEPER OF THE OIL'S YOUNG LORD LEERING AT ME.
MY WORST FEARS WERE REALIZED LAST NIGHT WHEN HE TRIED TO FORCE HIMSELF ON ME.
AND THAT'S WHY YOU RAN AWAY?
YES.
I STRUCK HIM WITH SOME FIREWOOD UNTIL HE LAY MOTIONLESS.

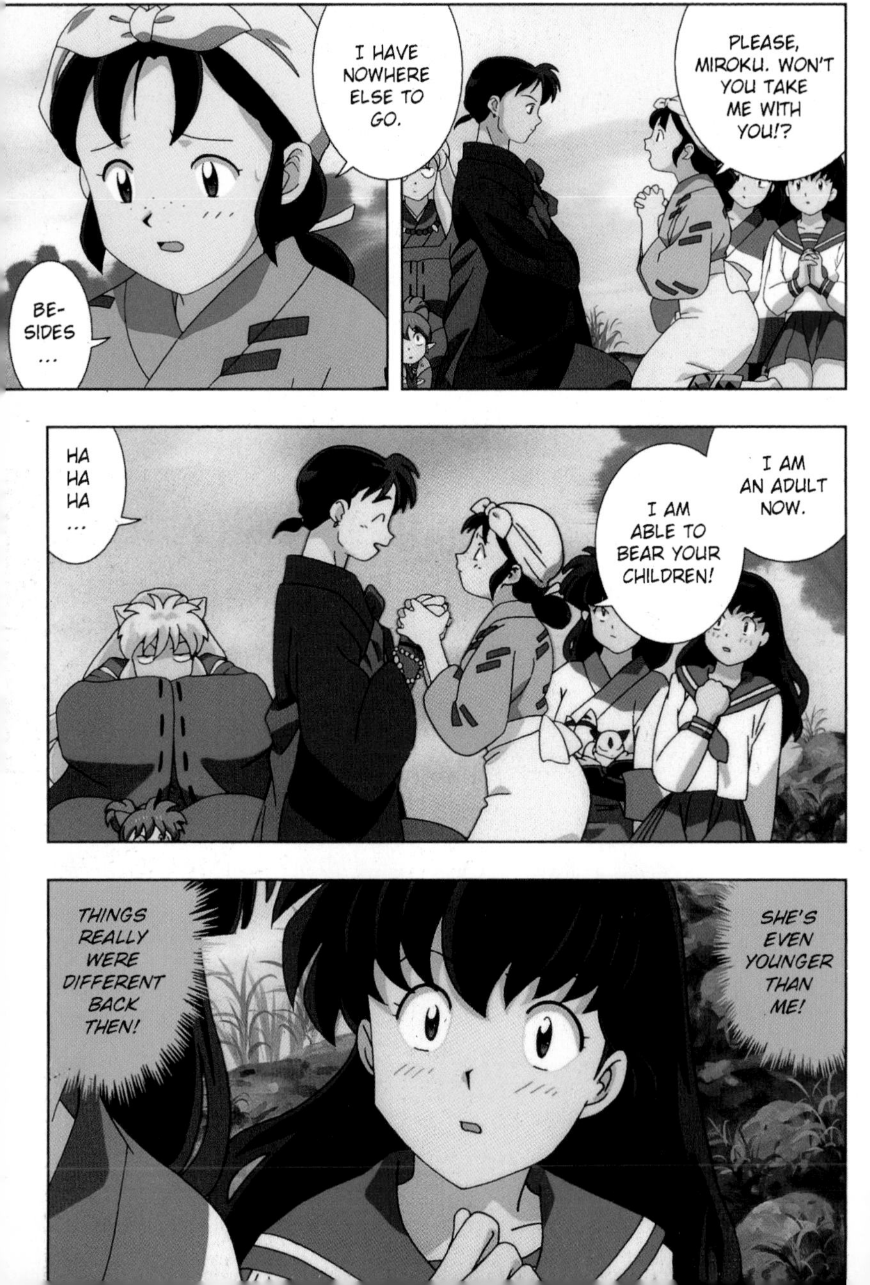
PLEASE, MIROKU. WON'T YOU TAKE ME WITH YOU!?
I HAVE NOWHERE ELSE TO GO.
BE-SIDES ...
I AM AN ADULT NOW.
I AM ABLE TO BEAR YOUR CHILDREN!
HA HA HA ...
SHE'S EVEN YOUNGER THAN ME!
THINGS REALLY WERE DIFFERENT BACK THEN!

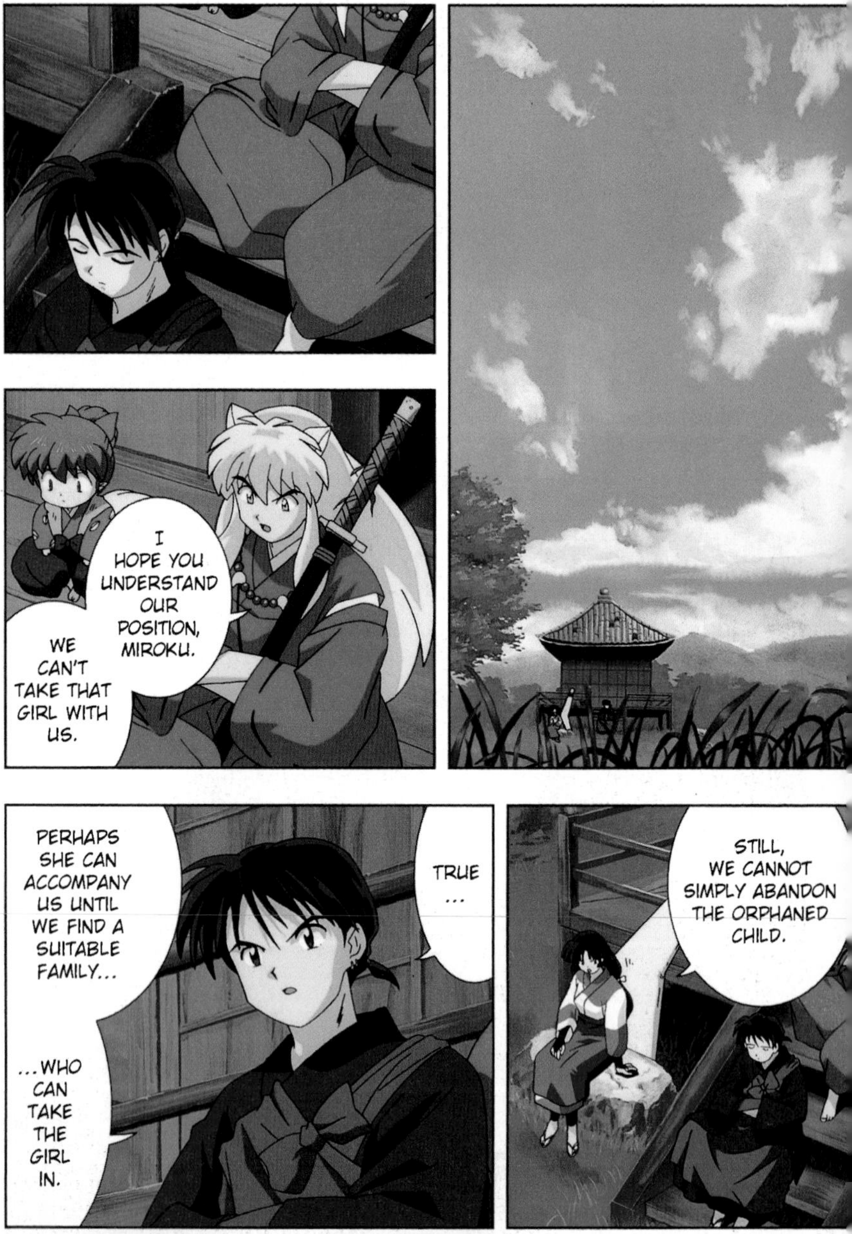
I HOPE YOU UNDERSTAND OUR POSITION, MIROKU.
WE CAN'T TAKE THAT GIRL WITH US.
STILL, WE CANNOT SIMPLY ABANDON THE ORPHANED CHILD.
TRUE ...
PERHAPS SHE CAN ACCOMPANY US UNTIL WE FIND A SUITABLE FAMILY...
...WHO CAN TAKE THE GIRL IN.

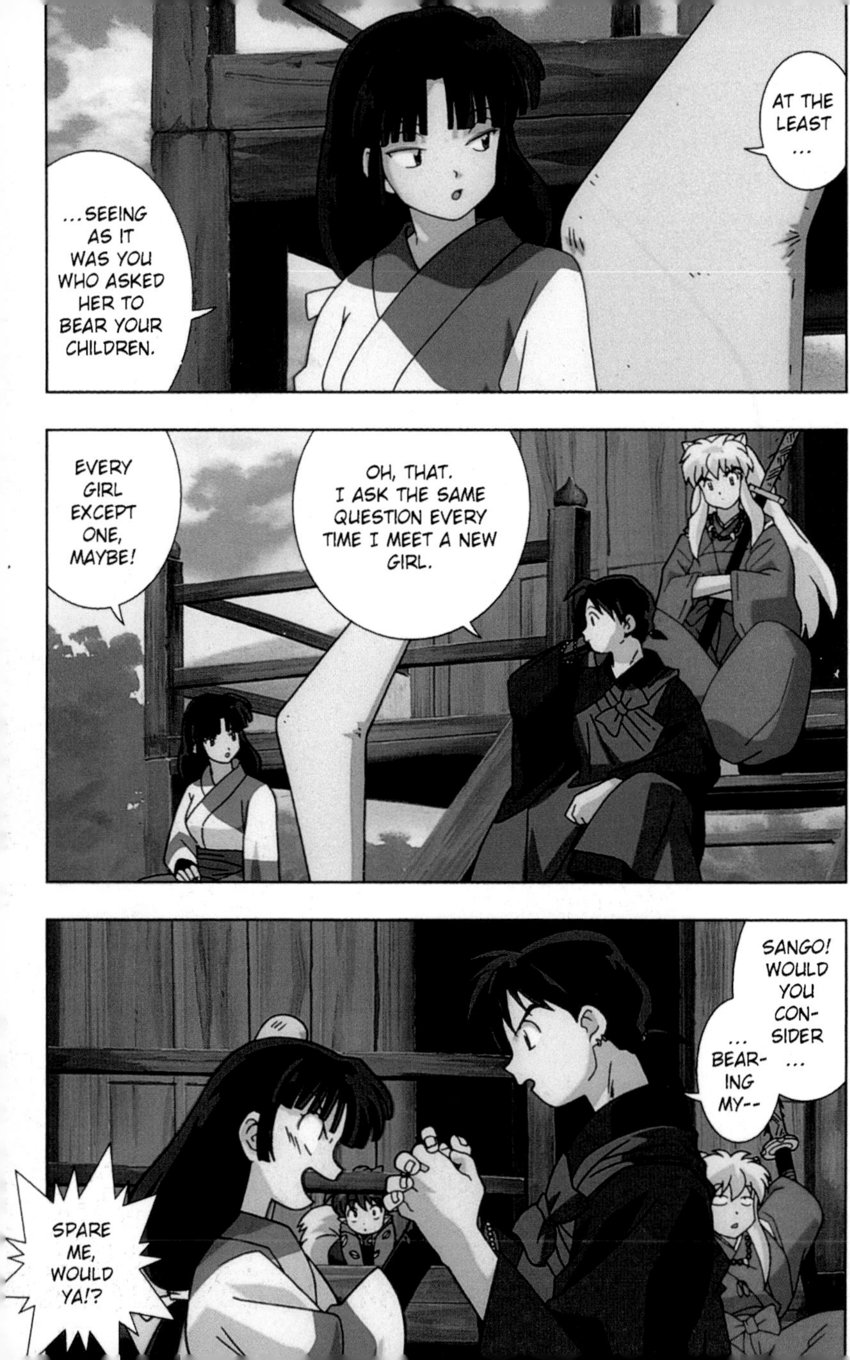
AT THE LEAST ...
...SEEING AS IT WAS YOU WHO ASKED HER TO BEAR YOUR CHILDREN.
OH, THAT. I ASK THE SAME QUESTION EVERY TIME I MEET A NEW GIRL.
EVERY GIRL EXCEPT ONE, MAYBE!
SANGO! WOULD YOU CON- SIDER ...
... BEAR- ING MY--
SPARE ME, WOULD YA!?

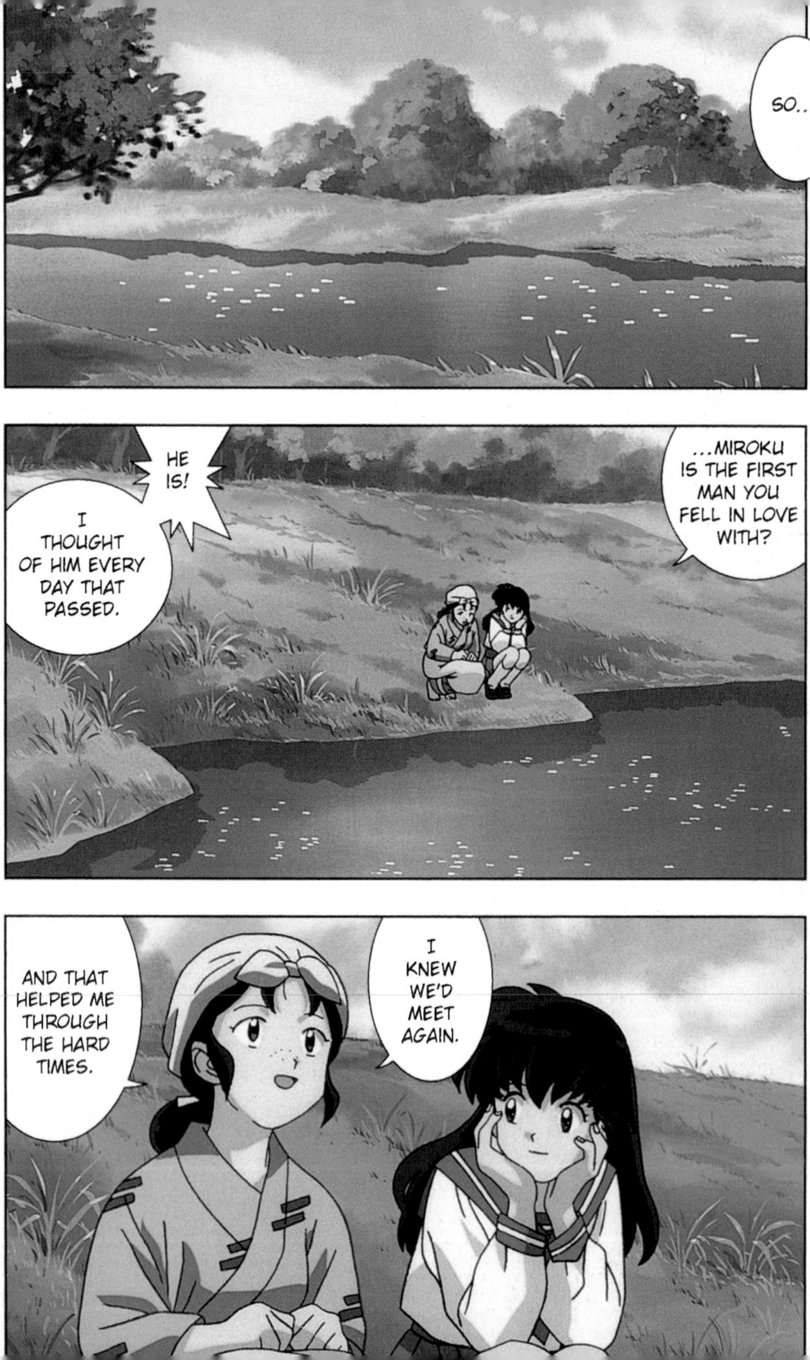
SO...
...MIROKU IS THE FIRST MAN YOU FELL IN LOVE WITH?
HE IS!
I THOUGHT OF HIM EVERY DAY THAT PASSED.
I KNEW WE'D MEET AGAIN.
AND THAT HELPED ME THROUGH THE HARD TIMES.

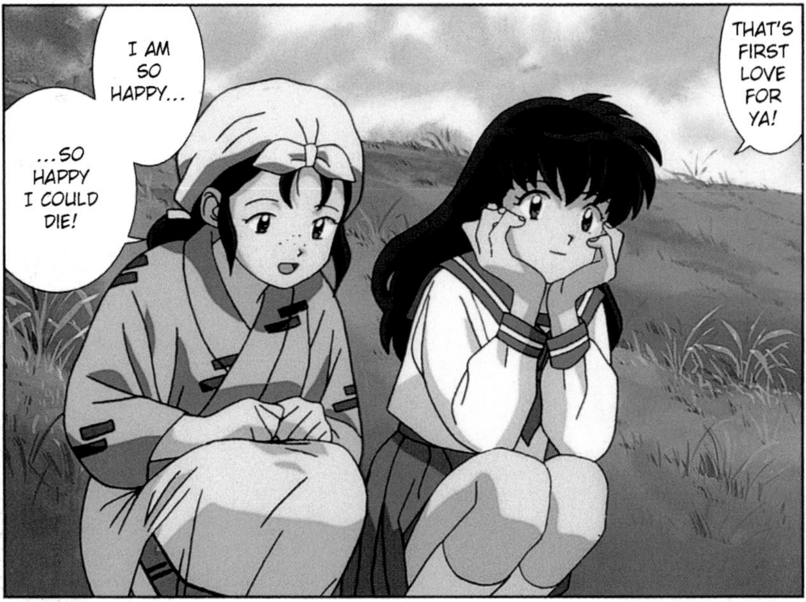
THAT'S FIRST LOVE FOR YA!
I AM SO HAPPY...
...SO HAPPY I COULD DIE!

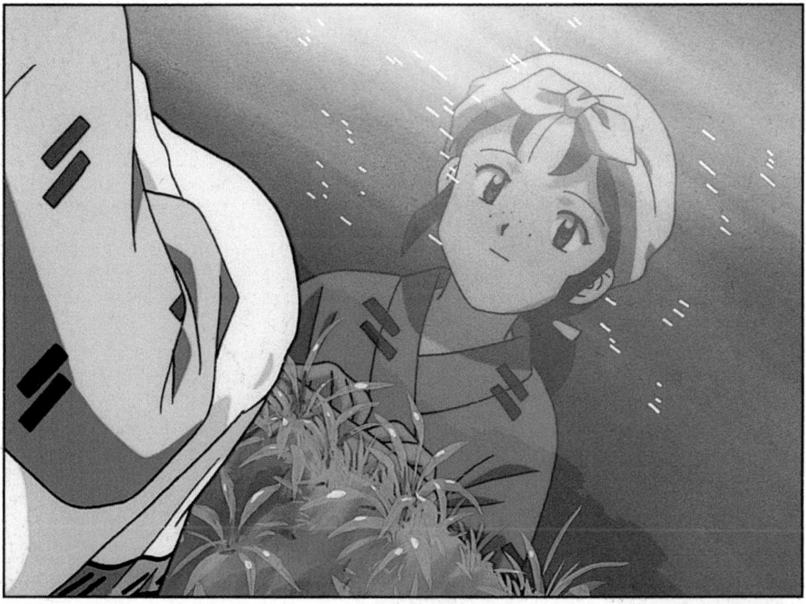

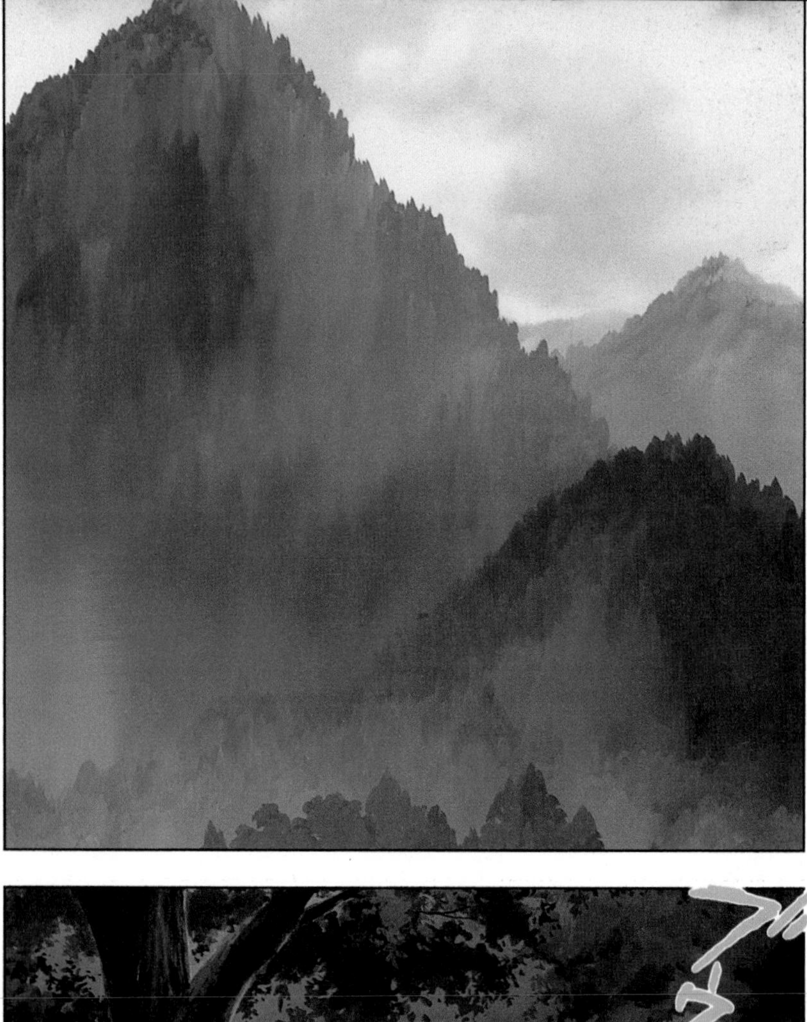

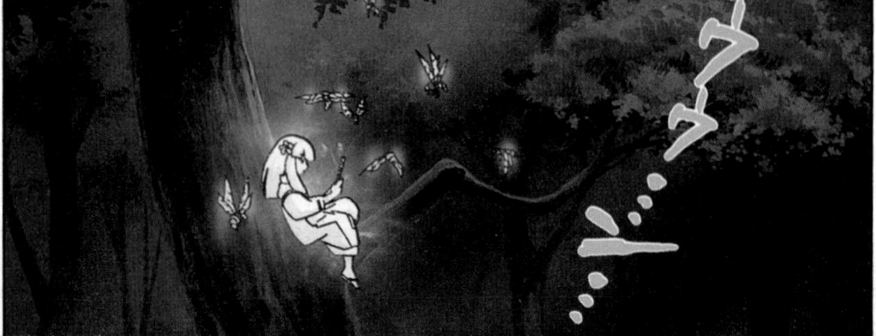
ブウウゥ…ン…

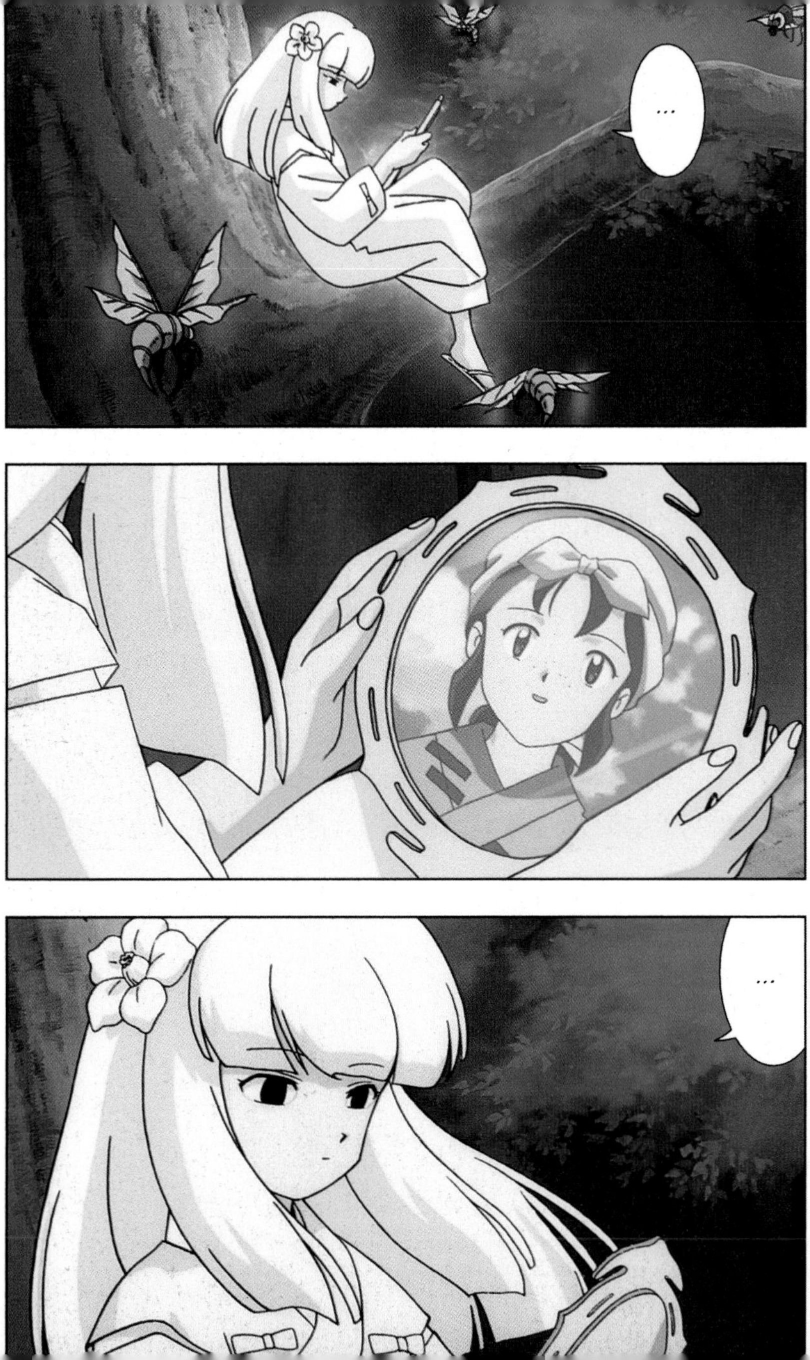
...
...

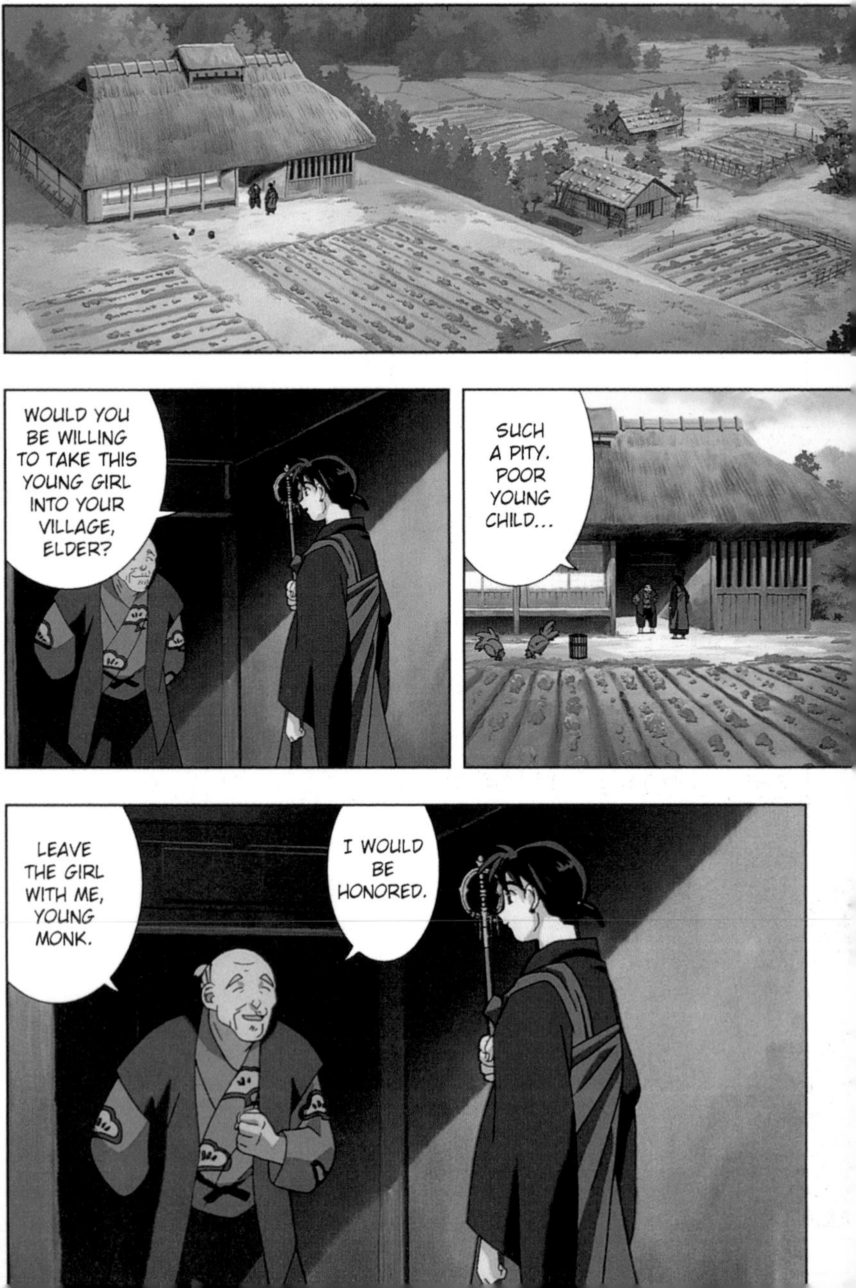
SUCH A PITY. POOR YOUNG CHILD...
WOULD YOU BE WILLING TO TAKE THIS YOUNG GIRL INTO YOUR VILLAGE, ELDER?
I WOULD BE HONORED.
LEAVE THE GIRL WITH ME, YOUNG MONK.

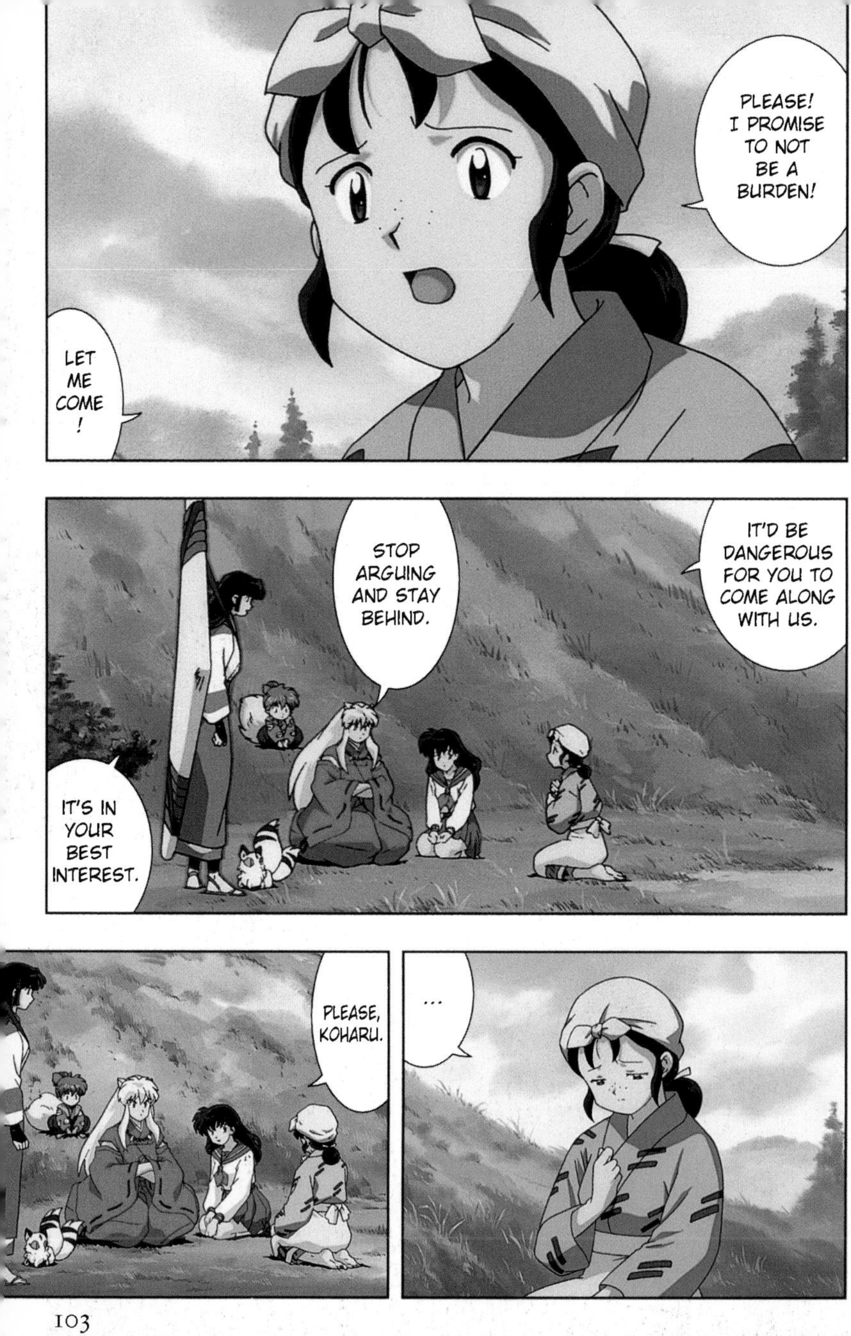

PLEASE! I PROMISE TO NOT BE A BURDEN!
LET ME COME!
IT'D BE DANGEROUS FOR YOU TO COME ALONG WITH US.
STOP ARGUING AND STAY BEHIND.
IT'S IN YOUR BEST INTEREST.
...
PLEASE, KOHARU.

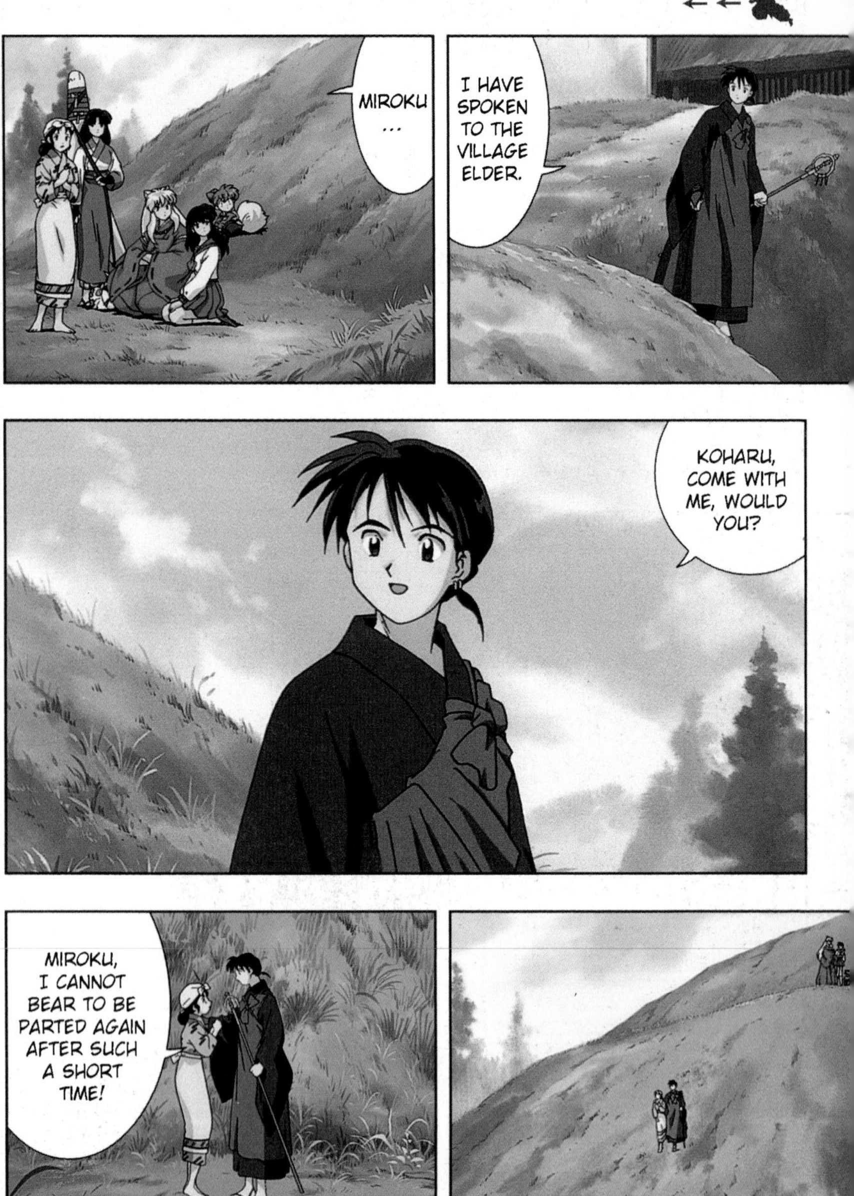

I HAVE SPOKEN TO THE VILLAGE ELDER.
MIROKU...
KOHARU, COME WITH ME, WOULD YOU?
MIROKU, I CANNOT BEAR TO BE PARTED AGAIN AFTER SUCH A SHORT TIME!

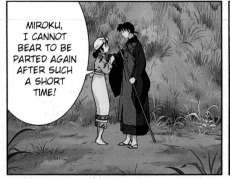

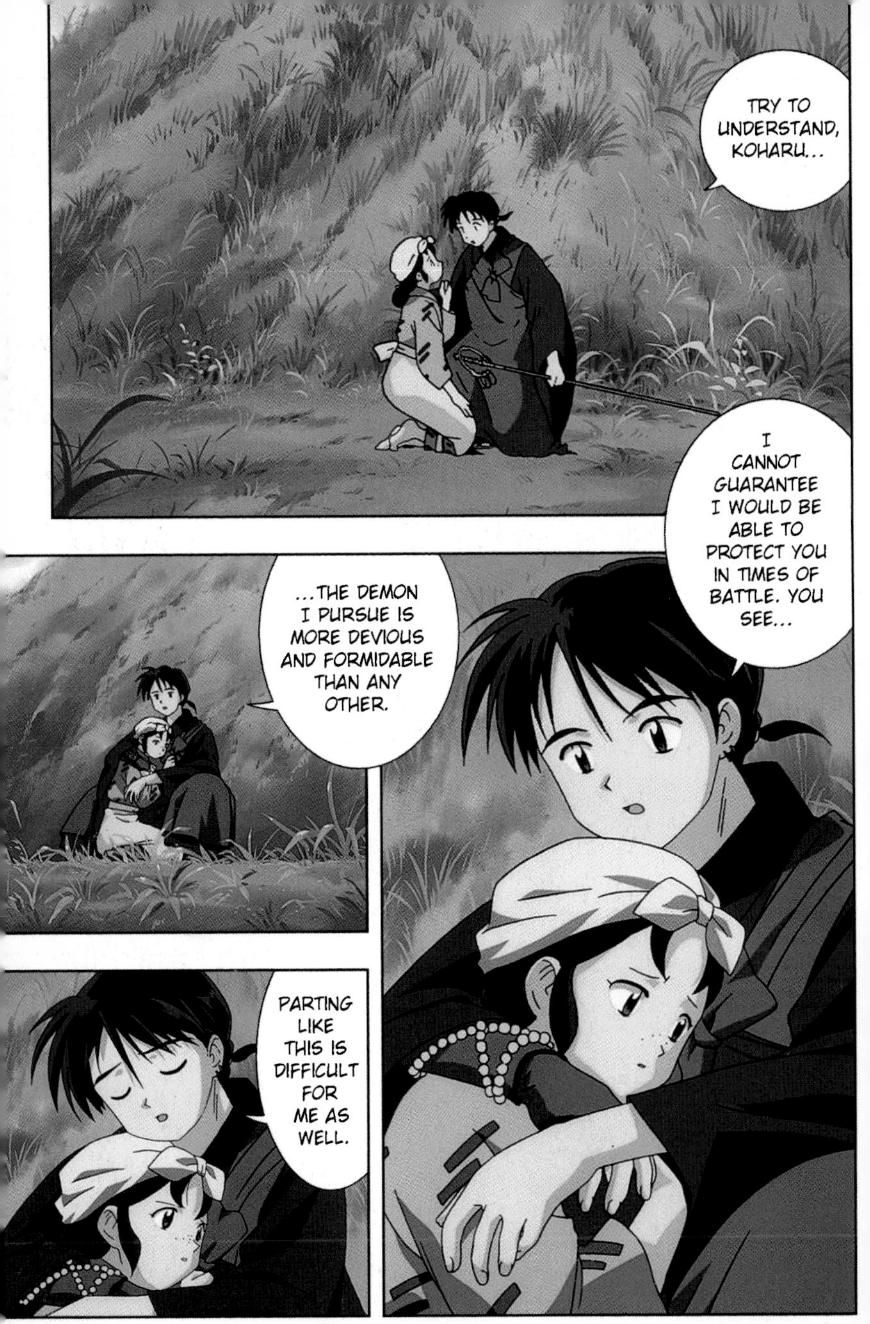
TRY TO UNDERSTAND, KOHARU...
I CANNOT GUARANTEE I WOULD BE ABLE TO PROTECT YOU IN TIMES OF BATTLE. YOU SEE...
...THE DEMON I PURSUE IS MORE DEVIOUS AND FORMIDABLE THAN ANY OTHER.
PARTING LIKE THIS IS DIFFICULT FOR ME AS WELL.

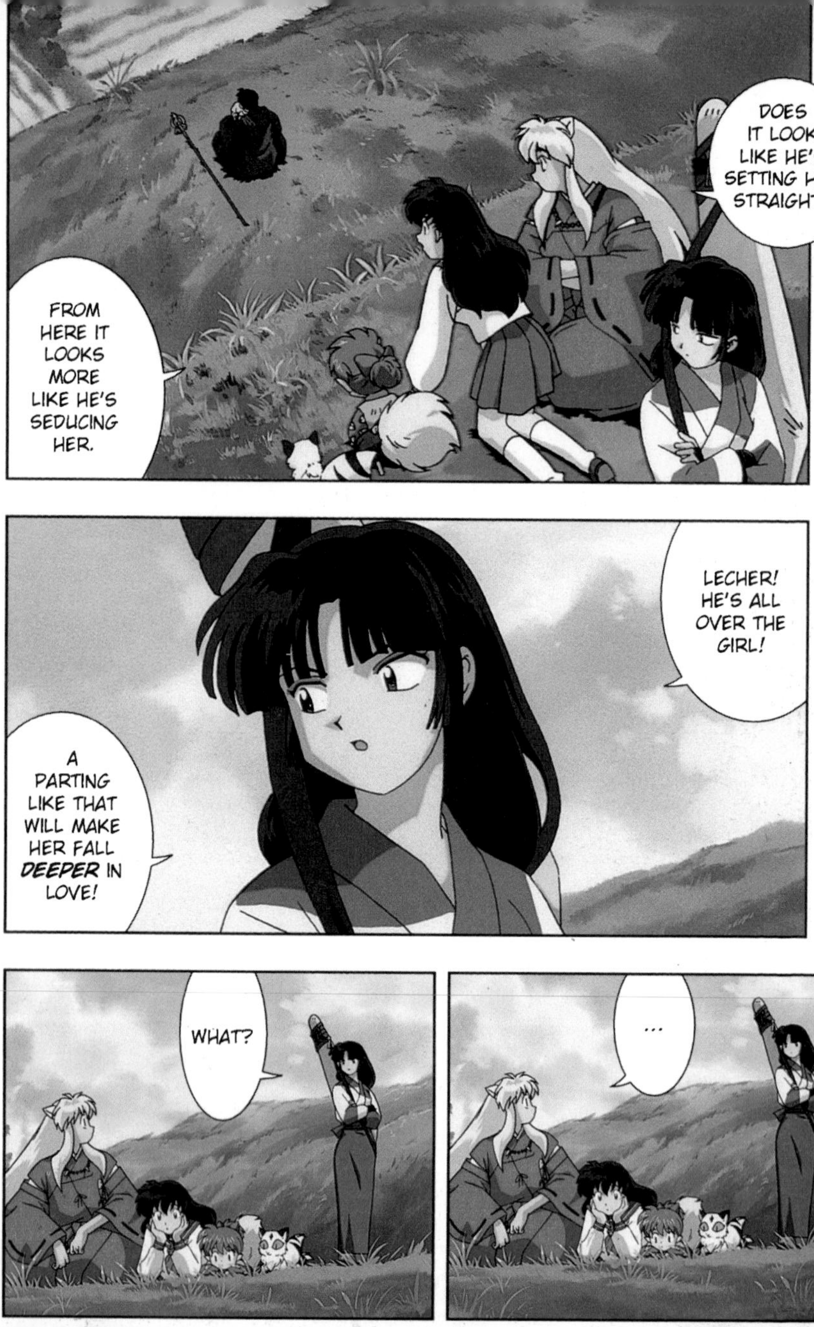
DOES IT LOOK LIKE HE'S SETTING HER STRAIGHT?
FROM HERE IT LOOKS MORE LIKE HE'S SEDUCING HER.
LECHER! HE'S ALL OVER THE GIRL!
A PARTING LIKE THAT WILL MAKE HER FALL ***DEEPER*** IN LOVE!
WHAT?
...

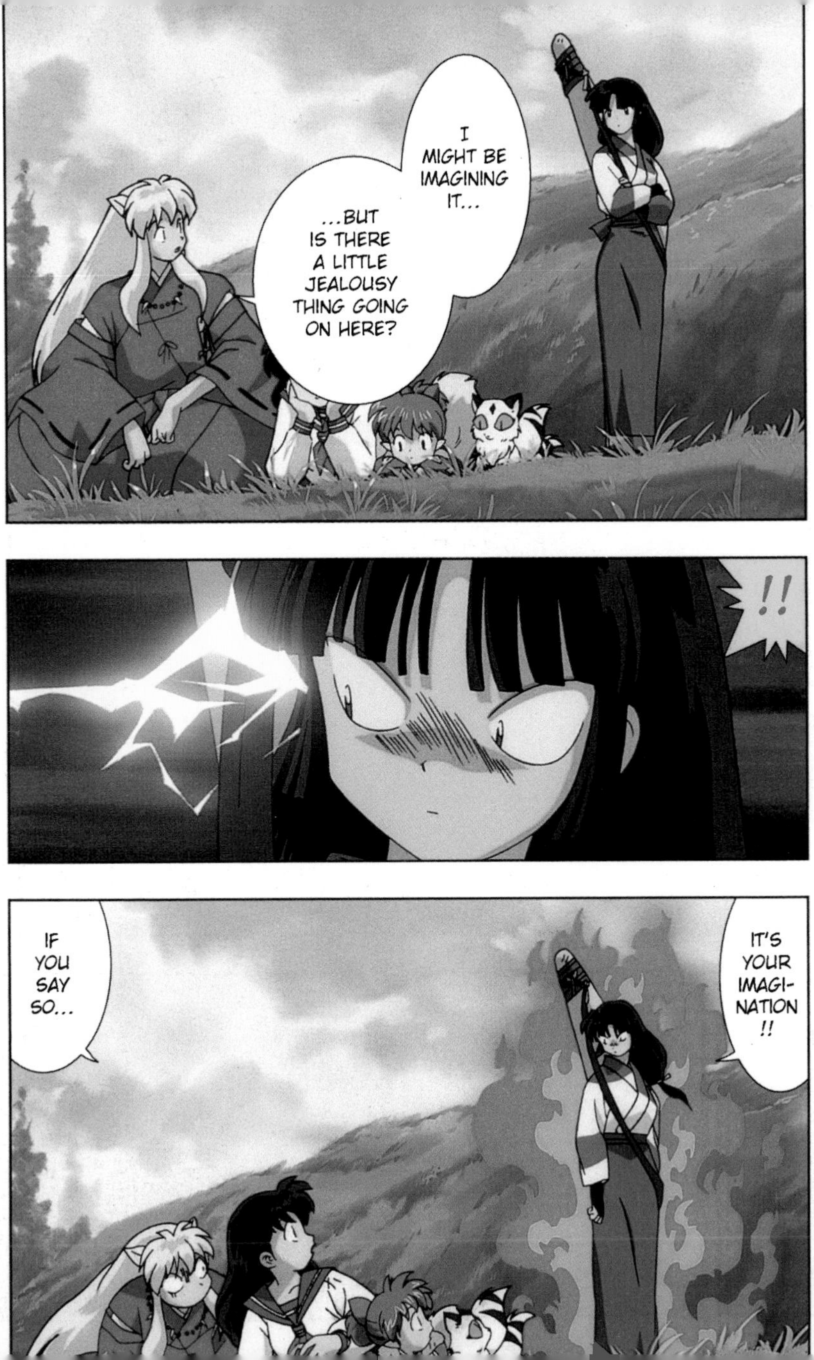
I MIGHT BE IMAGINING IT...
...BUT IS THERE A LITTLE JEALOUSY THING GOING ON HERE?
!!
IT'S YOUR IMAGI-NATION !!
IF YOU SAY SO...

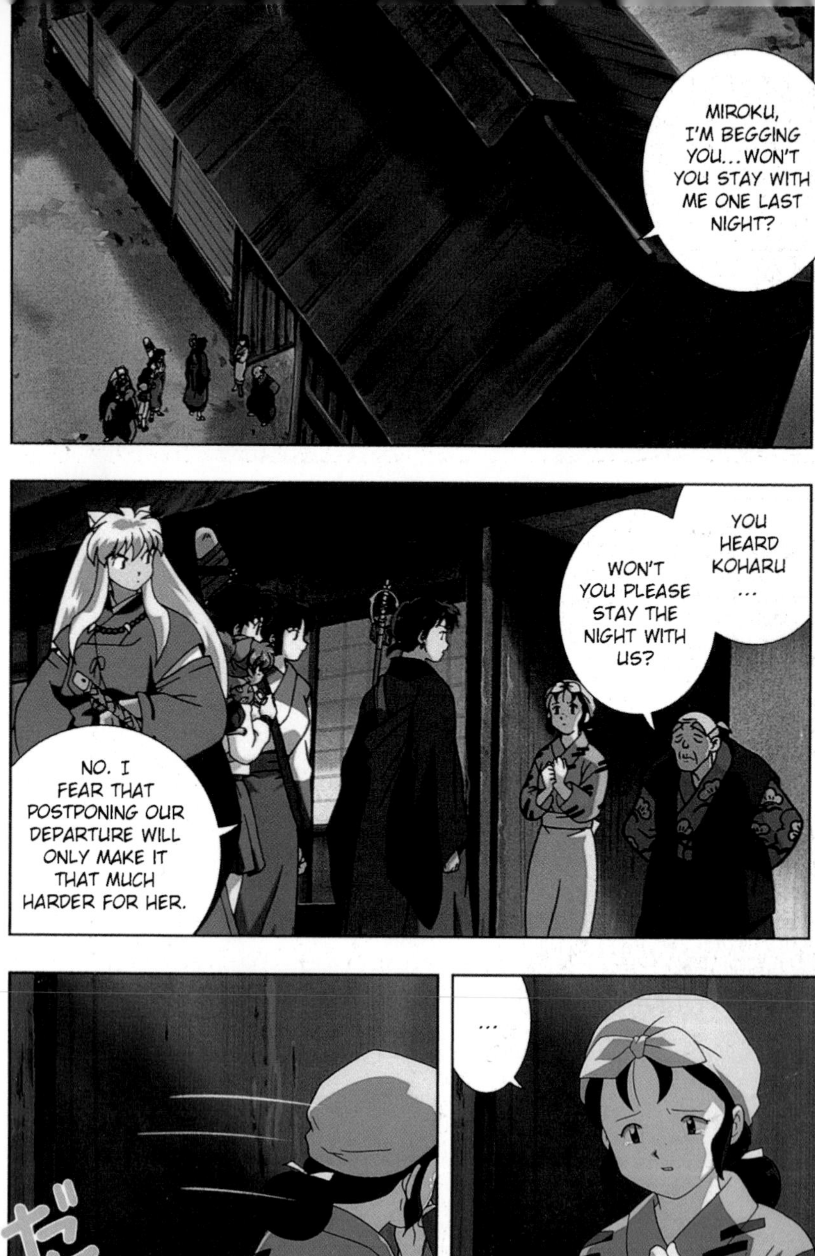

MIROKU, I'M BEGGING YOU...WON'T YOU STAY WITH ME ONE LAST NIGHT?
YOU HEARD KOHARU...
WON'T YOU PLEASE STAY THE NIGHT WITH US?
NO. I FEAR THAT POSTPONING OUR DEPARTURE WILL ONLY MAKE IT THAT MUCH HARDER FOR HER.
...
だっ

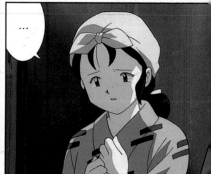

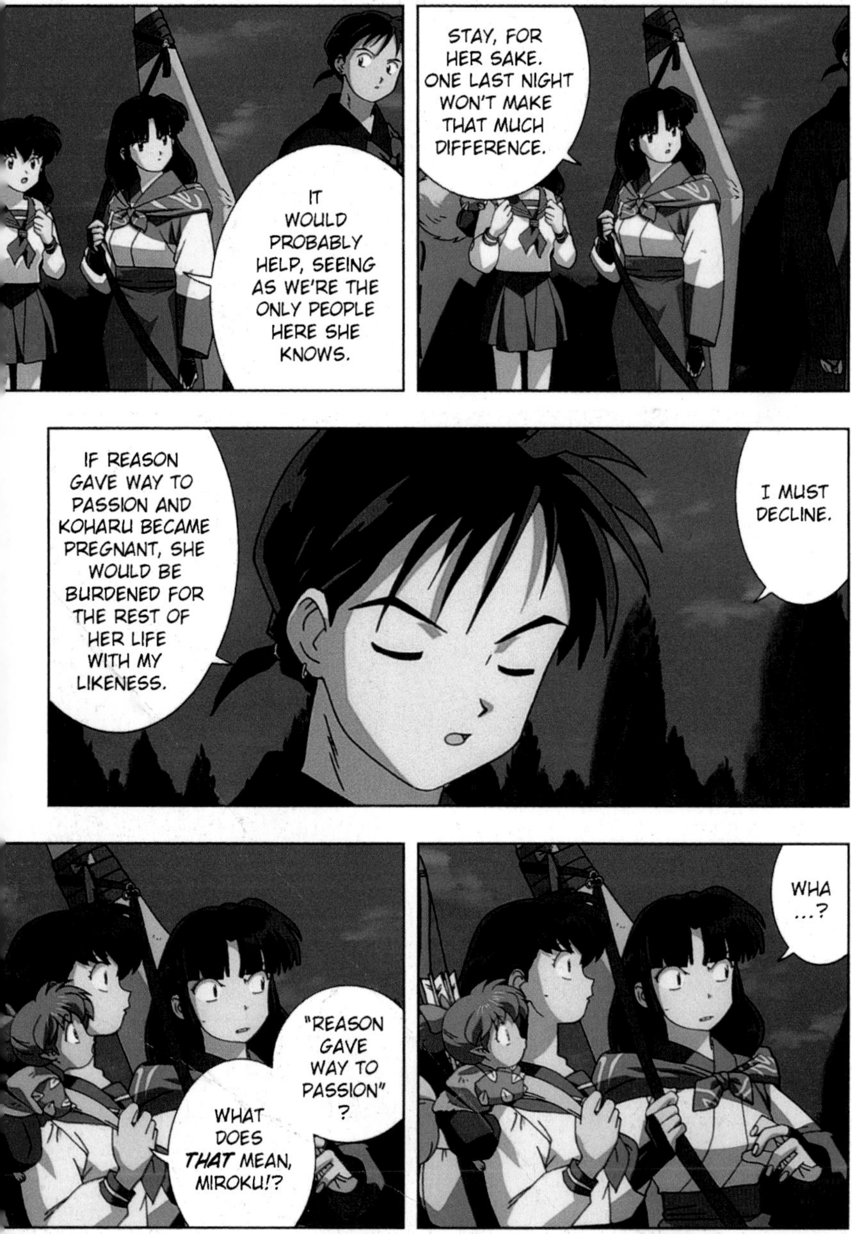
IT WOULD PROBABLY HELP, SEEING AS WE'RE THE ONLY PEOPLE HERE SHE KNOWS.
STAY, FOR HER SAKE. ONE LAST NIGHT WON'T MAKE THAT MUCH DIFFERENCE.
I MUST DECLINE.
IF REASON GAVE WAY TO PASSION AND KOHARU BECAME PREGNANT, SHE WOULD BE BURDENED FOR THE REST OF HER LIFE WITH MY LIKENESS.
"REASON GAVE WAY TO PASSION"?
WHAT DOES *THAT* MEAN, MIROKU!?
WHA...?

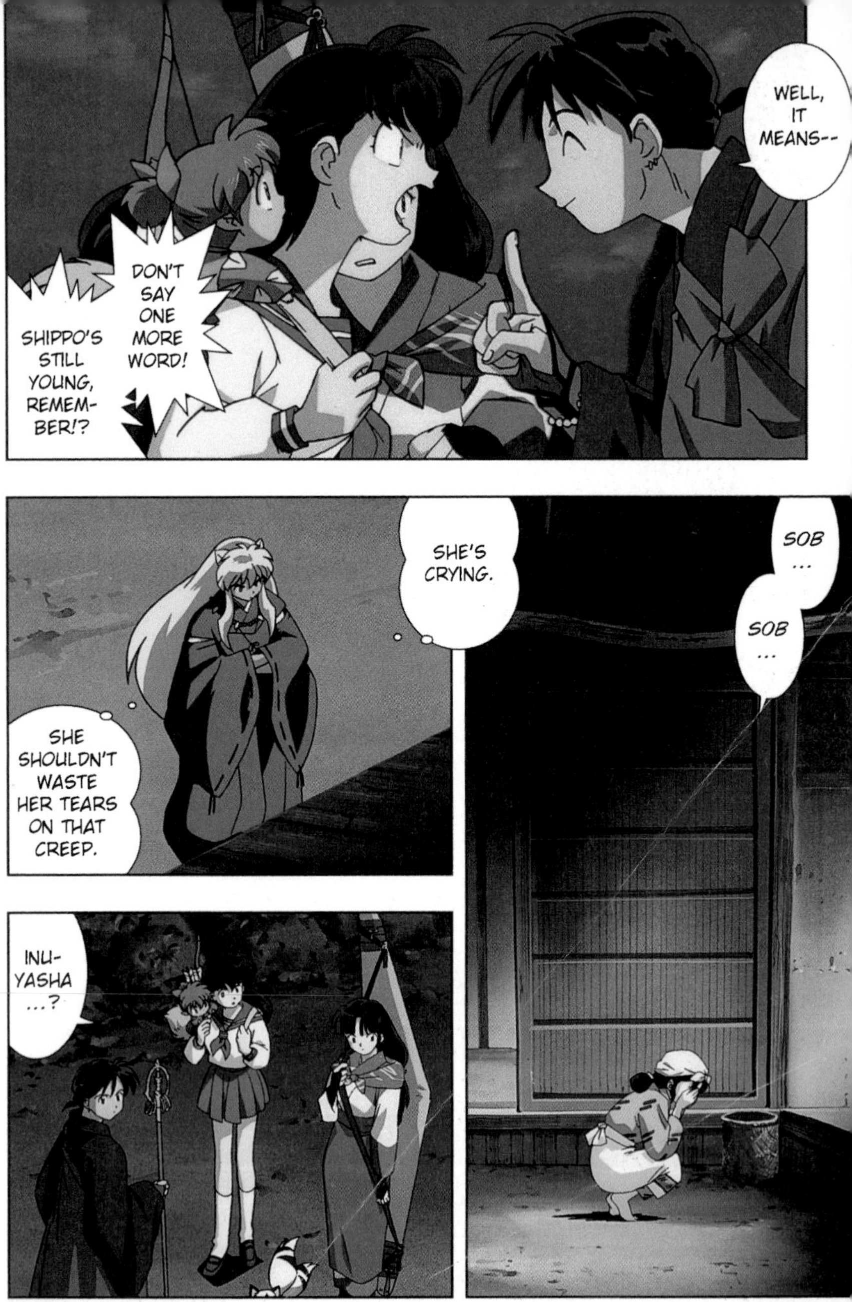
WELL, IT MEANS--
DON'T SAY ONE MORE WORD!
SHIPPO'S STILL YOUNG, REMEMBER!?
SOB...
SOB...
SHE'S CRYING.
SHE SHOULDN'T WASTE HER TEARS ON THAT CREEP.
INU-YASHA...?

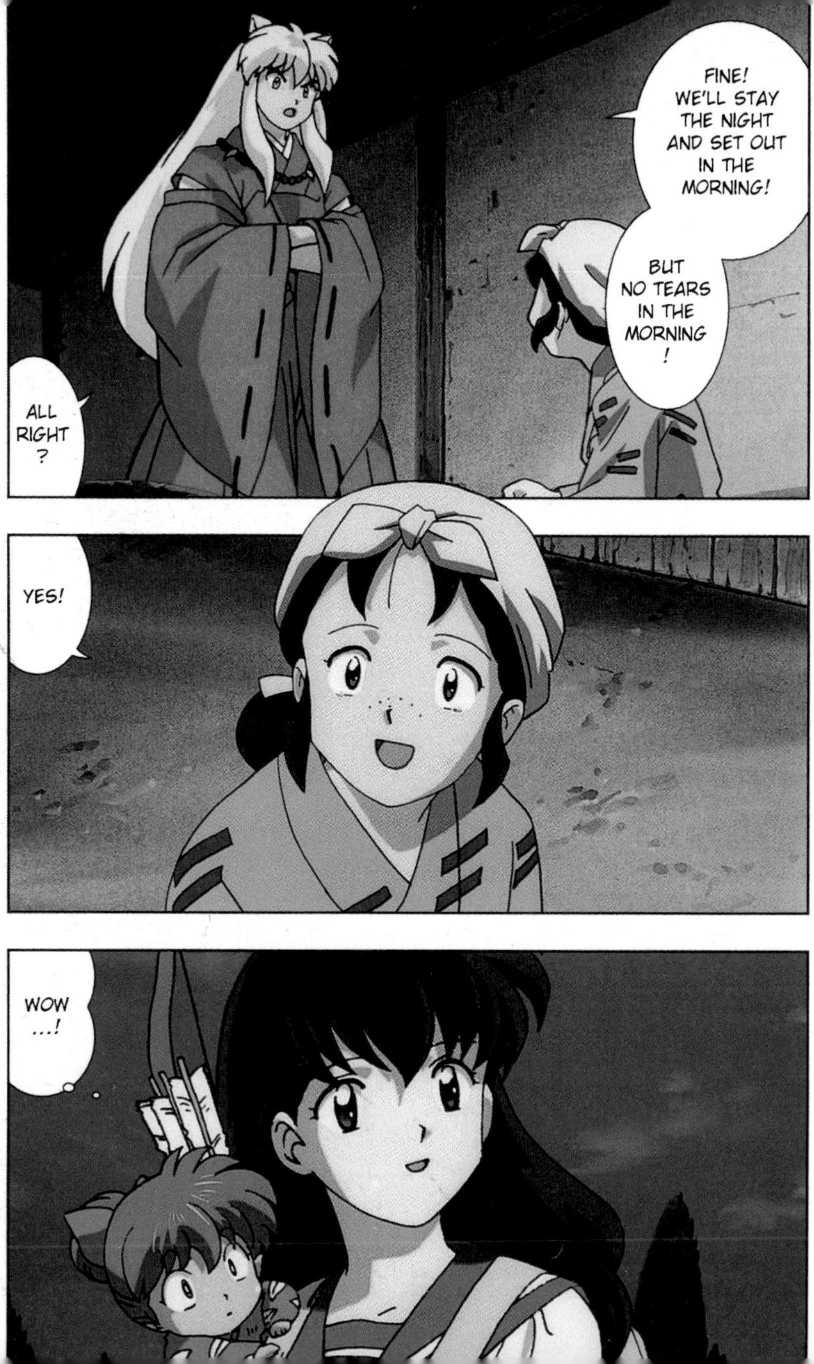
FINE! WE'LL STAY THE NIGHT AND SET OUT IN THE MORNING!
BUT NO TEARS IN THE MORNING!
ALL RIGHT?
YES!
WOW...!

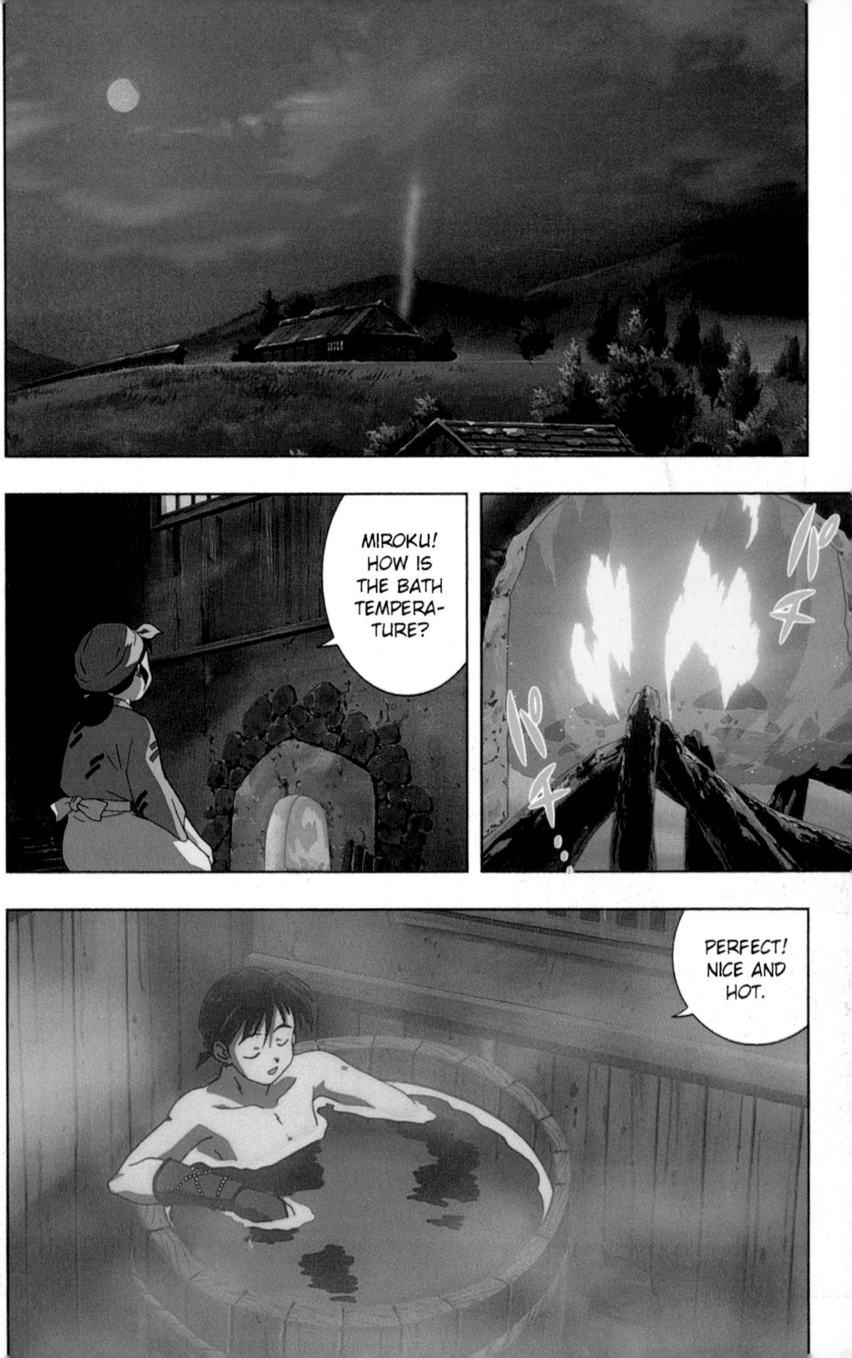
MIROKU! HOW IS THE BATH TEMPERA-TURE?
パチ
パチ
PERFECT! NICE AND HOT.

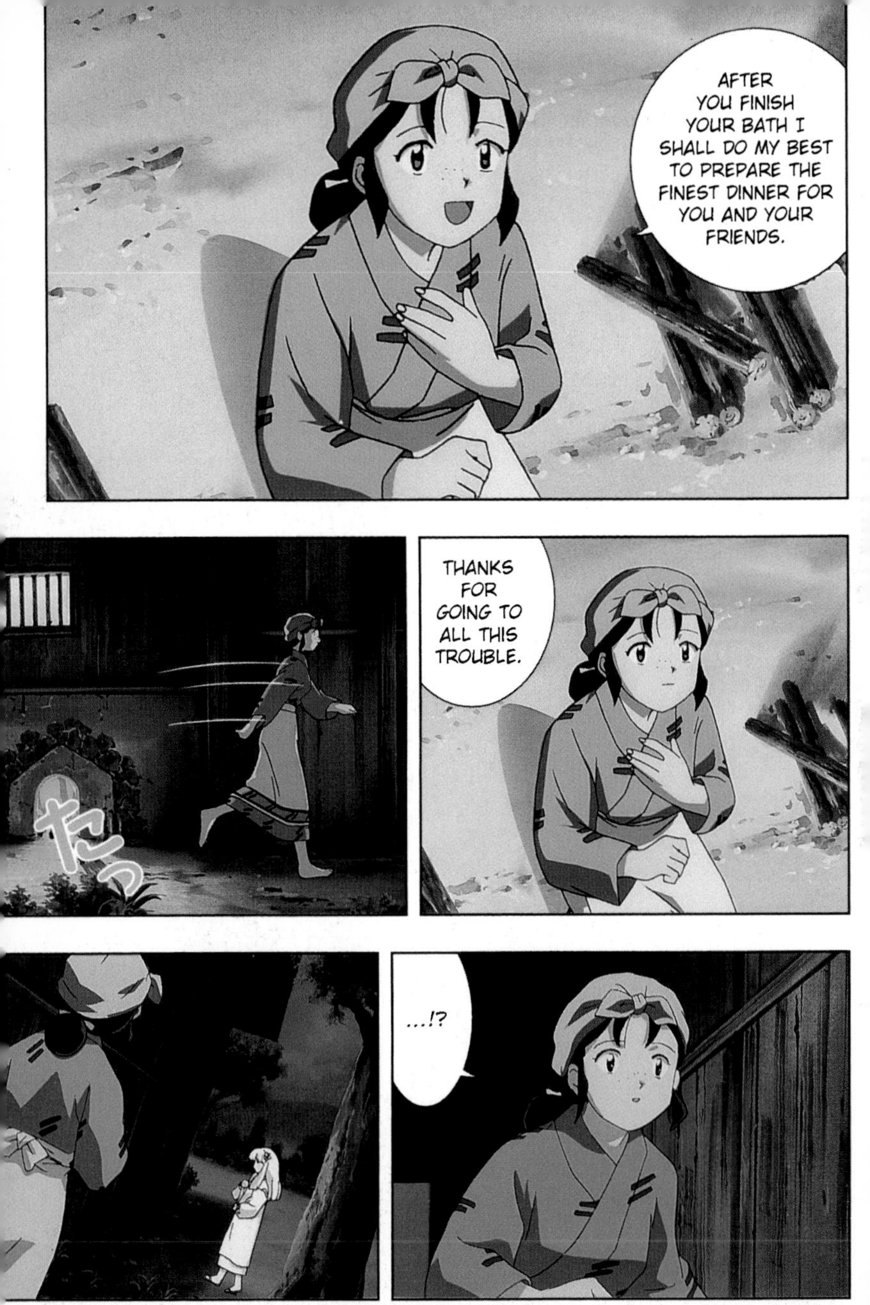
AFTER YOU FINISH YOUR BATH I SHALL DO MY BEST TO PREPARE THE FINEST DINNER FOR YOU AND YOUR FRIENDS.
THANKS FOR GOING TO ALL THIS TROUBLE.
たっ
...!?

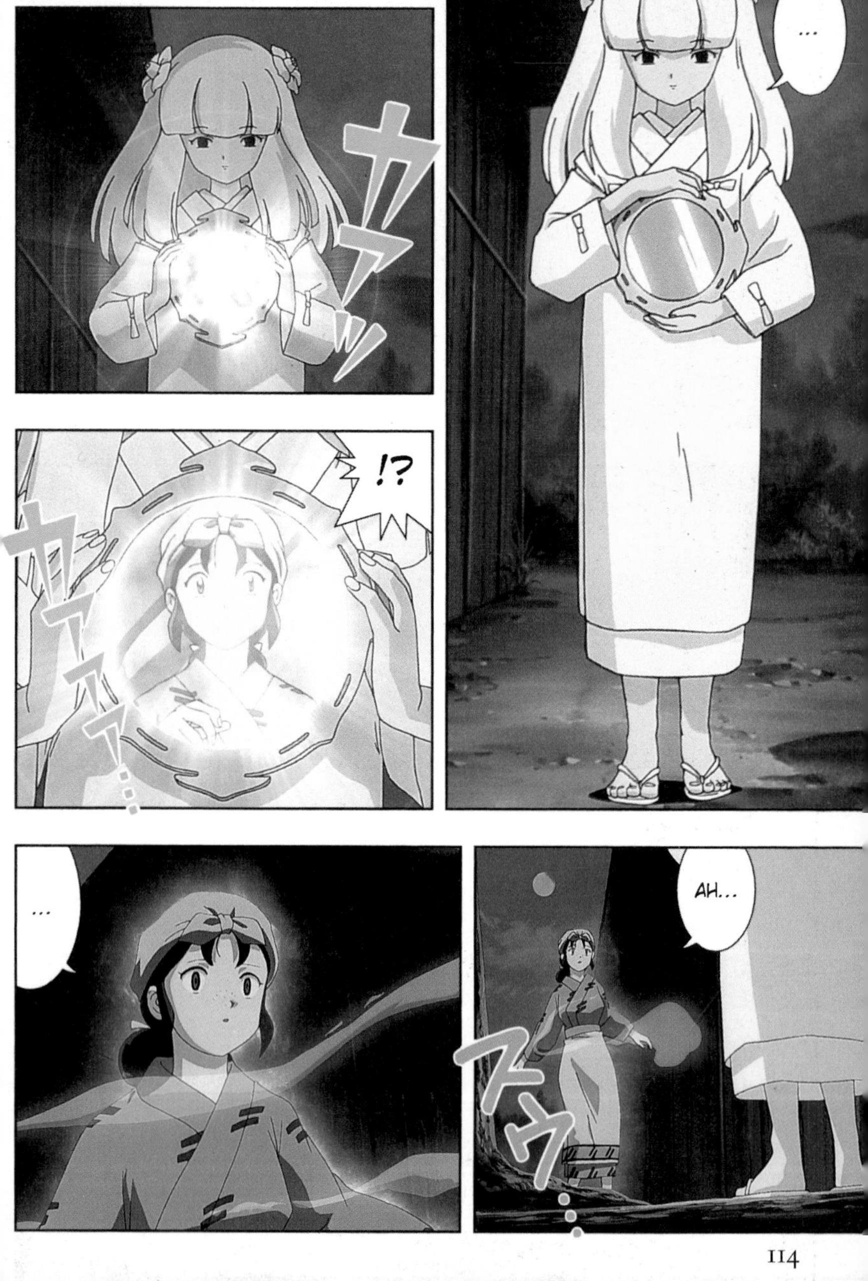
...
カァァッ
!?
カァァァァ...
AH...
スゥ...
...

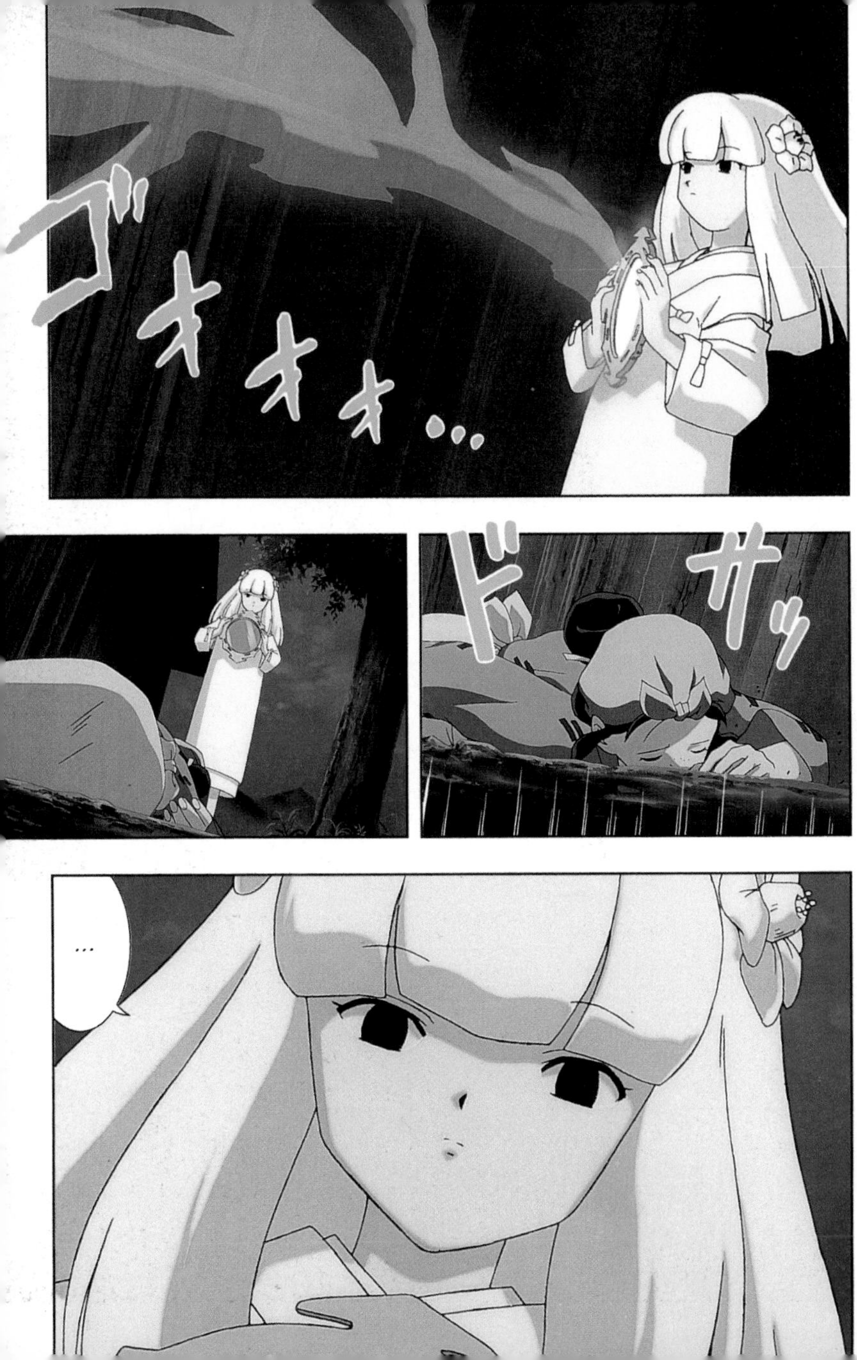
ゴオオオ…
ドサッ
...

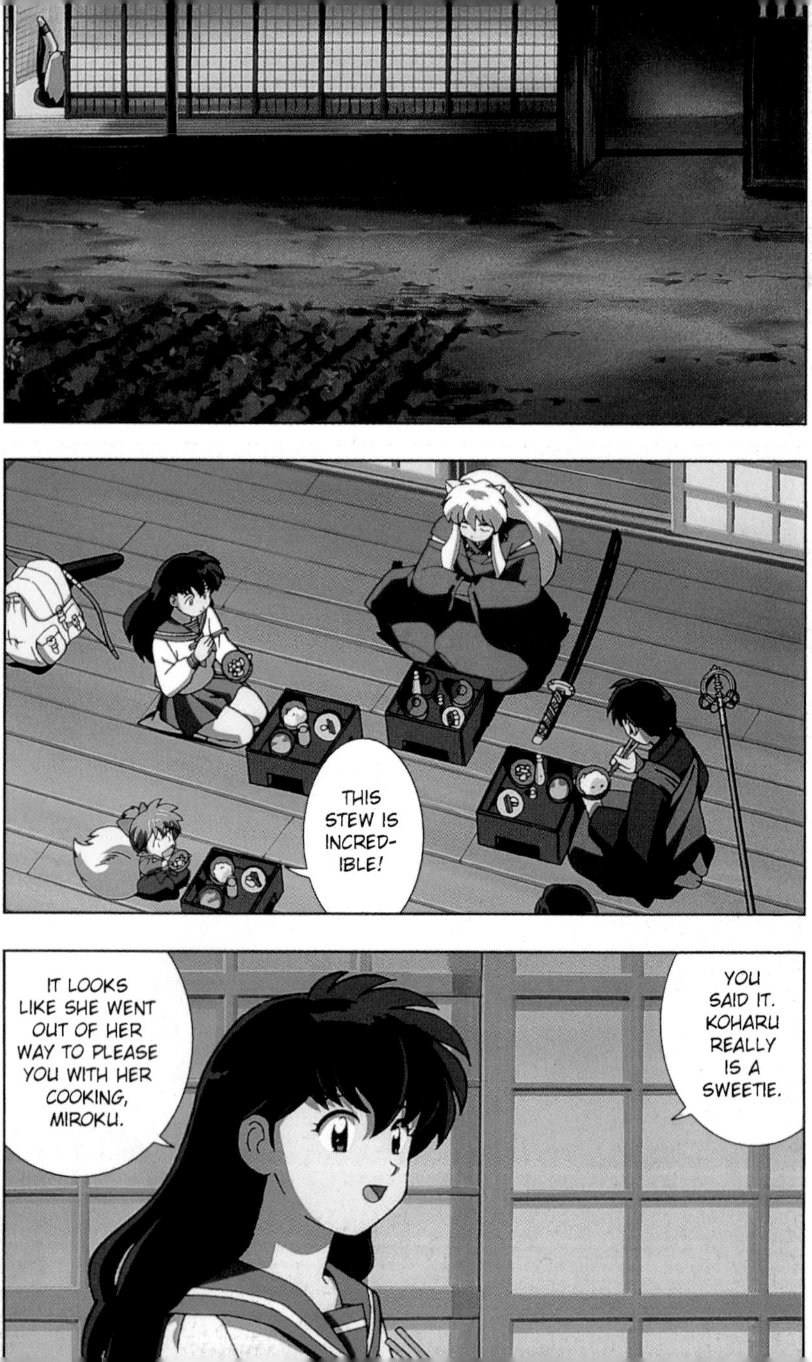
THIS STEW IS INCRED-IBLE!
YOU SAID IT. KOHARU REALLY IS A SWEETIE.
IT LOOKS LIKE SHE WENT OUT OF HER WAY TO PLEASE YOU WITH HER COOKING, MIROKU.

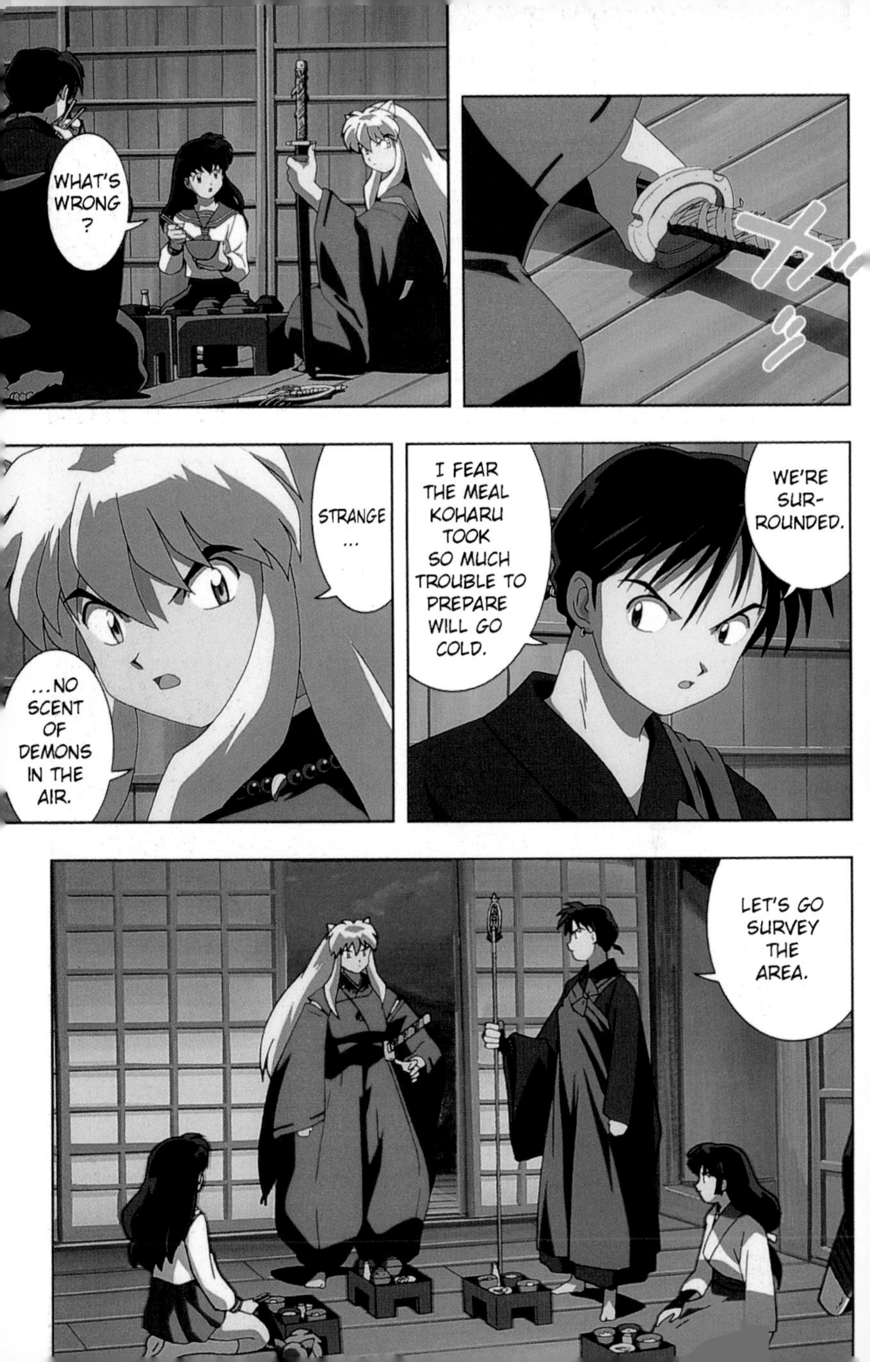
ガッ
WHAT'S WRONG?
WE'RE SUR-ROUNDED.
I FEAR THE MEAL KOHARU TOOK SO MUCH TROUBLE TO PREPARE WILL GO COLD.
STRANGE...
...NO SCENT OF DEMONS IN THE AIR.
LET'S GO SURVEY THE AREA.

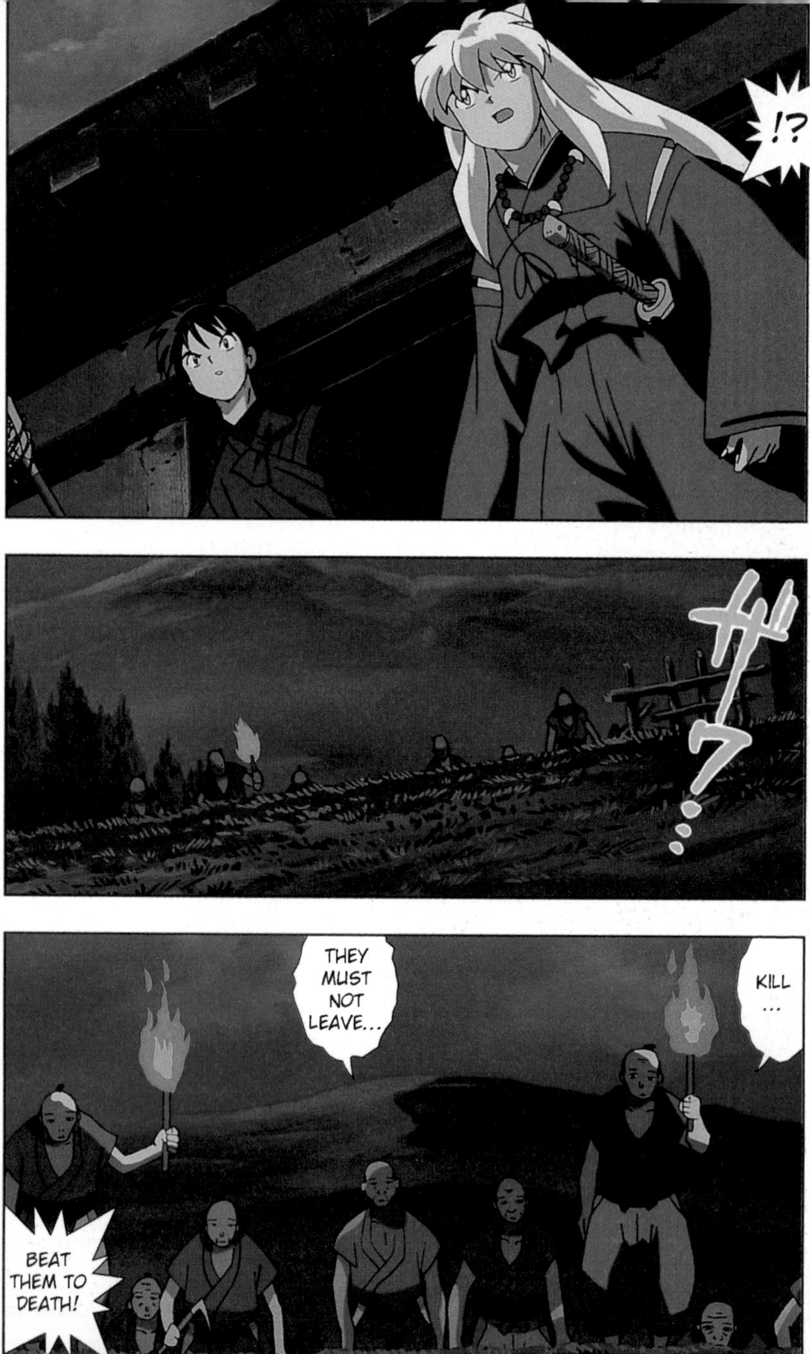
!?
ザワ…
KILL ...
THEY MUST NOT LEAVE...
BEAT THEM TO DEATH!

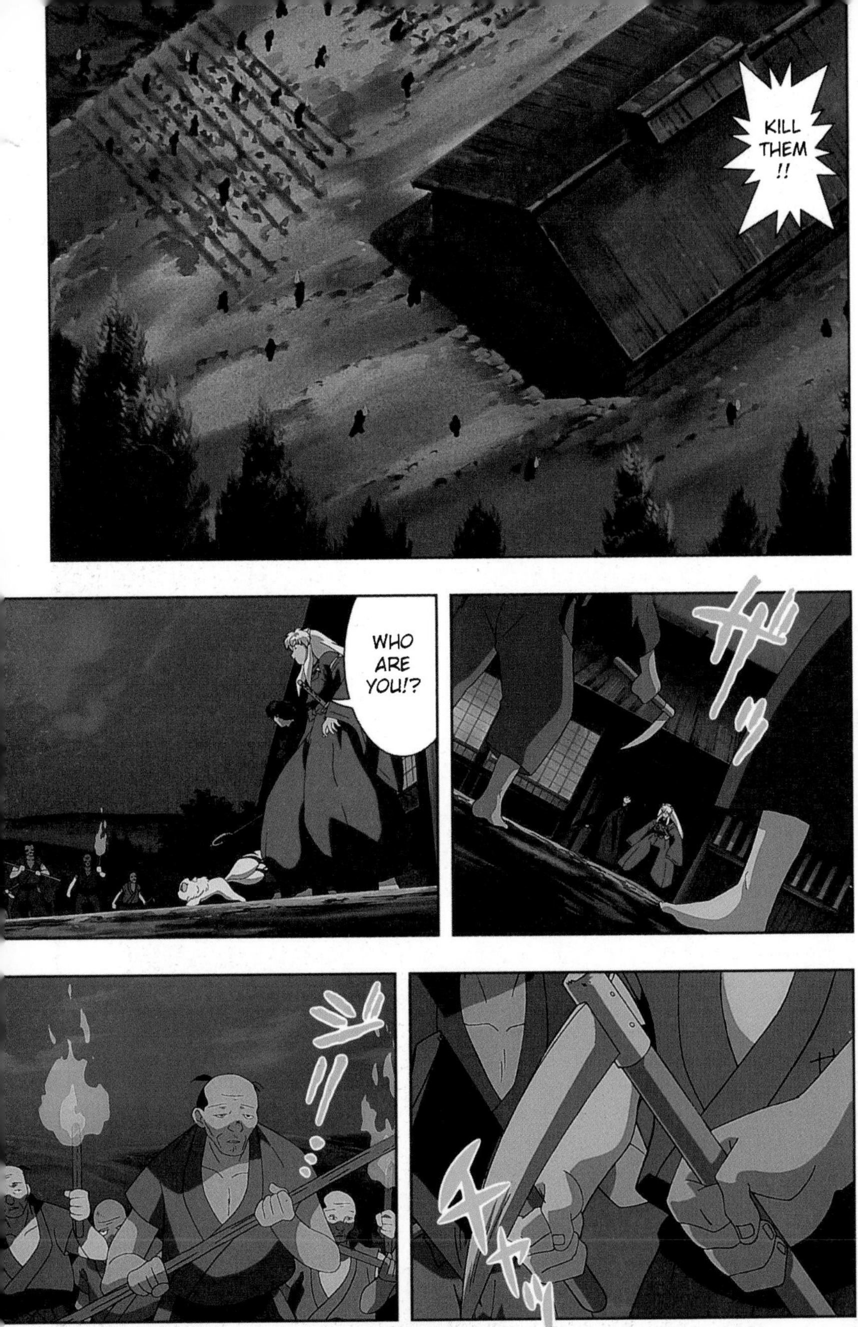
KILL THEM !!
WHO ARE YOU!?

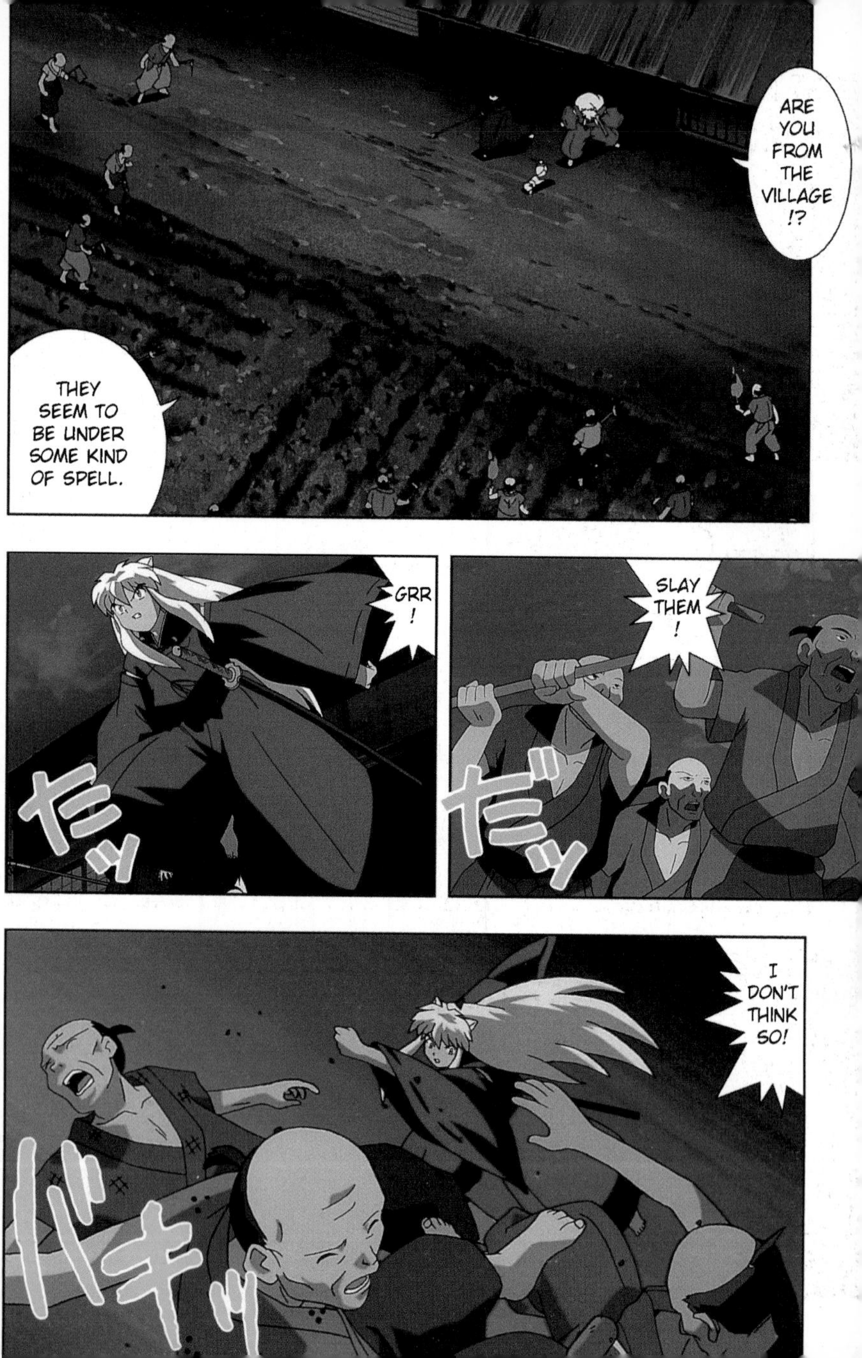
ARE YOU FROM THE VILLAGE !?
THEY SEEM TO BE UNDER SOME KIND OF SPELL.
SLAY THEM !
だッ
GRR !
たッ
I DON'T THINK SO!
バキッ

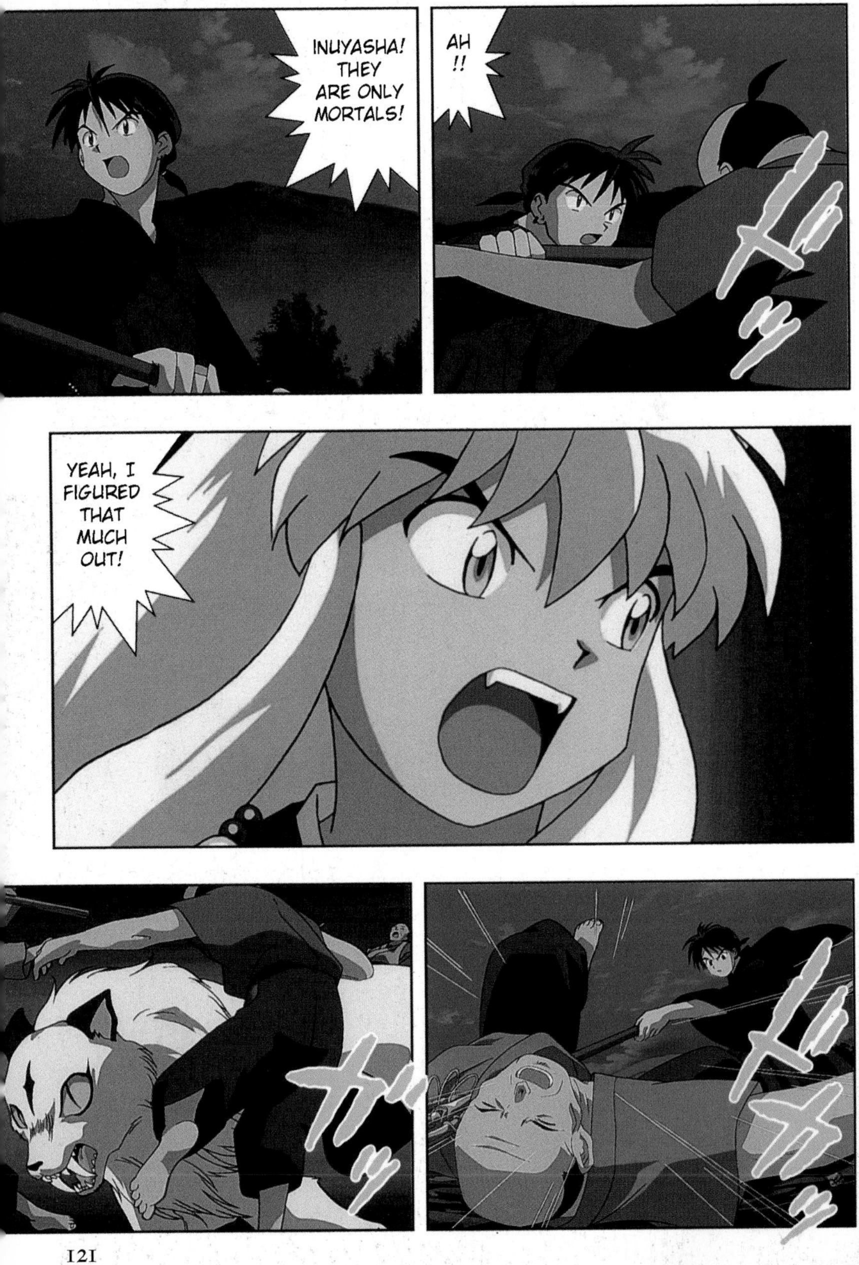
INUYASHA! THEY ARE ONLY MORTALS!
AH !!
YEAH, I FIGURED THAT MUCH OUT!

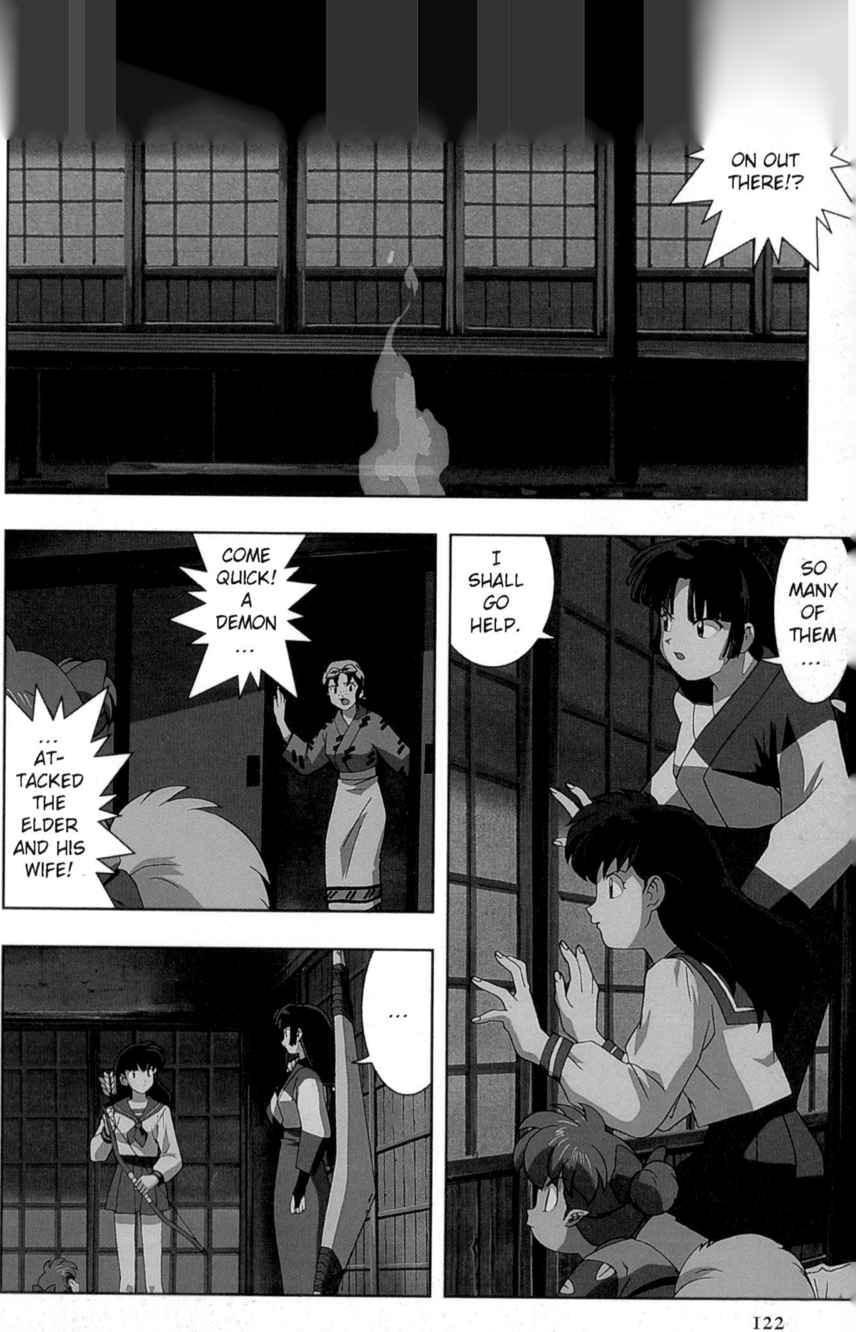
ON OUT THERE!?
COME QUICK! A DEMON ...
... AT-TACKED THE ELDER AND HIS WIFE!
SO MANY OF THEM ...
I SHALL GO HELP.
...

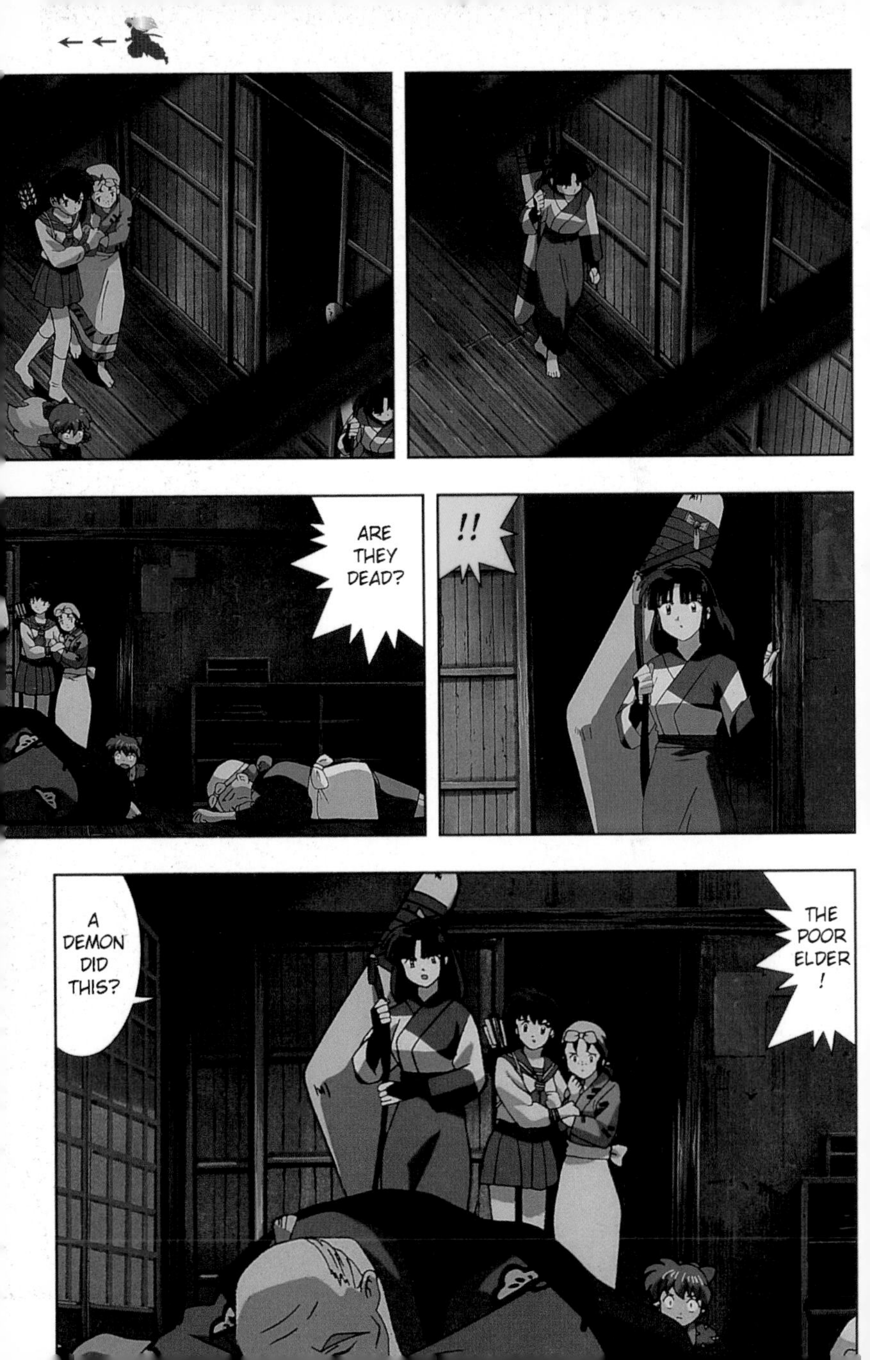
!!
ARE THEY DEAD?
THE POOR ELDER!
A DEMON DID THIS?

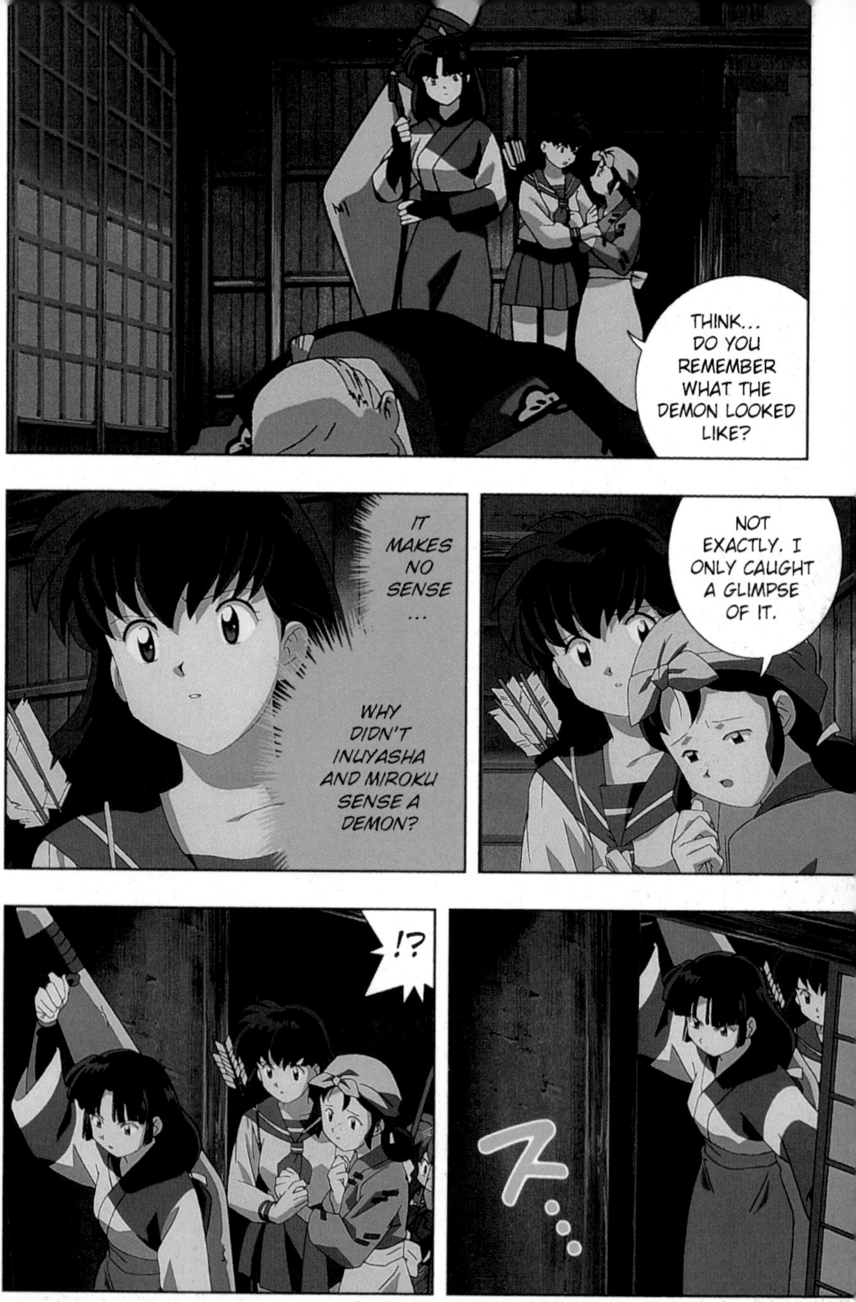
THINK... DO YOU REMEMBER WHAT THE DEMON LOOKED LIKE?
NOT EXACTLY. I ONLY CAUGHT A GLIMPSE OF IT.
IT MAKES NO SENSE ...
WHY DIDN'T INUYASHA AND MIROKU SENSE A DEMON?
ス...
!?

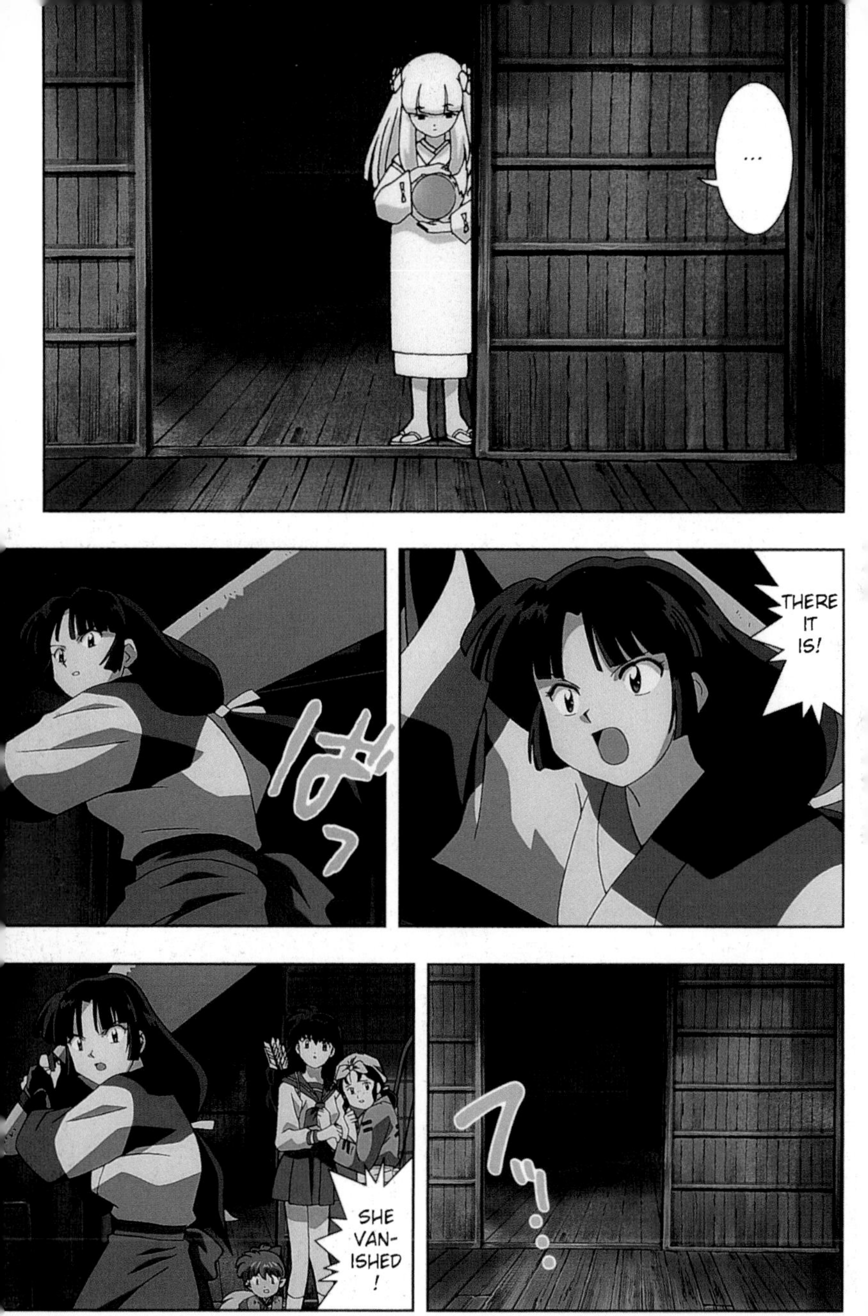
...
THERE IT IS!
SHE VAN-ISHED!

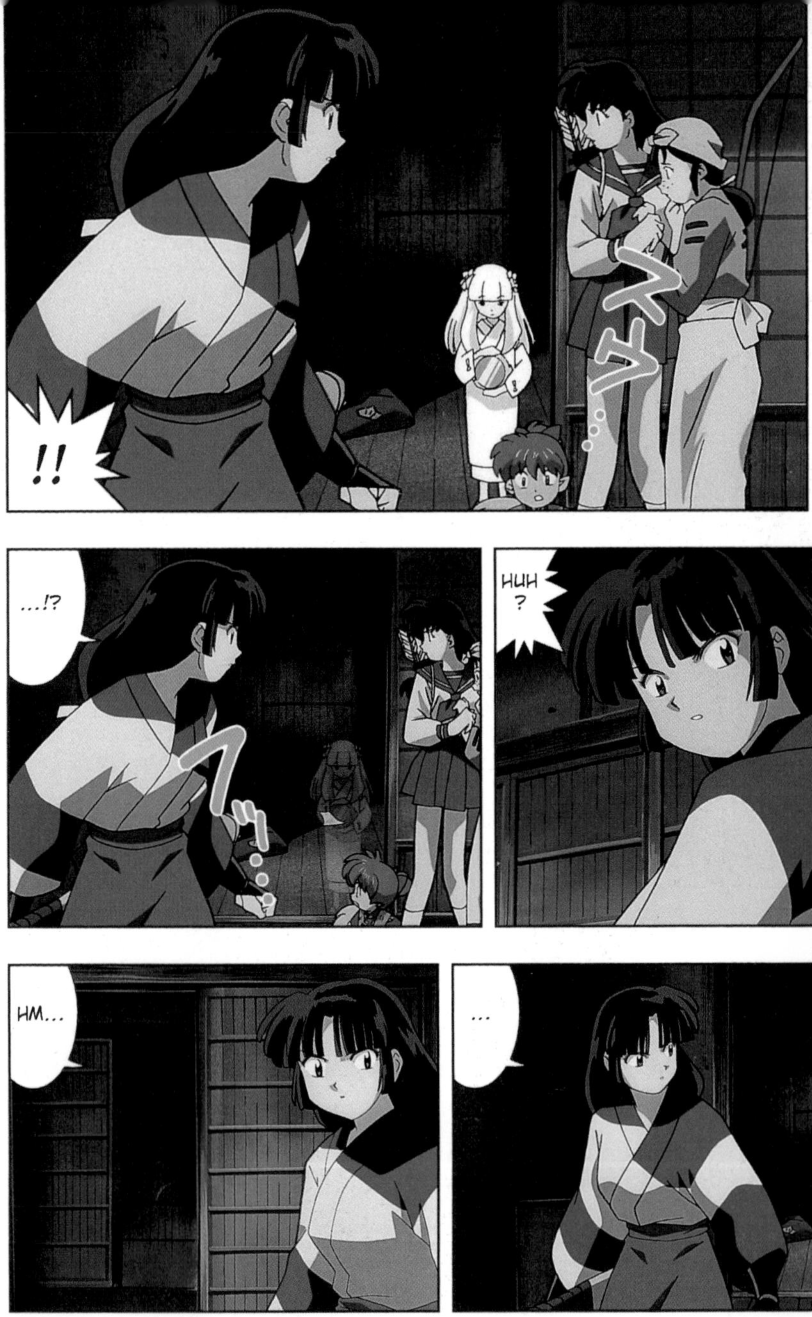
!!
HUH
?
...!?
...
HM...

AH
!!

スウッ···

HIRAI-
KOTSU
!

ブ···
ゥー
ン叫

ギ
ュ
ル
ル
ル···

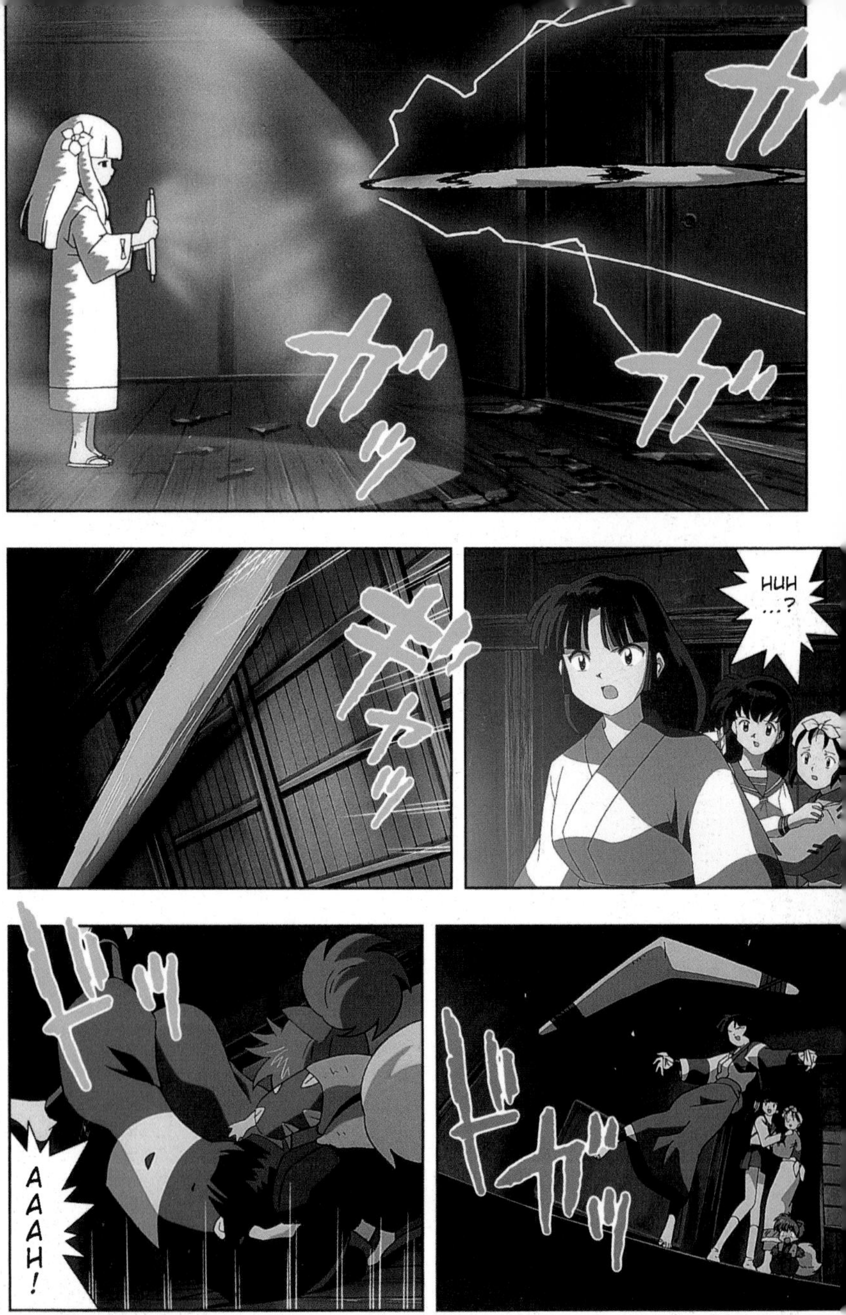
ガガッ
ガ
ガガ
ギャッ
HUH ...?
ドッ
AAAAH!
ドガッ

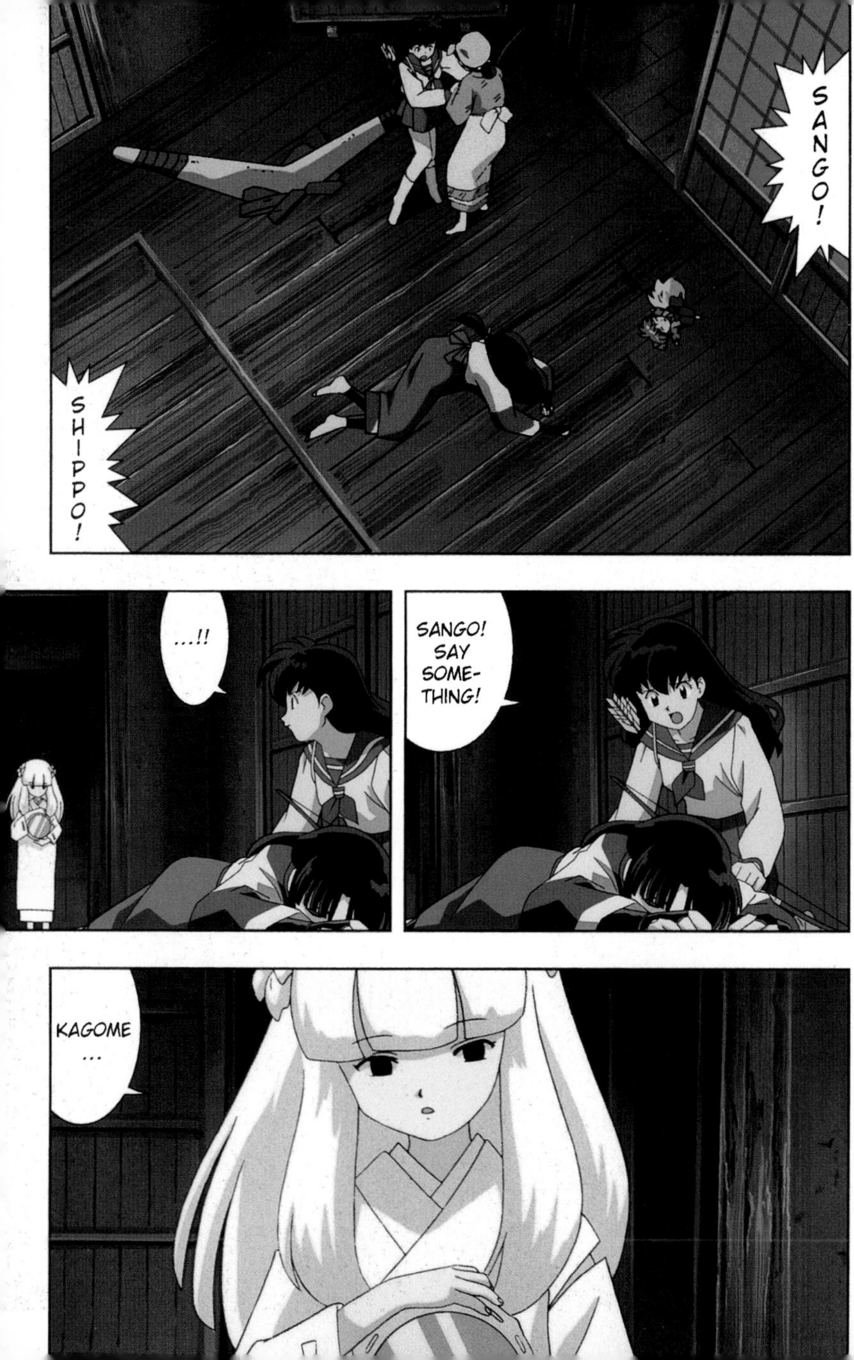
SANGO!
SHIPPO!
SANGO! SAY SOME-THING!
...!!
KAGOME ...

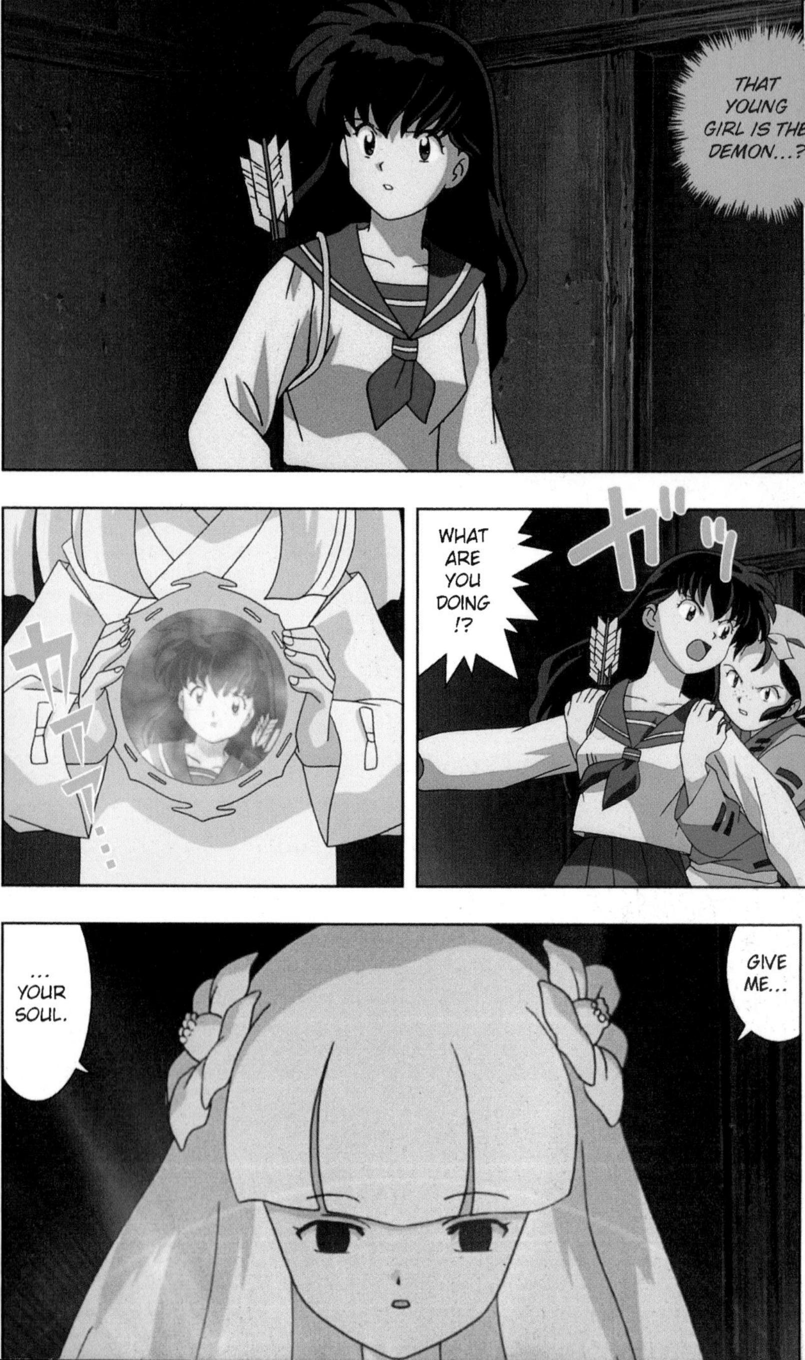
THAT YOUNG GIRL IS THE DEMON...?
ガッ
WHAT ARE YOU DOING!?
GIVE ME...
...YOUR SOUL.

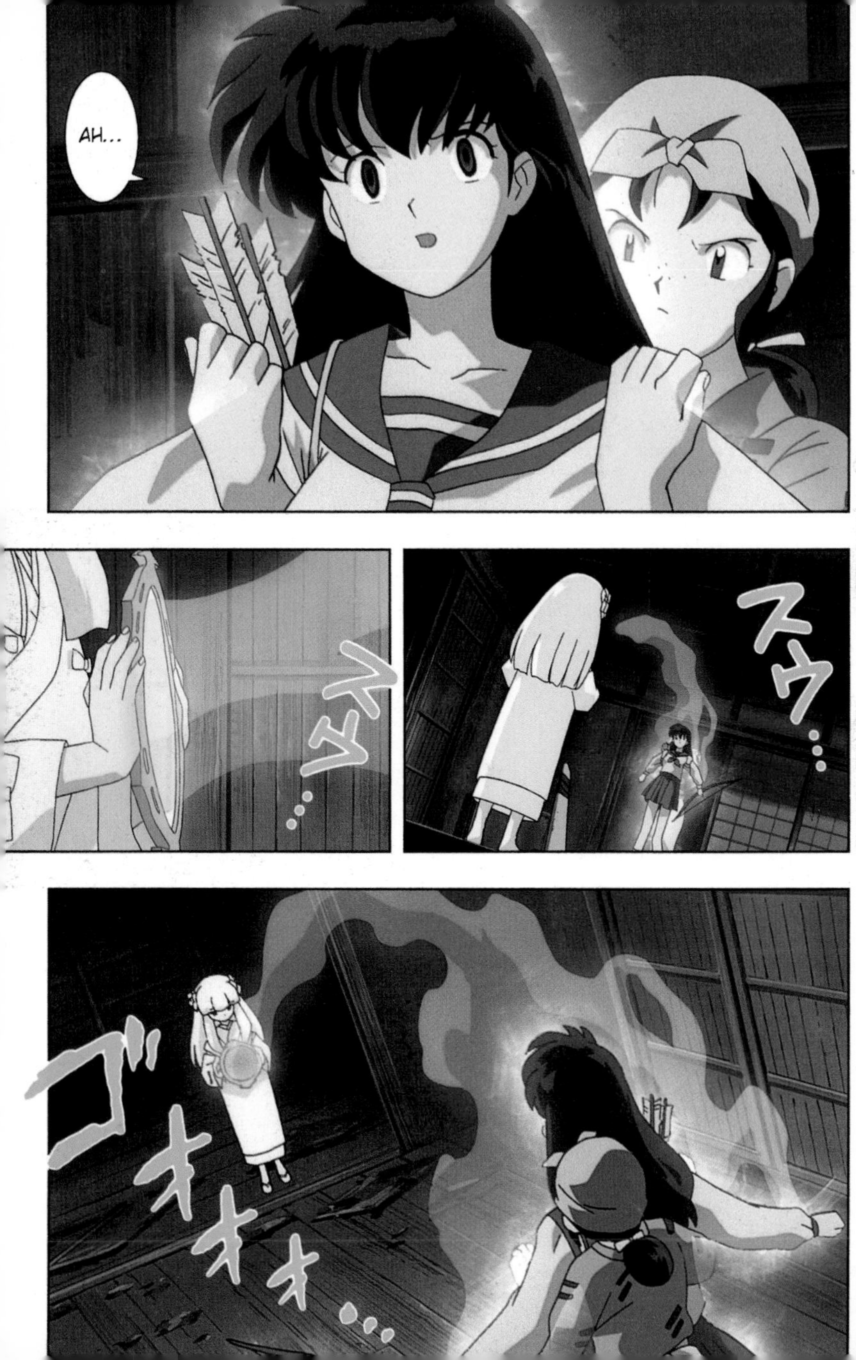
AH...
スゥ...
スッ...
ゴォォォ...

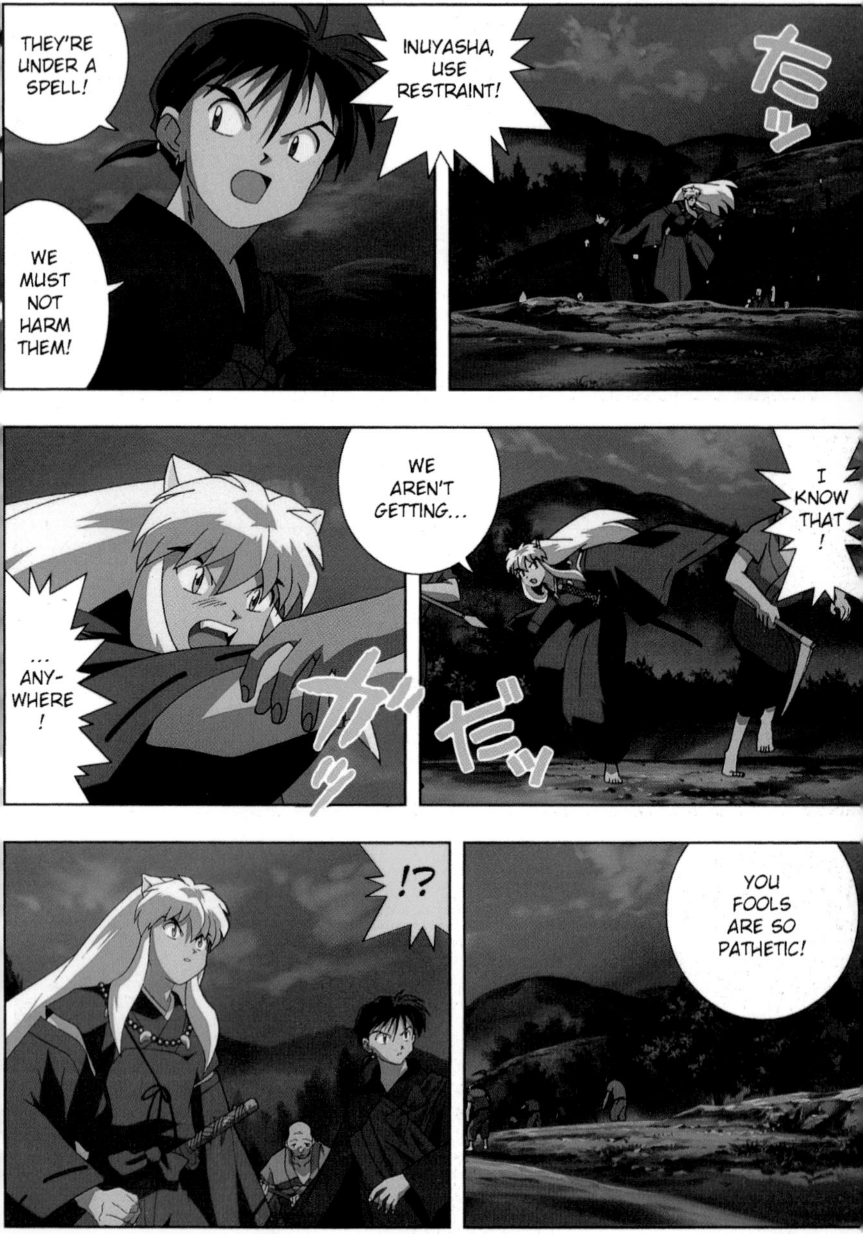
タッ
INUYASHA, USE RESTRAINT!
THEY'RE UNDER A SPELL!
WE MUST NOT HARM THEM!
I KNOW THAT!
WE AREN'T GETTING...
...ANYWHERE!
ダッ
ガッ
YOU FOOLS ARE SO PATHETIC!
!?

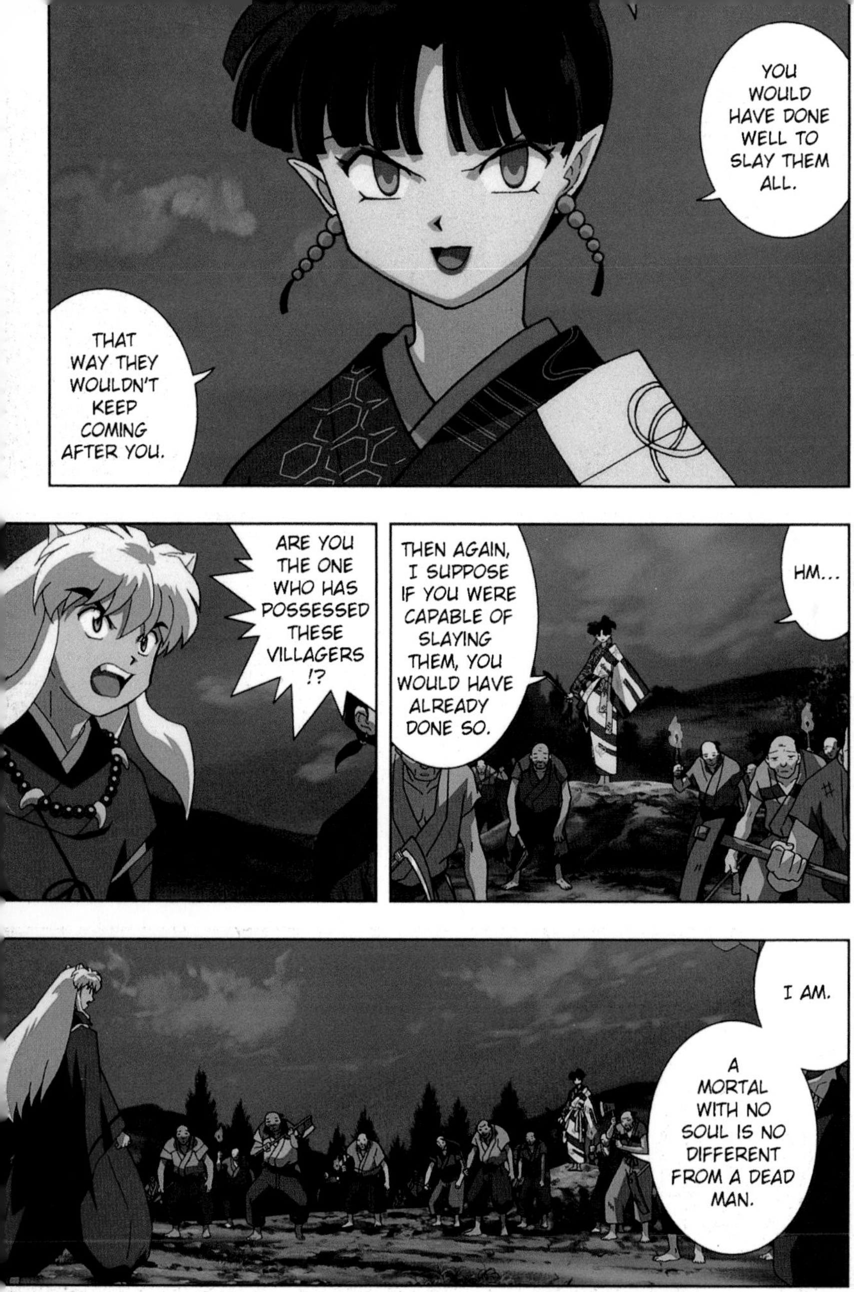

YOU WOULD HAVE DONE WELL TO SLAY THEM ALL.
THAT WAY THEY WOULDN'T KEEP COMING AFTER YOU.
HM...
THEN AGAIN, I SUPPOSE IF YOU WERE CAPABLE OF SLAYING THEM, YOU WOULD HAVE ALREADY DONE SO.
ARE YOU THE ONE WHO HAS POSSESSED THESE VILLAGERS !?
I AM.
A MORTAL WITH NO SOUL IS NO DIFFERENT FROM A DEAD MAN.

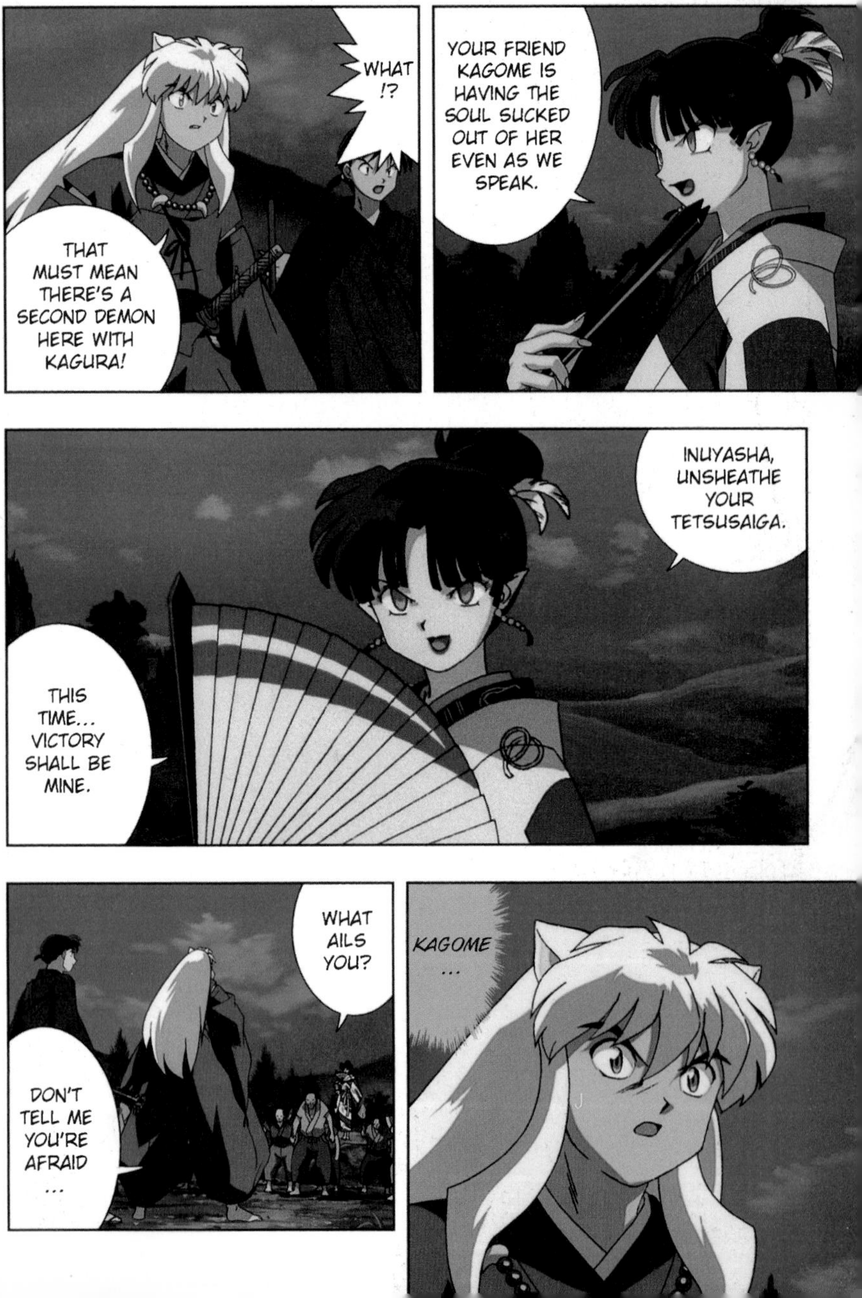
YOUR FRIEND KAGOME IS HAVING THE SOUL SUCKED OUT OF HER EVEN AS WE SPEAK.
WHAT !?
THAT MUST MEAN THERE'S A SECOND DEMON HERE WITH KAGURA!
INUYASHA, UNSHEATHE YOUR TETSUSAIGA.
THIS TIME... VICTORY SHALL BE MINE.
KAGOME ...
WHAT AILS YOU?
DON'T TELL ME YOU'RE AFRAID ...

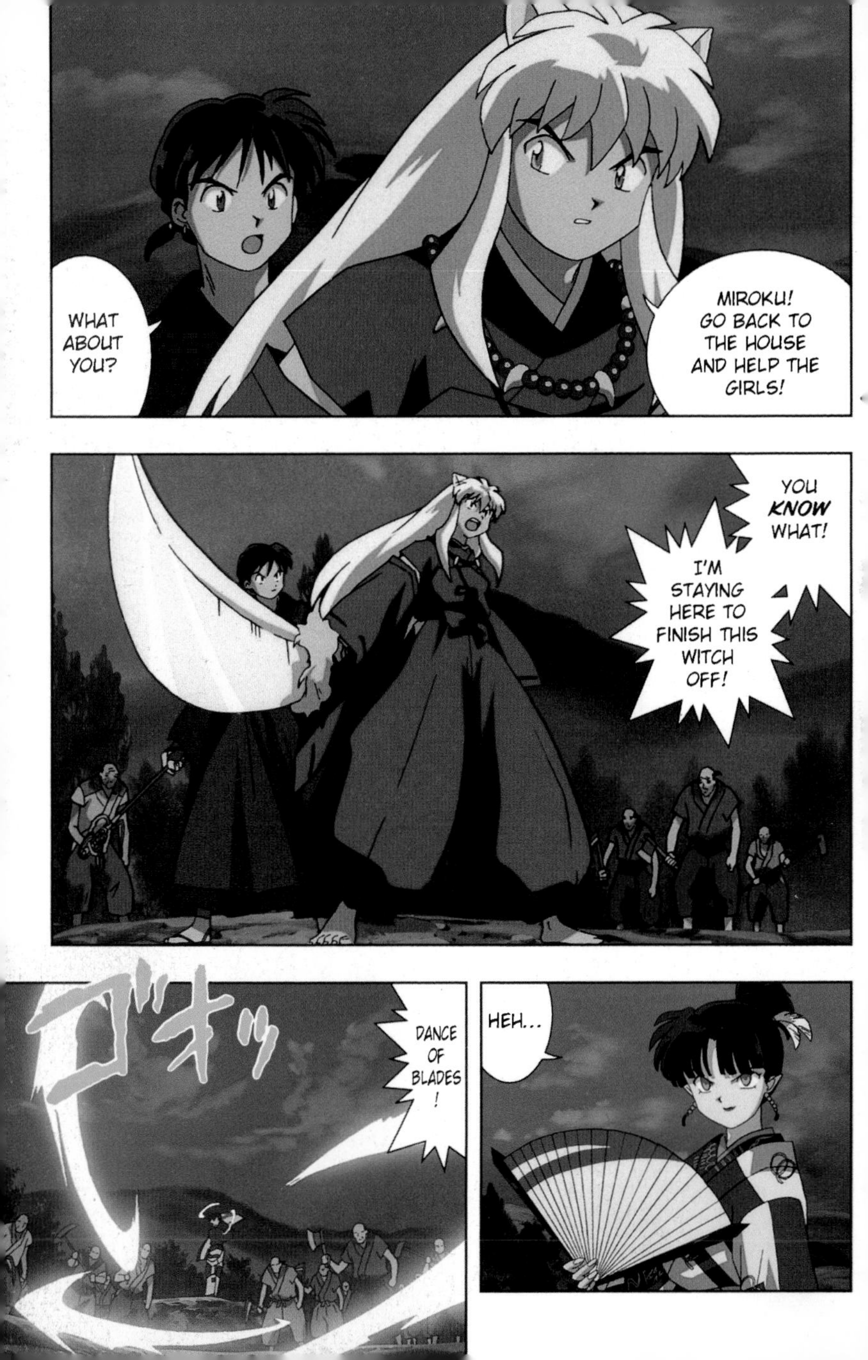
MIROKU! GO BACK TO THE HOUSE AND HELP THE GIRLS!
WHAT ABOUT YOU?
YOU KNOW WHAT!
I'M STAYING HERE TO FINISH THIS WITCH OFF!
HEH...
DANCE OF BLADES!
ゴオッ

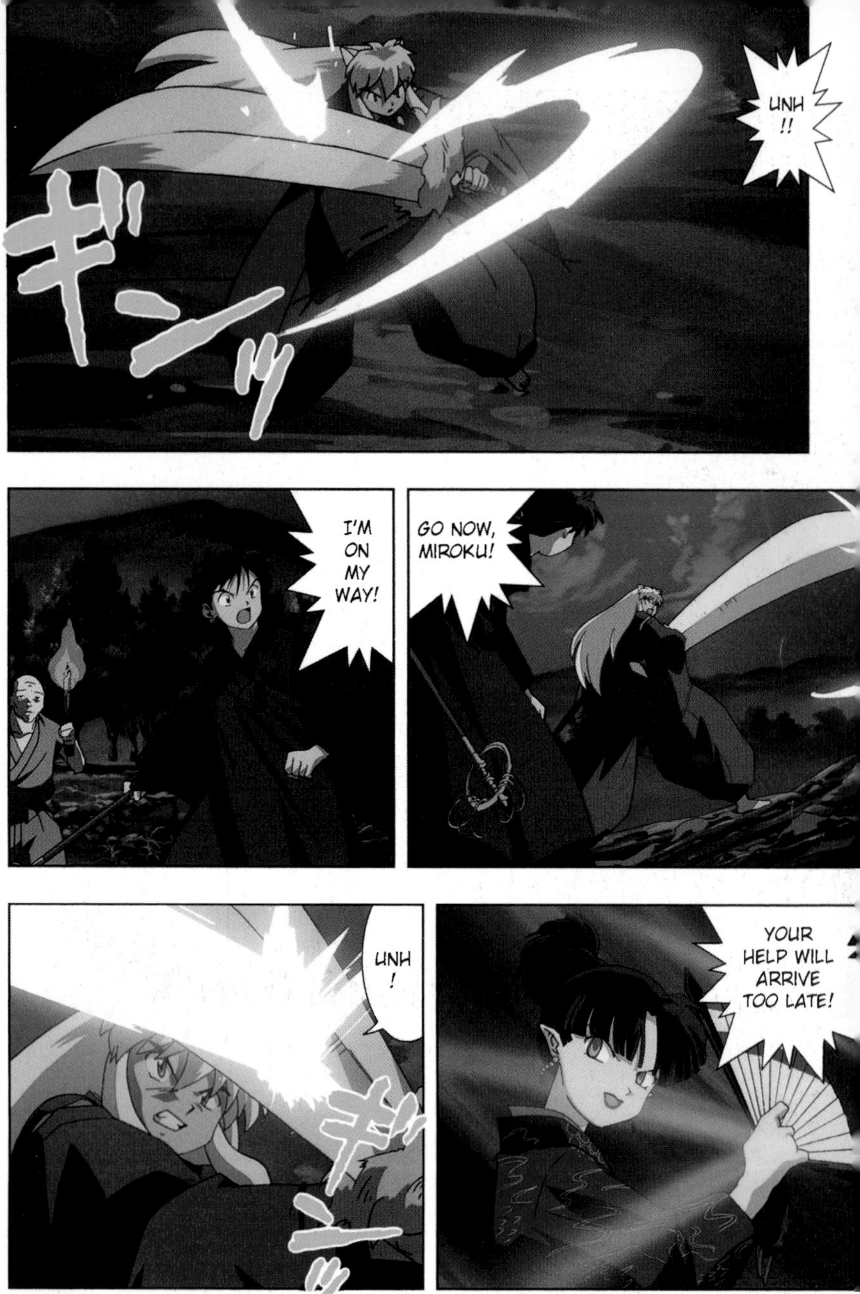
UNH !!
ギンッ
GO NOW, MIROKU!
I'M ON MY WAY!
YOUR HELP WILL ARRIVE TOO LATE!
UNH !
ギンッ

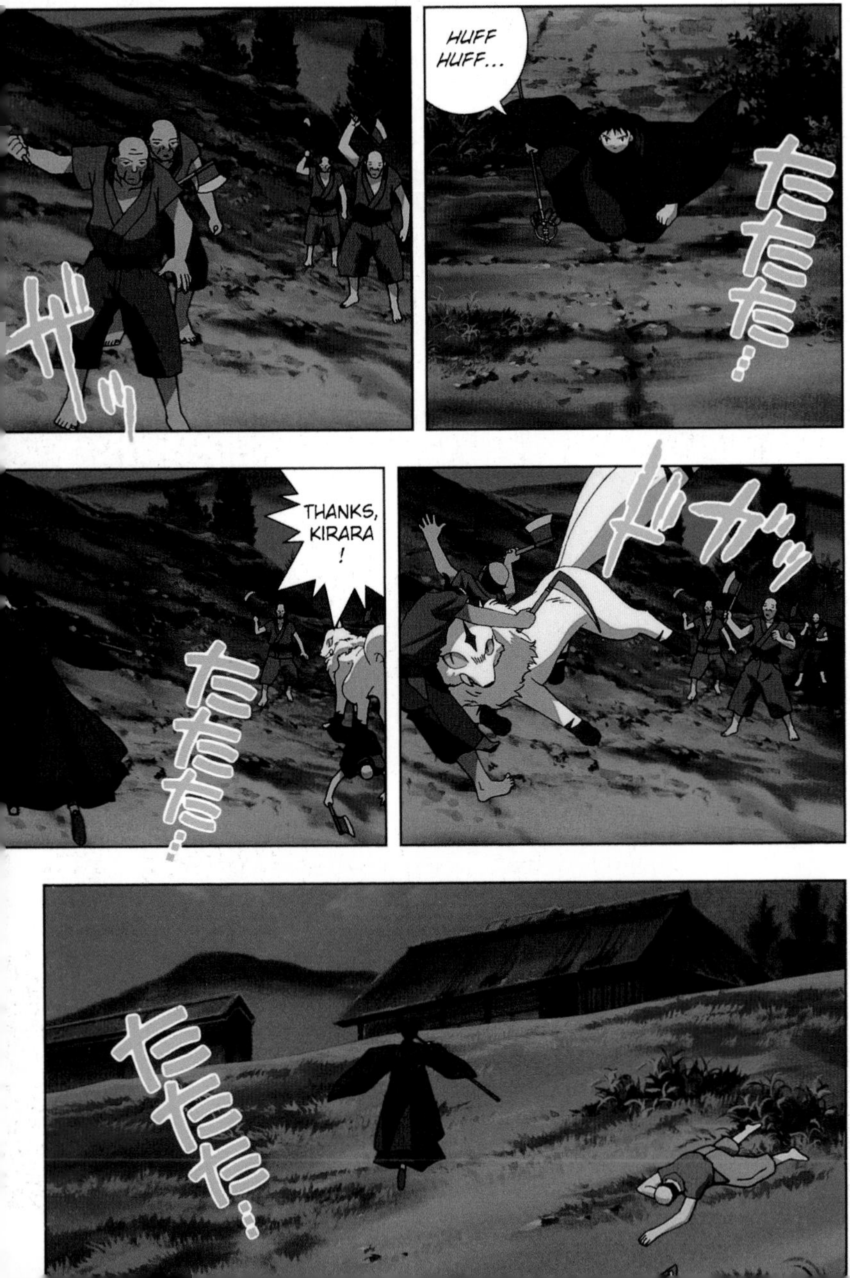
HUFF HUFF...
たたたた..
ザッ
ドガッ
THANKS, KIRARA!
たたたた..
たたたた..

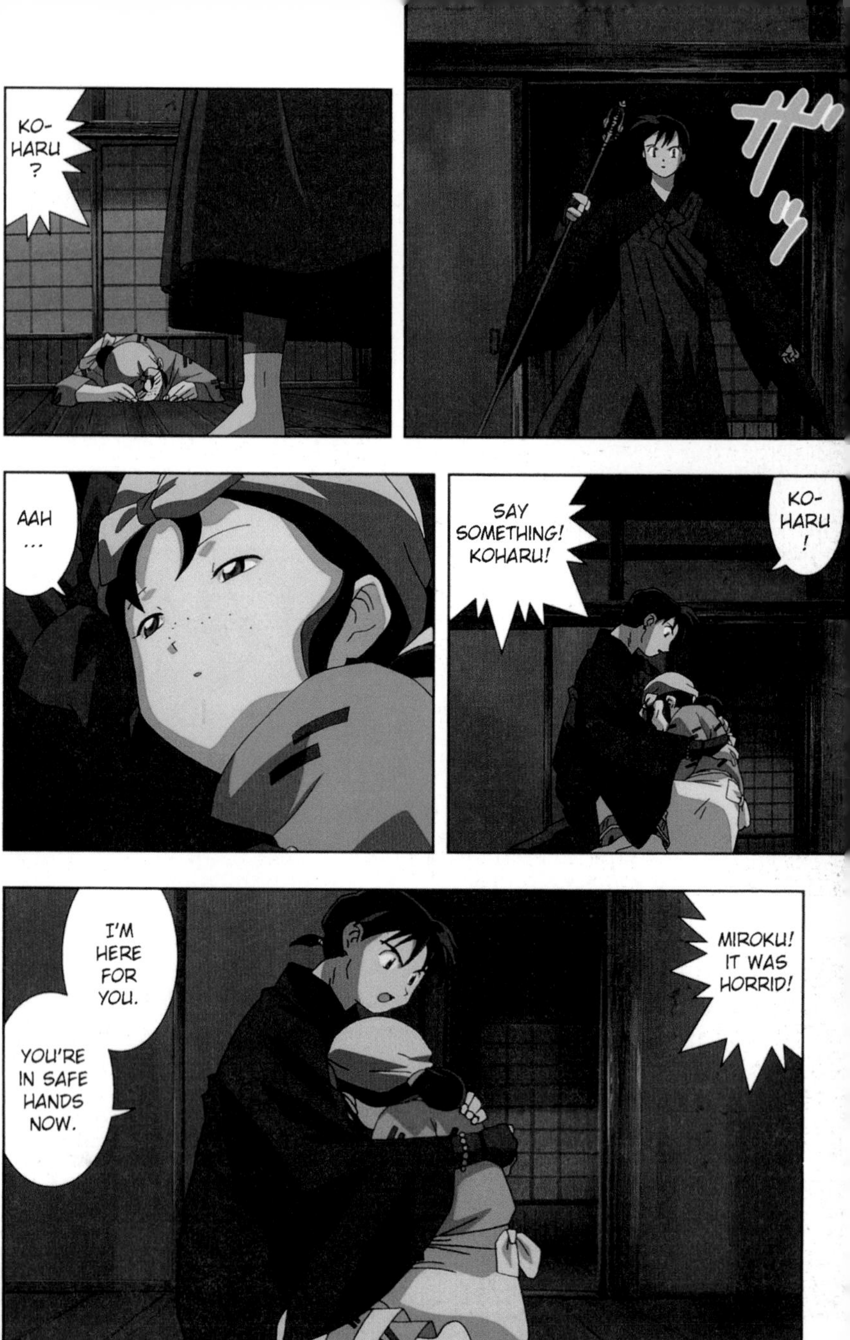
ザッ
KO-HARU?
KO-HARU!
SAY SOMETHING! KOHARU!
AAH ...
MIROKU! IT WAS HORRID!
I'M HERE FOR YOU.
YOU'RE IN SAFE HANDS NOW.

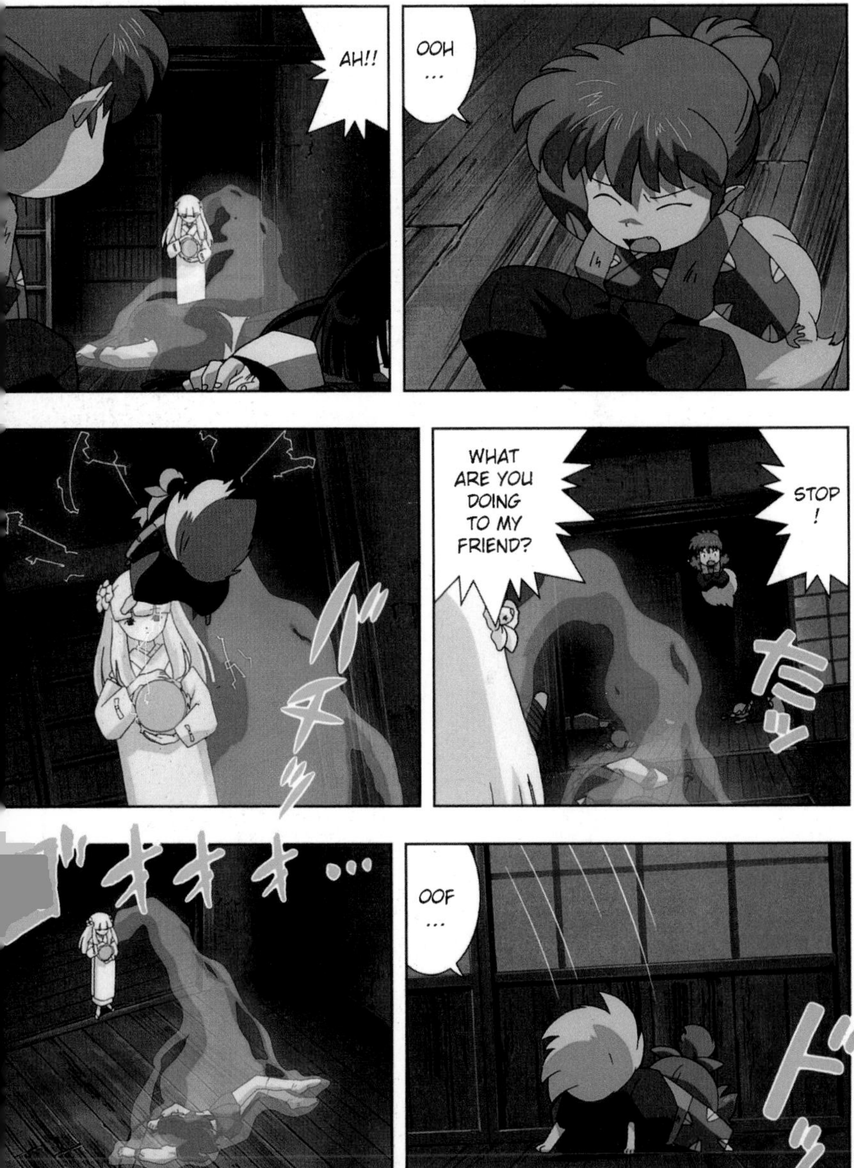
OOH ...
AH!!
WHAT ARE YOU DOING TO MY FRIEND?
STOP!
タッ
OOF ...
ドッ
ゴオオオ…

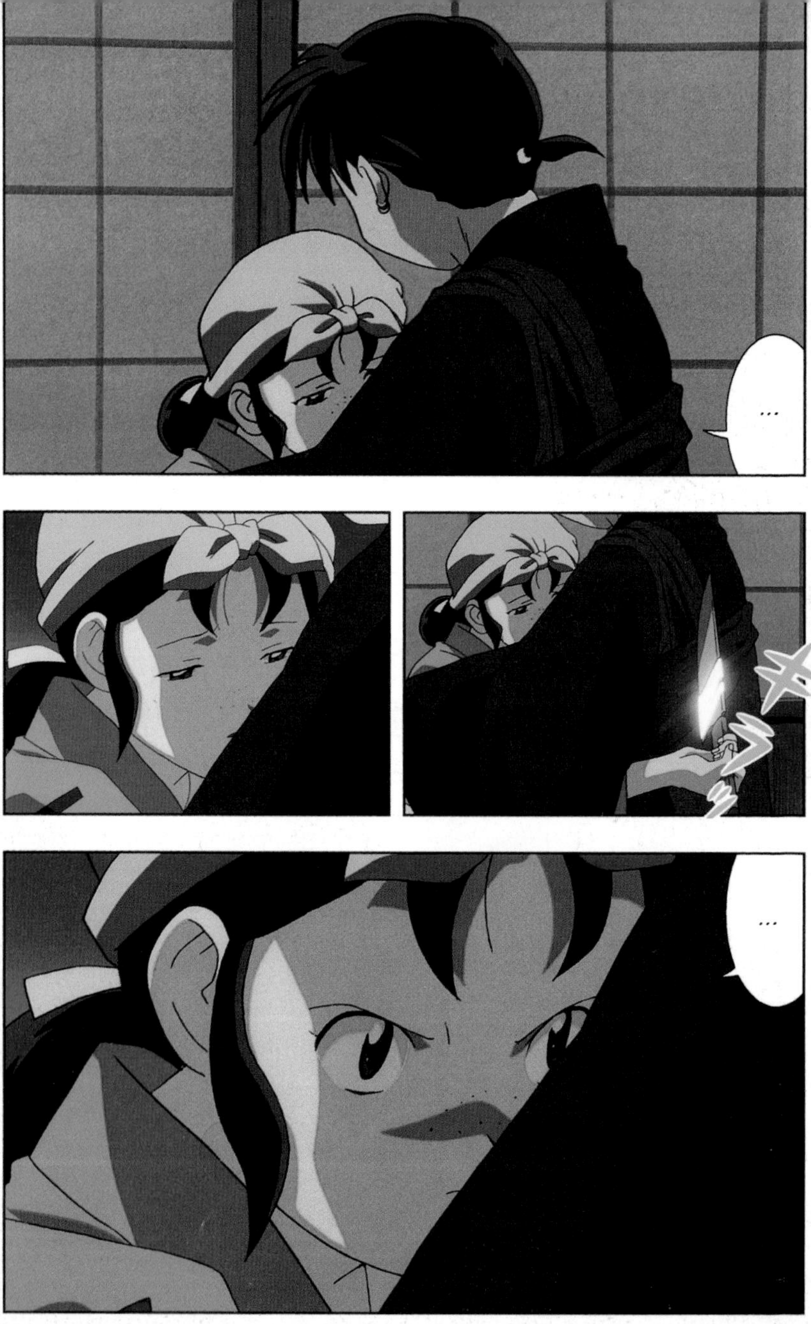
...
...

# 42 The Wind Scar, Defeated

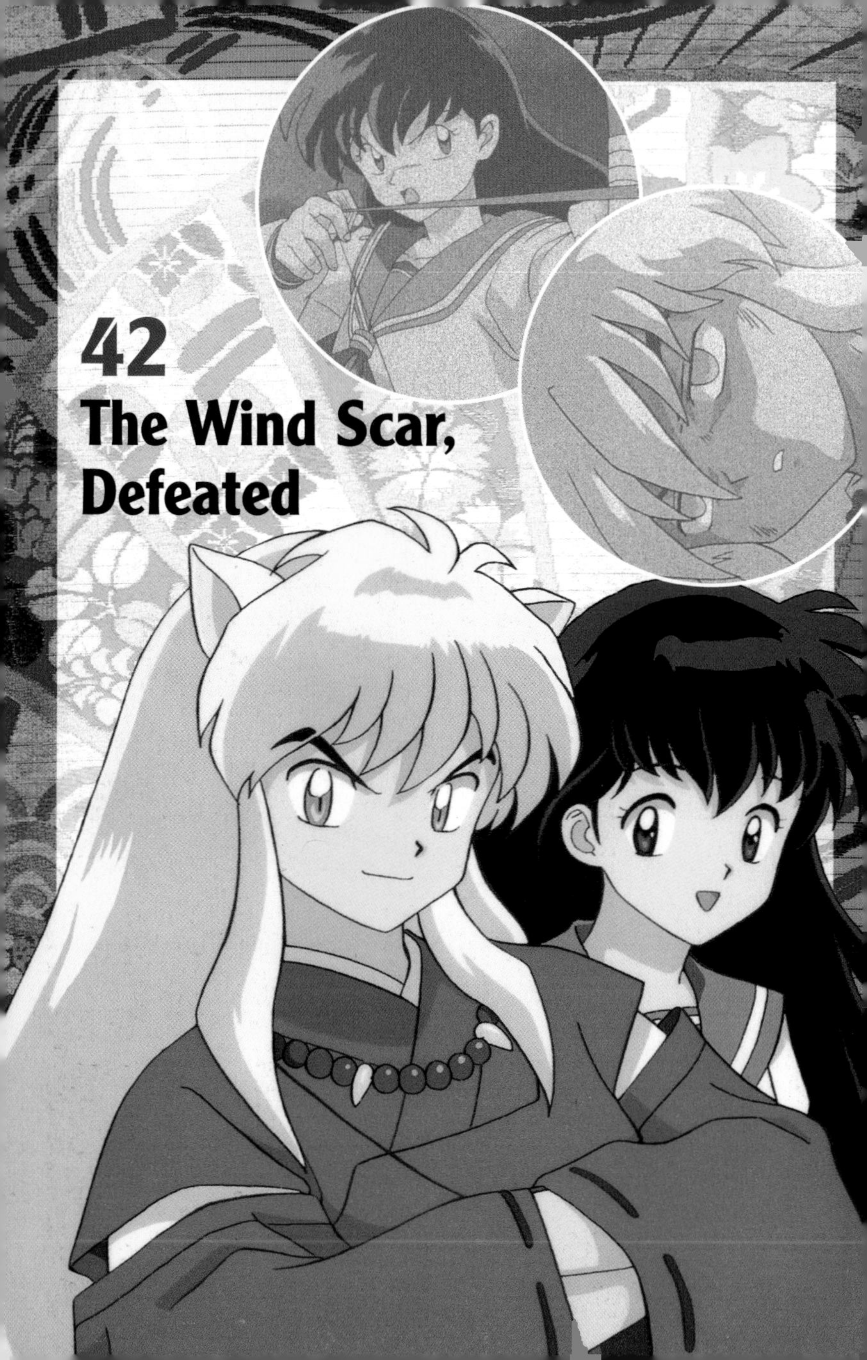

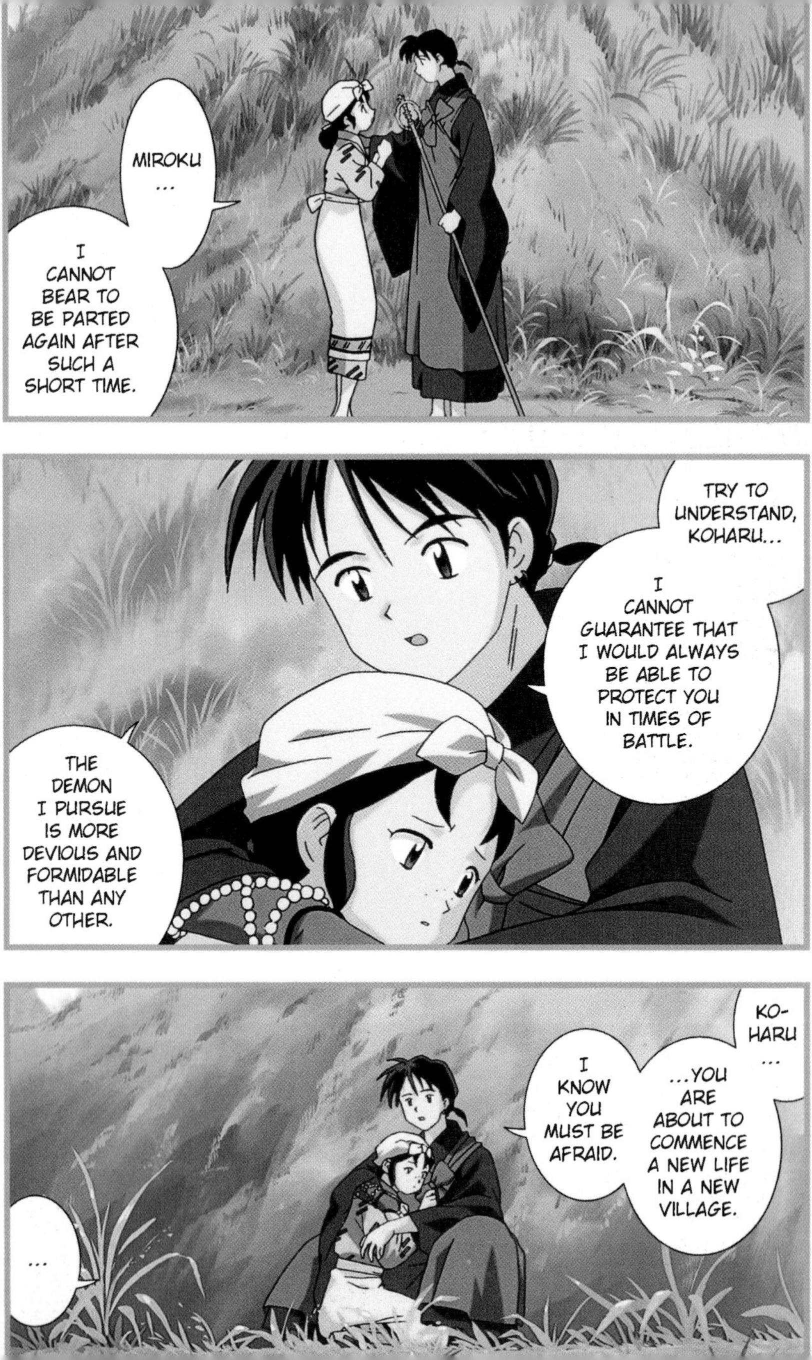
MIROKU ...
I CANNOT BEAR TO BE PARTED AGAIN AFTER SUCH A SHORT TIME.
TRY TO UNDERSTAND, KOHARU...
I CANNOT GUARANTEE THAT I WOULD ALWAYS BE ABLE TO PROTECT YOU IN TIMES OF BATTLE.
THE DEMON I PURSUE IS MORE DEVIOUS AND FORMIDABLE THAN ANY OTHER.
KO-HARU ...
...YOU ARE ABOUT TO COMMENCE A NEW LIFE IN A NEW VILLAGE.
I KNOW YOU MUST BE AFRAID.
...

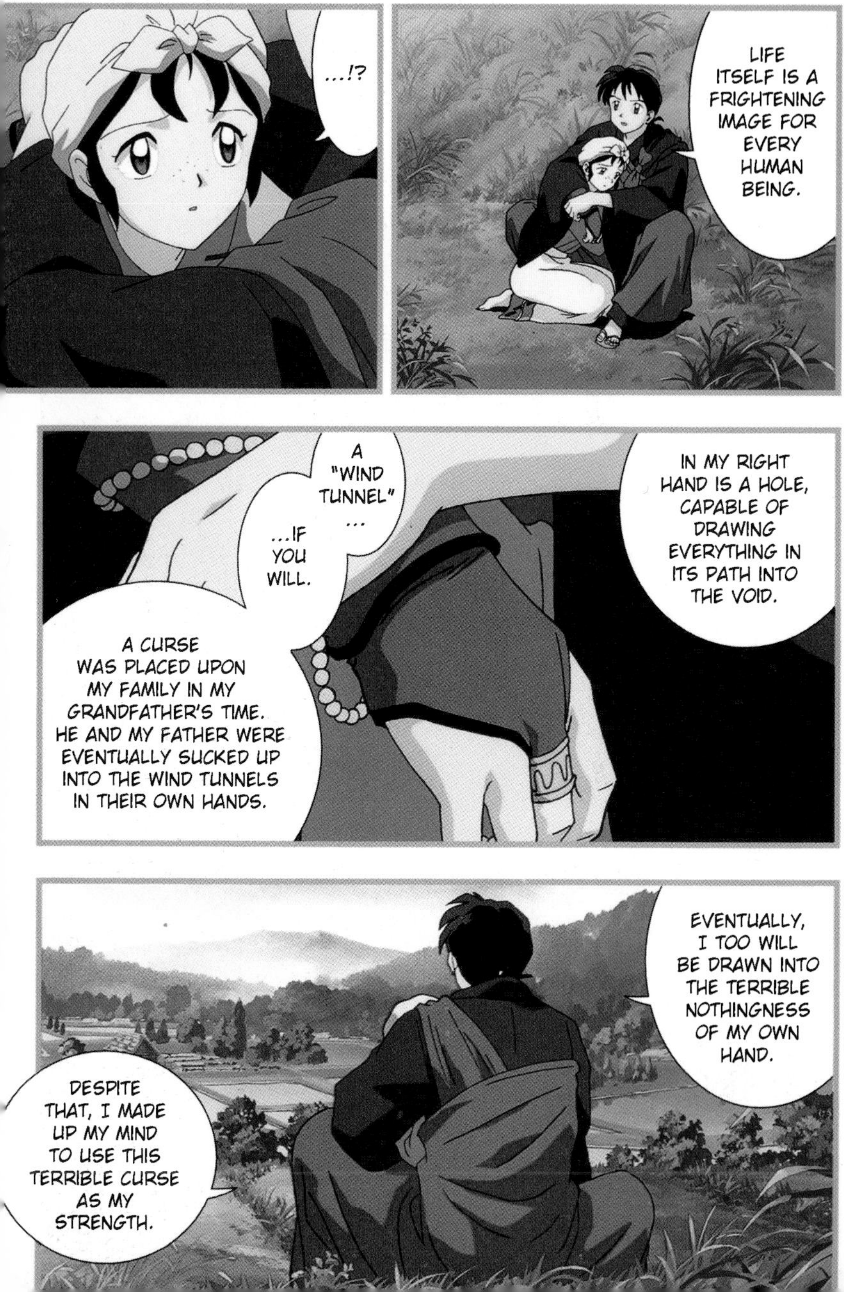
LIFE ITSELF IS A FRIGHTENING IMAGE FOR EVERY HUMAN BEING.
...!?
IN MY RIGHT HAND IS A HOLE, CAPABLE OF DRAWING EVERYTHING IN ITS PATH INTO THE VOID.
A "WIND TUNNEL" ...
...IF YOU WILL.
A CURSE WAS PLACED UPON MY FAMILY IN MY GRANDFATHER'S TIME. HE AND MY FATHER WERE EVENTUALLY SUCKED UP INTO THE WIND TUNNELS IN THEIR OWN HANDS.
EVENTUALLY, I TOO WILL BE DRAWN INTO THE TERRIBLE NOTHINGNESS OF MY OWN HAND.
DESPITE THAT, I MADE UP MY MIND TO USE THIS TERRIBLE CURSE AS MY STRENGTH.

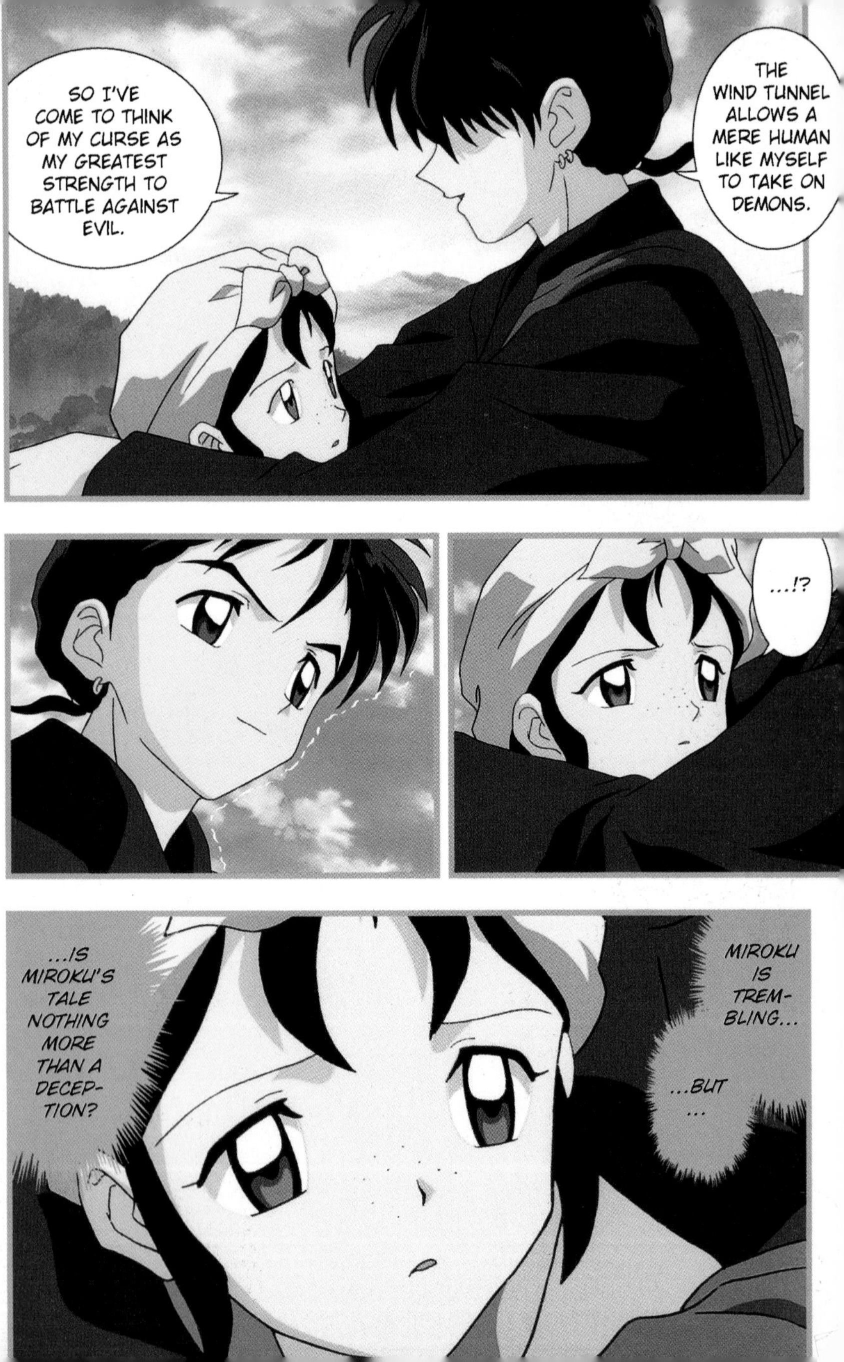
THE WIND TUNNEL ALLOWS A MERE HUMAN LIKE MYSELF TO TAKE ON DEMONS.
SO I'VE COME TO THINK OF MY CURSE AS MY GREATEST STRENGTH TO BATTLE AGAINST EVIL.
...!?
MIROKU IS TREM-BLING...
...BUT...
...IS MIROKU'S TALE NOTHING MORE THAN A DECEP-TION?

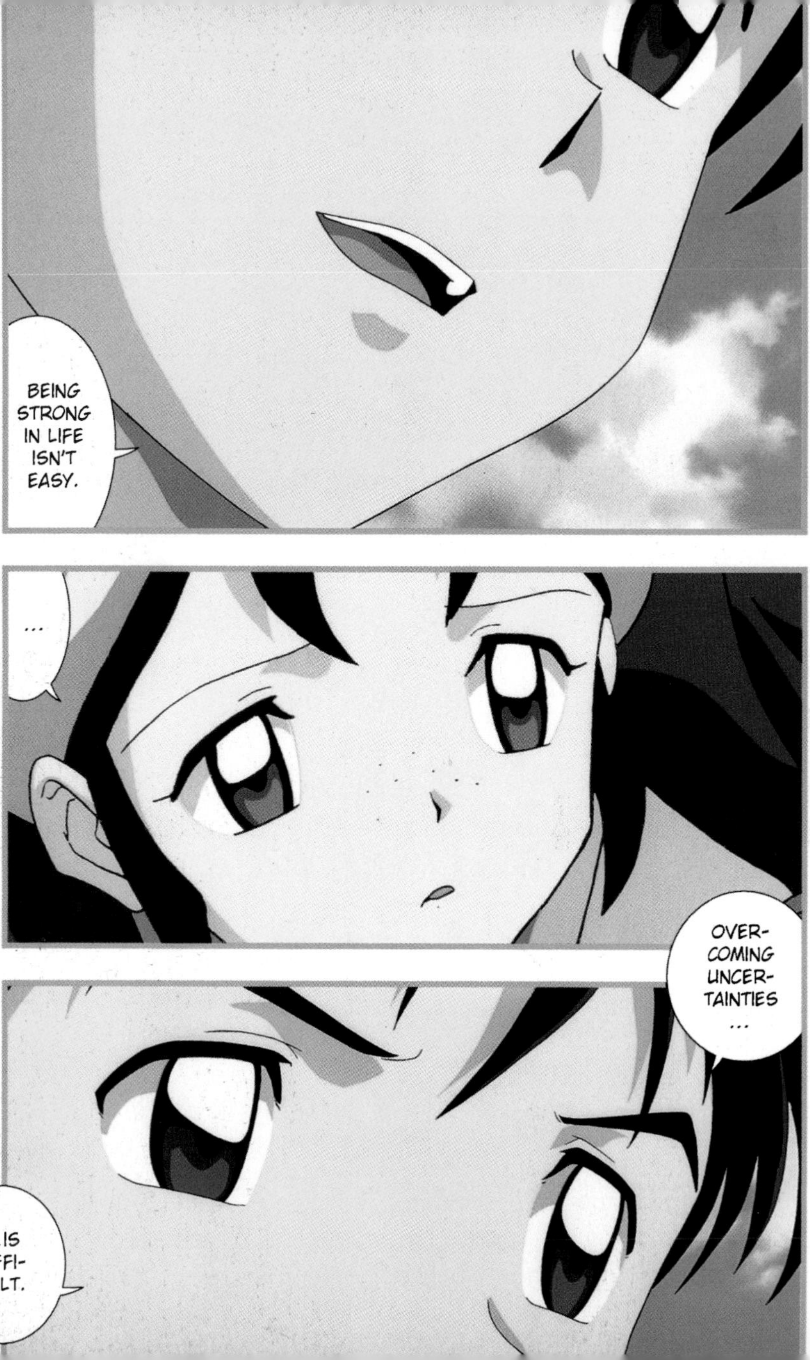
BEING STRONG IN LIFE ISN'T EASY.
...
OVER-COMING UNCER-TAINTIES ...
...IS DIFFI-CULT.

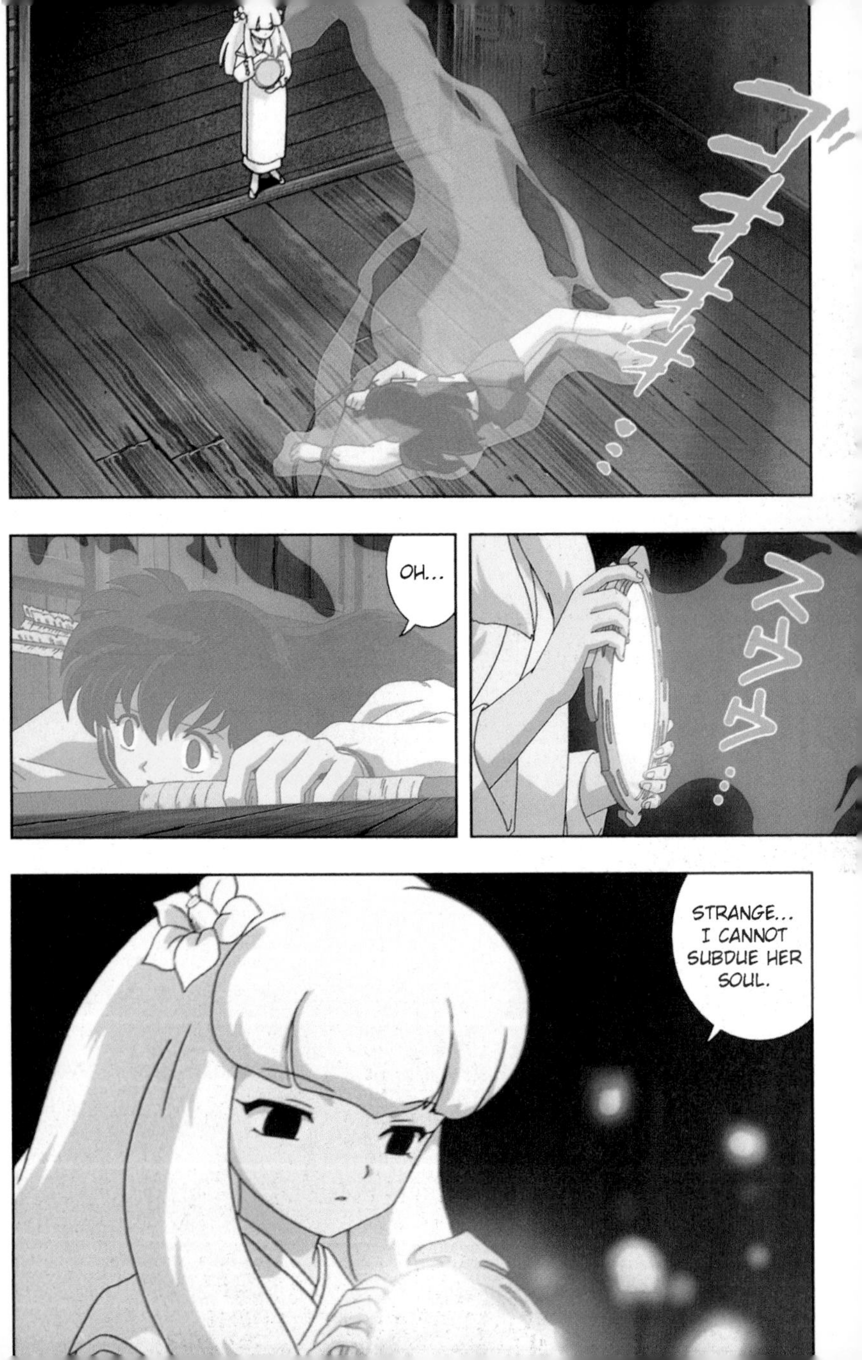
OH...
STRANGE... I CANNOT SUBDUE HER SOUL.

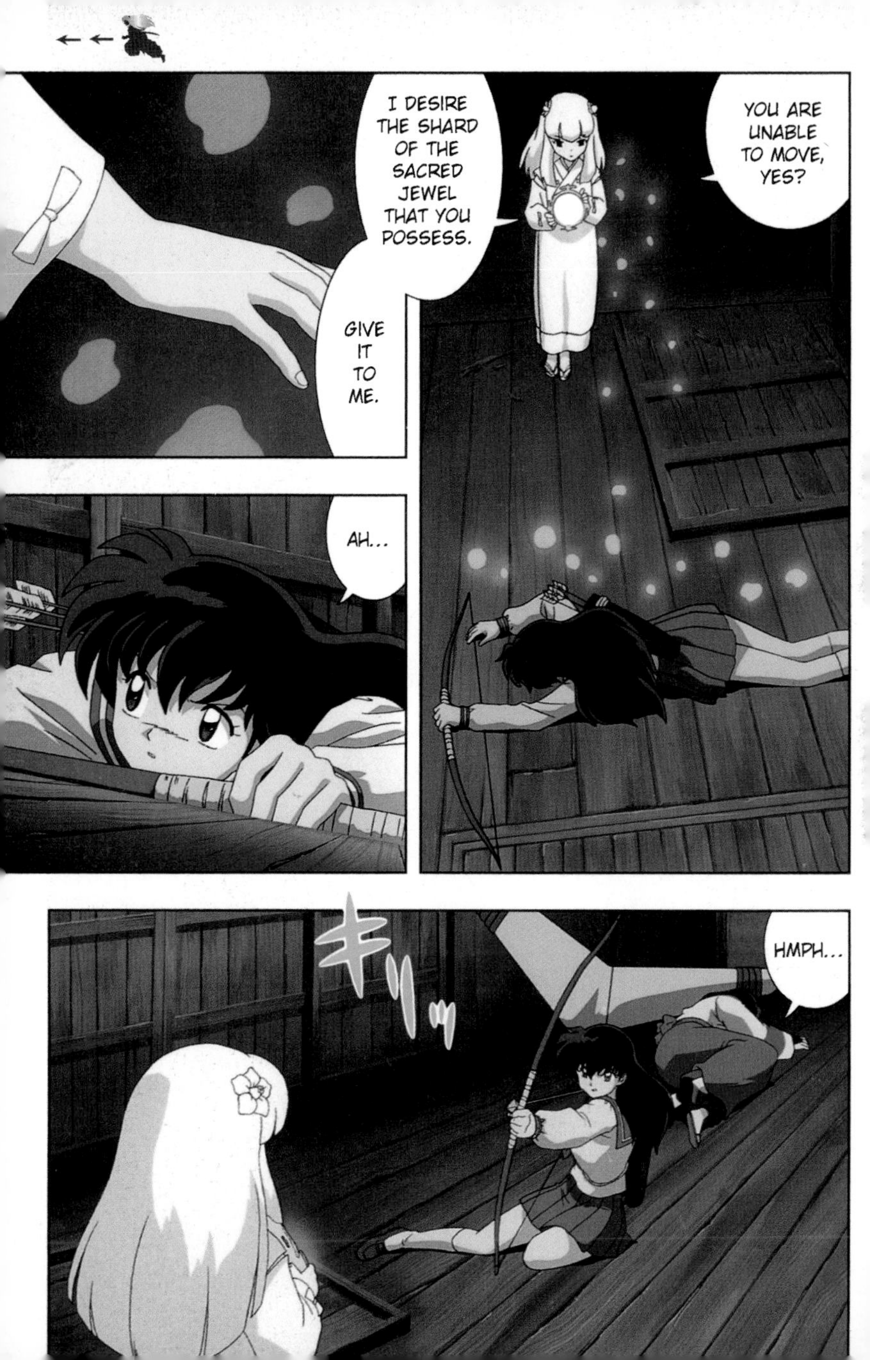
YOU ARE UNABLE TO MOVE, YES?
I DESIRE THE SHARD OF THE SACRED JEWEL THAT YOU POSSESS.
GIVE IT TO ME.
AH...
HMPH...

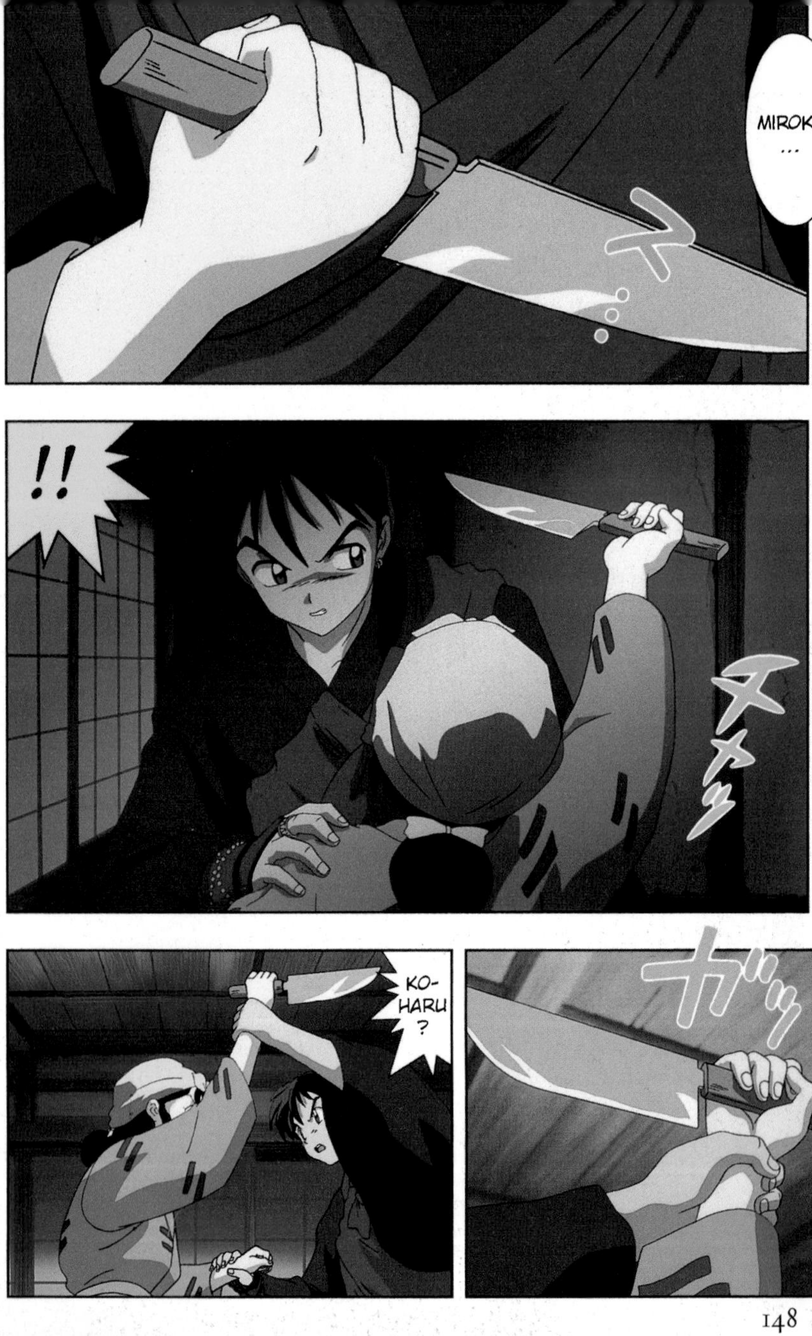
MIROKU ...
ス…
!!
ガッ
KO-HARU?

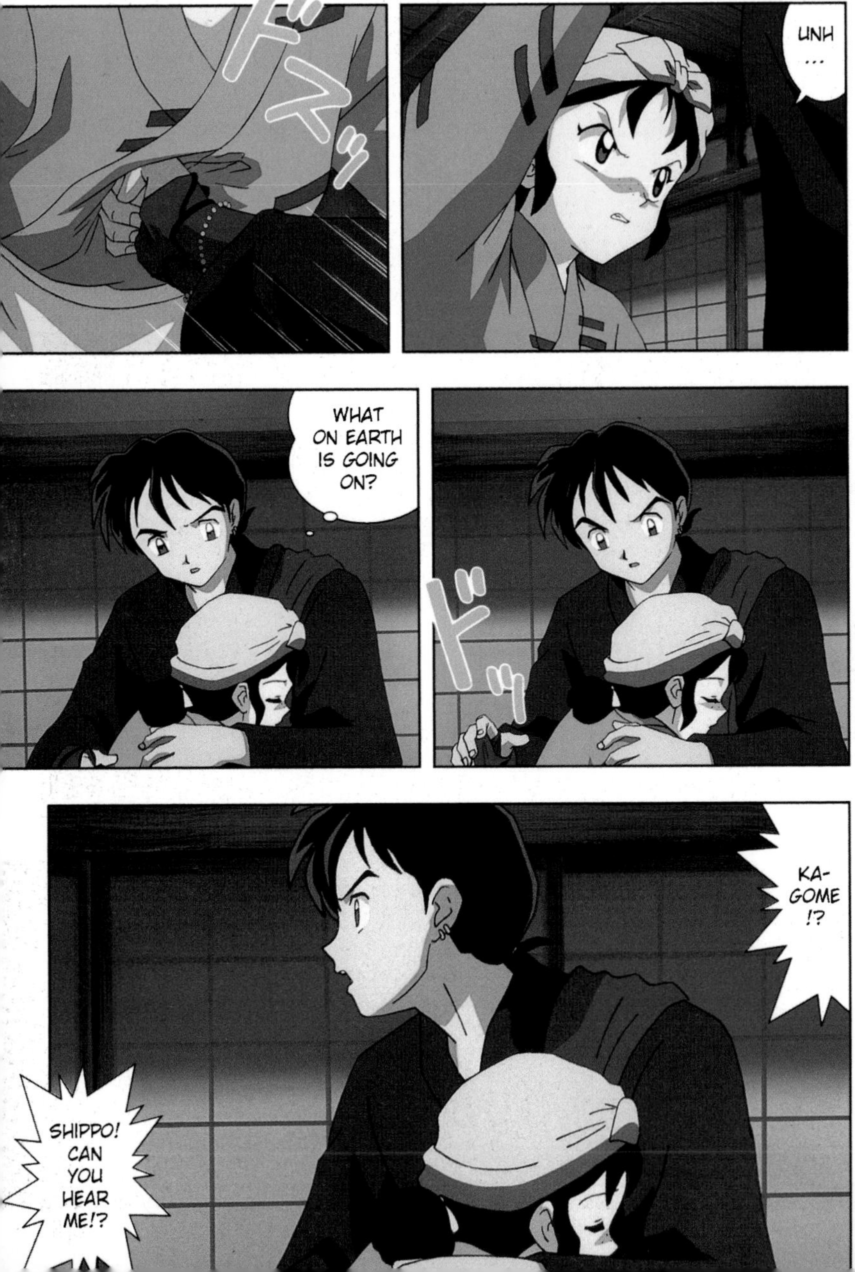
UNH ...
ドスッ
ドッ
WHAT ON EARTH IS GOING ON?
KA-GOME!?
SHIPPO! CAN YOU HEAR ME!?

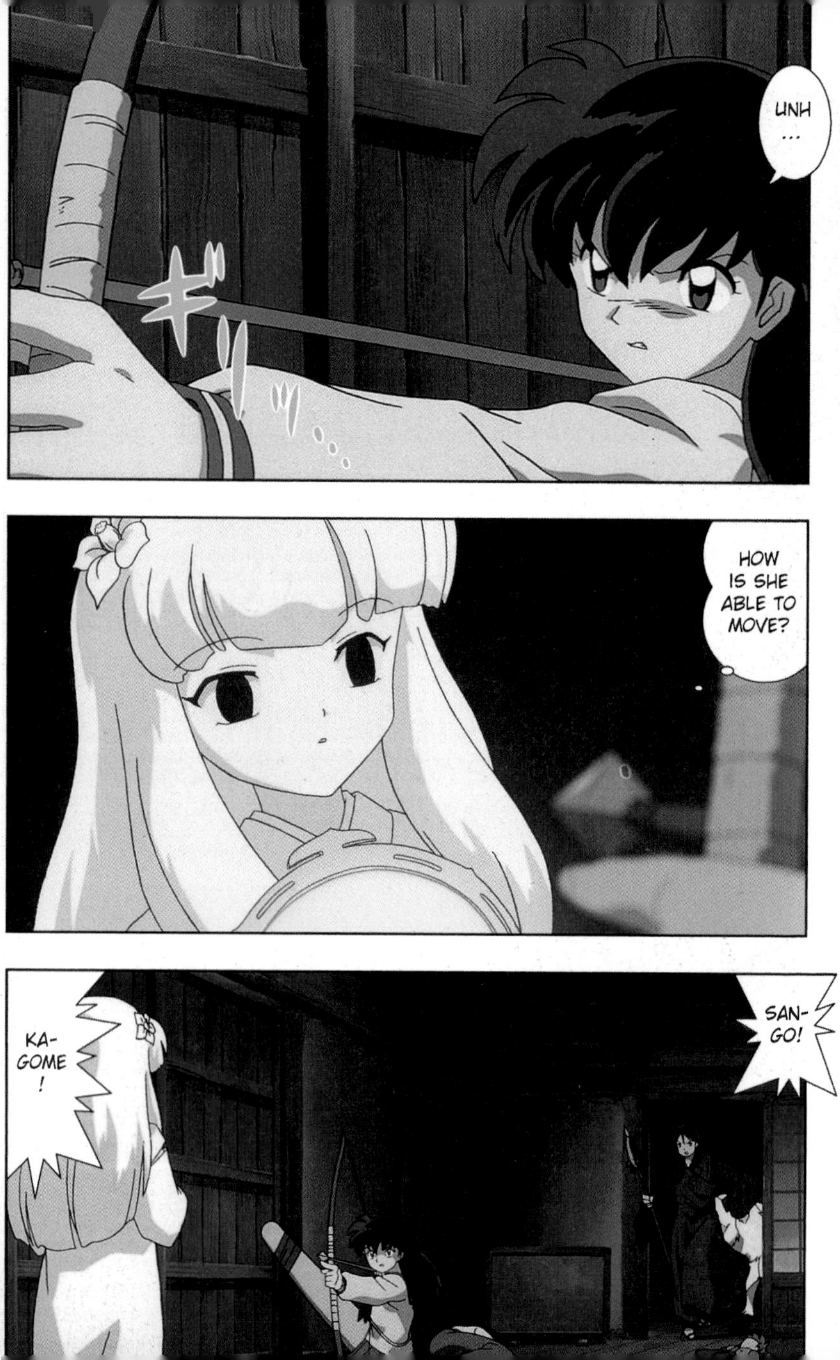
UNH ...
ギリッ
HOW IS SHE ABLE TO MOVE?
SAN-GO!
KA-GOME!

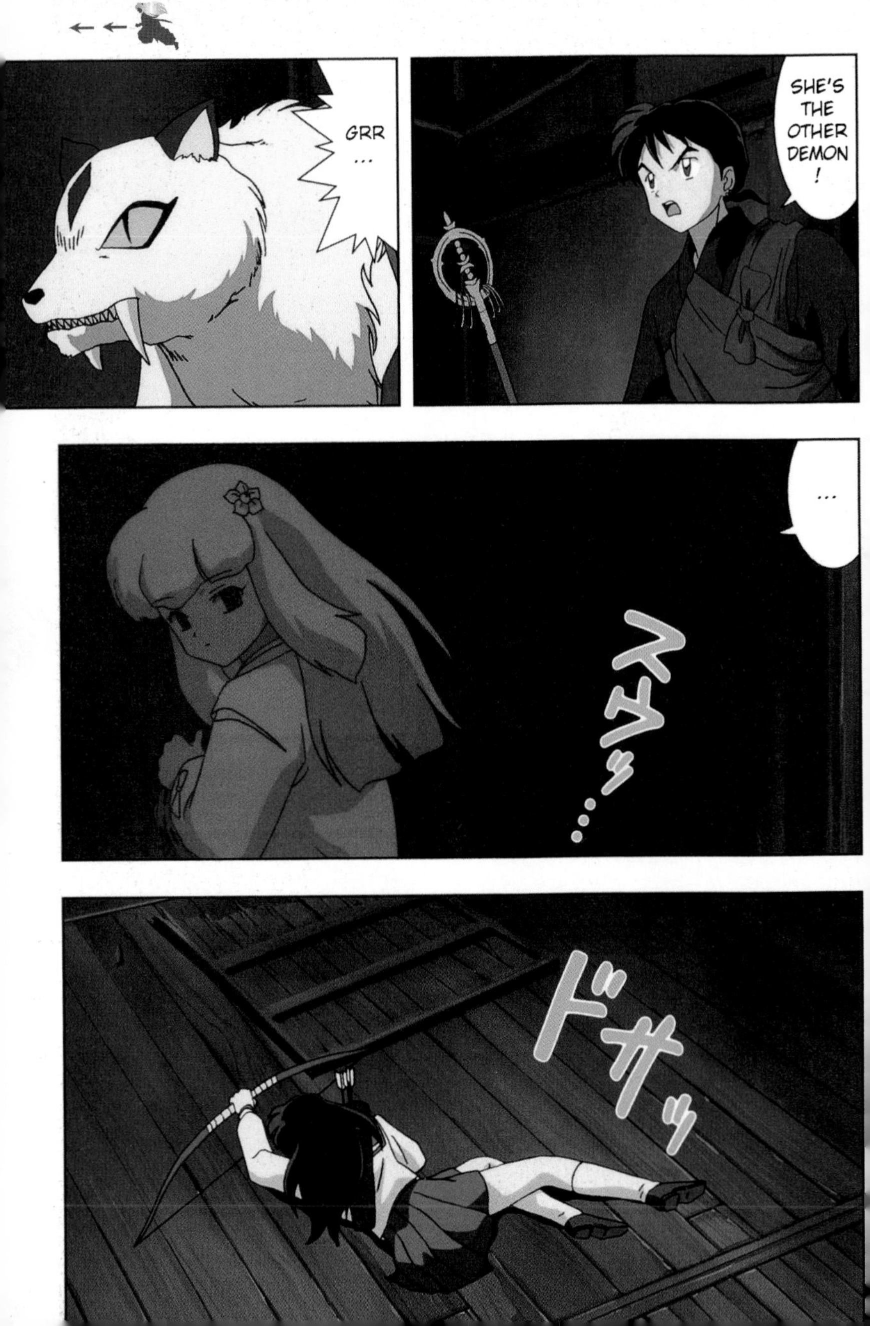
SHE'S THE OTHER DEMON!
GRR ...
...
スタッ...
ドサッ

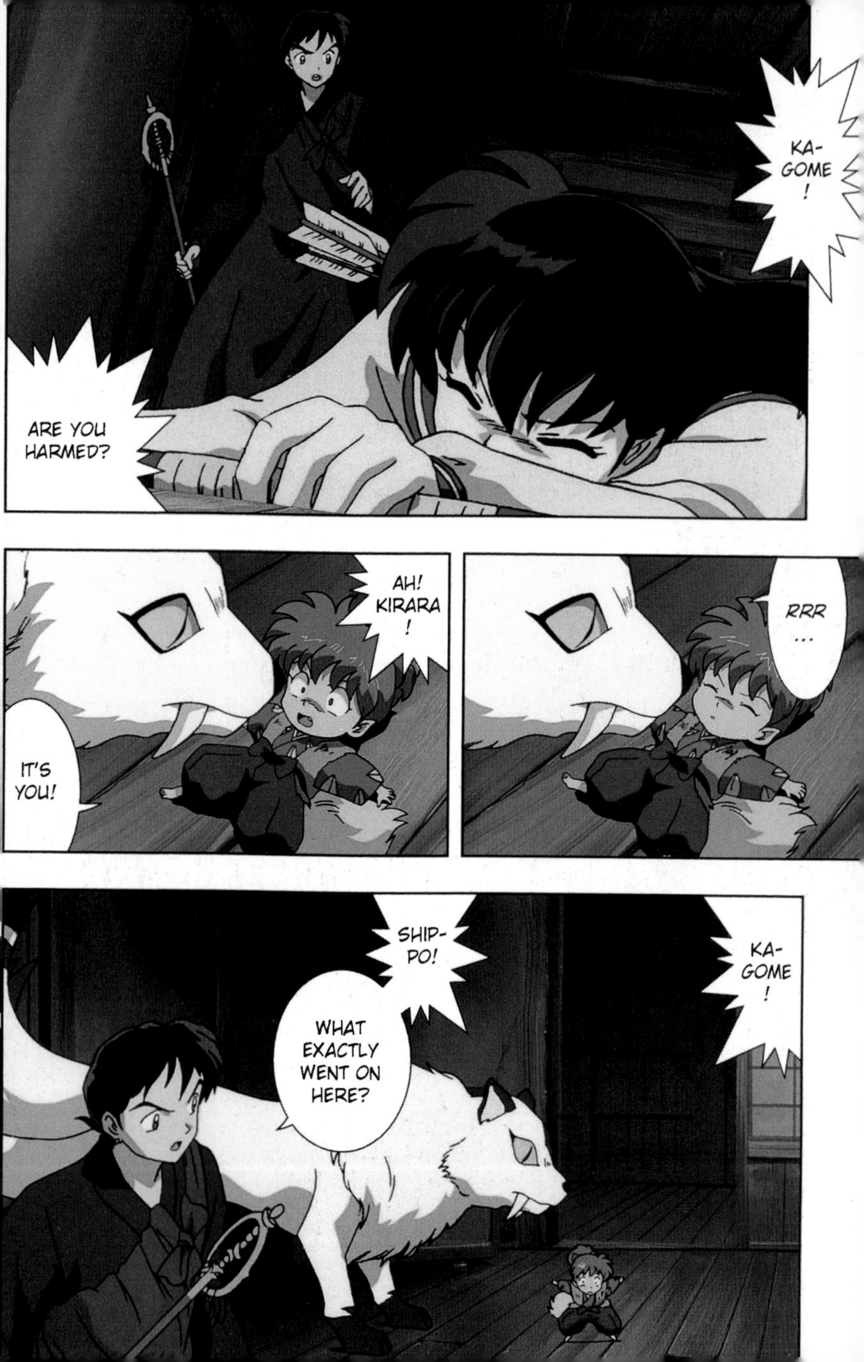

ARE YOU HARMED?
KA-GOME!
AH! KIRARA!
IT'S YOU!
RRR...
SHIP-PO!
WHAT EXACTLY WENT ON HERE?
KA-GOME!

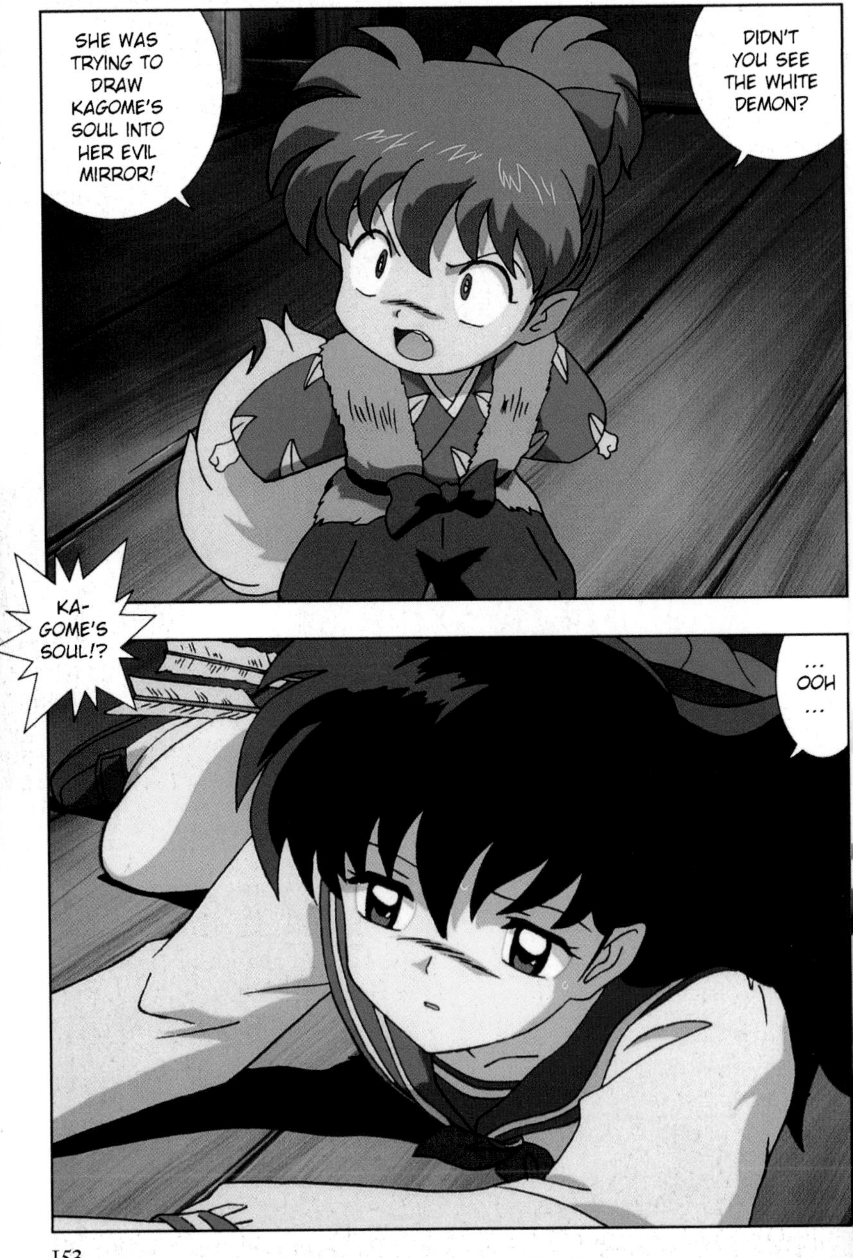
DIDN'T YOU SEE THE WHITE DEMON?
SHE WAS TRYING TO DRAW KAGOME'S SOUL INTO HER EVIL MIRROR!
KA-GOME'S SOUL!?
... OOH ...

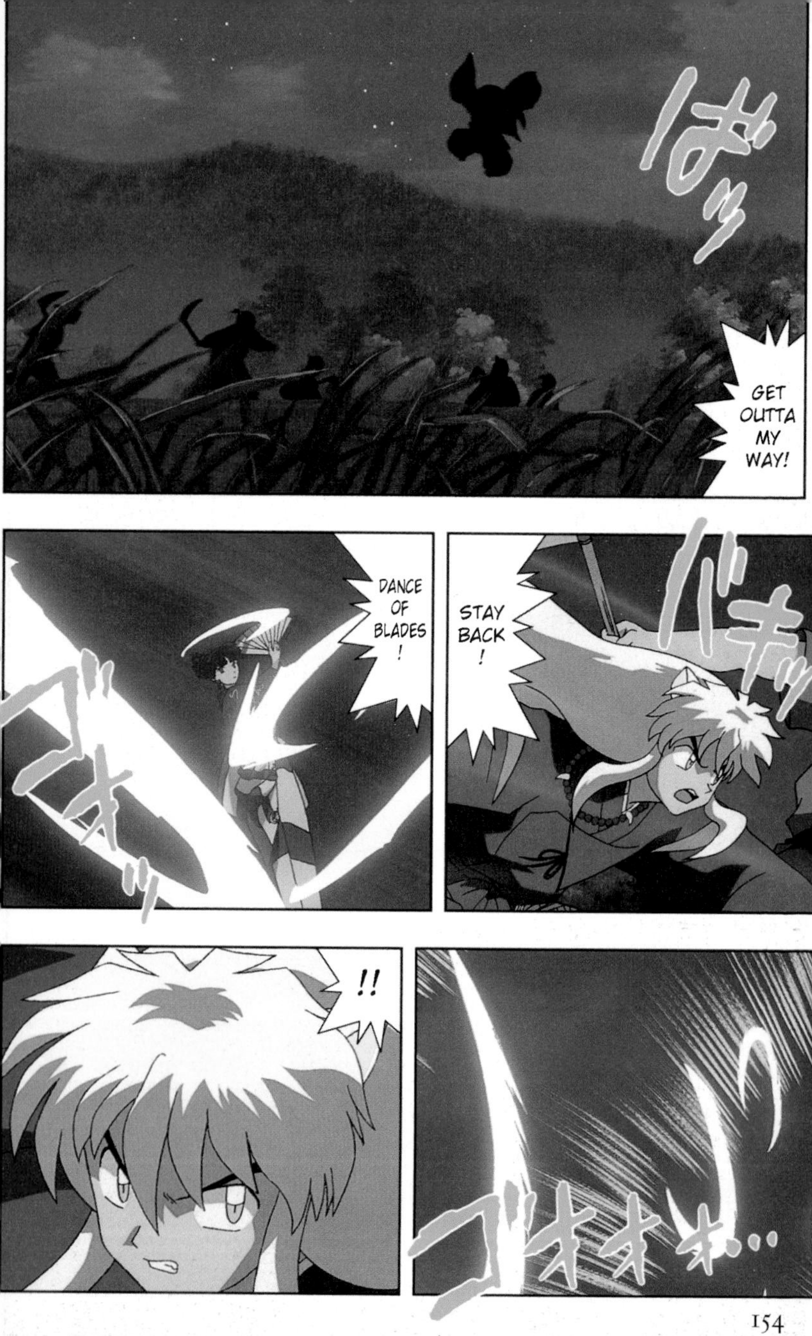
ばッ
GET OUTTA MY WAY!
バキッ
STAY BACK!
DANCE OF BLADES!
ゴオッ
ゴオオオ…
!!

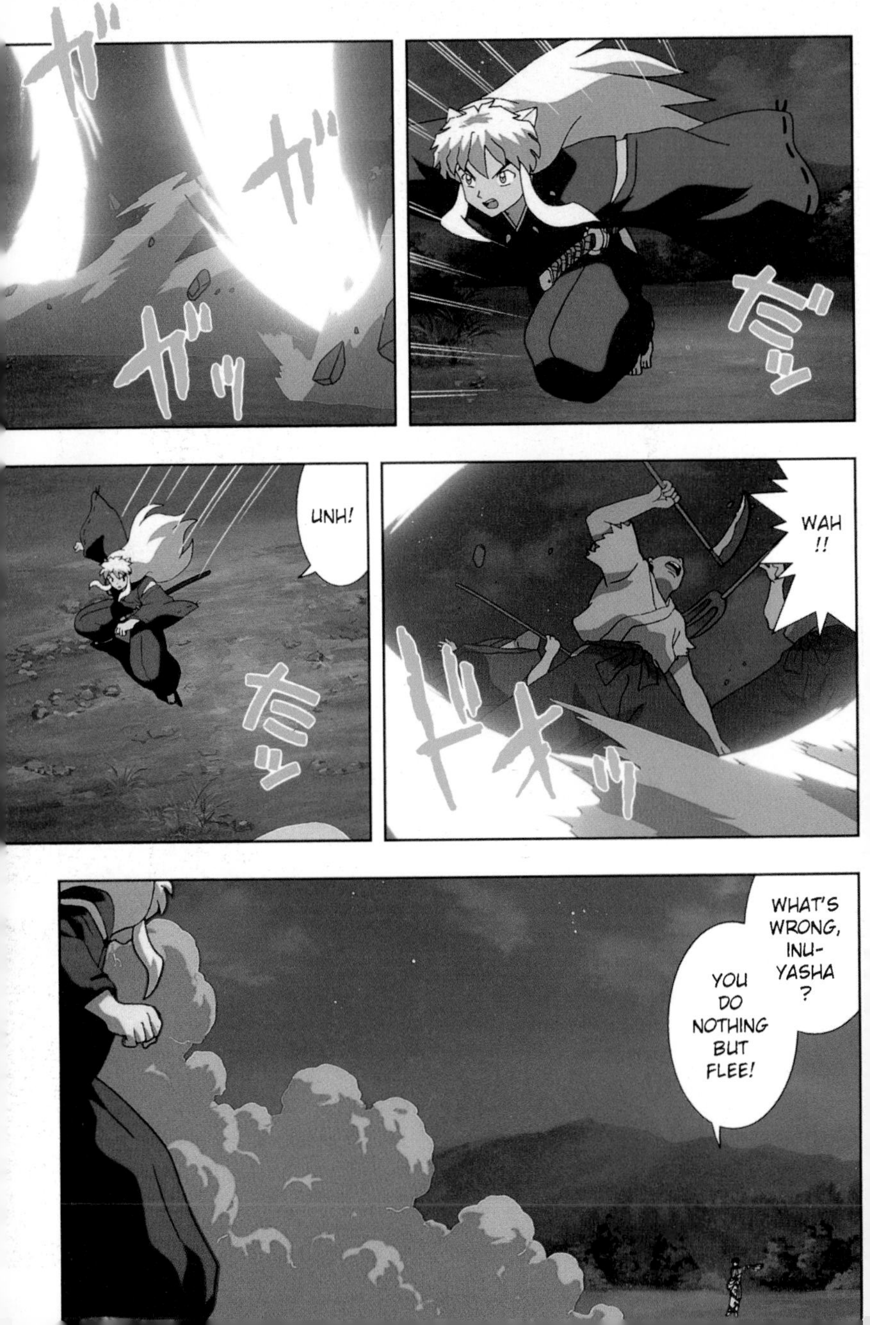
ダッ
ガ
ガ
ガッ
WAH !!
ドオッ
UNH!
ダッ
WHAT'S WRONG, INU-YASHA?
YOU DO NOTHING BUT FLEE!

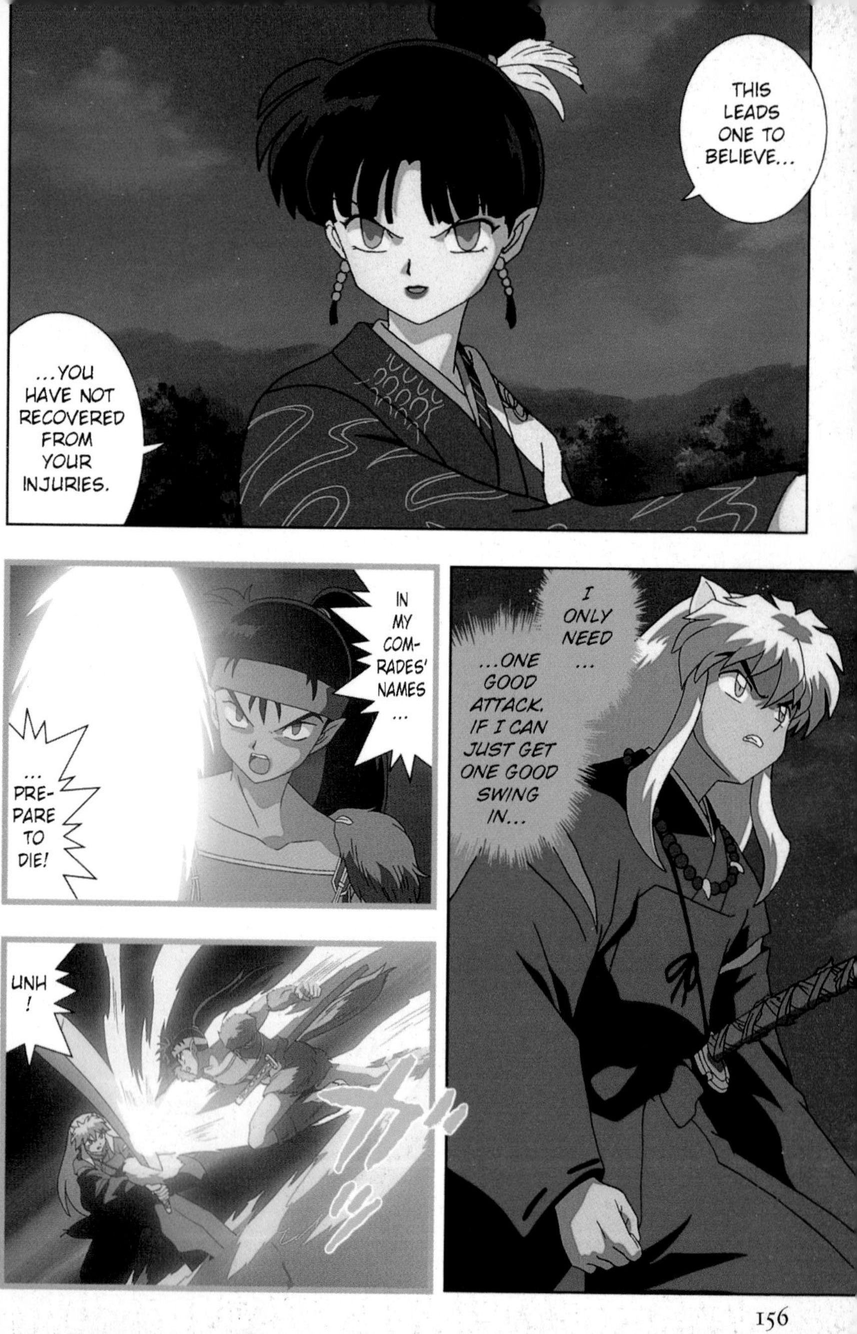
THIS LEADS ONE TO BELIEVE...
...YOU HAVE NOT RECOVERED FROM YOUR INJURIES.
I ONLY NEED...
...ONE GOOD ATTACK. IF I CAN JUST GET ONE GOOD SWING IN...
IN MY COM-RADES' NAMES...
...PRE-PARE TO DIE!
UNH!

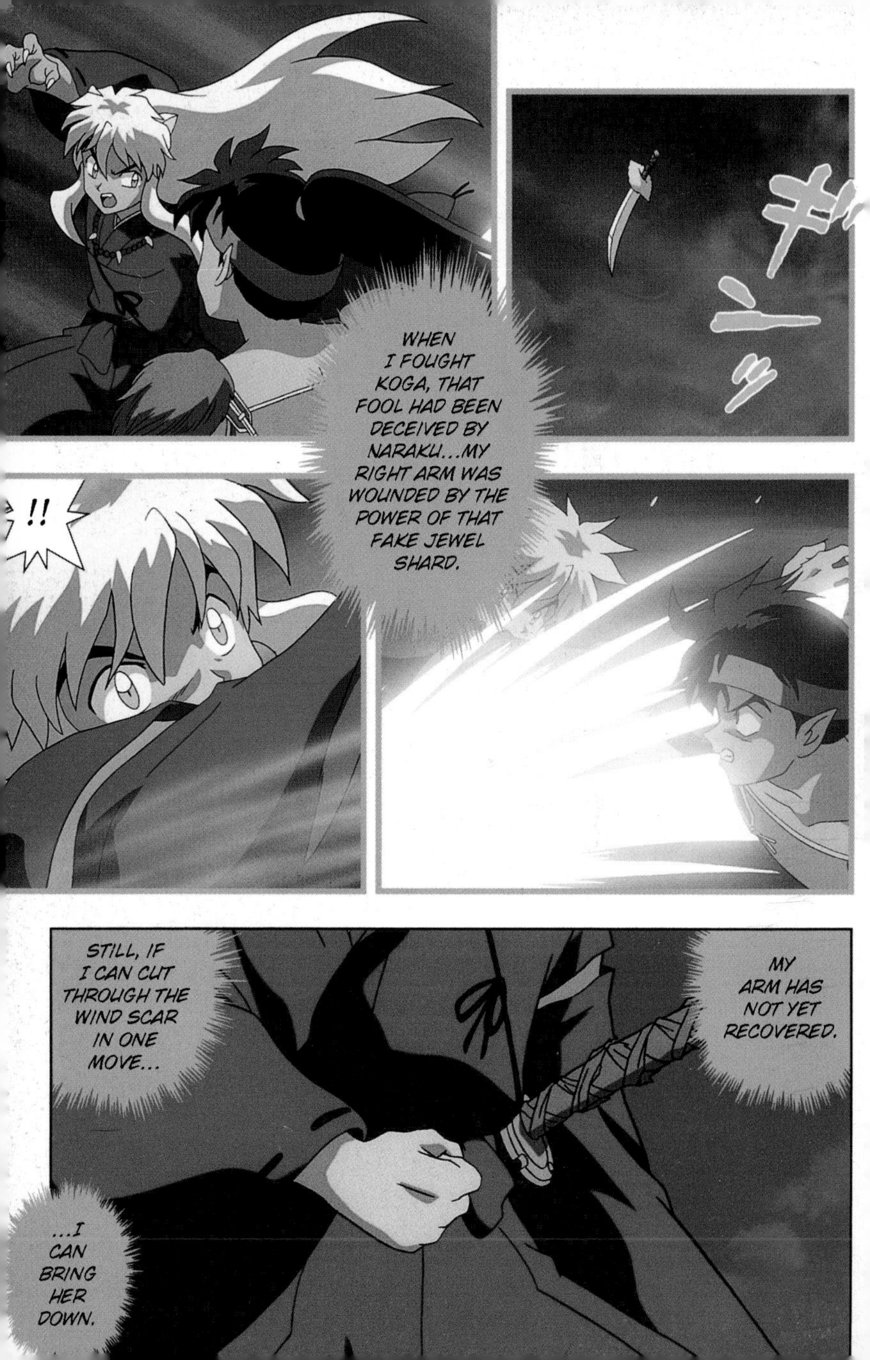
ギンッ
WHEN I FOUGHT KOGA, THAT FOOL HAD BEEN DECEIVED BY NARAKU...MY RIGHT ARM WAS WOUNDED BY THE POWER OF THAT FAKE JEWEL SHARD.
!!
MY ARM HAS NOT YET RECOVERED.
STILL, IF I CAN CUT THROUGH THE WIND SCAR IN ONE MOVE...
...I CAN BRING HER DOWN.

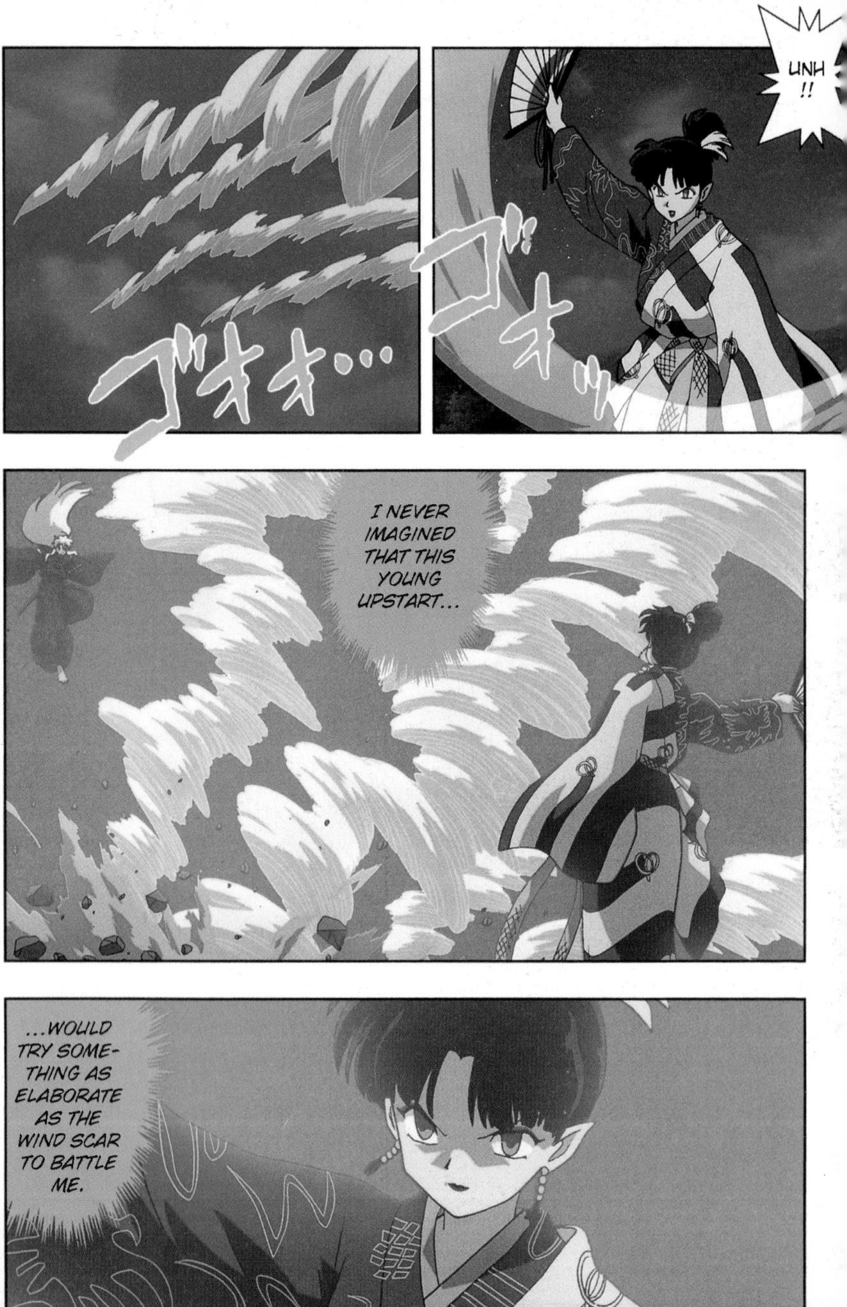
UNH !!
ゴオオッ
ゴオオ…
I NEVER IMAGINED THAT THIS YOUNG UPSTART...
...WOULD TRY SOME-THING AS ELABORATE AS THE WIND SCAR TO BATTLE ME.

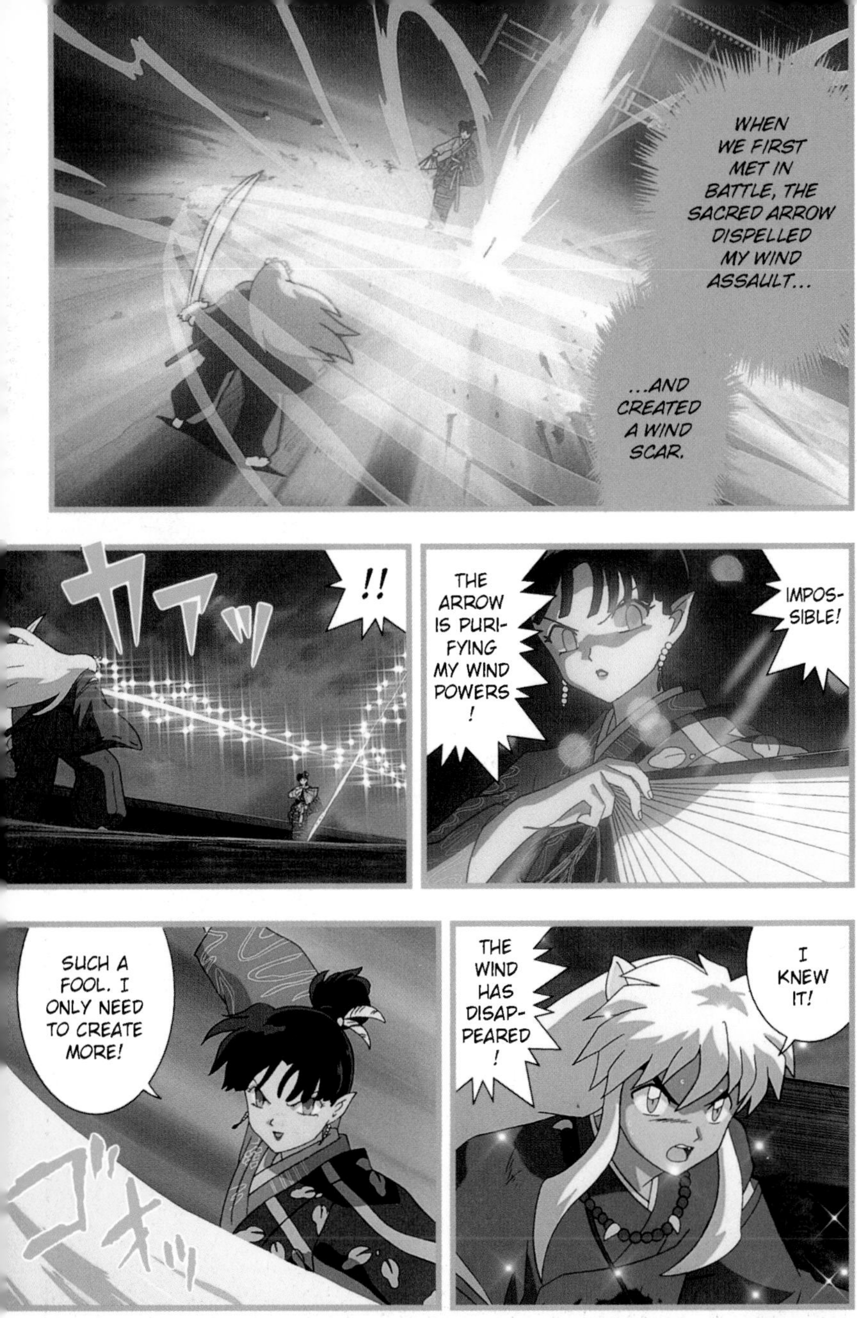
WHEN WE FIRST MET IN BATTLE, THE SACRED ARROW DISPELLED MY WIND ASSAULT...
...AND CREATED A WIND SCAR.
IMPOSSIBLE!
THE ARROW IS PURIFYING MY WIND POWERS!
!!
カァッ
I KNEW IT!
THE WIND HAS DISAPPEARED!
SUCH A FOOL. I ONLY NEED TO CREATE MORE!
ゴォッ

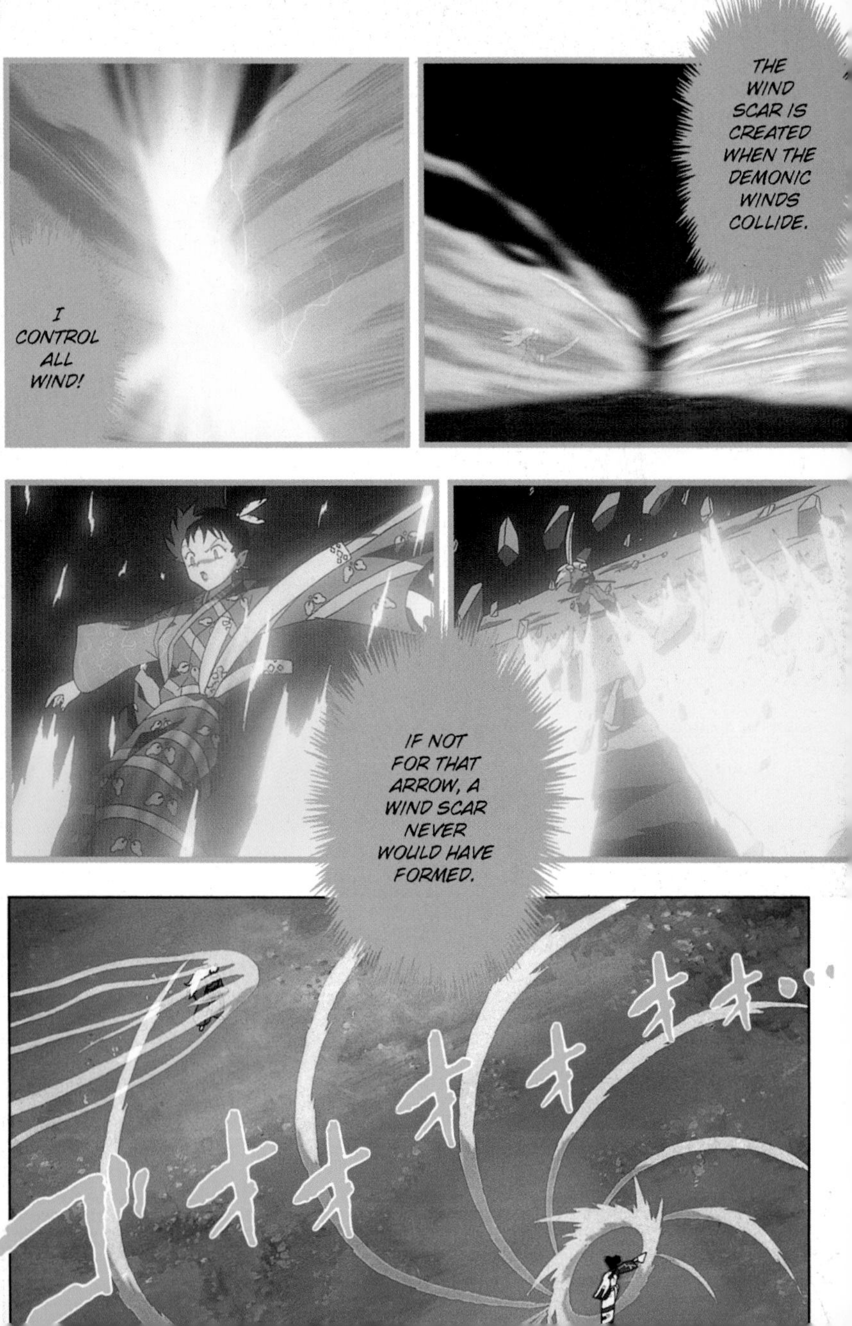
THE WIND SCAR IS CREATED WHEN THE DEMONIC WINDS COLLIDE.
I CONTROL ALL WIND!
IF NOT FOR THAT ARROW, A WIND SCAR NEVER WOULD HAVE FORMED.
ゴオオオオオオ…

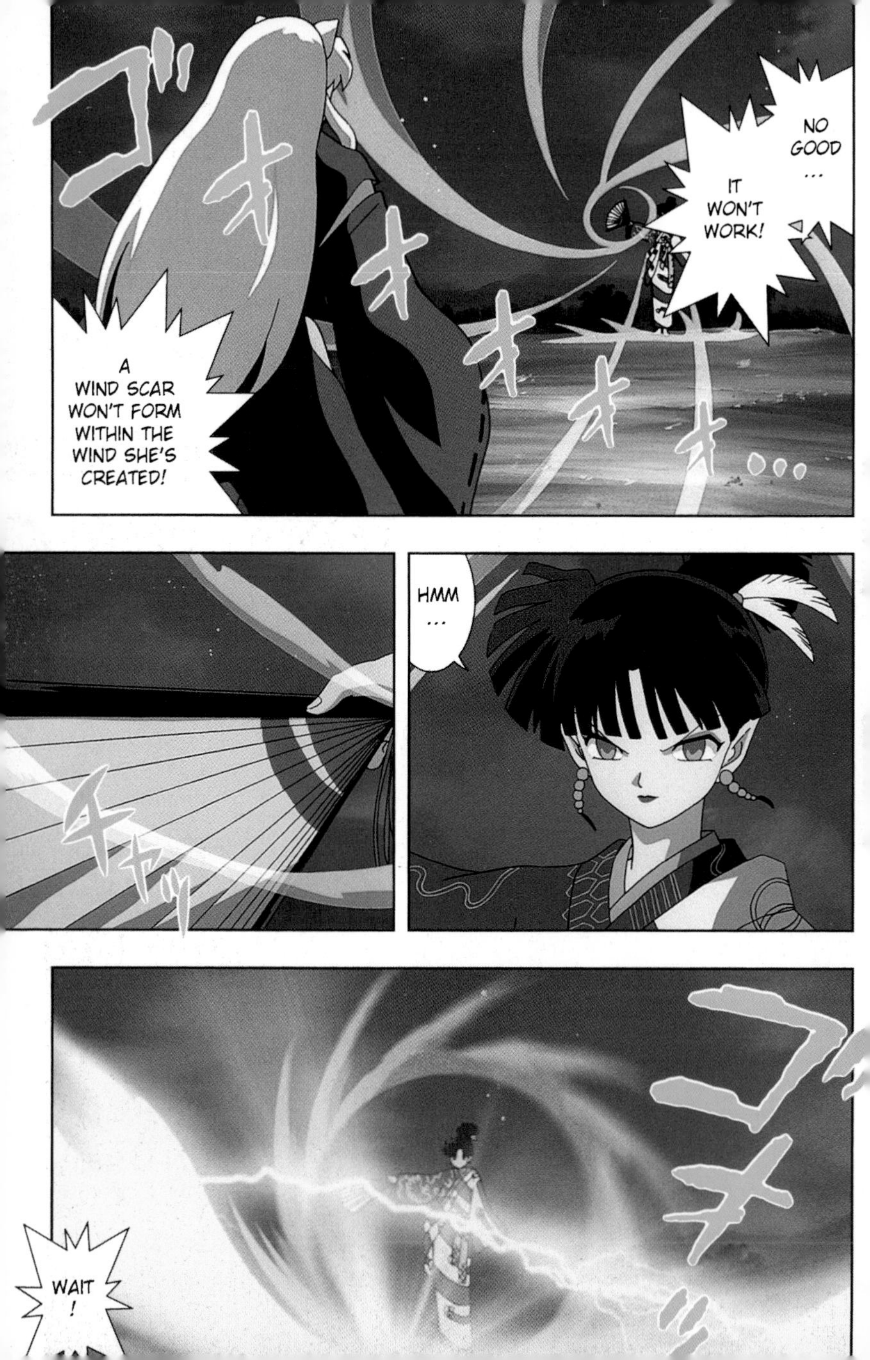
NO GOOD...
IT WON'T WORK!
A WIND SCAR WON'T FORM WITHIN THE WIND SHE'S CREATED!
HMM...
WAIT!

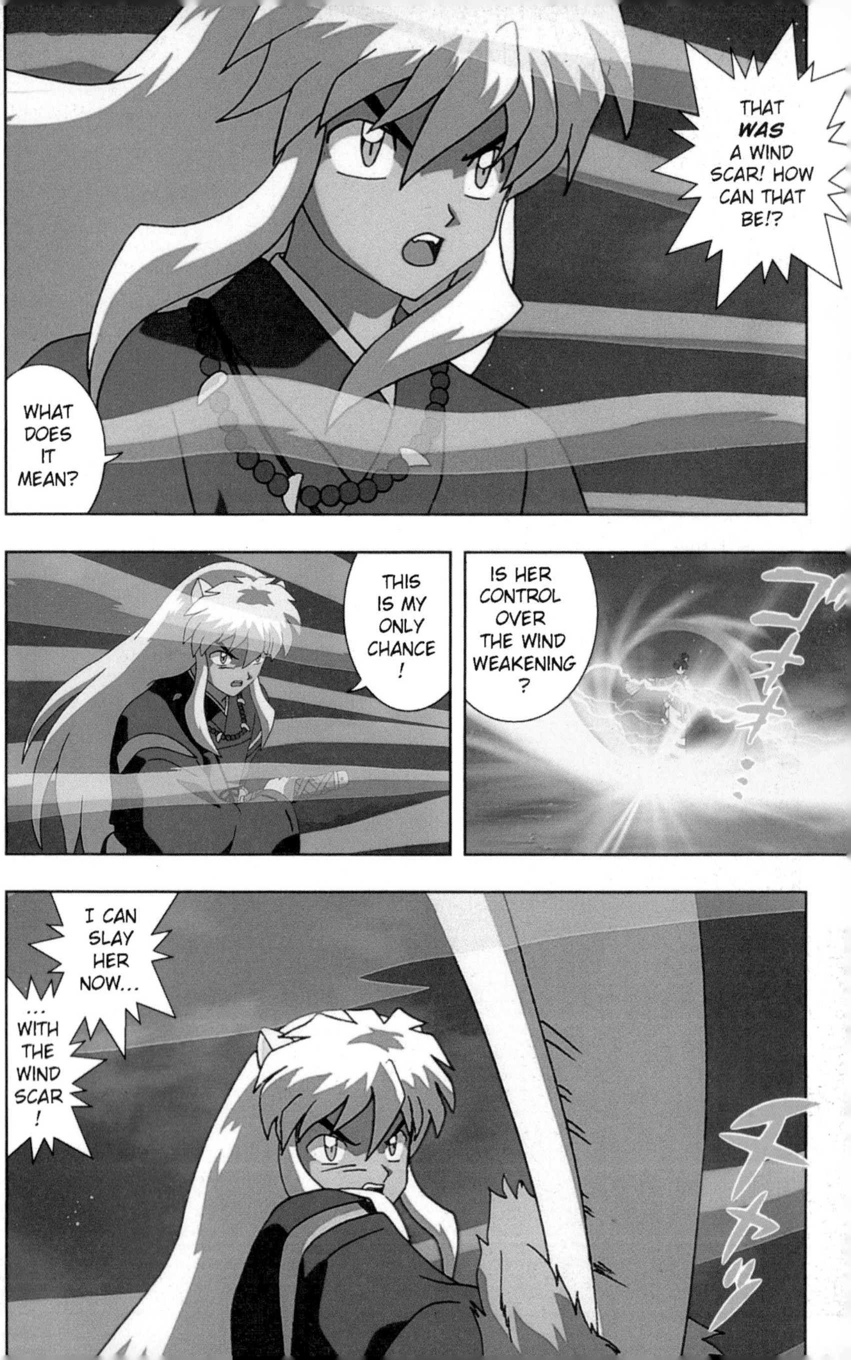
THAT WAS A WIND SCAR! HOW CAN THAT BE!?
WHAT DOES IT MEAN?
THIS IS MY ONLY CHANCE!
IS HER CONTROL OVER THE WIND WEAKENING?
I CAN SLAY HER NOW...
...WITH THE WIND SCAR!

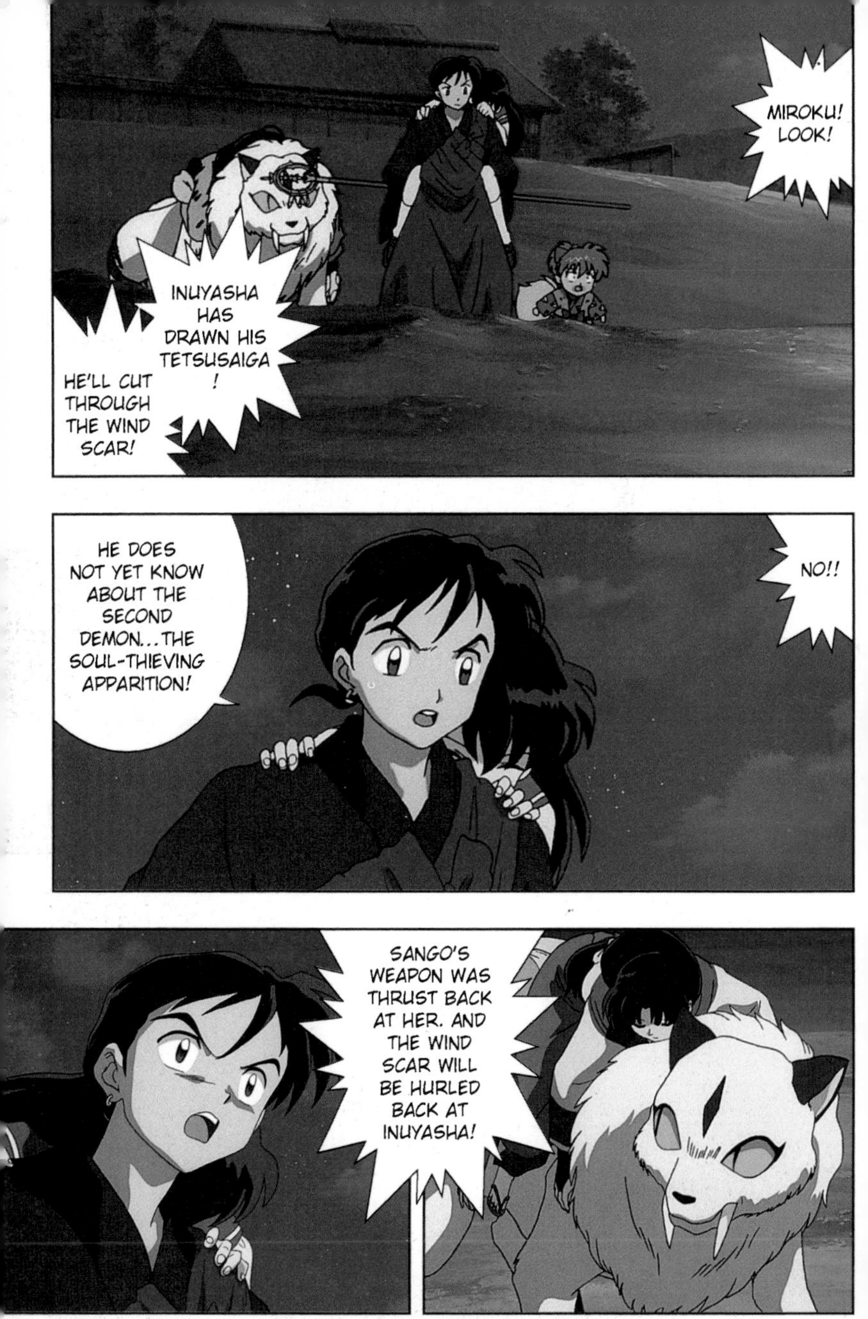
MIROKU! LOOK!
INUYASHA HAS DRAWN HIS TETSUSAIGA!
HE'LL CUT THROUGH THE WIND SCAR!
NO!!
HE DOES NOT YET KNOW ABOUT THE SECOND DEMON...THE SOUL-THIEVING APPARITION!
SANGO'S WEAPON WAS THRUST BACK AT HER. AND THE WIND SCAR WILL BE HURLED BACK AT INUYASHA!

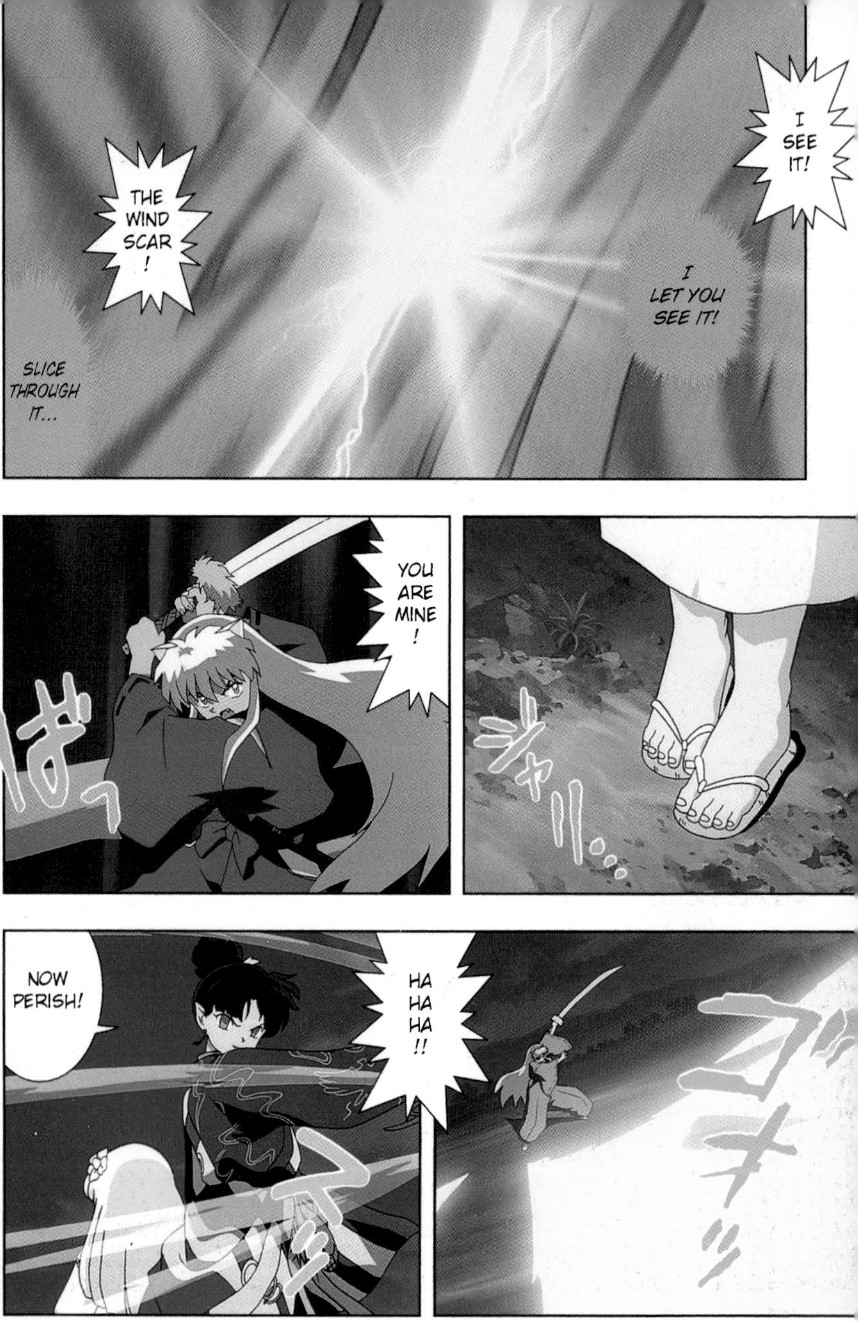
I SEE IT!
I LET YOU SEE IT!
THE WIND SCAR!
SLICE THROUGH IT...
ジャリ…
YOU ARE MINE!
ばっ
HA HA HA!!
NOW PERISH!

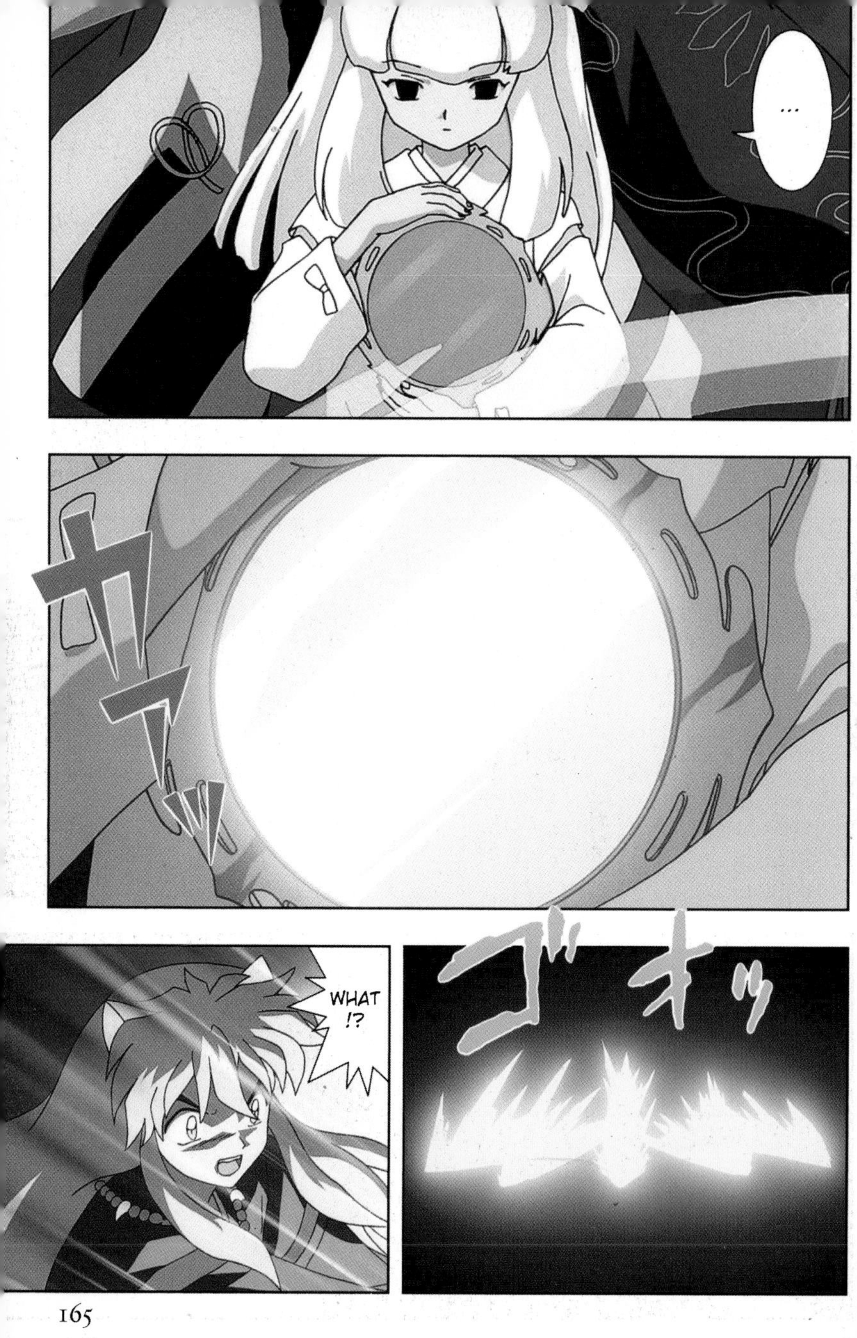
...
カァッ
WHAT !?
ゴオッ

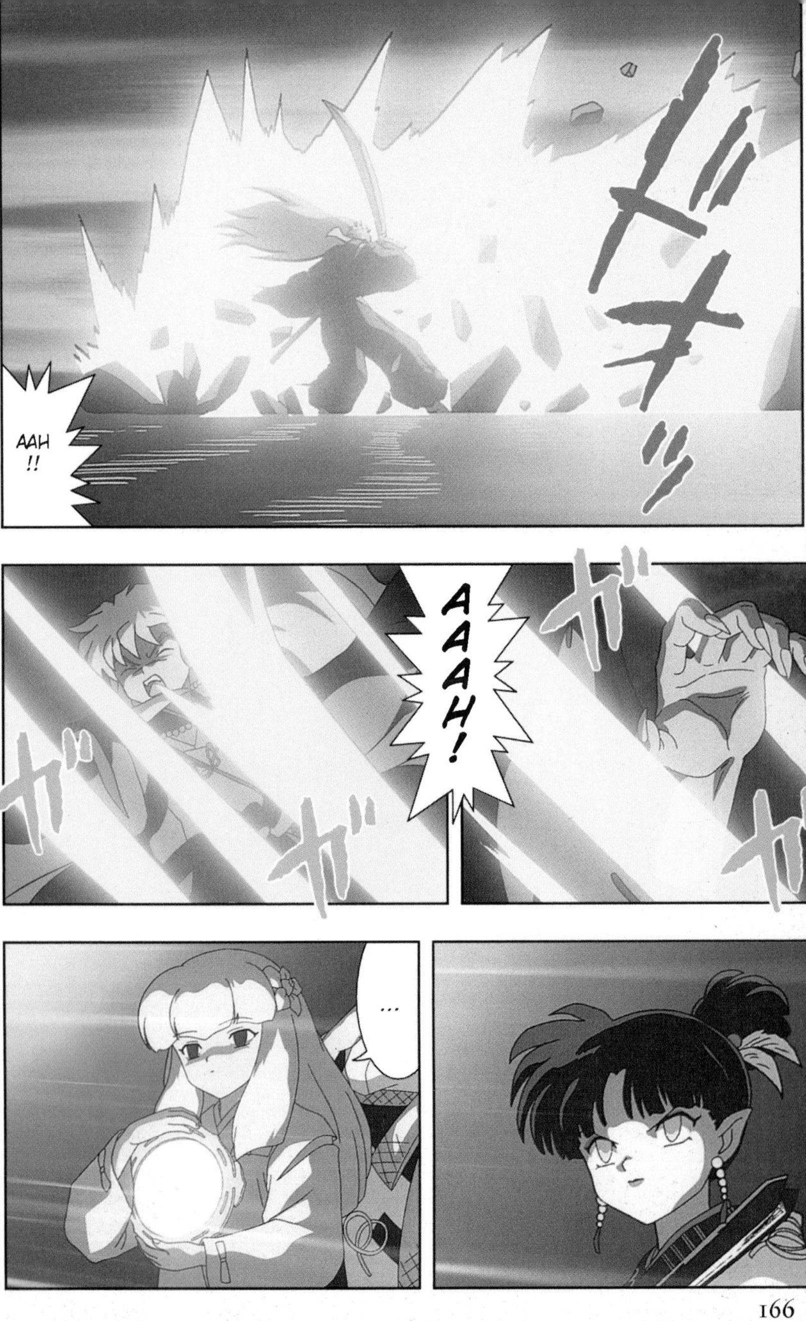
AAH !!
AAAAH!
...

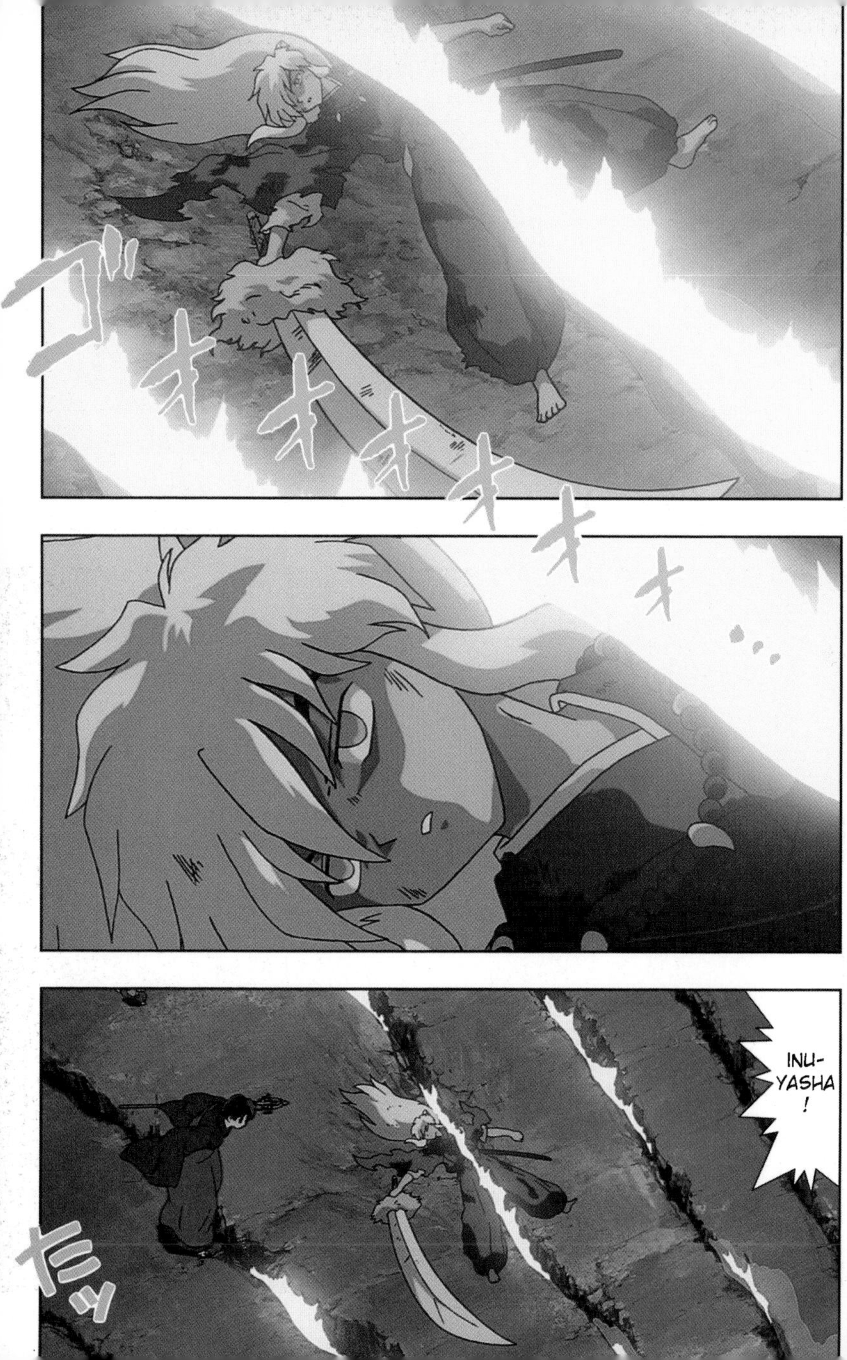
ゴオオオオオオ...
INU-YASHA!
ダッ

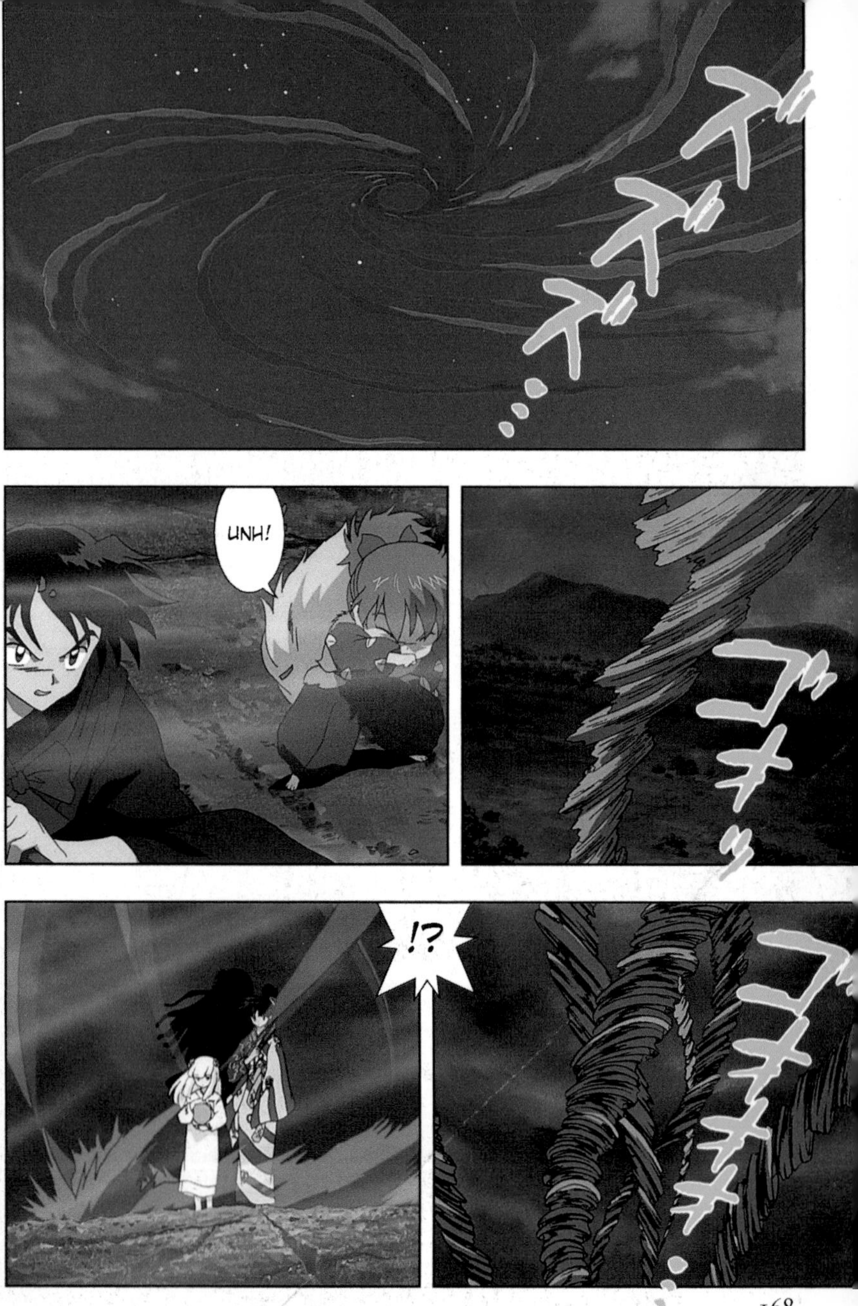
ズズズ…
ゴオッ
UNH!
ゴオオオ…
!?

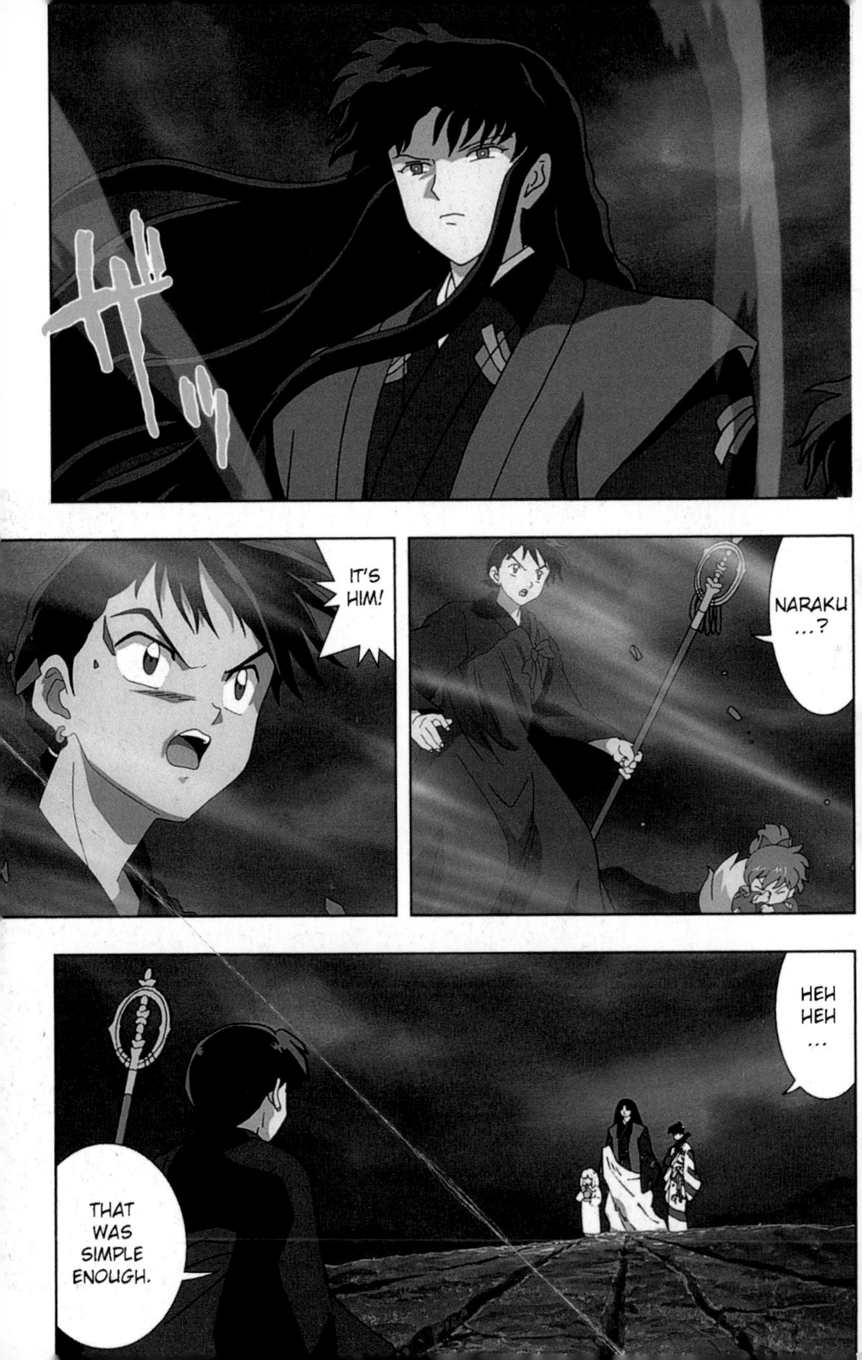
ザッ
NARAKU ...?
IT'S HIM!
HEH HEH ...
THAT WAS SIMPLE ENOUGH.

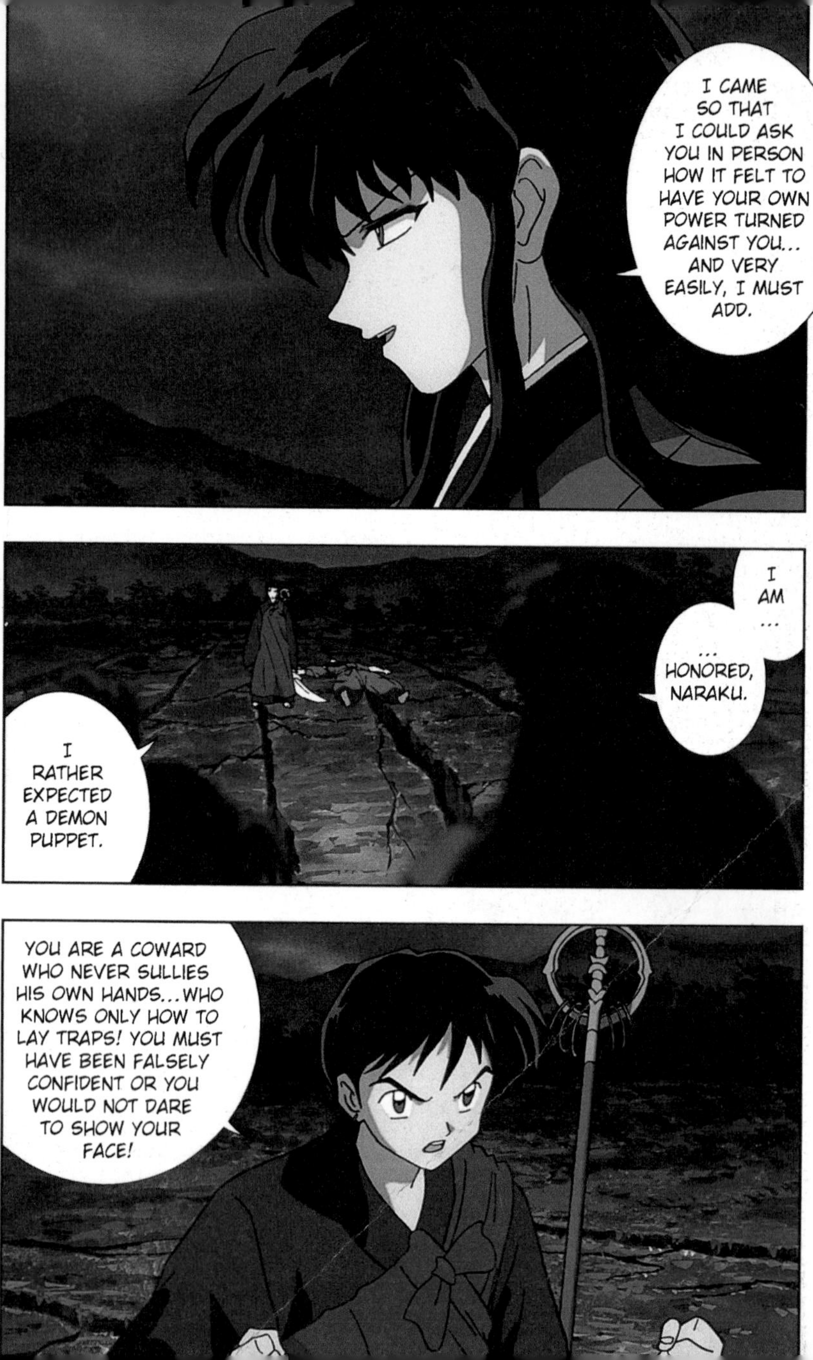
I CAME SO THAT I COULD ASK YOU IN PERSON HOW IT FELT TO HAVE YOUR OWN POWER TURNED AGAINST YOU... AND VERY EASILY, I MUST ADD.
I AM ...
... HONORED, NARAKU.
I RATHER EXPECTED A DEMON PUPPET.
YOU ARE A COWARD WHO NEVER SULLIES HIS OWN HANDS...WHO KNOWS ONLY HOW TO LAY TRAPS! YOU MUST HAVE BEEN FALSELY CONFIDENT OR YOU WOULD NOT DARE TO SHOW YOUR FACE!

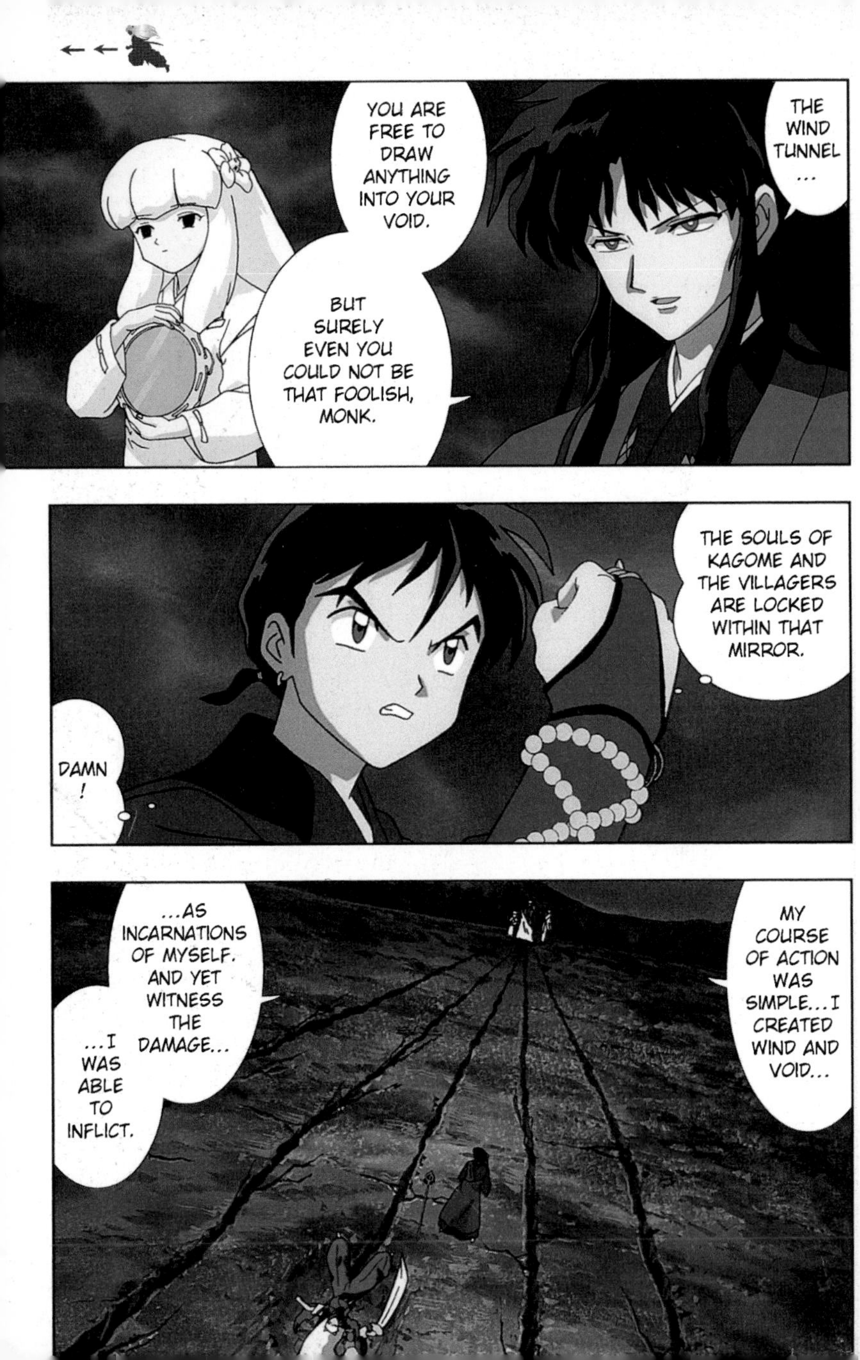
THE WIND TUNNEL...
YOU ARE FREE TO DRAW ANYTHING INTO YOUR VOID.
BUT SURELY EVEN YOU COULD NOT BE THAT FOOLISH, MONK.
THE SOULS OF KAGOME AND THE VILLAGERS ARE LOCKED WITHIN THAT MIRROR.
DAMN!
MY COURSE OF ACTION WAS SIMPLE...I CREATED WIND AND VOID...
...AS INCARNATIONS OF MYSELF. AND YET WITNESS THE DAMAGE...
...I WAS ABLE TO INFLICT.

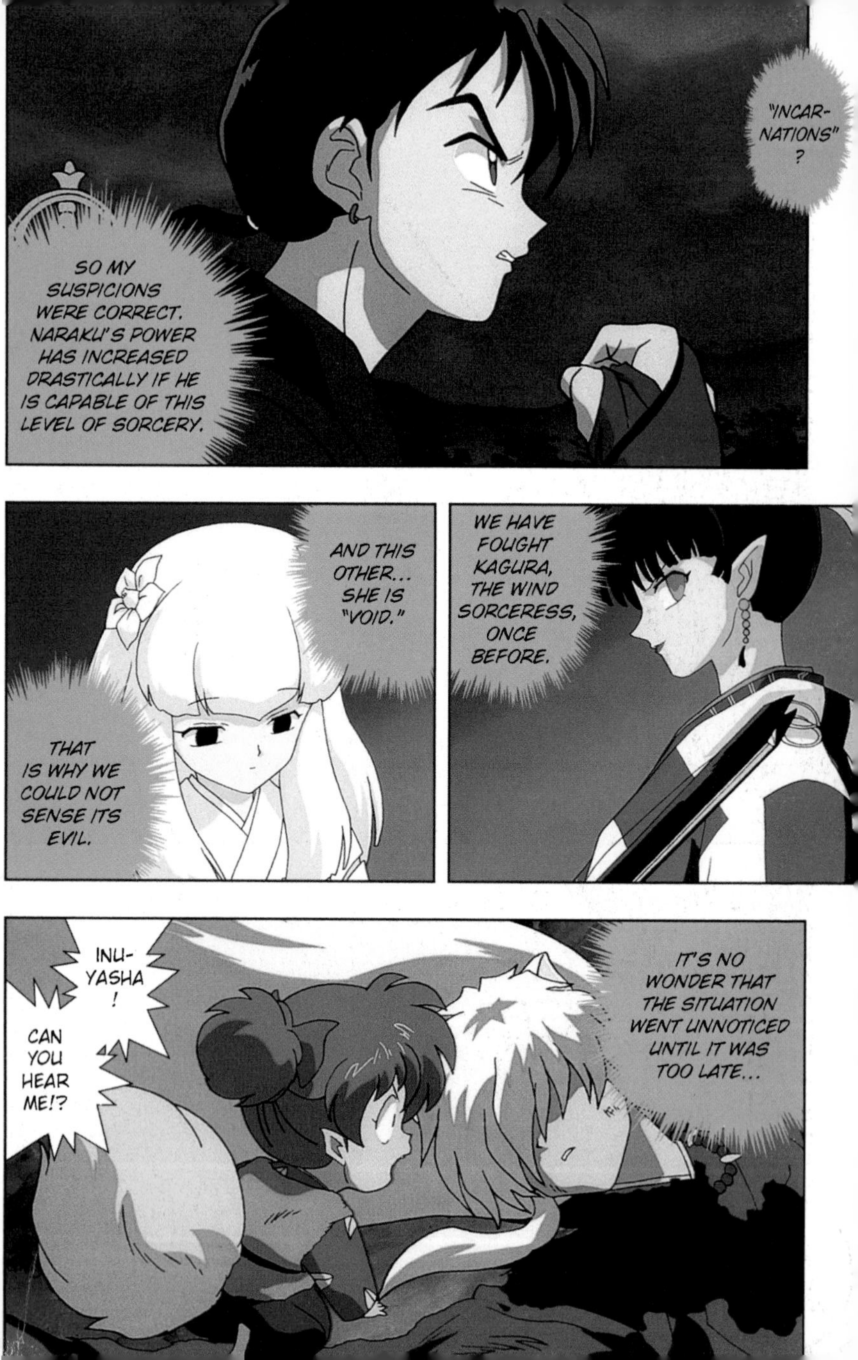
"INCARNATIONS"?
SO MY SUSPICIONS WERE CORRECT. NARAKU'S POWER HAS INCREASED DRASTICALLY IF HE IS CAPABLE OF THIS LEVEL OF SORCERY.
WE HAVE FOUGHT KAGURA, THE WIND SORCERESS, ONCE BEFORE.
AND THIS OTHER... SHE IS "VOID."
THAT IS WHY WE COULD NOT SENSE ITS EVIL.
IT'S NO WONDER THAT THE SITUATION WENT UNNOTICED UNTIL IT WAS TOO LATE...
INU-YASHA!
CAN YOU HEAR ME!?

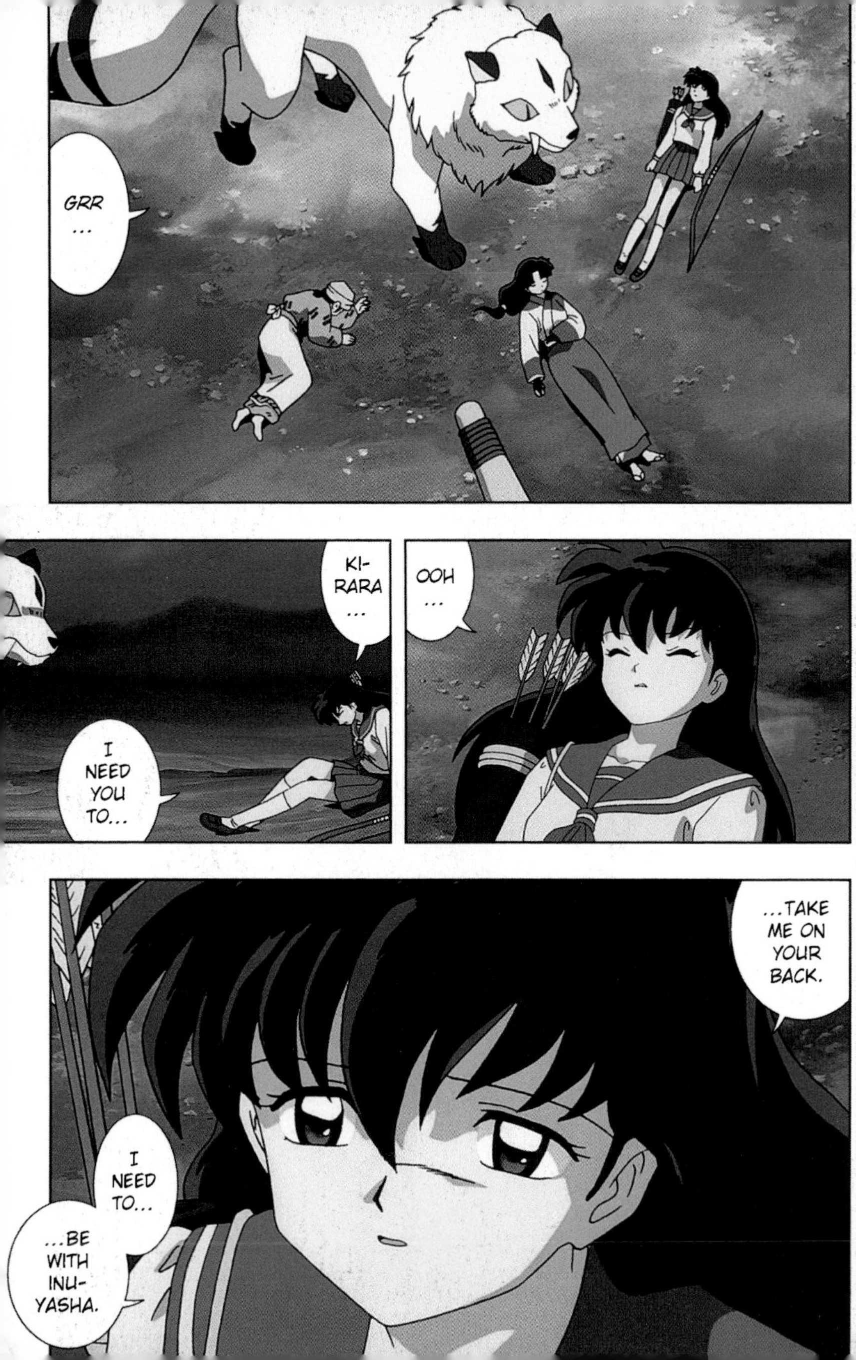
GRR ...
OOH ...
KI-RARA ...
I NEED YOU TO...
...TAKE ME ON YOUR BACK.
I NEED TO...
...BE WITH INU-YASHA.

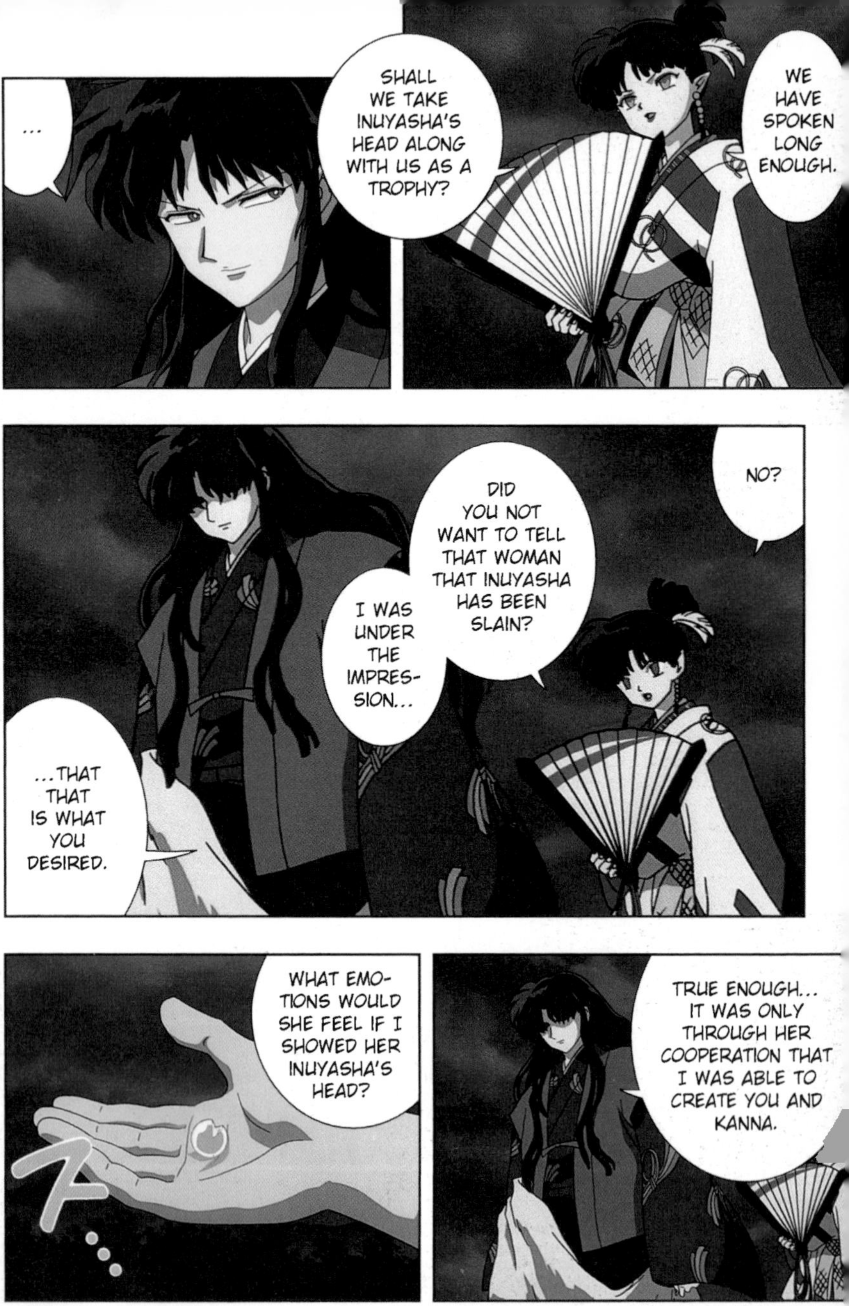
WE HAVE SPOKEN LONG ENOUGH.
SHALL WE TAKE INUYASHA'S HEAD ALONG WITH US AS A TROPHY?
...
NO?
DID YOU NOT WANT TO TELL THAT WOMAN THAT INUYASHA HAS BEEN SLAIN?
I WAS UNDER THE IMPRESSION...
...THAT THAT IS WHAT YOU DESIRED.
TRUE ENOUGH... IT WAS ONLY THROUGH HER COOPERATION THAT I WAS ABLE TO CREATE YOU AND KANNA.
WHAT EMOTIONS WOULD SHE FEEL IF I SHOWED HER INUYASHA'S HEAD?

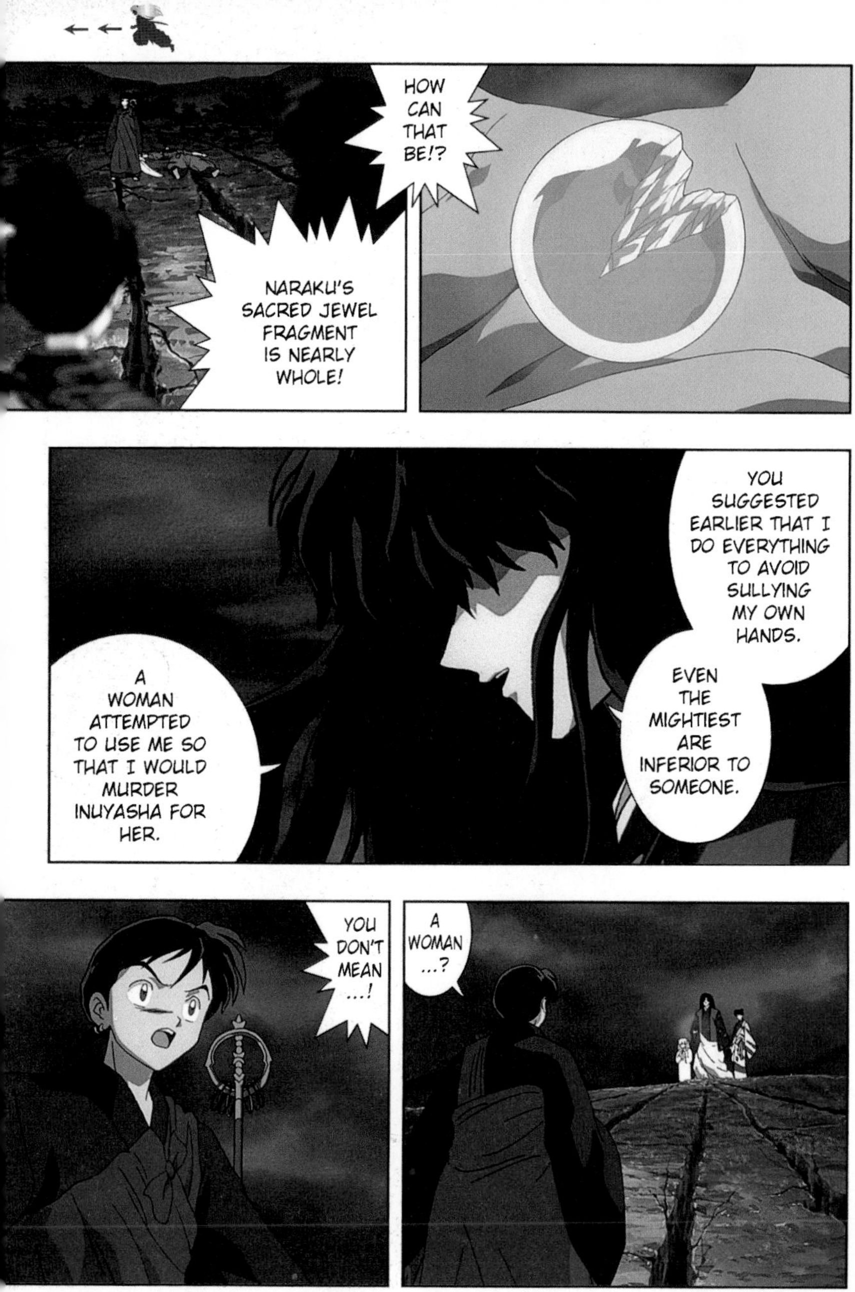
HOW CAN THAT BE!?
NARAKU'S SACRED JEWEL FRAGMENT IS NEARLY WHOLE!
YOU SUGGESTED EARLIER THAT I DO EVERYTHING TO AVOID SULLYING MY OWN HANDS.
EVEN THE MIGHTIEST ARE INFERIOR TO SOMEONE.
A WOMAN ATTEMPTED TO USE ME SO THAT I WOULD MURDER INUYASHA FOR HER.
A WOMAN ...?
YOU DON'T MEAN ...!

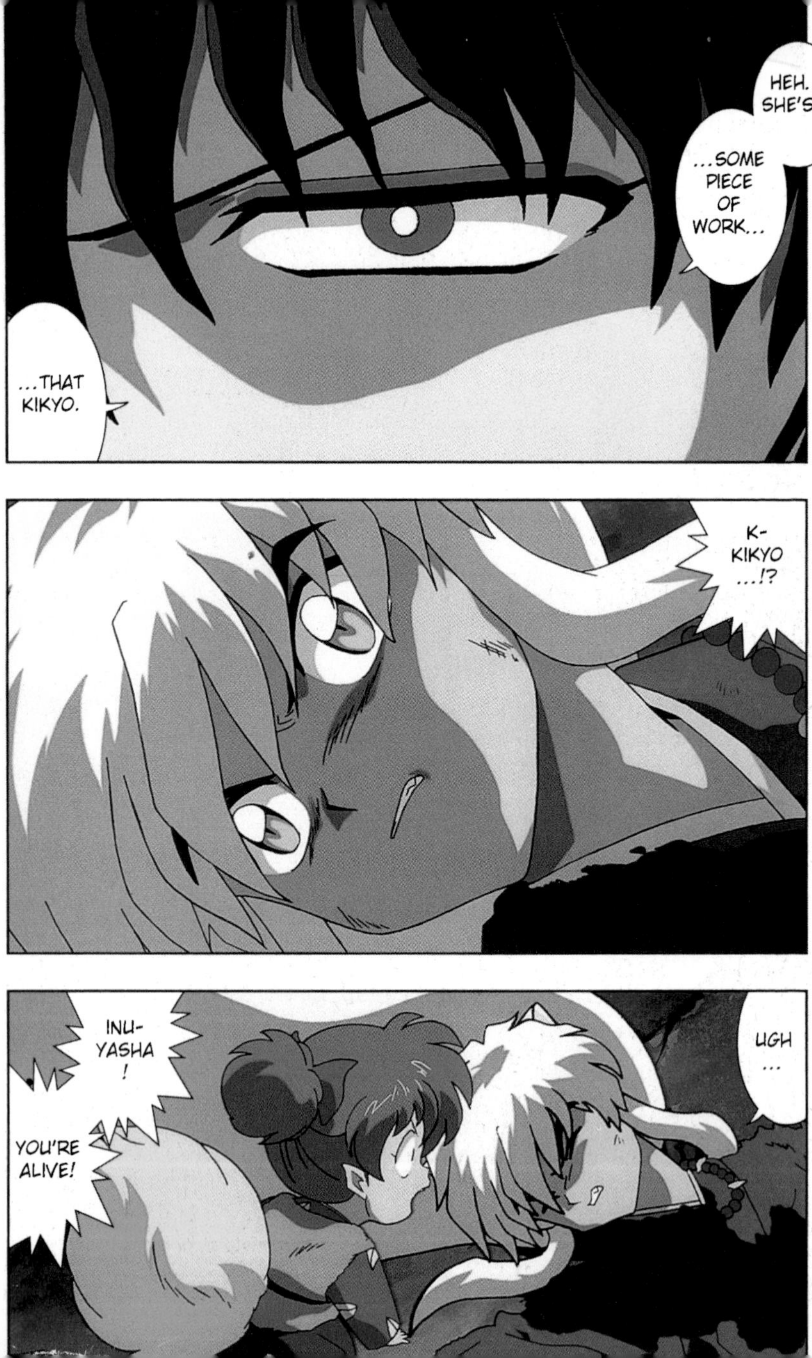
HEH... SHE'S...
...SOME PIECE OF WORK...
...THAT KIKYO.
K-KIKYO ...!?
UGH ...
INU-YASHA !
YOU'RE ALIVE!

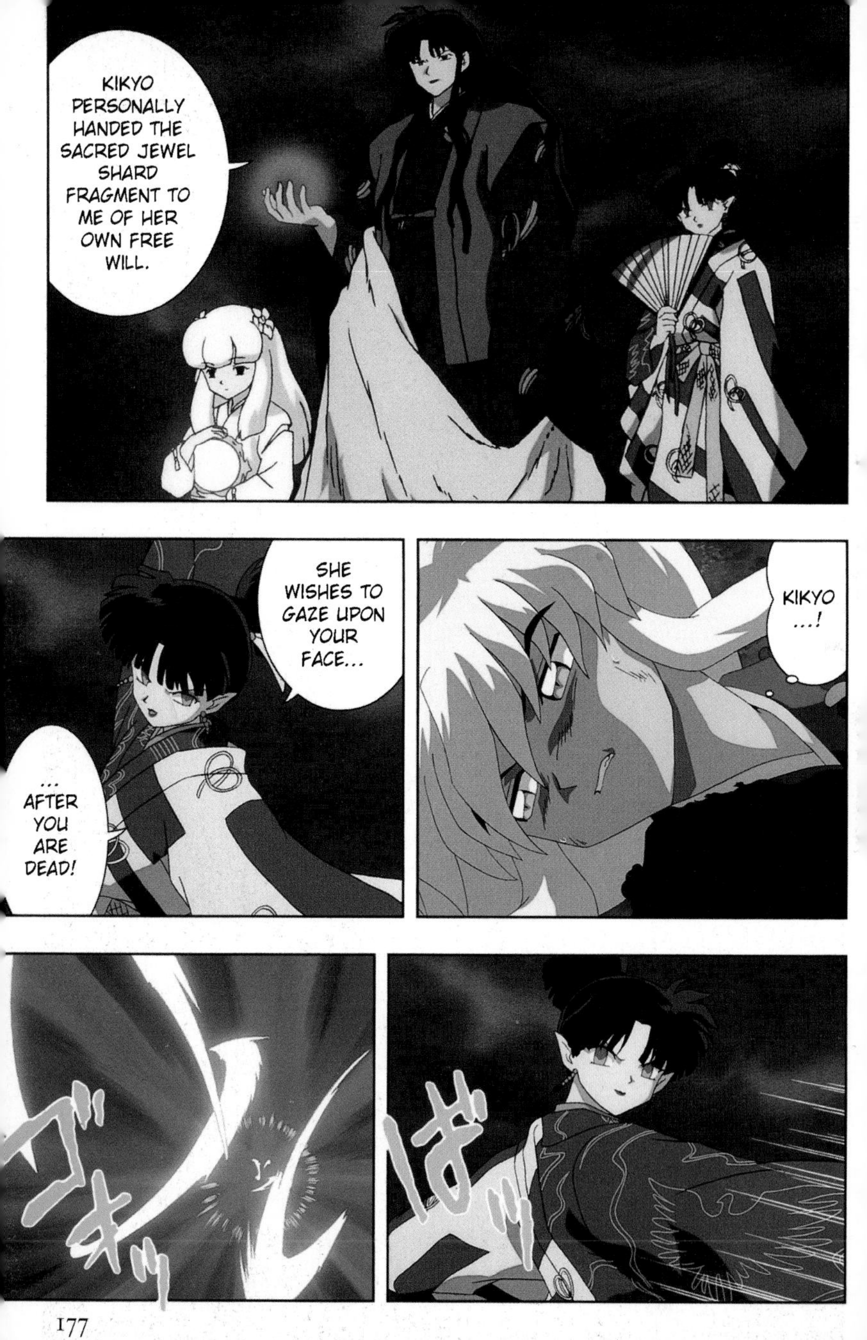
KIKYO PERSONALLY HANDED THE SACRED JEWEL SHARD FRAGMENT TO ME OF HER OWN FREE WILL.
SHE WISHES TO GAZE UPON YOUR FACE...
KIKYO ...!
... AFTER YOU ARE DEAD!
ゴキッ
ばッ

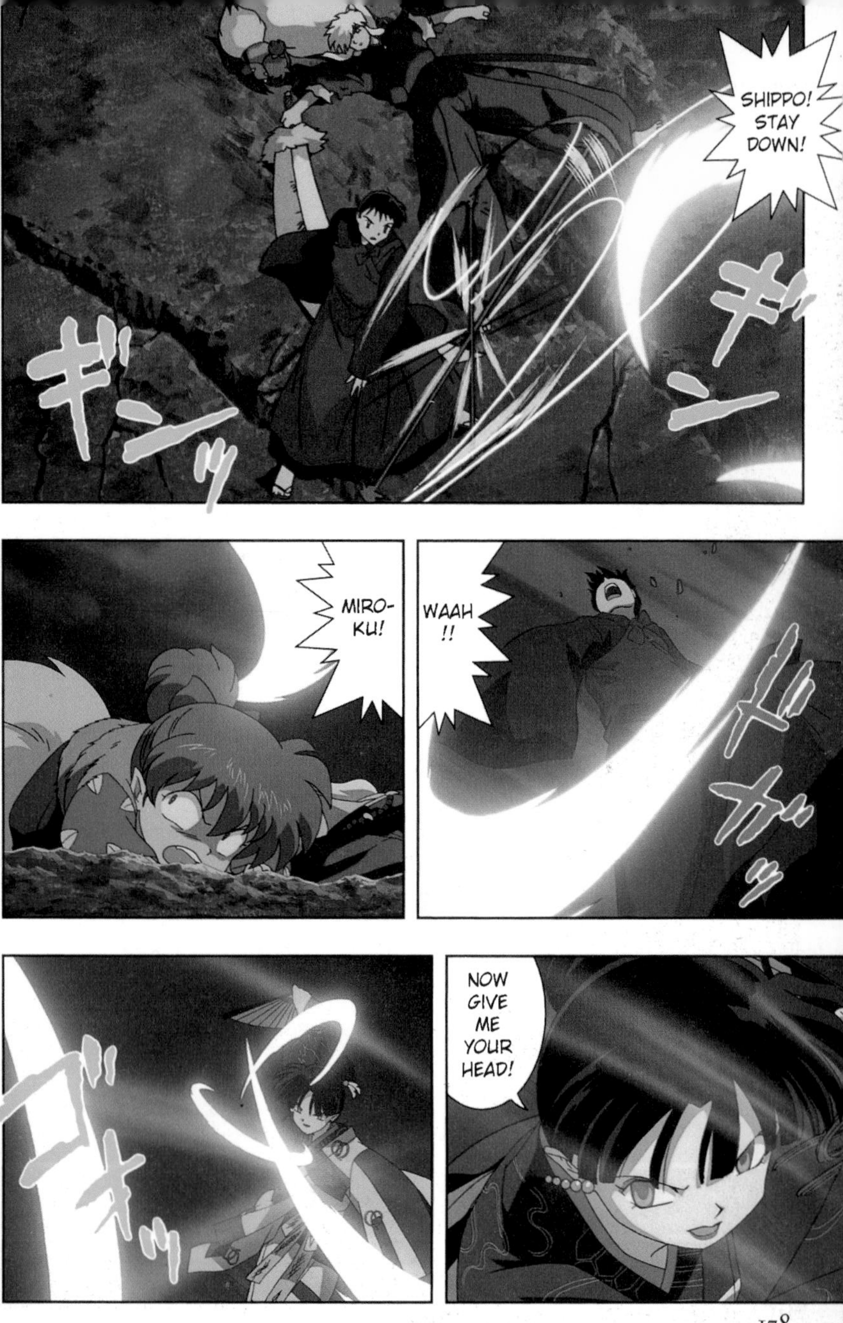
SHIPPO! STAY DOWN!
ギーン
ギンッ
WAAH!!
ドガッ
MIRO-KU!
NOW GIVE ME YOUR HEAD!
ゴオッ

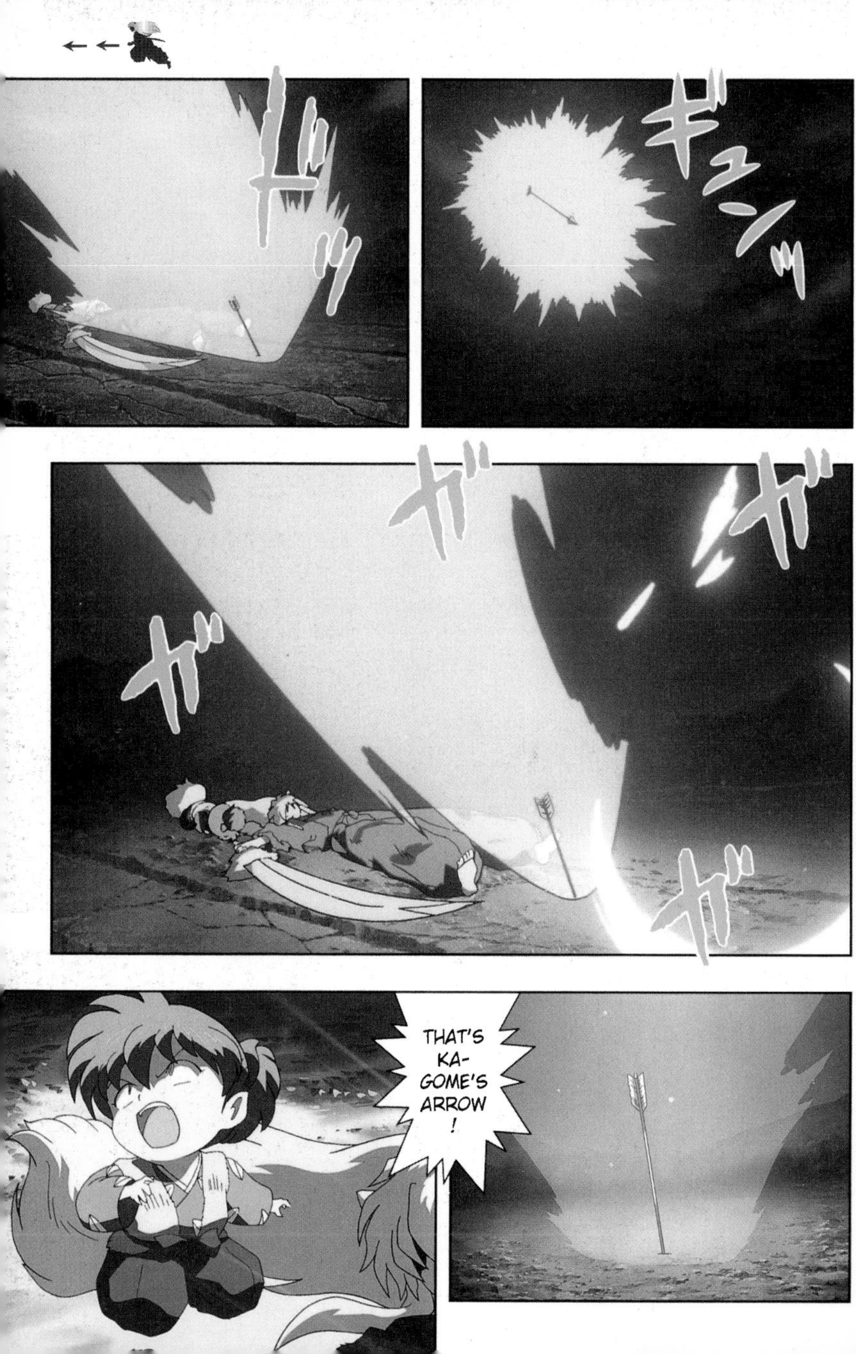
ドッ
ギュンッ
ガ
ガ
ガ
ガ
THAT'S KA-GOME'S ARROW!

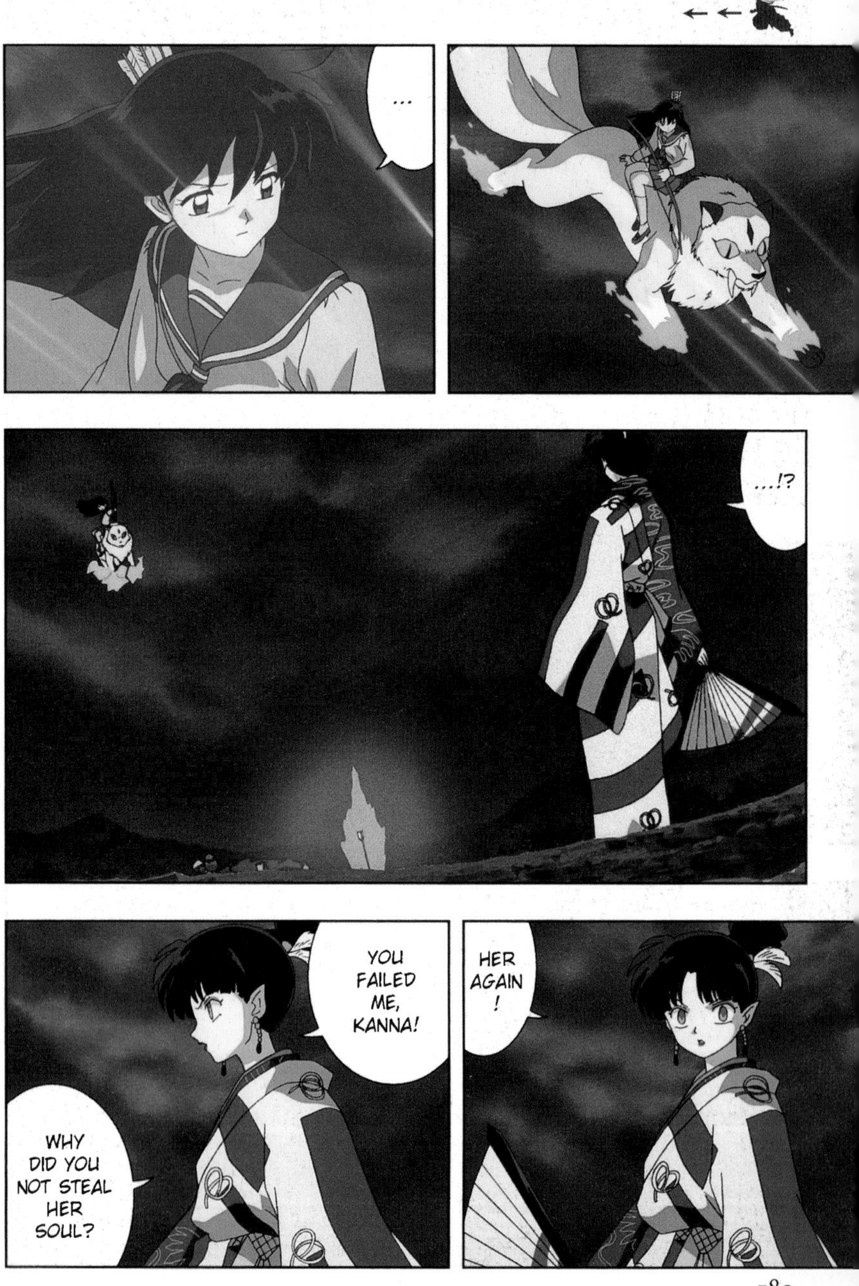
...
...!?
HER AGAIN!
YOU FAILED ME, KANNA!
WHY DID YOU NOT STEAL HER SOUL?

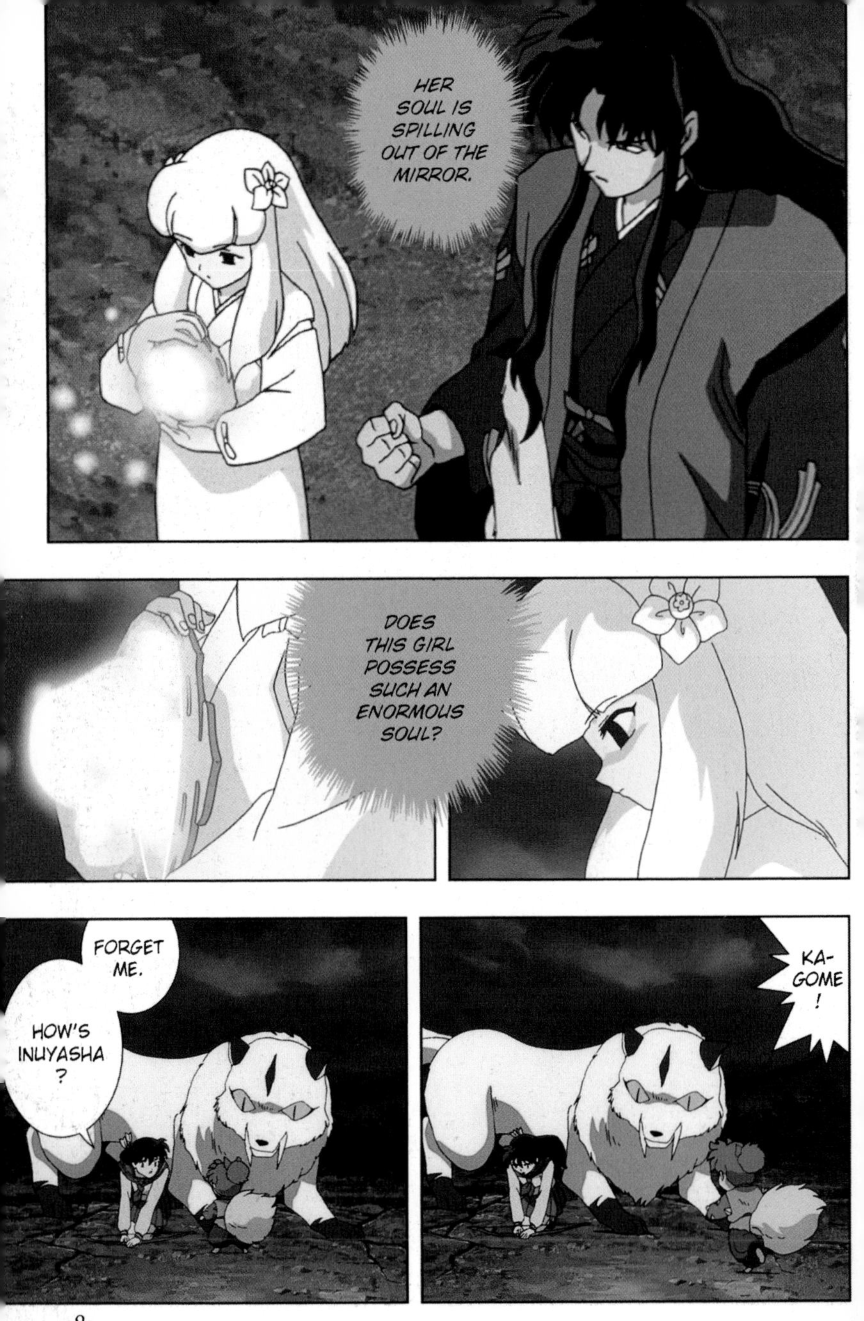
HER SOUL IS SPILLING OUT OF THE MIRROR.
DOES THIS GIRL POSSESS SUCH AN ENORMOUS SOUL?
FORGET ME.
HOW'S INUYASHA?
KA-GOME!

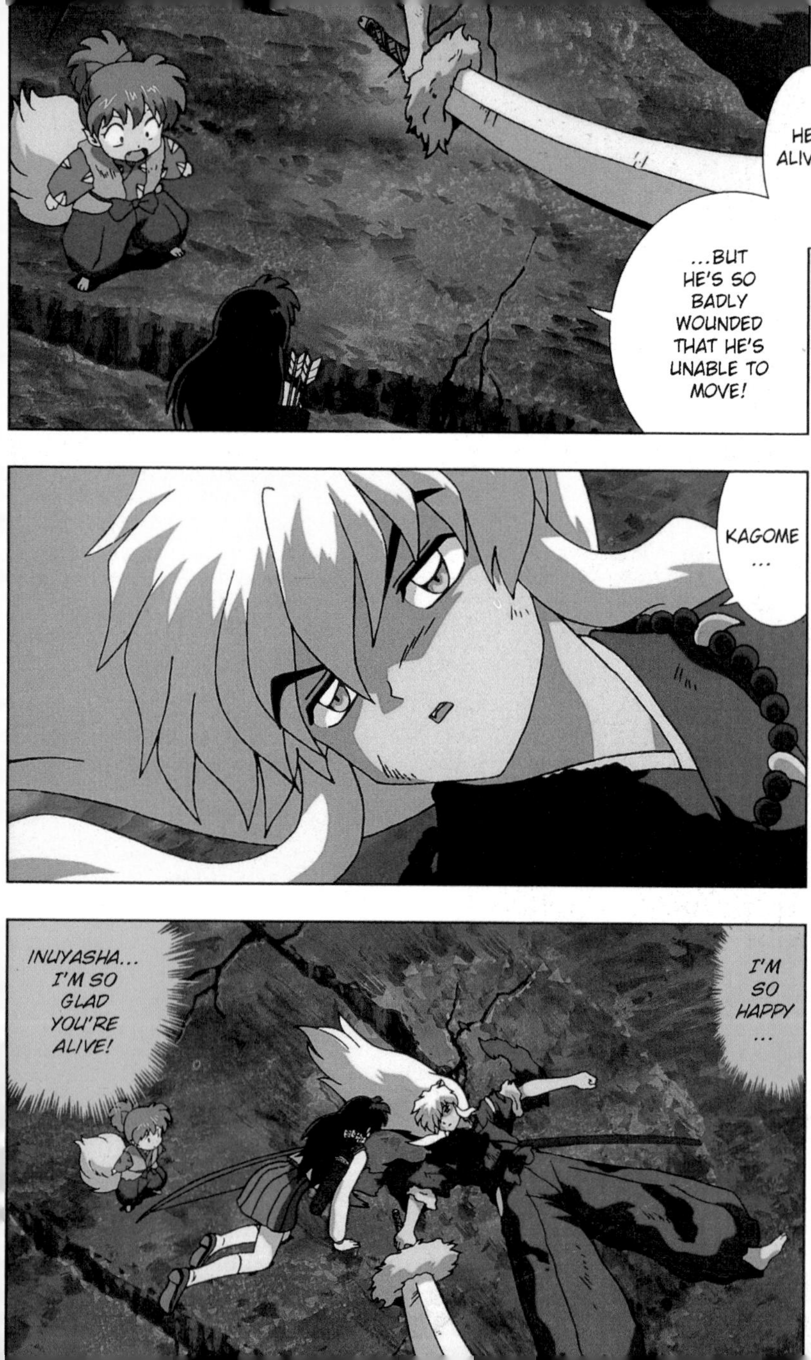
HE'S ALIVE...
...BUT HE'S SO BADLY WOUNDED THAT HE'S UNABLE TO MOVE!
KAGOME ...
I'M SO HAPPY ...
INUYASHA... I'M SO GLAD YOU'RE ALIVE!

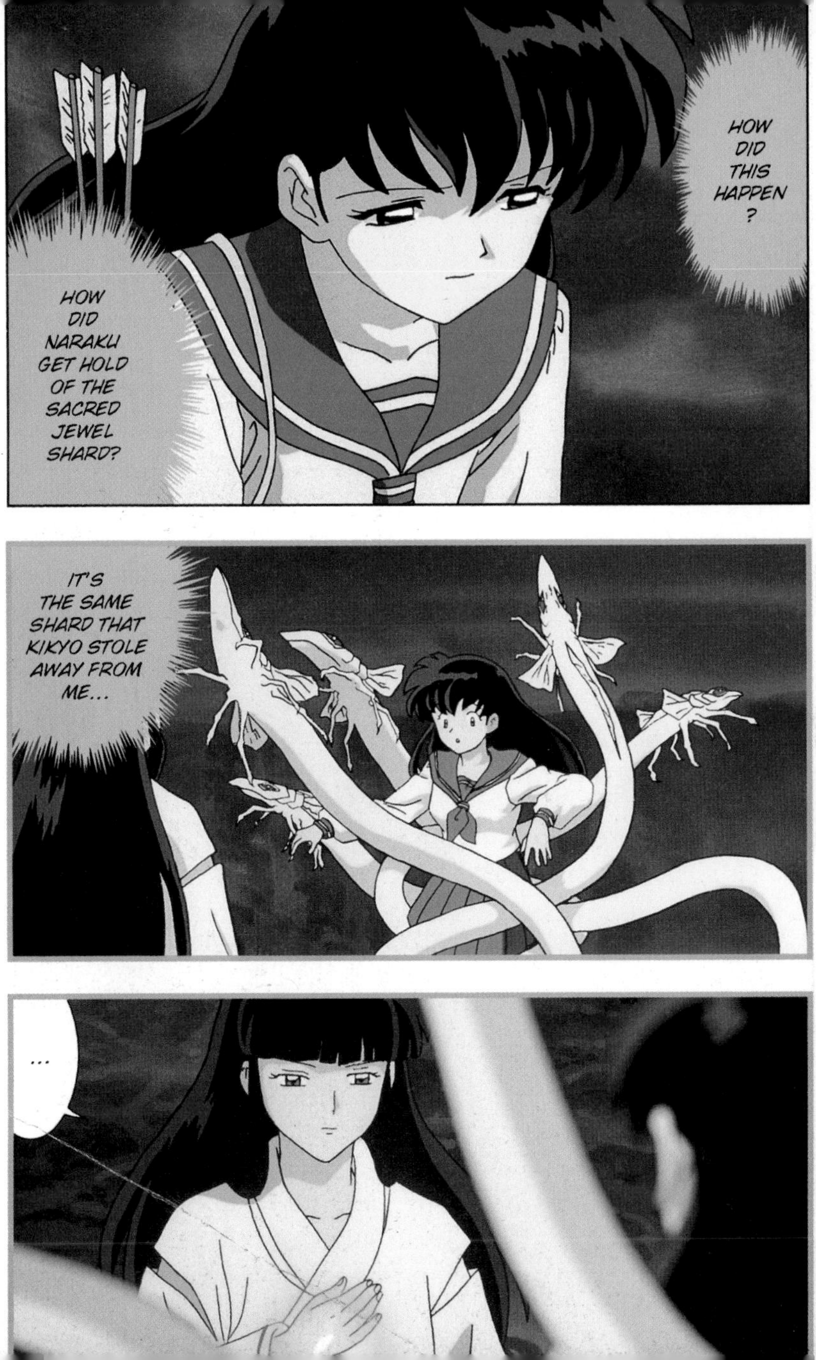
HOW DID THIS HAPPEN?
HOW DID NARAKU GET HOLD OF THE SACRED JEWEL SHARD?
IT'S THE SAME SHARD THAT KIKYO STOLE AWAY FROM ME...
...

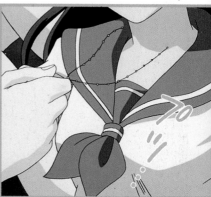

WAS IT KIKYO WHO GAVE IT TO NARAKU?

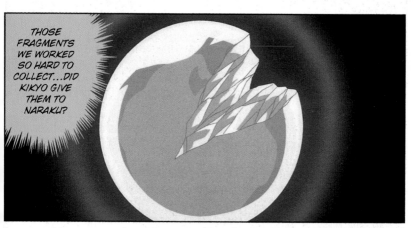

THOSE FRAGMENTS WE WORKED SO HARD TO COLLECT...DID KIKYO GIVE THEM TO NARAKU?

BUT...

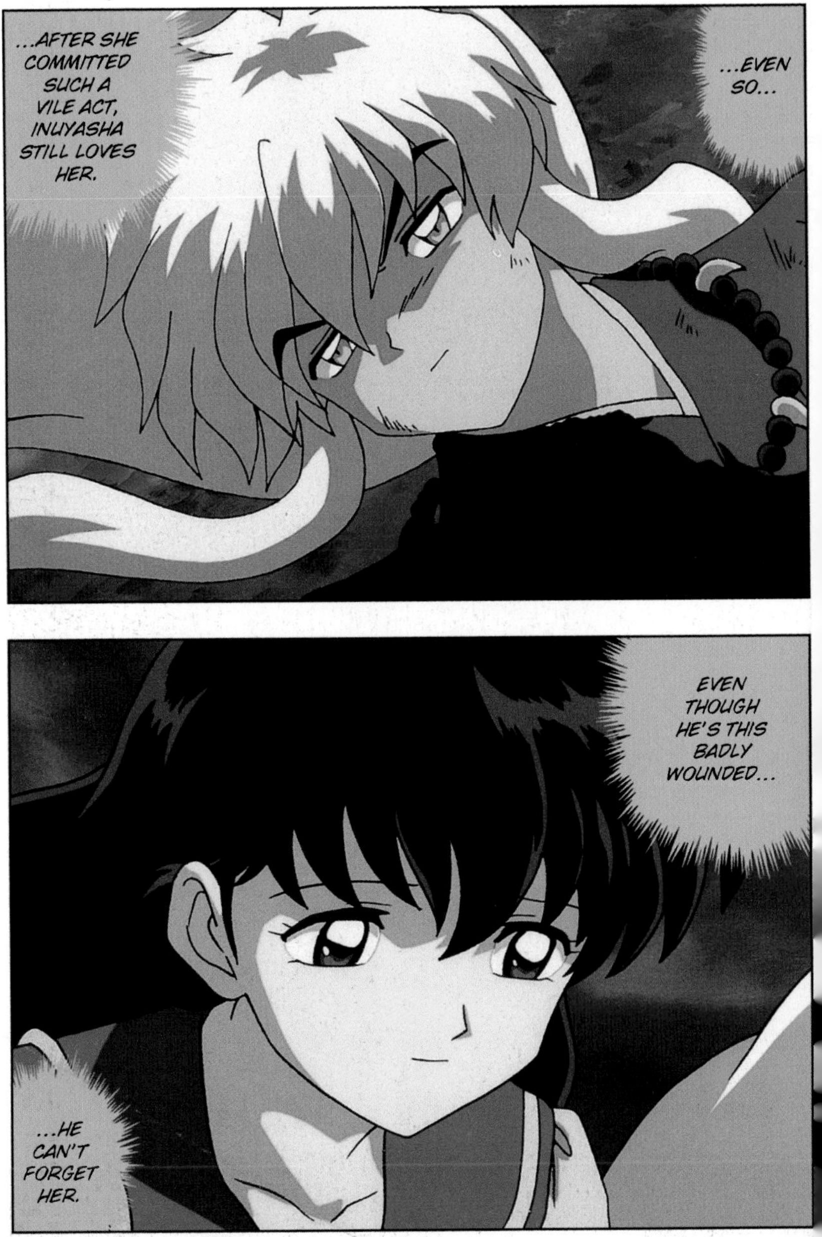
...EVEN SO...
...AFTER SHE COMMITTED SUCH A VILE ACT, INUYASHA STILL LOVES HER.
EVEN THOUGH HE'S THIS BADLY WOUNDED...
...HE CAN'T FORGET HER.

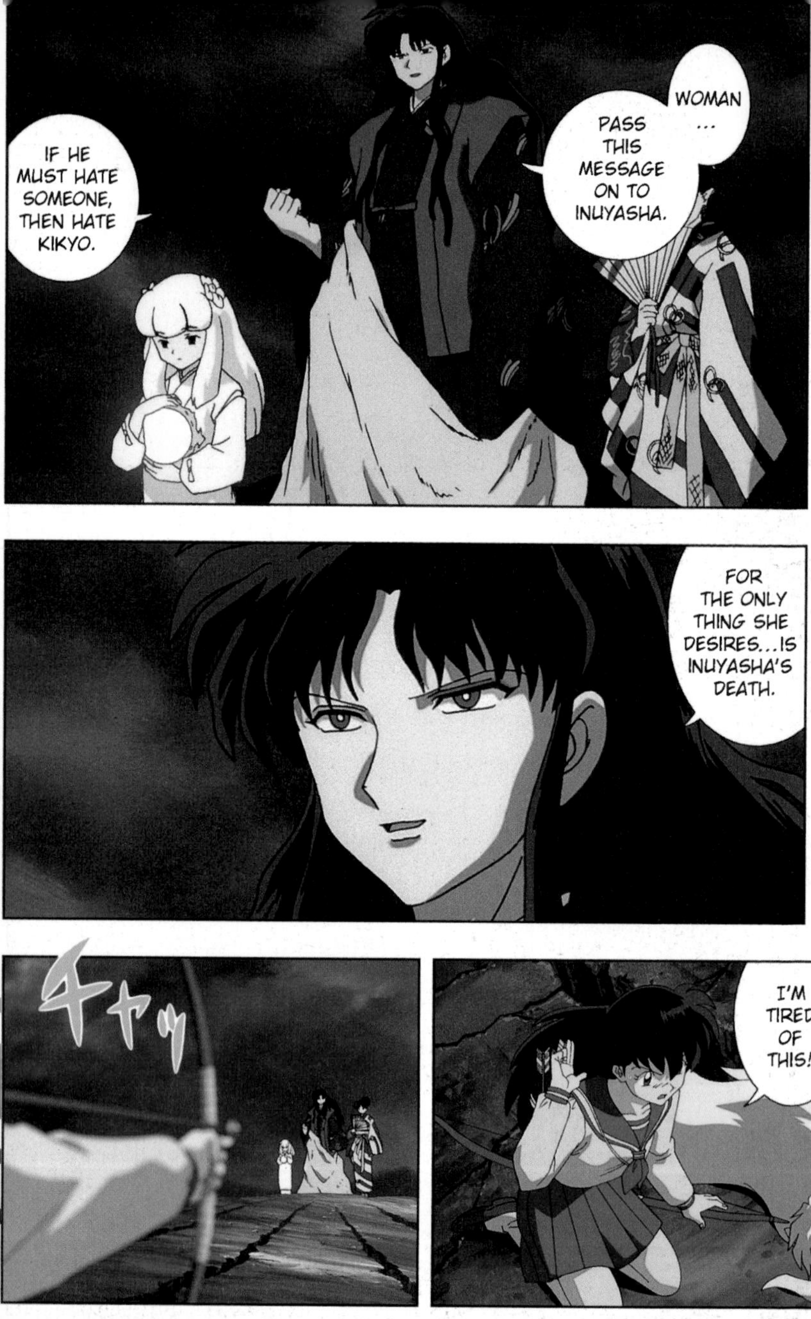
WOMAN ...
PASS THIS MESSAGE ON TO INUYASHA.
IF HE MUST HATE SOMEONE, THEN HATE KIKYO.
FOR THE ONLY THING SHE DESIRES...IS INUYASHA'S DEATH.
I'M TIRED OF THIS!
キャッ

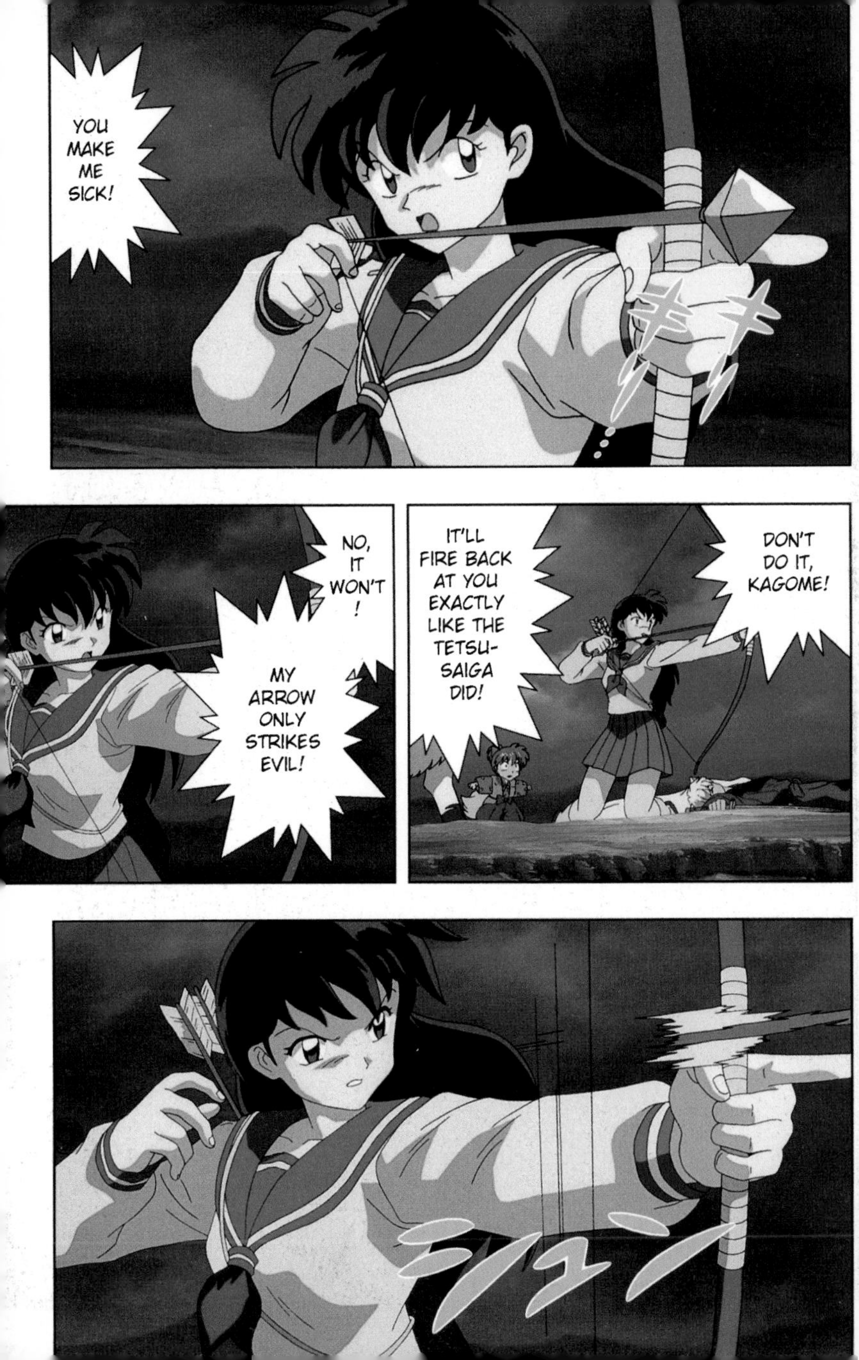
YOU MAKE ME SICK!
DON'T DO IT, KAGOME!
IT'LL FIRE BACK AT YOU EXACTLY LIKE THE TETSU-SAIGA DID!
NO, IT WON'T!
MY ARROW ONLY STRIKES EVIL!

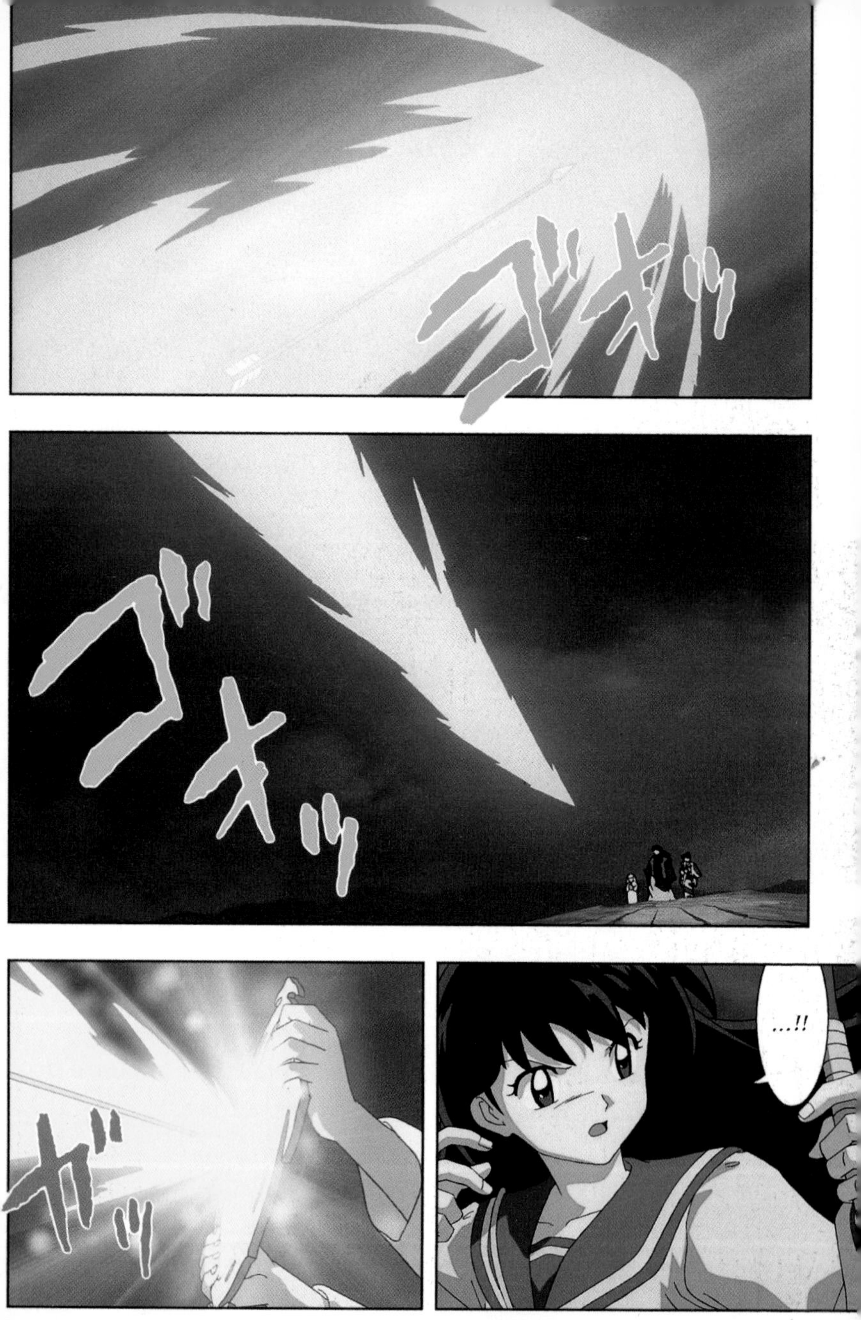
ゴォッ
ゴォッ
ザッ
...!!

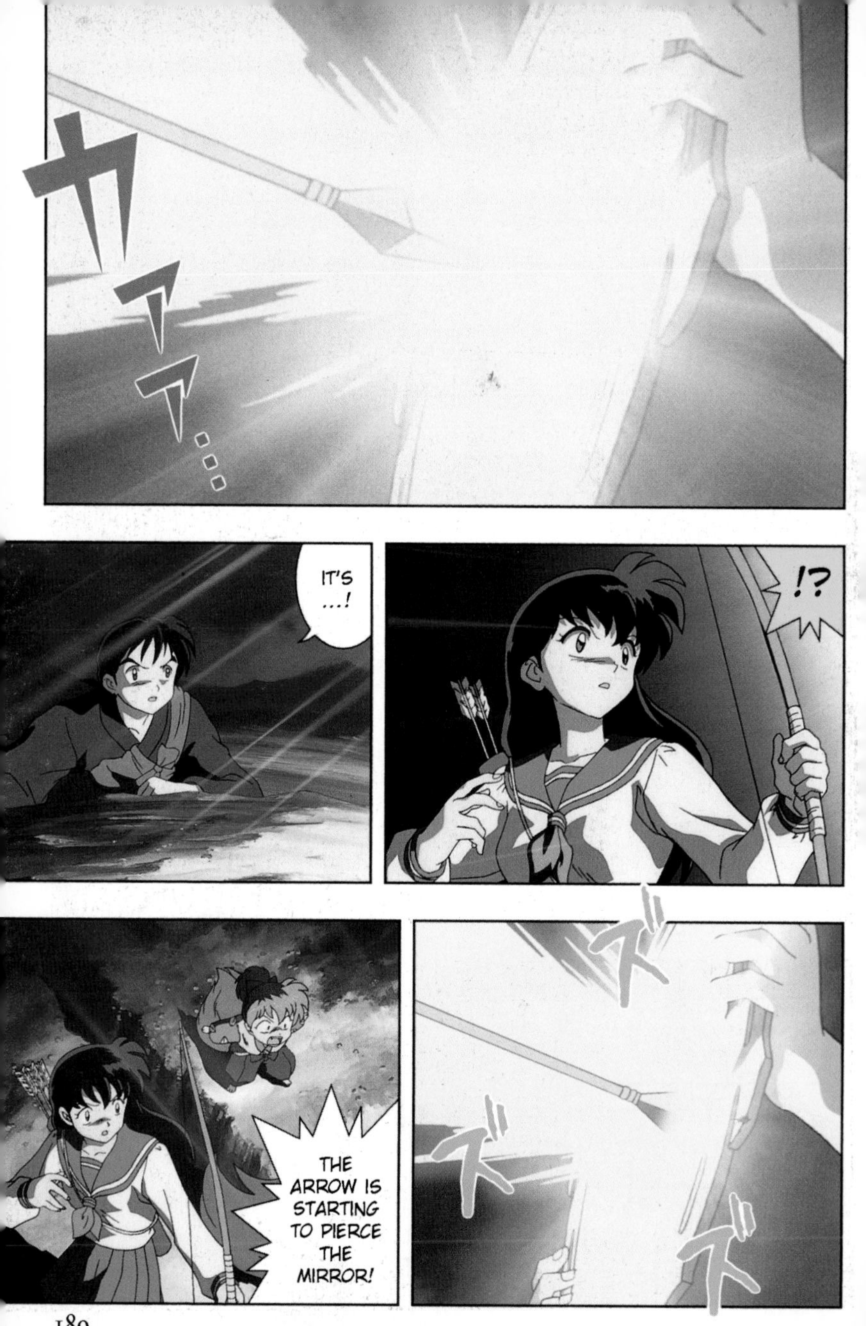
カァァ…
!?
IT'S ...!
ズズズ
THE ARROW IS STARTING TO PIERCE THE MIRROR!

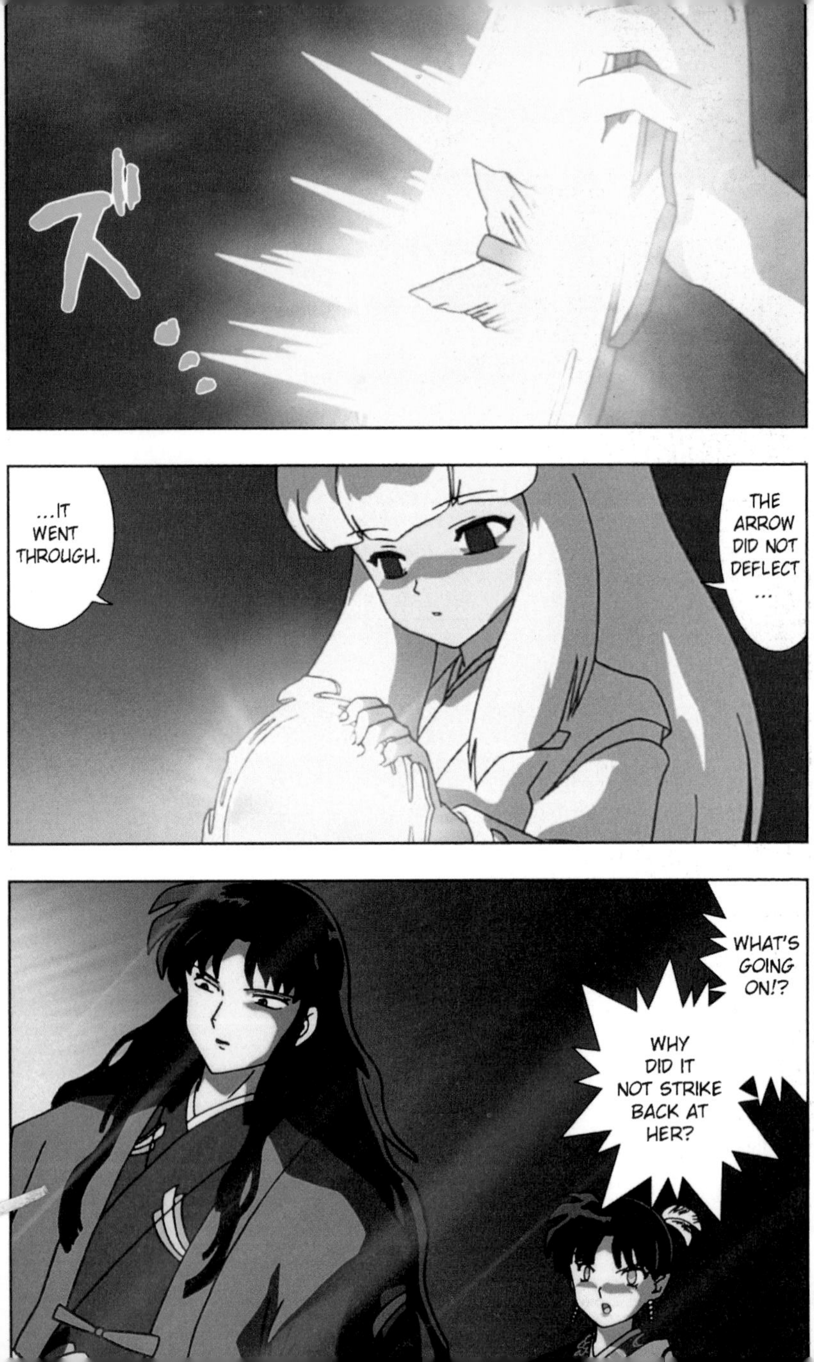
ズ
THE ARROW DID NOT DEFLECT ...
...IT WENT THROUGH.
WHAT'S GOING ON!?
WHY DID IT NOT STRIKE BACK AT HER?

I UNDER-
STAND.

THE
ARROW
IS MADE
UP OF
SOULS.

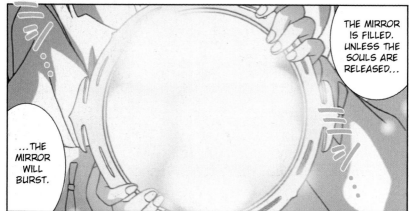

THE MIRROR
IS FILLED.
UNLESS THE
SOULS ARE
RELEASED...

...THE
MIRROR
WILL
BURST.

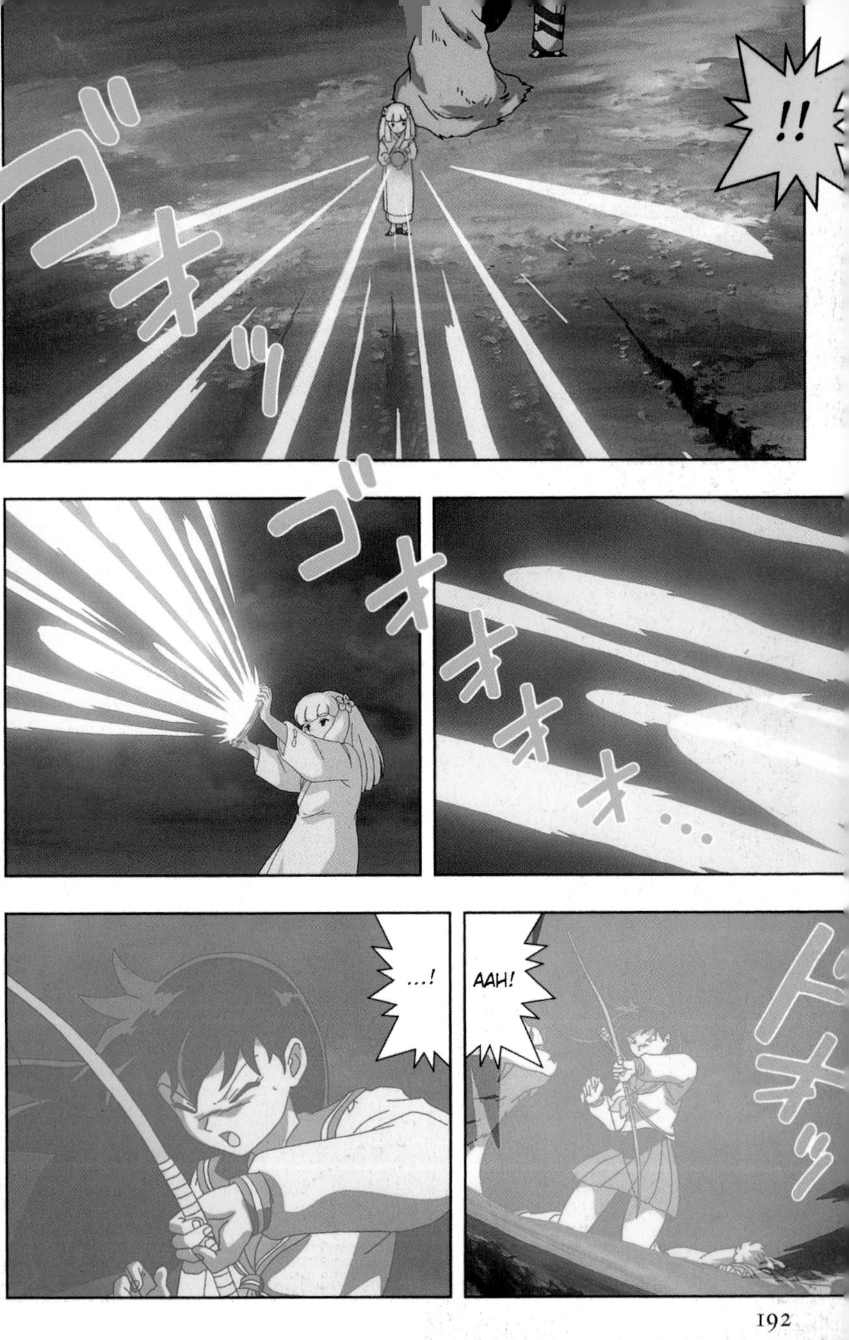
!!
ゴオッ
ゴオオオオ…
AAH!
ドキッ
...!

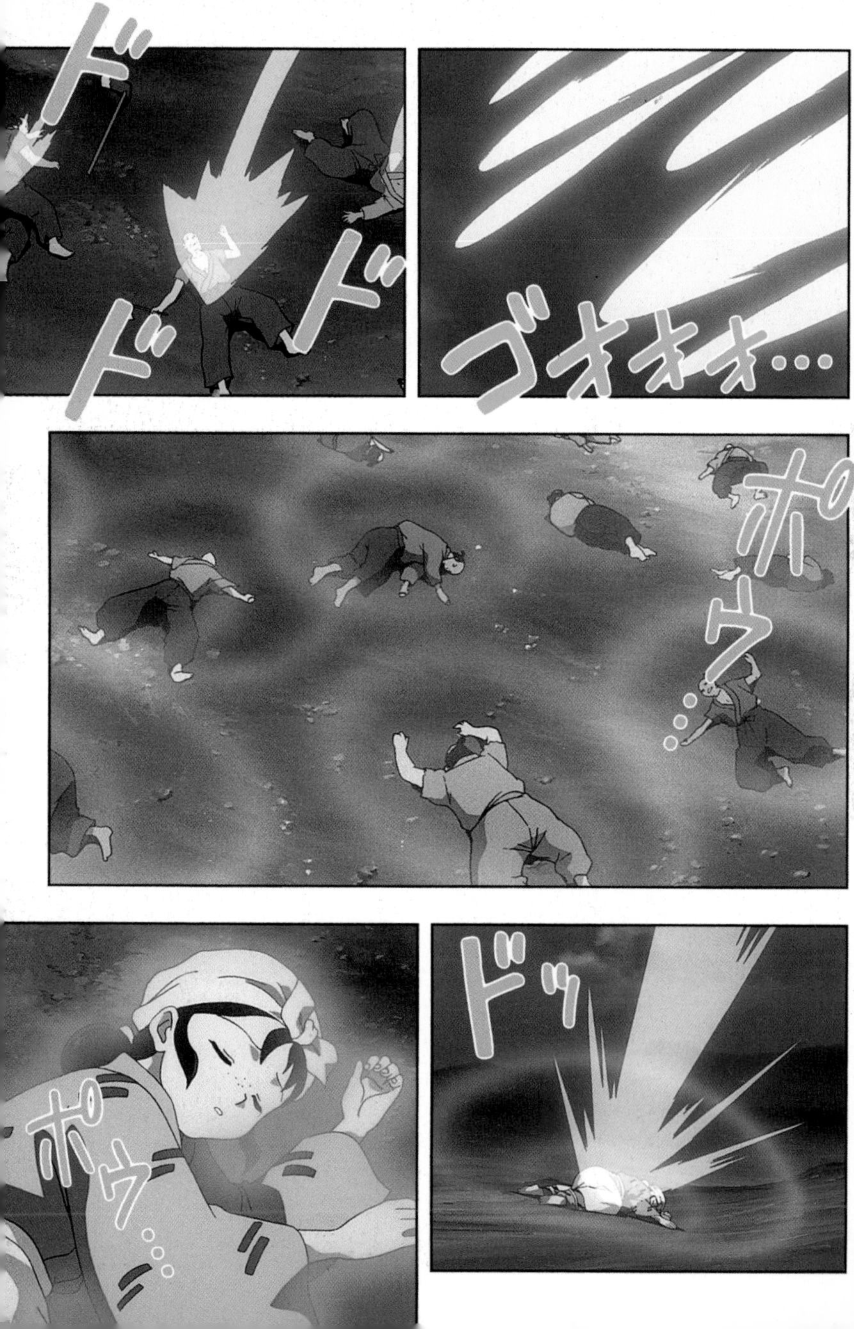
ゴオォォ…
ドドド
ポゥ…
ドッ
ポゥ…

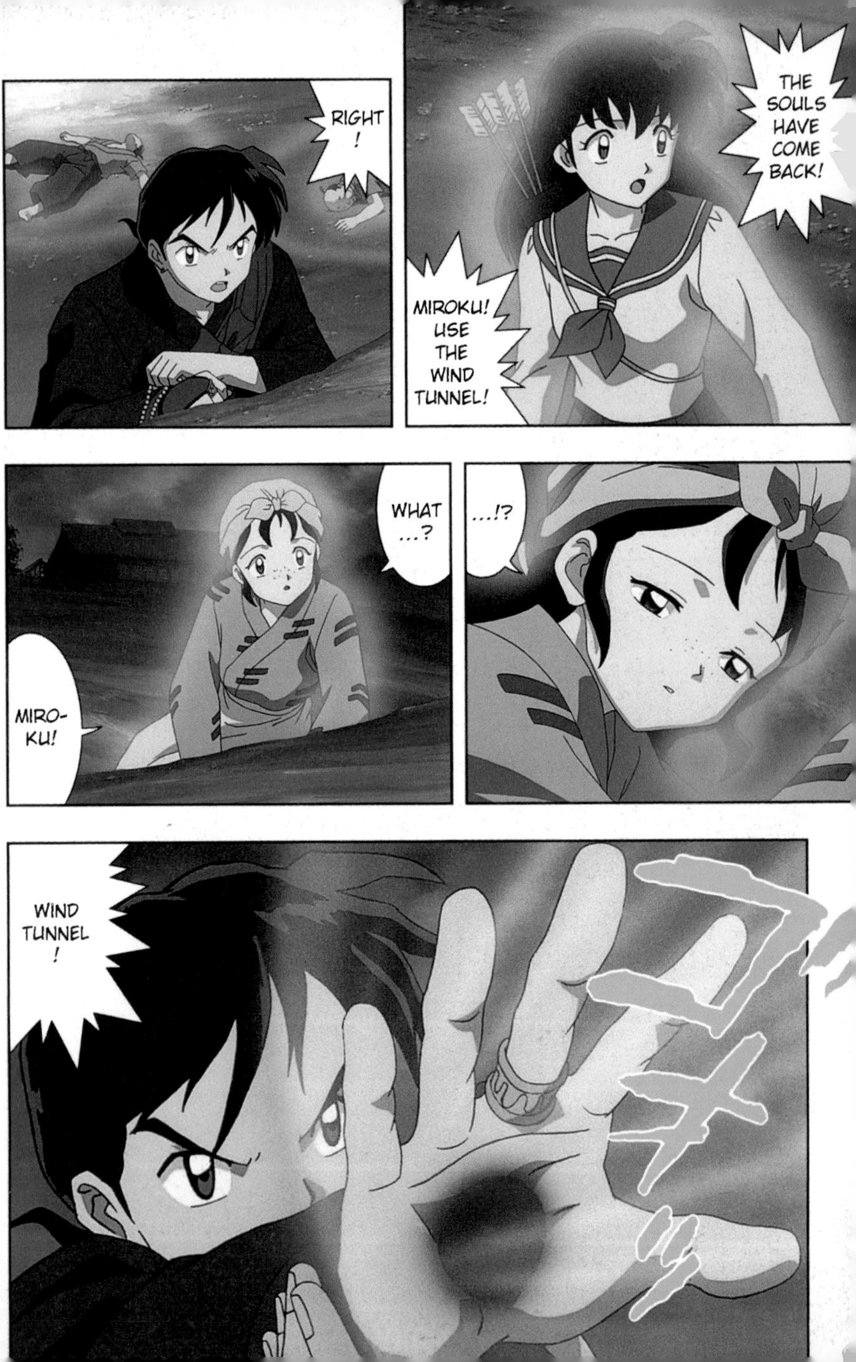
THE SOULS HAVE COME BACK!
MIROKU! USE THE WIND TUNNEL!
RIGHT!
...!?
WHAT...?
MIRO-KU!
WIND TUNNEL!

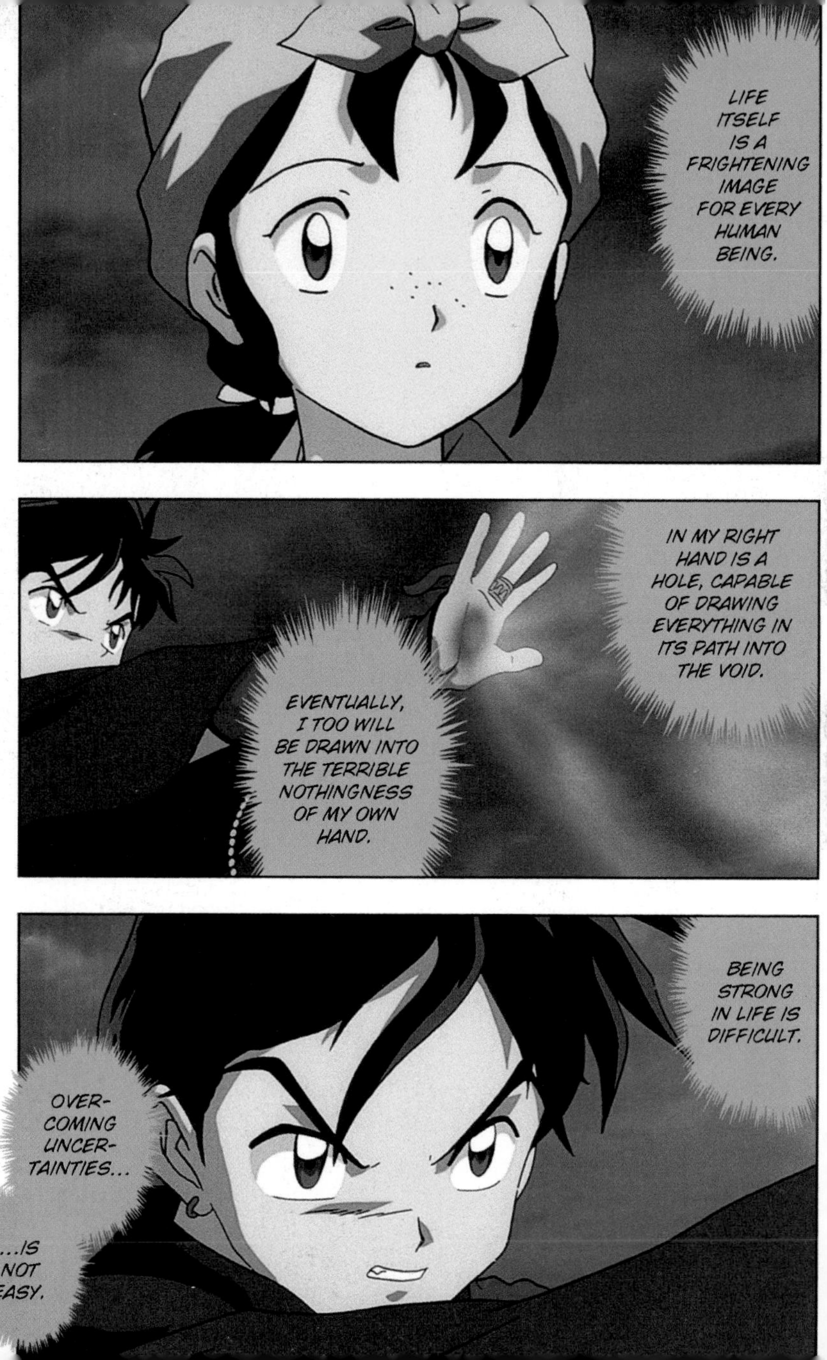
LIFE ITSELF IS A FRIGHTENING IMAGE FOR EVERY HUMAN BEING.
IN MY RIGHT HAND IS A HOLE, CAPABLE OF DRAWING EVERYTHING IN ITS PATH INTO THE VOID.
EVENTUALLY, I TOO WILL BE DRAWN INTO THE TERRIBLE NOTHINGNESS OF MY OWN HAND.
BEING STRONG IN LIFE IS DIFFICULT.
OVER-COMING UNCER-TAINTIES...
...IS NOT EASY.

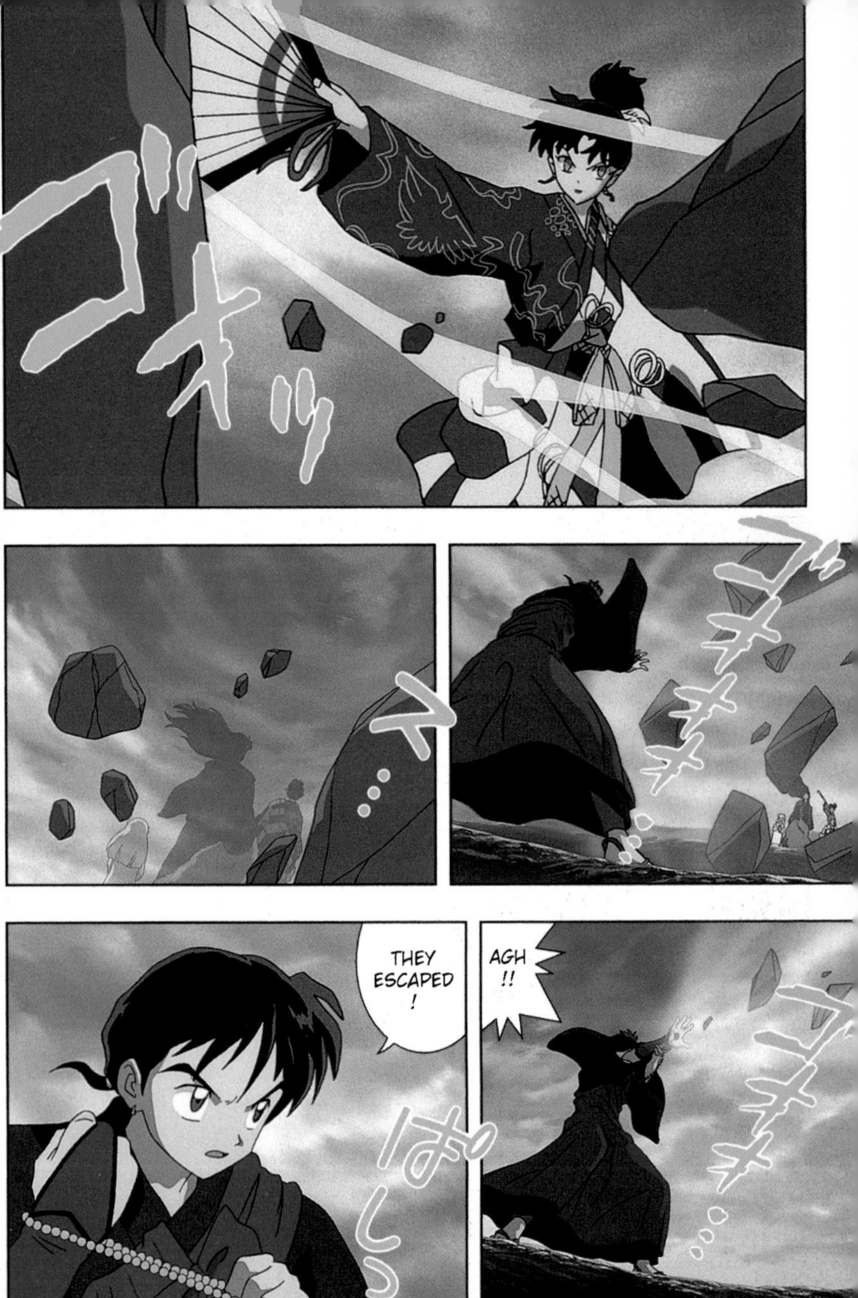
AGH !!
THEY ESCAPED !

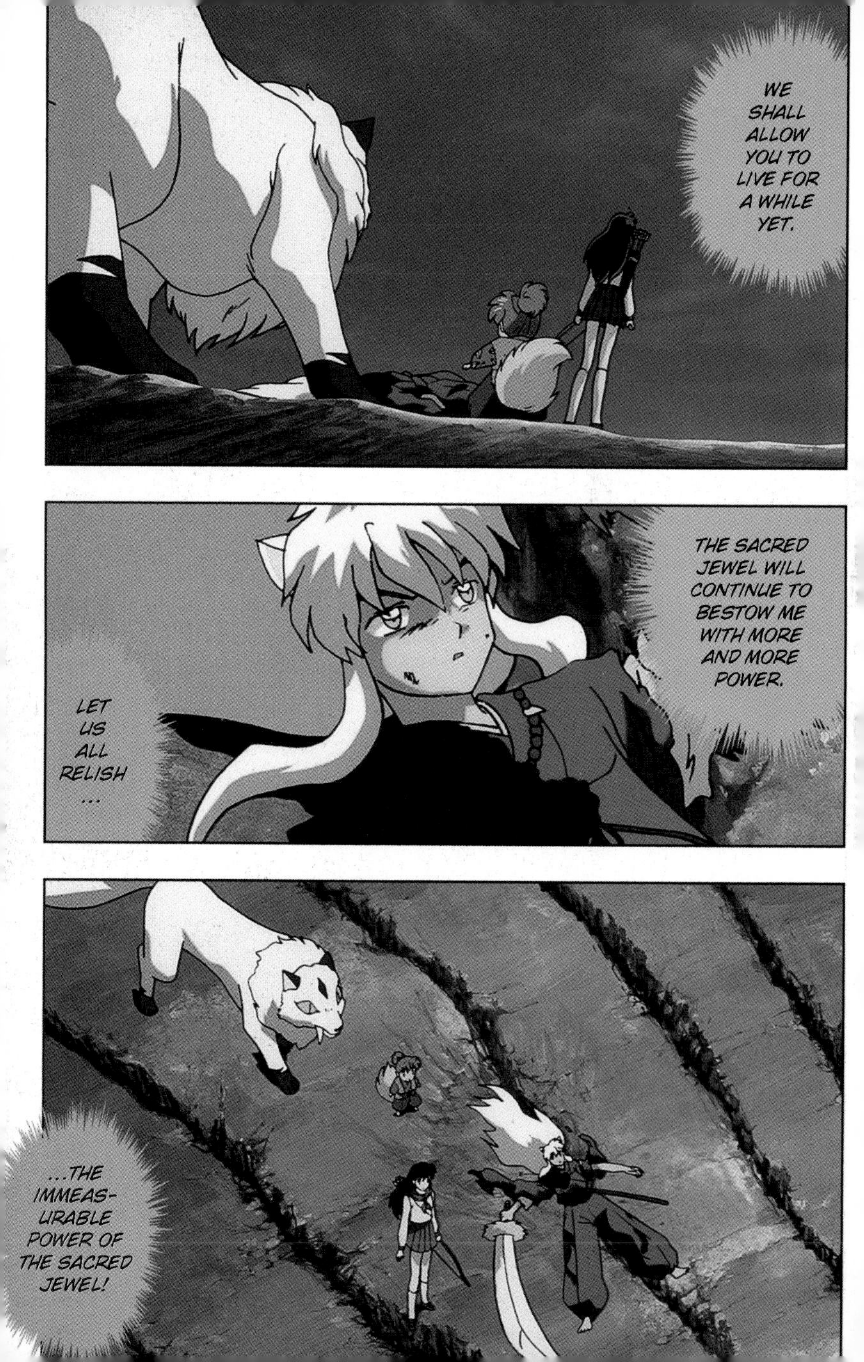
WE SHALL ALLOW YOU TO LIVE FOR A WHILE YET.
THE SACRED JEWEL WILL CONTINUE TO BESTOW ME WITH MORE AND MORE POWER.
LET US ALL RELISH ...
...THE IMMEAS-URABLE POWER OF THE SACRED JEWEL!

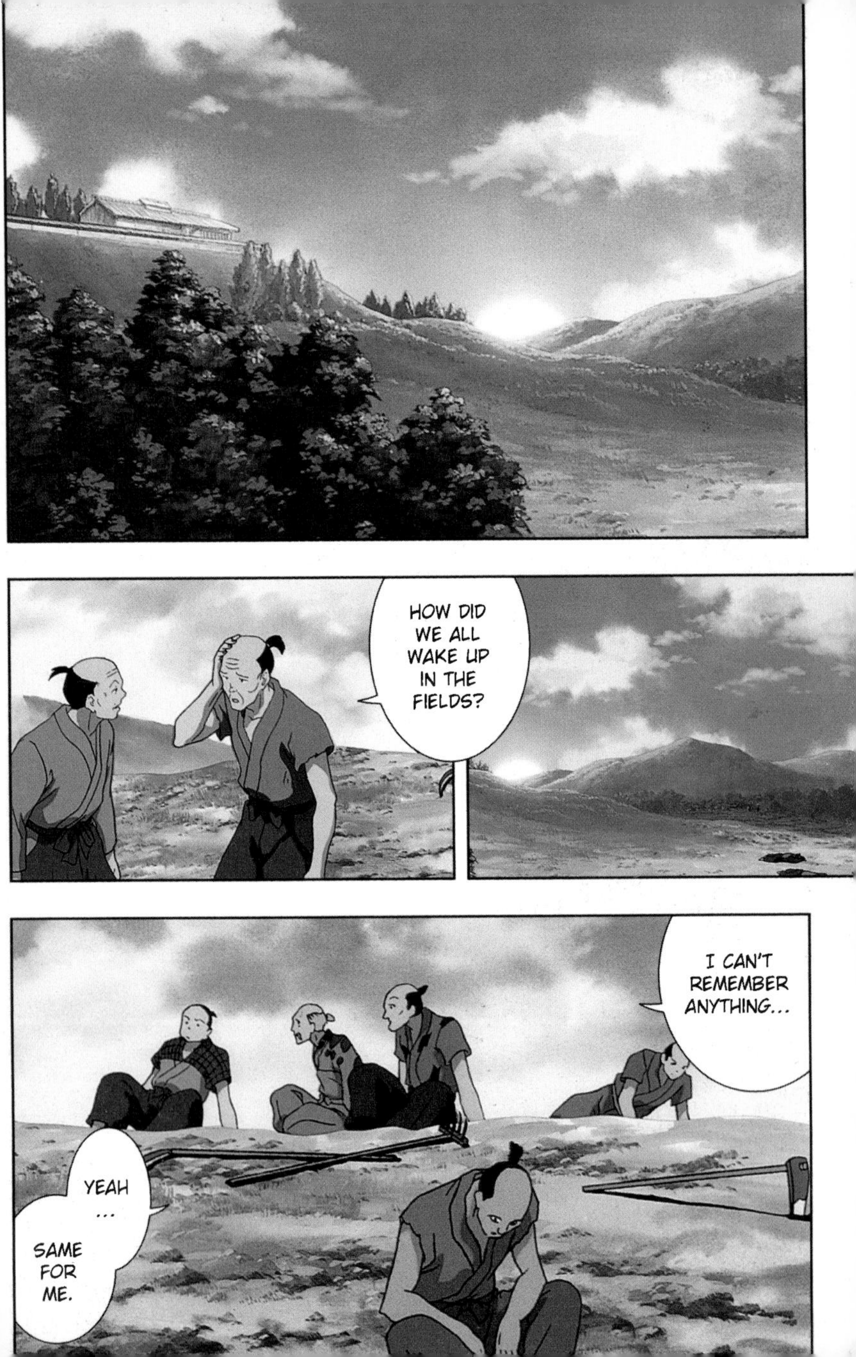
HOW DID WE ALL WAKE UP IN THE FIELDS?
I CAN'T REMEMBER ANYTHING...
YEAH ... SAME FOR ME.

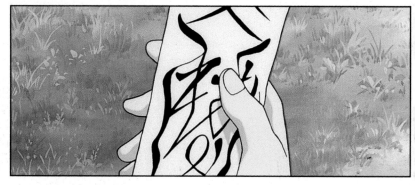

...

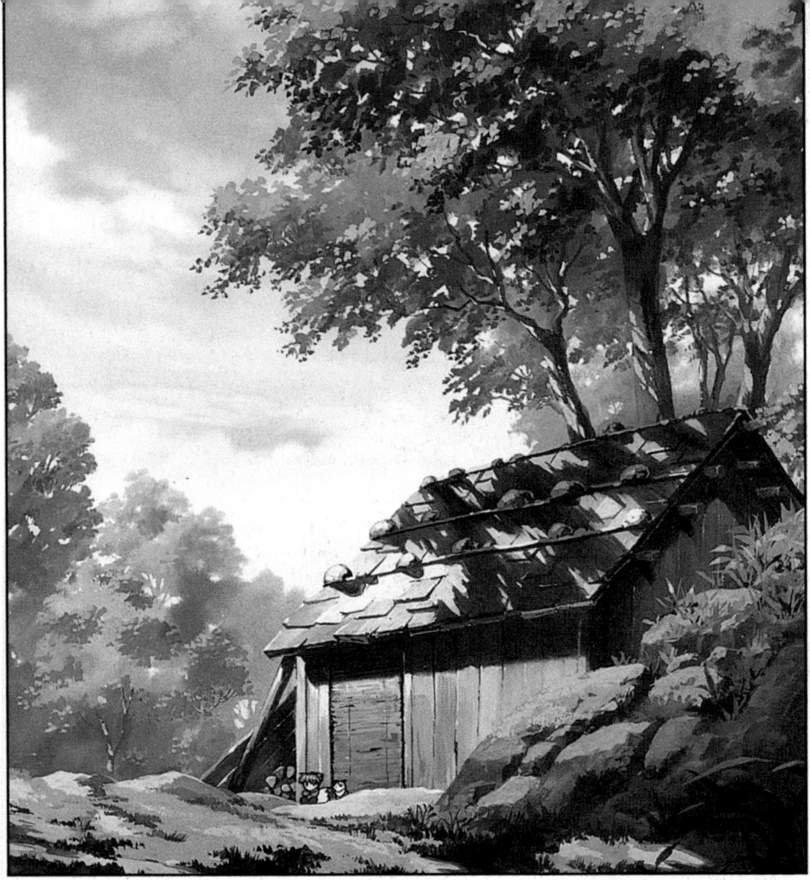

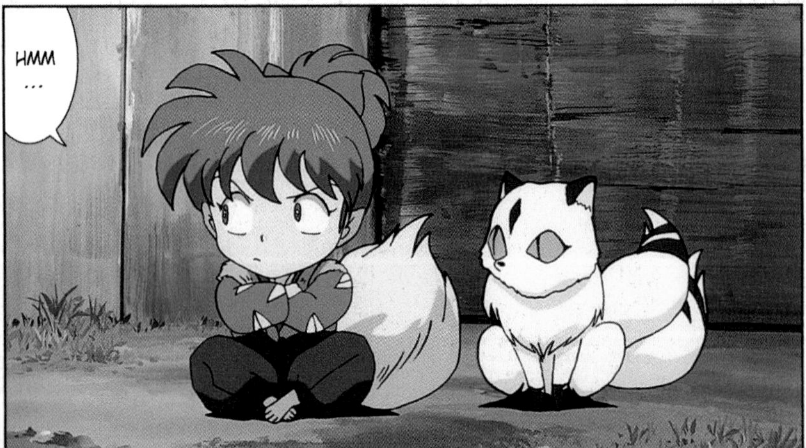
HMM
...

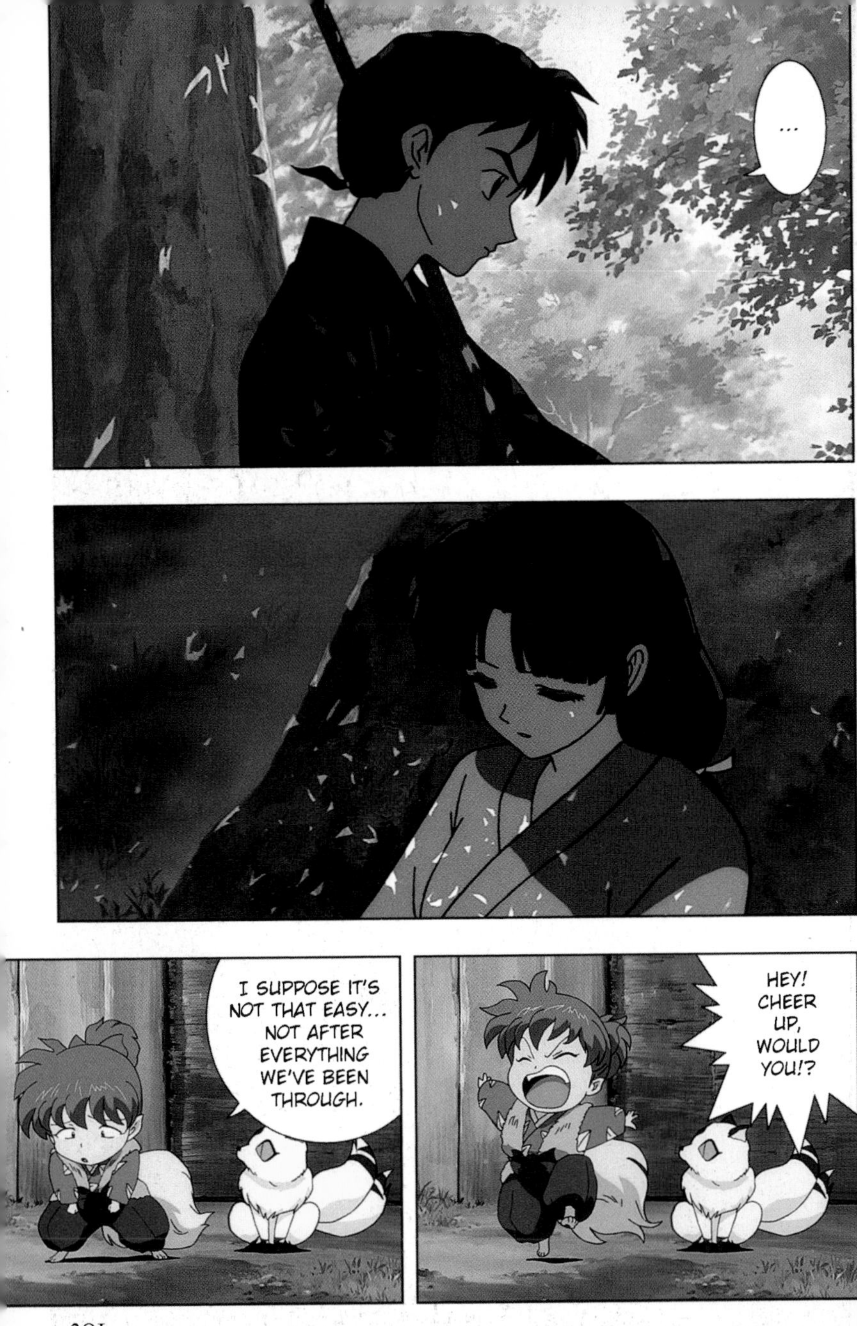
...
I SUPPOSE IT'S NOT THAT EASY... NOT AFTER EVERYTHING WE'VE BEEN THROUGH.
HEY! CHEER UP, WOULD YOU!?

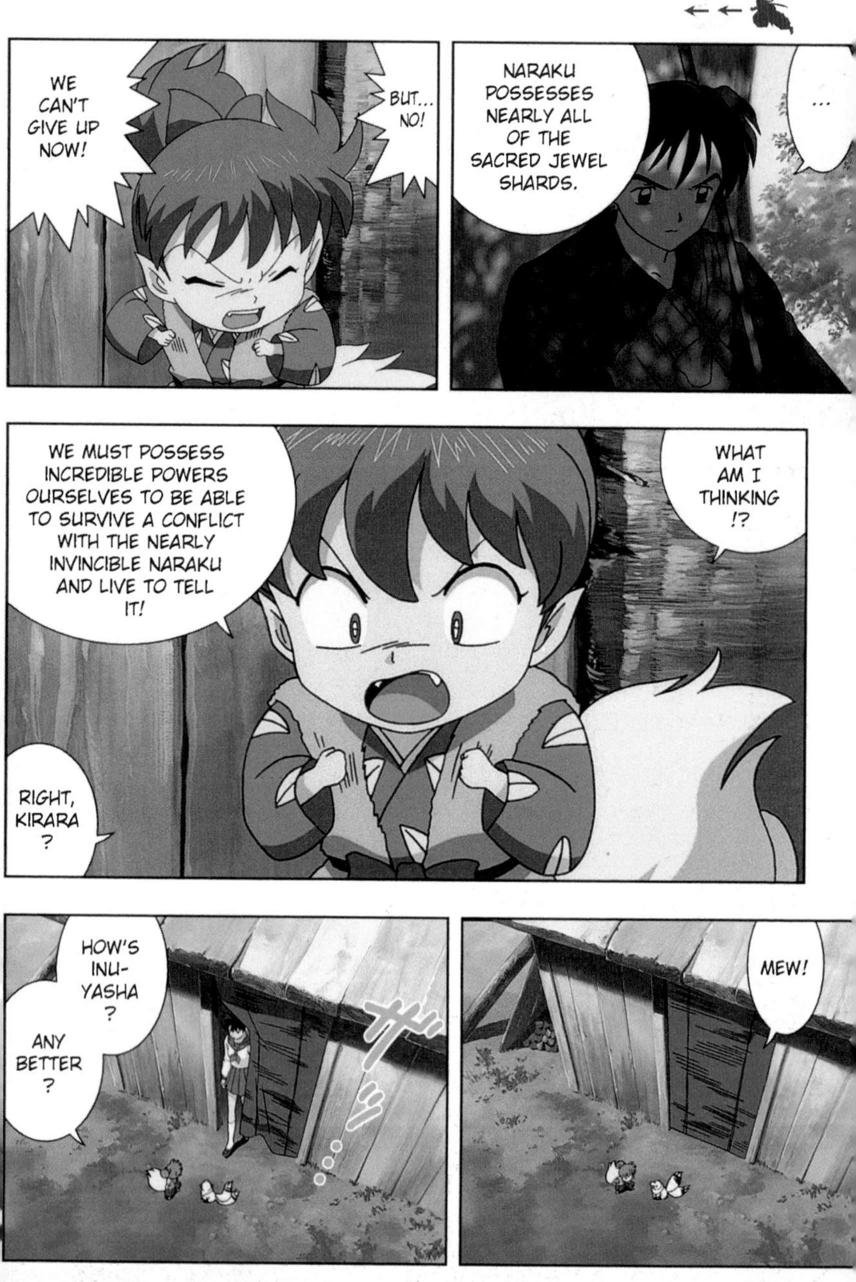
...
NARAKU POSSESSES NEARLY ALL OF THE SACRED JEWEL SHARDS.
BUT... NO!
WE CAN'T GIVE UP NOW!
WHAT AM I THINKING!?
WE MUST POSSESS INCREDIBLE POWERS OURSELVES TO BE ABLE TO SURVIVE A CONFLICT WITH THE NEARLY INVINCIBLE NARAKU AND LIVE TO TELL IT!
RIGHT, KIRARA?
MEW!
HOW'S INU-YASHA?
ANY BETTER?

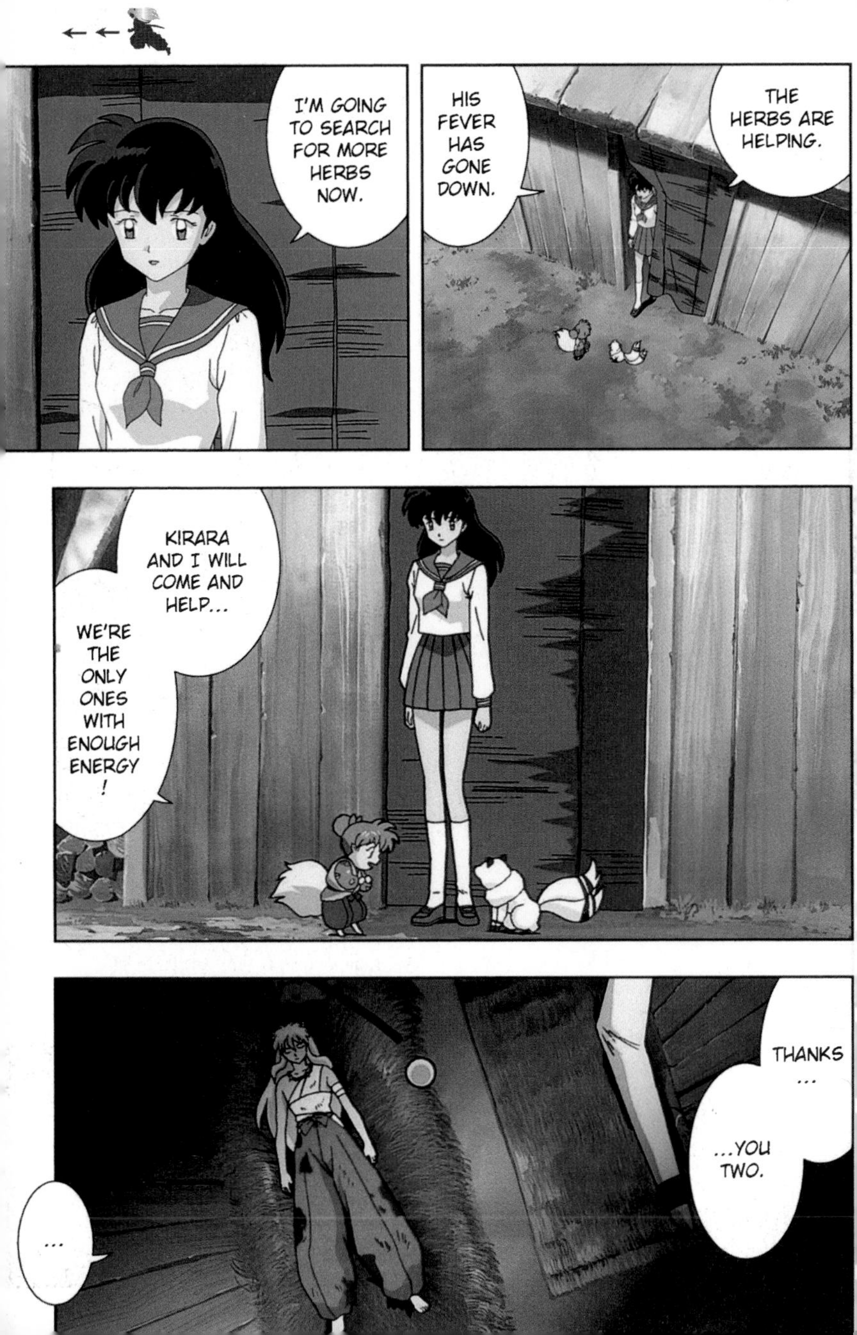
THE HERBS ARE HELPING.
HIS FEVER HAS GONE DOWN.
I'M GOING TO SEARCH FOR MORE HERBS NOW.
KIRARA AND I WILL COME AND HELP...
WE'RE THE ONLY ONES WITH ENOUGH ENERGY!
THANKS...
...YOU TWO.
...

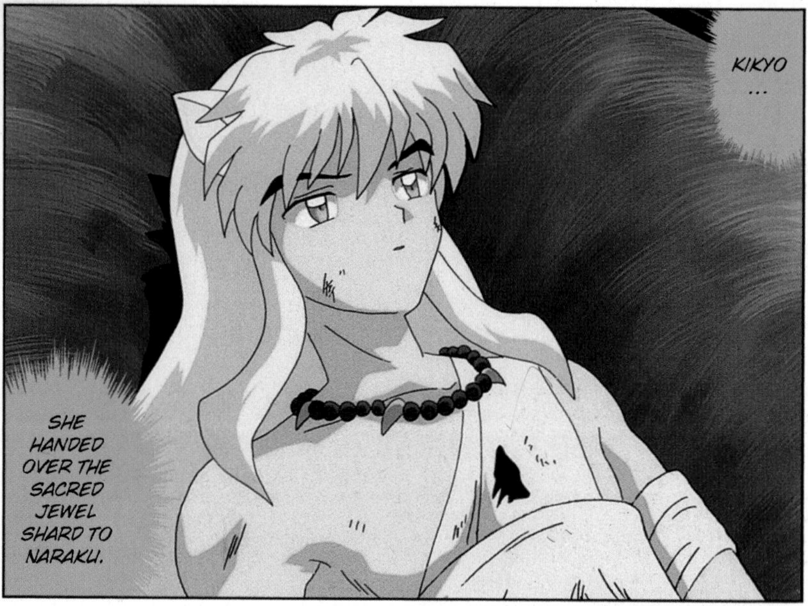
KIKYO ...
SHE HANDED OVER THE SACRED JEWEL SHARD TO NARAKU.

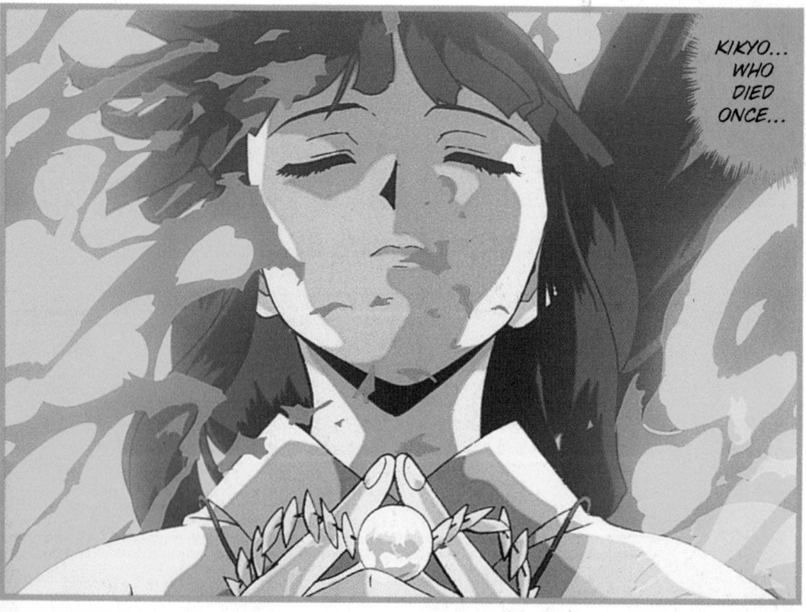
KIKYO... WHO DIED ONCE...

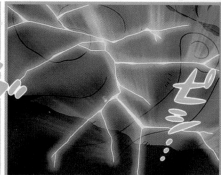

...AND THEN ROSE AGAIN.

KIKYO... WHO DESPISES ME...

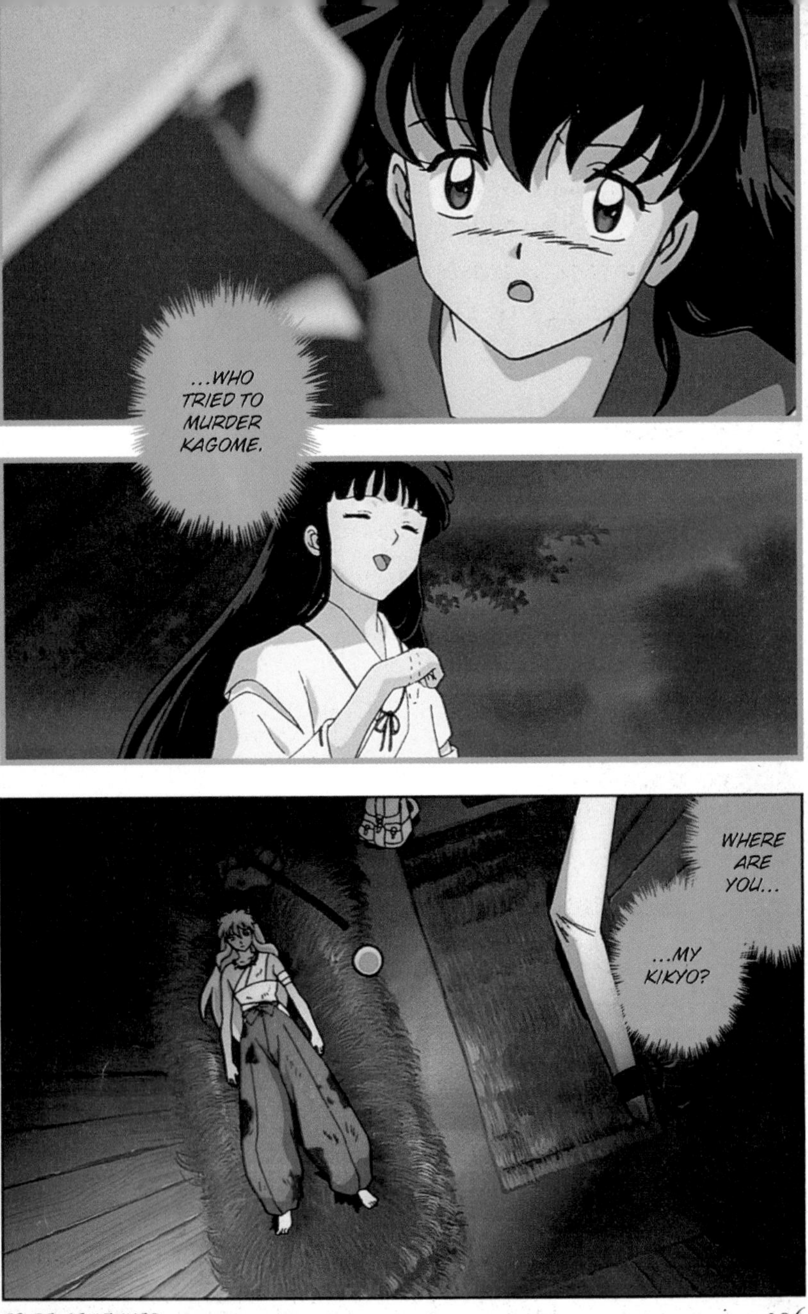
...WHO TRIED TO MURDER KAGOME.
WHERE ARE YOU...
...MY KIKYO?

TO BE CONTINUED...

# Glossary of Sound Effects

Each entry includes: the location, indicated by page number and panel number (so 3.1 means page 3, panel number 1); the phonetic romanization of the original Japanese; and our English "translation"—we offer as close an English equivalent as we can.

16.1 FX: Zuga (wham)
16.2 FX: Ga ga ga ga (rumbling rocks)
16.4 FX: Da (grab)

17.2 FX: Ga ga ga (rumbling)
17.3 FX: Suu... (gliding)
17.4 FX: Toh (landing)

19.2 FX: Da (lunge)
19.4 FX: Ga (smack)
19.5 FX: Giin (sword ringing)

20.1 FX: Ga (smack)
20.4 FX: Za (skidding)

21.3 FX: Doga (punch)
21.4 FX: Baki (crunch)
21.5 FX: Bun (punch)

22.1 FX: Da (leap)
22.2 FX: Ga (punch)
22.3 FX: Zuzaza... (skidding)
22.4 FX: Da (leap)
22.5 FX: Gohh (whoosh)

23.1 FX: Dogo (punch)
23.2 FX: Gohhhhh... (whooshing)

24.1 FX: Gohhh... (whooshing)
24.2 FX: Kaaaa... (shining)

25.4 FX: Za (Kagura appears)

**Chapter 40:**
**The Deadly Trap of the Wind Sorceress, Kagura**

6.2 FX: Zawa...
(crackling of Naraku's tentacles)
6.4 FX: Zawa zawa (crackling)

8.2 FX: Ta (leap)
8.3 FX: Dohh (slam)
8.4 FX: Zuba (slash)
8.5 FX: Zan (whoosh)

9.1 FX: Toh (landing)
9.4 FX: Doka (striking out with staff)
9.5 FX: Zuba (slash)

10.1 FX: Ta ta ta... (running)
10.2 FX: Ta (jump)
10.3 FX: Doh (boom)

11.1 FX: Doga (explosion through roof)
11.2 FX: Gohhhh... (whooshing)
11.4 FX: Ta (landing)

12.1 FX: Gohhhh... (whoosh)

14.2 FX: Da (leap)
14.4 FX: Dogo (smash)
14.5 FX: Da (running)

15.1 FX: Doga (explosive attack)
15.2 FX: Dogo (explosive attack)
15.5 FX: Da (punch)

26.4 FX: Ba (fan opening)
26.5 FX: Yura… (wobble as zombies stand)

28.2 FX: Su… (brandishing fan)
28.3 FX: Gohh (whoosh)
28.4 FX: Da (leap)
28.5 FX: Doga (tackle)
28.6 FX: Ta (landing)

29.1 FX: Poh… (scar starts to burn)
29.2 FX: Kiin… (jewel shard shines)
29.3 FX: Gaku (startled, pained reaction)

30.2 FX: Ba (blades whip through air)
30.3 FX: Doh doh doh (zap zap zap)
30.4 FX: Ba (blood spurts)

31.1 FX: Doh (collapsing)

32.3 FX: Shurururu… (arrow flies)
32.5 FX: Gohh (whoosh)
32.6 FX: Ba (arrow hits)

33.1 FX: Doh (zombies explode)
33.4 FX: Bun (slashing with fan)
33.5 FX: Gohh (whoosh of blades)

34.1 FX: Doh doh doh doh (blades fly around)
34.2 FX: Zu zu zu (dust clears)

35.2 FX: Ga (staggering)
35.3 FX: Jari… (grasping sword like a cane)

38.2 FX: Ba (lunge)
38.3 FX: Gin (clang)
38.5 FX: Ga (bang)

39.3 FX: Suu… (swishing of fan)
39.4 FX: Gohh (swoosh)

40.1 FX: Gohhhh… (whoosh)
40.2-3 FX: Gohhhhh… (whoosh)
40.4 FX: Doh doh doh doh (rumbling)

41.1 FX: Ba (swishing of fan)
41.3 FX: Doga (cyclones touch down)
41.3 FX: Ta (leap)

42.3 FX: Cha (fan opens)
42.4 FX: Goh (whoosh)

43.3 FX: Giri (creak of arrow string)
43.4 FX: Shu (arrow shot)
43.5 FX: Gyun (arrow lands)

44.1 FX: Hyu (arrow takes effect)
44.3 FX: Gohh (Whoosh)

45.5 FX: Giri (creak of arrow string)

46.1 FX: Shun… (arrow flies)
46.3 FX: Dohn (arrow and wind collide)
46.5 FX: Buwa (arrow disperses wind)

47.3 FX: Gohhh… (whoosh)
47.5 FX: Goh (whoosh)

48.1 FX: Goh (whoosh)
48.2 FX: Gohhh… (whoosh)
48.3 FX: Da (stepping forward)
48.4 FX: Ba (slash)
48.5 FX: Kaa (shining)

49.1 FX: Goh (whoosh)
49.2-3 FX: Go go go go (whooshing)
49.5 FX: Gohhhh… (whoosh)

50.1 FX: Zu zu zu zu (clothes burning)
50.2 FX: Ba (tossing feather)
50.3 FX: Goh (whoosh)

51.2-3 FX: Gohhhhh… (whoosh)

52.1 FX: Doh (smack)
52.3 FX: Zuba (slash)
52.4 FX: Shuuu… (disintegrating)

85.5 FX: Da (running)

87.4 FX: Ta (running)

91.1 FX: Niko… (smiling)
91.4 FX: Zuza (sliding backward)

100.2 FX: Buuuu…n… (insects buzzing)

108.4 FX: Da (dashing out of room)

112.2 FX: Pachi pachi… (flames crackling)

113.3 FX: Ta (trotting away)

114.2 FX: Kaa (shining)
114.3 FX: Kaaaa… (shining)
114.4 FX: Suu… (soul being drawn in)

115.1 FX: Gohhhh… (whoosh)
115.2 FX: Dosa (collapsing)

117.1 FX: Ga (grabbing sword)

118.2 FX: Zawa… (mob appears)

119.2 FX: Za (mob approaches)
119.4 FX: Cha (metal clinking)
119.5 FX: Jiri… (torches crackling)

120.2 FX: Da (lunge)
120.3 FX: Ta (leap)
120.4 FX: Baki (punch)

121.1 FX: Doh (hitting)
121.4 FX: Doka (smack)
121.5 FX: Ga (colliding)

124.4 FX: Su… (door slides open)

125.3 FX: Ba (gripping weapon)
125.4 FX: Fu… (disappearing)

53.1-2 FX: Zu zu zu zu zu (castle dissolves)
53.4 FX: Zu zu zu zu… (dissolving)

56.1 FX: Bachi (deflecting)

58.3 FX: Za (arrow penetrates barrier)
58.4 FX: Kaaaa… (shining)

59.1 FX: Suu… (jewel pops out)
59.2 FX: Pa—n (jewel disintegrates)
59.3 FX: Suuu… (dissipating)

60.1-2 FX: Gohhhhh… (wind blowing)
60.4 FX: Yoro… (Koga being unsteady on his feet)

62.3 FX: Zuki (nudge)

68.1 FX: Goh (whoosh)

70.3 FX: Bun (swatting with fan)
70.4-5 FX: Doh doh doh doh doh doh (blades whirl through air)

71.3 FX: Su… (gripping something)
71.5 FX: Poh… (glowing darkly)
71.6 FX: Giri (squeezing)

72.4-5 FX: Dokun dokun… (heartbeats)

**Chapter 41:**
**Kagura's Dance and Kanna's Mirror**

82.1 FX: Da (running)
82.3 FX: Suka (dodging)
82.4 FX: Baki (smack)
82.5 FX: Za (splash)

84.5 FX: Za (splashing)

85.1 FX: Za (splashing)
85.2 FX: Baki (smack)
85.3 FX: Doka (punch)

**Chapter 42:**
**The Wind Scar, Defeated**

146.1 FX: Gohhhh… (whoosh)
146.2 FX: Suuu… (soul enters mirror)

147.3 FX: Kiri (creak of bowstring)

148.1 FX: Su (pulling out knife)
148.2 FX: Cha (brandishing knife)
148.3 FX: Ga (grab)

149.2 FX: Dosu (punch)
149.3 FX: Doh (collapsing)

150.1 FX: Giri (bowstring pulls taut)

151.3 FX: Suu… (disappearing)
151.4 FX: Dosa (collapsing)

154.1 FX: Ba (leap)
154.2 FX: Baki (dodging blow)
154.3 FX: Goh (whoosh)
154.4 FX: Gohhh… (blades whooshing)

155.1 FX: Da (running)
155.2 FX: Ga ga ga (blade strikes)
155.3 FX: Dohh (blade strikes villager)
155.4 FX: Ta (leaping)

156.4 FX: Ga (strike)

157.1 FX: Gin (clang)

158.1 FX: Goh (whoosh of fan)
158.2 FX: Gohh… (whoosh)

159.3 FX: Kaa (shining)
159.5 FX: Goh (whoosh)

160.5 FX: Gohhhhhh… (whoosh)

126.1 FX: Suu… (reappearing)
126.3 FX: Fu… (disappearing)

127.1 FX: Suu… (reappearing)
127.3 FX: Bun (throwing)
127.4 FX: Kyurururu… (whirling through the air)
127.5 FX: Kaa (mirror shining)

128.1 FX: Ga ga ga (striking force field)
128.3 FX: Gya (force field deflects weapon)
128.4 FX: Doga (strike)
128.5 FX: Doh (whump)

130.2 FX: Ga (grab)
130.3 FX: Kaa (shining)

131.2 FX: Suu… (soul being drawn in)
131.3 FX: Suu… (mirror draws in soul)
131.4 FX: Gohhh… (whoosh)

132.1 FX: Ta (running)
132.3 FX: Da (running)
132.4 FX: Ga (punch)

135.4 FX: Goh (blades whoosh)

136.1 FX: Gin (clang)
136.5 FX: Gin (clang)

137.1 FX: Ta ta ta… (running)
137.2 FX: Za (zombies aproaching)
137.3 FX: Doga (smack)
137.4 FX: Ta ta ta… (running)
137.5 FX: Ta ta ta… (running)

138.1 FX: Za (door opening)

139.3 FX: Ta (leap)
139.4 FX: Bachi (hitting force field)
139.5 FX: Doh (hitting the ground)
139.6 FX: Gohhh… (whoosh)

140.2 FX: Kira (knife glinting)

186.5 FX: Cha (arrow pulled back)

187.1 FX: Kiri kiri… (bowstring creaking)
187.4 FX: Shun (arrow flies)

188.1 FX: Goh (whoosh)
188.1 FX: Goh (whoosh)
188.3 FX: Ga (arrow hits mirror)

189.1 FX: Kaa… (shining)
189.4 FX: Zu zu zu zu (arrow pierces mirror)

190.1 FX: Zu… (arrow disappears into mirror)

191.2 FX: Mishi… mishi… (mirror expanding)
191.3 FX: Kaaaaa… (mirror shining)
191.4 FX: Bishi (mirror starts to crack)

192.1 FX: Goh (whoosh)
192.2-3 FX: Gohhhh… (whoosh)
192.4 FX: Dohh (smack)

193.1 FX: Gohhh… (whoosh)
193.2 FX: Doh doh doh (souls hit villagers)
193.3 FX: Poh… (souls reabsorbed into bodies)
193.4 FX: Doh (soul hits body)
193.5 FX: Poh… (bodies glowing)

194.5 FX: Goh (whoosh)

196.1 FX: Goh (slashing with fan)
196.2 FX: Gohhh… (whooshing)
196.3 FX: Su… (getting sucked into wind tunnel)
196.4 FX: Gohh… (whooshing)
196.5 FX: Pashi (closing wind tunnel)

202.5 FX: Za… (stepping outside)

205.1 FX: Pishi… (cracking)
205.2 FX: Ga (breaking)

161.1 FX: Gohhhhh… (whoosh)
161.3 FX: Chari (partially closing fan)
161.4 FX: Goh (whoosh)

162.2 FX: Gohh… (whoosh)
162.4 FX: Chari (drawing sword)

164.2 FX: Jari… (light crunching of footsteps)
164.3 FX: Ba (wielding sword)
164.4 FX: Goh (whoosh)
164.5 FX: Su (swipe)

165.2 FX: Kaa (mirror shining)
165.3 FX: Goh (whoosh)

166.1 FX: Dohh (wham)
166.2-3 FX: Ga ga ga ga (strike of fire bolts)

167.1-2 FX: Gohhhhhh… (whoosh)
167.3 FX: Ta (running)

168.1 FX: Zu zu zu… (thundering)
168.2 FX: Gohh (whooshing)
168.4 FX: Gohhh… (whoosh)

169.1 FX: Za (stepping forward)

174.5 FX: Su… (opening hand to reveal jewel)

177.4 FX: Ba (slashing with fan)
177.5 FX: Goh (blades whoosh)

178.1 FX: Gin gin (blades clang)
178.2 FX: Doga (strike)
178.5 FX: Goh (whoosh)

179.1 FX: Gyun (arrow flying)
179.2 FX: Doh (arrow strikes)
179.3 FX: Ga ga ga ga (blades are deflected)

184.1 FX: Pu… (chain breaking)

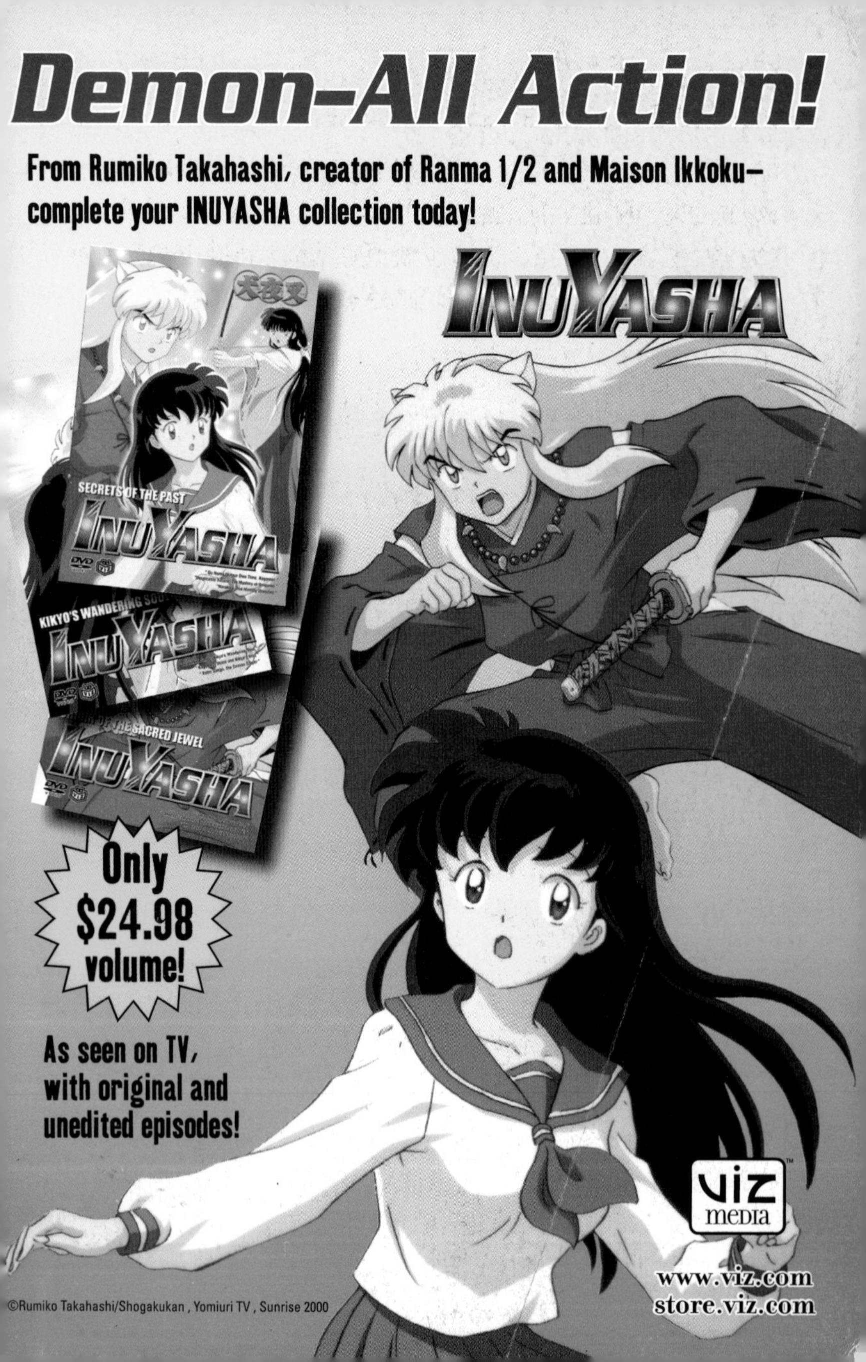
Demon-All Action!
From Rumiko Takahashi, creator of Ranma 1/2 and Maison Ikkoku–
complete your INUYASHA collection today!
INUYASHA
SECRETS OF THE PAST
INUYASHA
KIKYO'S WANDERING SOUL
INUYASHA
SACRED JEWEL
INUYASHA
Only
$24.98
volume!
As seen on TV,
with original and
unedited episodes!
VIZ MEDIA
www.viz.com
store.viz.com
©Rumiko Takahashi/Shogakukan , Yomiuri TV , Sunrise 2000

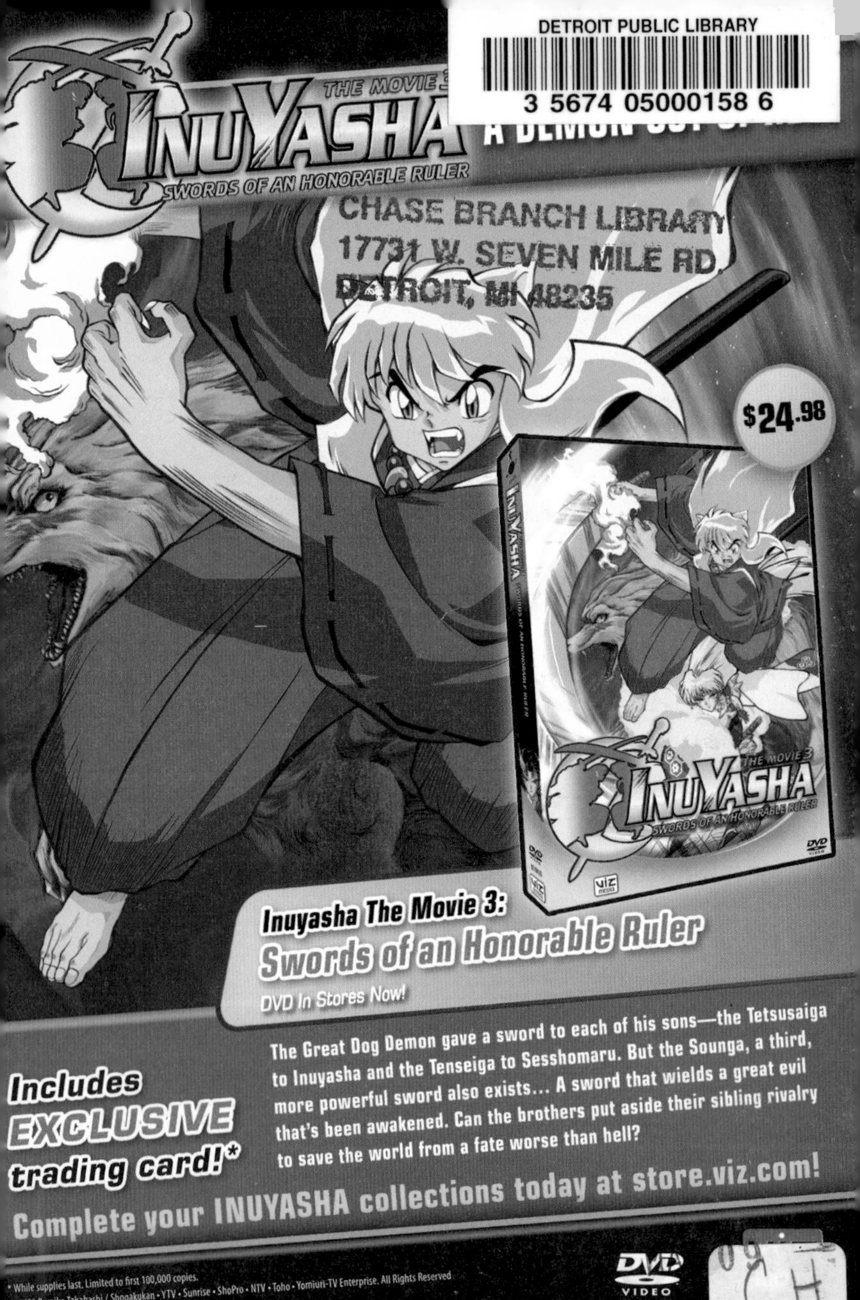
THE MOVIE 3
INUYASHA
SWORDS OF AN HONORABLE RULER
$24.98
Inuyasha The Movie 3:
Swords of an Honorable Ruler
DVD In Stores Now!
The Great Dog Demon gave a sword to each of his sons—the Tetsusaiga to Inuyasha and the Tenseiga to Sesshomaru. But the Sounga, a third, more powerful sword also exists... A sword that wields a great evil that's been awakened. Can the brothers put aside their sibling rivalry to save the world from a fate worse than hell?
Includes EXCLUSIVE trading card!*
Complete your INUYASHA collections today at store.viz.com!
DVD VIDEO